[WetFeet.com's]
Industry Insider Guide

[WetFeet.com's]
Industry Insider Guide
The Inside Scoop on the Job You Want

Jossey-Bass Publishers
San Francisco

Jossey-Bass books and products are available through most bookstores. To contact Jossey-Bass directly, call (888) 378-2537, fax to (800) 605-2665, or visit our website at www.josseybass.com.

Substantial discounts on bulk quantities of Jossey-Bass books are available to corporations, professional associations, and other organizations. For details and discount information, contact the special sales department at Jossey-Bass.

Text design by Seventeenth Street Studios

 Manufactured in the United States of America.
The text is printed on acid-free recycled paper containing
a minimum of 10 percent postconsumer waste.

Library of Congress Cataloging-in-Publication Data

WetFeet.com's industry insider guide: the inside scoop on the job you want.
      p. cm.
   ISBN 0-7879-5195-1 (alk. paper)
   1. Vocational guidance—United States: 2. Job descriptions—United States. I.
WetFeet.com (Firm)

HF5382.5.U5 W46 1999
331.7'02—dc21   99-047336

first edition
PB Printing   10 9 8 7 6 5 4 3 2 1

Contents

[WetFeet.com's]
Industry Insider Guide

Introduction

Many people do a job search the wrong way. They prepare a résumé, look for job listings, and start applying for positions. At a minimum, they get rejections—even when they would be a good fit with a position. Worse, they may land a job but find that the work, the culture, and the career path are very different from what they had originally expected. What seemed like the short, straight-line distance between résumé submission and new job ends up being a long and winding path to another job search and another position.

This guide is designed to offer readers a shortcut to conducting a better, more successful job search. Over the course of the last five years, we've spoken to tens of thousands of job seekers—and millions more have used our materials. Our experience tells us that the most successful candidates are those people who have done their homework about industries and companies before they start applying for positions. They understand what the work in a particular industry or company is really like (both what's great and what isn't so great), they have a feeling for the culture and workplace environment, and they know how to present their personal experiences in a way that will make them attractive to prospective employers.

The challenge to conducting this type of job search is that most career information resources are useless. They are written for the entire job-seeking universe, and therefore offer sweeping advice that applies to everyone, but is not particularly helpful to anyone. Or they talk about workplace trends and opportunities—without offering an in-the-trenches understanding of what it's really like to work for a specific industry or company. In particular, there's almost nothing written for the smart, college-educated individual who is either new to the job search or who has worked for several years and is trying to understand the range of career paths available and the way to pursue those options. This guide is written to fill this hole. Our hope is that it will help you learn what you need to know to find and land the job you want—even if you don't yet know it's the job you want.

What We Cover

This book profiles thirty growing industries from the inside out. Each industry is presented in a similar format. The profile begins with an overview of the industry. This top-level view covers the trends shaping the industry as well as the different segments that compose it, and provides a context for understanding what people in the industry do on a day-to-day basis. It is followed by a summary of the key pros and cons about the industry. Based on our conversations with hundreds of people working in these industries, this What's Great/What's to Hate section offers insight into factors that will affect a person's work experience. The industry profile concludes with a list of the types of jobs available, typical salary ranges, and tips for actually landing a position.

Accompanying each industry profile are two Real People Profiles. Although we've changed the names and some identifying details of each person, these profiles are actual interviews with real people working in the industry. They are not designed to be comprehensive, but they offer a taste of what it's really like to work in each industry. We designed our interview questions to give readers an inside look at the job-search process and the career opportunities available—and to provoke readers to think about how the industry fits their own career aspirations.

The book concludes with three resources to help you apply the information in this book to your job search. The first of these is a self-assessment tool that contains questions and worksheets designed to help you identify industries of particular interest. This resource will help you better understand your personal goals, as well as how the industries profiled in this book stack up against those goals. The second offers general advice about schmoozing and the job seeker's real secret weapon: the informational interview. By applying these skills effectively, you may be able to land a job before it hits the market—especially if you've already done your homework about the industry and company. The final appendix includes a list of resources we recommend. You'll want to use all the tools at your disposal to help you land a job, and this list will get you started in that direction.

Who This Book Is For

When WetFeet.com started out, we designed our products to serve the student audience, especially MBAs and business-oriented undergraduates. However, we soon discovered that job seekers of all stripes were enthusiastically using our materials to research industries and prepare for interviews—so we expanded our coverage to serve a much wider range of candidates. Today, undergraduates, MBAs, advanced-degree candidates, job-changers, and midcareer job seekers all use WetFeet.com research as an essential tool for the job search. The common denominator for all of these people is that they seek carefully researched information about the companies and industries they are considering—before they go about applying for a job. This book, our website (www.wetfeet.com), and our other publications are researched and written with this in mind. Although our content still focuses primarily on the needs of the college-educated job seeker, we've tried to present information that will help people who are trying to find—and land—a position that really fits their personal career goals.

A Word About WetFeet.com

Since 1994, WetFeet.com has been the number one provider of objective information about companies, industries, and careers to college-educated job seekers. WetFeet.com research has been used by millions of the country's top candidates as they prepare to interview with the most competitive employers in the world. We have a well-trafficked website where candidates can further research companies, industries, and careers and find more information about WetFeet.com and our other products for job seekers. We currently license our content to Yahoo, Excite, Career Central, BridgePath, and other key job sites on the Internet and work with a variety of corporate partners, including Amazon.com, Bank of America, The Boston Consulting Group, Citibank, Ernst & Young, Merrill Lynch, and PeopleSoft. We are committed to delivering the highest-quality information available, and we welcome your comments and suggestions for improvement. We're also eager to hear about your experiences in the job market.

Acknowledgment

This book wouldn't have been possible without the time and help of the hundreds of industry insiders we interviewed during our research. We thank them for their support. We also appreciate the generous assistance and support of Susan Williams, Lisa Shannon, JoAnne Skinner, Julianna Gustafson, and the many others at Jossey-Bass who have worked to bring this title to life.

At WetFeet.com, a host of people contributed their time and energy to completing this project. In particular, Frank Marquardt, Robin Platt, Steve Pollock, Michael Ribas, and Eric Wilinski all contributed as writers and editors, shaping and sharpening the research of the many contributing writers and researchers for the IndustryQuick series (from which this book has been adapted). Dave Bracken, Elizabeth Givens, Aparna Kumar, and many freelance writers contributed time and energy to the development of sections contained here. And without the vision and execution of Steve Pollock and Gary Alpert—who in the process of founding WetFeet.com invented a whole new category of job research products—we wouldn't have been able to offer you this book.

Advertising and Public Relations

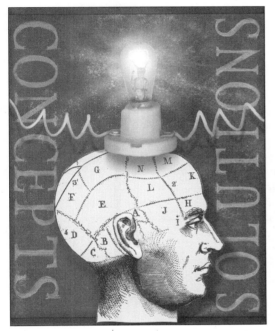

Advertising isn't mysterious. You hear it on the radio, find it in the Yellow Pages, and see it on billboards and TV. It's the omnipresent industry—enticing consumers to buy the products that other industries produce—and its players are measured by the prominence of the clients they serve. The top one hundred ad agencies billed out more than $62 billion in 1997. Estimated total ad spending exceeds $180 billion per year in the United States—about $750 for every American. No wonder everywhere you look, you see an ad. About a quarter of this money goes to newspaper ads, another quarter to TV commercials, and about a fifth to direct mail. Revenues in all but three of the fifty biggest were up in 1997. As a general rule, the fortunes of the advertising industry follow those of the economy, so as long as the economy stays strong ad agencies can expect to continue to profit.

The first thing job seekers should know about advertising: It isn't easy to break into and it doesn't pay well when you start. Second, expect to work in New York City, Chicago, San Francisco, or Los Angeles, where the biggest agencies—or, in the case of San Francisco, numerous boutique agencies—are headquartered. Third, the industry is undergoing significant change. A rash of mergers and acquisitions have been consolidating firms into a few big players with a global reach, and many of these are offering an ever-widening array of services—

REAL PEOPLE PROFILE

BILL WARD

OCCUPATION:
Account executive for a
public relations agency

YEARS IN BUSINESS: 5

AGE: 28

EDUCATION: BS in public
relations, Ohio State
University

HOURS PER WEEK:
45, 9:00 A.M. to 6:00 P.M.;
30 minutes for lunch

SIZE OF COMPANY: 20

CERTIFICATION: None

ANNUAL SALARY:
$30,000

How did you get your job?

Initially I wanted to be a chiropractor. But when I got to college I couldn't cut the math and science courses. I took an introduction to public relations course, a 100–level course, for a university-wide requirement, and I liked it. PR was more in line with what I was good at: writing, speaking, dealing with people in different situations, and dealing with the media. Between my junior and senior years, I did an unpaid internship at a small agency, and after graduating I did an internship at a very large firm. That paid about seven bucks an hour. I learned a lot about how a big corporation works; there were a lot of office politics. I hoped to find something permanent there, but I didn't have the experience to qualify for anything other than the media department in advertising, where they start people. Another firm offered me a job, so I took it. I managed the account for a national award that recognized individuals who significantly increased the quality of life for the disabled. I really felt good about my job, but I was paid only $21,000. After a short search, I found my present job.

Describe a typical day.

9:00 Get to work. Read the local paper and the *Wall Street Journal* while drinking coffee. Check e-mails and online database for news about our clients, trying to keep an eye out for anything that might be advantageous to them. Also check Profnet, an e-mail service used by journalists looking for expert leads to quote for articles they're writing.

9:45 It's better to call journalists and other media people in the morning because in the afternoon they're usually on deadline, so I make the calls I have to make. These include making sure a press release or press kit was received or pitching a story. After the calls—or if I don't have any—I write press releases, press kits, and pitch letters . . . a lot of pitch letters.

1:00 Lunch. Usually I run out and grab a sandwich and eat it at my desk while reading the papers more carefully and looking at MSNBC and other online stuff. It's pretty important in PR to know what's up in the companies and industries of your client. It's also important to be familiar with what's going on in the local and world economies.

1:30 Most afternoons, I'm in meetings, sometimes until five. If we're developing a new program for a client, we talk about the client's strengths and weaknesses, brainstorm communication strategies for how to get the media to cover their story, and think about what we can do for the client. Sometimes we have meetings to update each other on a client project. If I don't have any meetings,

public relations, direct marketing, promotions. Some of the best-known independent agencies of yesteryear (BBDO, McCann-Erickson, and Ogilvy & Mather, to name a few) are now owned by huge holding companies with less-familiar names (Interpublic Group, Omnicom Group, and WPP Group). Meantime, a few hot shops have been stealing business away from some of the big fish, only to become acquisition candidates for agencies hungry to strengthen their offerings. Relationship marketing—focusing on building long-term partnerships with clients and end-users to build brand loyalty—and global marketing are getting bigger.

then I'll usually spend the time writing.

3:00 More writing. Also, I might call a client. I generally talk to at least one a day. Today, for instance, I talked to a client about his trip to New York. I provided some information about the journalists whom I'd arranged for him to meet and faxed him magazine articles I thought he might have missed.

4:00 Oversee the preparation of a press release or earnings release due to go out the following day, coordinate with the client to get approval, and coordinate with Business Wire to get the copy ready. This sort of thing never just takes an hour.

5:00 I push a lot of papers during the day, so around five I begin filing them and doing other administrative tasks, then I clean my desk, go through my inbox, and read trade magazines in client industries such as *Chemical Week* and *Wireless Communication Technology*. These give me background on the client and industry competition.

6:00 I make a task list for tomorrow and go home.

What are your career aspirations?

I like the path that I'm on. In the future, I'd like to specialize in writing or get into interactive media with a communications slant. There's more money if you specialize and I don't think I'm slick enough to specialize in media relations. I'd like to use PR through the Web more, designing websites friendly to journalists and using e-mail to distribute information.

What kinds of people do well in this business?

People who are outgoing, who aren't passive. Risk takers do well. You need to thrive on stress and challenges and be able to handle pressure to get a press release out. It's also important that you can visualize abstract concepts, because the results of your work are never seen. You can't touch or feel a company's reputation, and although it's your job to enhance it, the enhancements that you bring to it aren't tangible.

What do you really like about your job?

It's diverse. My agency is smaller than the big ones, where an account executive might have one or two clients. At a place that's smaller, you get to work on more types of programs. I've become an expert on a lot of little things, from the smokestack industry to the rubber industry to wireless communications. The people, both in the agency and the clients, are interesting and intelligent. Every day there's a new challenge and something new to explore. Also, I get a charge out of the pressure; you're doing something where if you fail, it could have serious consequences, but you pull through. I get a rush out of that.

What do you dislike?

Sometimes not seeing the results of my work wears me down. And no one knows what you do. Otherwise, there's not much that I dislike.

What's the biggest misconception about this job?

At parties, when you tell people what you do, you get a nodding, a blank stare. People have no idea what you do. So the biggest misconception is that there is no conception.

How can someone get a job like yours?

Internships are the best way to get your foot in the door. A lot of people won't take somebody without experience. PR firms usually hire at the bottom, so the internship is critical. The exception is if you're a writer or journalist, then you can transfer in pretty easily. But developing some experience is the best way to get into it. For college students contemplating a public relations career, getting involved in student organizations and especially writing for the college newspaper are beneficial. Beyond that, the PRSA (Public Relations Society of America) offers an APR, or Accredited Public Relations, which is like the CPA, but I don't think it's really necessary; so few people do it. It's not recognized outside the industry.

And there has been an explosion in the number of vehicles through which advertisers are taking aim at their target audiences. The Internet, for instance, has opened up new opportunities to advertise directly to specific audiences. Although online advertising is still in its infancy, industry observers expect it to grow quickly.

Public relations is a closely related industry that is also growing quickly. A number of big agencies offer both advertising and PR services (although there are also PR specialists), and you should think of the two as different sides of the same coin. The key difference is that in advertising, the agency pays to place the ad. In public relations, the agency gets the exposure for free—or at least it doesn't pay the media outlets for it. The PR agency works with the media to create a positive and compelling image for their client by trying to place positive stories about the client in newspapers and magazines or on radio and TV. One favorite vehicle for exposure is through sponsorship of media events, such as IBM's pitting of Big Blue, its supercomputer, against chess grandmaster Gary Kasparov. For job seekers, the outlook is similar to advertising in several ways. You'll typically start at the bottom (an internship is a favorite way to break into the industry), and you probably won't make a huge salary to start, but the work can be interesting and rewarding.

How It Breaks Down

Though boutique agencies are growing in number and revenue, the big names continue to handle most of the accounts—and earn most of the dollars. They also are the primary source of employment opportunities. In addition to the size of the firm, you'll need to think about its location and its client list. Although many firms have branches, the location of the headquarters has a strong impact on corporate culture.

Large Marketing-Oriented Shops

Here we're not talking about the holding companies identified above. Rather, this group includes players such as J. Walter Thompson, Grey, Leo Burnett, BBDO, DDB Needham, Ogilvy & Mather, TBWA Chiat/Day, and Saatchi & Saatchi. Most of these agencies have billings of hundreds of millions of dollars per year, employ one thousand or more people around the world, boast at least one if not many offices overseas, service a Fortune 500 client list, and provide a full range of services to clients. Of the one hundred biggest shops, thirty-seven are headquartered in New York City, seven in Los Angeles, six in Chicago, five in Minneapolis, and four in San Francisco. At bigger agencies, the account-management team usually runs the show.

Small Creative Shops

The boutique shops may have a big client or two—or, more likely, a particular product line for a big client—but will frequently only have one office and may outsource some of the functions. Boutiques are typically started by ad executives who have broken away from a larger agency, taking a prime client or two with them. In general, the creative people—art directors and copywriters—tend to have more control than the account folks do. Although scores of firms populate this segment, some of the better-known small shops include Goodby Silverstein, Gotham, and Organic. Often, these players will specialize in a certain type of account or media. For example, Organic is a leading player in interactive advertising.

Public Relations

As mentioned above, a number of the larger full-service ad agencies offer PR capabilities to their clients. In addition, there are a number of firms that specialize in providing PR services. Well-known names include Edelman, Ketchum PR, and Hill and Knowlton (owned by WPP). Internally, one difference between PR and ad agencies is that PR firms tend to organize themselves around practice areas such as public affairs, investor relations, labor relations, crisis communications, entertainment, media relations, consumer-product marketing, and corporate-reputation management. Smaller PR firms, like ad agencies, may specialize in a particular field, such as the Internet, health care, telecommunications, or consumer-product marketing.

Nonagency Opportunities

Beyond the traditional ad and PR agencies, a number of other players could be lumped in with this field. Research firms, such as IRI (Information Resources, Inc.), Nielsen (of TV-ratings fame), Gallup, and J. D. Powers all provide data measuring the success of agency campaigns. Other firms specialize in certain aspects of the advertising world, such as direct marketing, media, or promotions. Although some of these are independent, others, like the ad agencies, are owned by the big players.

What's Great

Not a Typical Desk Job

Advertising and PR attract high-energy creative types who can be fun to work with. "People are wacky and crazy and it's okay," says an insider. Plus, advertising was one of the first industries to embrace casual dress codes. And because of the nature of the work, hallway conversation tends toward pop culture.

Your Work on TV

Advertising is one of the few fields where you can say you worked on a project seen by millions of people. At parties, you'll be able to point to a TV commercial and say, "I worked on that." Ads are a fun topic that everybody relates to. (In PR, the reward is usually clandestine: you may have helped place an article that shows up in a big-city daily, but nobody will know you had a hand in it.)

Huge Variety

In advertising and PR, you need to know your client, its industry, and its competition, which means you'll learn a little about a lot of different things. Plus, your work varies. If you're on the account-management side, you might be writing a creative strategy one day, studying competitive-market data the next, and managing a production shoot the day after that.

The Adventure

The challenge of coming up with a big idea for a campaign—and implementing it—can be exhilarating. If you can come up with the right message for your target audiences, you'll have a chance to sell millions of people on a product.

On a Leash

This is a service industry. If your client doesn't like your great idea, then it's not a great idea. And if the client calls at 8 P.M. and wants something by 7 A.M., guess who's going to cancel plans for the symphony.

The Creativity Trap

Lots of would-be novelists and other creative types enter advertising, hoping to get a start in life before making their mark artistically—but not all get off the gravy train once it starts rolling. Your essential task is to help the client sell more of whatever it makes, and in the long run many don't find this creatively fulfilling. A career helping Purina sell Dog Chow isn't, after all, going to win you a Pulitzer Prize.

Long Hours, Low Pay

In advertising, everybody starts at the bottom. It's hierarchical, so it takes a long time to get to the top. In the meantime, to paraphrase David Ogilvy, it's not what you earn; it's what you learn—at least to start. This means you won't make much money until you've paid your dues. And you'll work long hours to pay them.

"Well, Excuse Moi!"

Ad agencies can be a minefield of strong personalities. This can be fun, but you're going to have to learn to work with these people—and some can be a major problem. Frustrated novelists and prize-winning creatives tend to have very complicated egos.

KEY JOBS

A lot of people outside the industry think that advertising is all about creative work. In fact, there are three primary career tracks: creative, account management, and media. In each of these areas (and in PR as well), there is a fairly standard hierarchy of positions. Generally, new hires start out as an account coordinator or assistant fill-in-the-blank, then the "assistant" is dropped from the title (assistant copywriter becomes copywriter), then you are promoted to senior fill-in-the-blank, vice president, and then senior vice president. Account-management and media positions require a BA or BS, preferably in communications, English, journalism, business, or economics. Jobs on the creative side often only require a two-year degree and a strong portfolio, although a BA won't hurt, especially for copywriters. For those without a degree the industry is full of administrative jobs.

Account Executive and Account Supervisor

These are the suits who manage the relationship with the client and develop advertising strategy. In advertising, account executives manage the creation of the pitch and ad campaign. In public relations, the account executives generally take responsibility for the implementation of the public relations program, working with the client, drafting press releases, and pitching stories to the media. Salary range: assistant account executive, $21,000 to $30,000; account executive, $30,000 to $55,000; account supervisors, $55,000 to $100,000. In public relations the account executive range is from $28,000 to $40,000; account supervisors start a little lower than in advertising, and the range is smaller.

Copywriter

Working with the art director, you come up with the copy (words or script) based on the defined strategy for the ad campaigns. The ads you create go into your portfolio, something you'll need if you want to switch jobs. Salary range: junior copywriters make between $22,000 and $35,000; copywriters $35,000 and $60,000; and really good ones make more.

Art Director

Art directors work with the copywriters to develop the story line and they are responsible for the visuals of an advertisement. They prepare layouts for print ads and television storyboards and oversee filming of television commercials. As with the copywriter, moving up is based on the strength of the portfolio. Salary range: assistant art directors, $22,000 to $35,000; art directors earn somewhere between $40,000 and $60,000.

Media Planner and Media Buyer

The media planner learns about people's viewing and media habits in order to plan how and where to place ads based on the client's objectives and budget. This is very numbers-oriented work with little client contact. The media buyer negotiates with media sales reps to buy and place ads for the client, calculating rates and budgets and making sure that ads appear correctly. Although these jobs are considered less glamorous than account or creative positions, they have some good perks: the media department is frequently wined and dined by ad reps hungry for clients' advertising dollars. In PR, the equivalent position is media relations, and this person is responsible for calling up members of the media and "pitching" or selling them on story ideas in an effort to get media coverage for a client. Salary range: assistant media planners or media buyers, $20,000 to $30,000; media planner and media buyer, $30,000 to $55,000; the media director, $50,000 to $60,000 and up.

Communications Director or Public Relations Manager

This type of job is more specific to PR firms. Many companies hire media spokespeople or communications experts to handle all media contact, event publicity, and media requests. You can find these positions by working up through a company's communications or public relations department, or by transferring from an agency. Salary range: $40,000 to $150,000.

REAL PEOPLE PROFILE

JOY POLLACK

OCCUPATION:
Account supervisor for an
advertising agency

YEARS IN BUSINESS: 6

AGE: 28

EDUCATION: BS in mass
communication, specialty in
advertising and marketing,
Boston University

HOURS PER WEEK: 55 to
60, 8:30 A.M. to 7:30 P.M.;
30 minutes for lunch

SIZE OF COMPANY: 400 at
headquarters; offices in more
than 70 countries

CERTIFICATION: None

ANNUAL SALARY:
$70,000

How did you get your job?

I did a lot of networking. I spent all of spring break during my senior year getting my résumé into every big New York agency and doing informational interviews. I got a job directly after graduation, after extensive networking throughout the city. I started out as an assistant account executive, made a lateral move to another agency, and in eight months was promoted to account executive. After two years as an account executive I was promoted to account supervisor and made another lateral move to my present agency. As account supervisor, I manage the relationship between the client and the agency and manage the creative development process, including strategy development and the timetable. I also supervise the work of my assistant and account executive.

Describe a typical day.

8:30 Drink Starbucks coffee while checking voice mail and e-mail. On slow days, I'll read the newspaper for fifteen to twenty minutes. Then I'll start writing strategies or presentations, which I'll later give to a group assistant, who will type them up, stylize them, and put them into PowerPoint. Typically, I'll make two presentations at the client's offices in a month.

9:30 Early in the day and late in the afternoon is when I do my work. During the day, I can never get anything done: I'm talking to clients and coordinating with different departments. For instance, today I spent three hours with the research department. My account team is working with them to come up with some new strategies to market one of my brands. Many of these strategies have been tested. Right now we're evaluating new ways of testing fifty statements to determine a winner—a marketing strategy that best positions the product or promotes its benefits. We'll use the one we think will best sell products in an ad.

12:30 Talk to clients about ongoing advertising campaigns. We might discuss the number of 30-second commercials versus 15-second commercials to run, which product line to advertise, what to name a new product the client's launching. There's a ton of these types of issues.

1:30 Usually I eat lunch in the building cafeteria, and I always eat healthy—low fat, following a strict vegetarian diet.

2:15 Stop by the creative department to talk about changes in the storyboard. Creative does the executional creative work. On the account side, we do the strategy and figure out how to position the product. Sometimes I'll suggest another way to word something or let them know it sounds too much like another ad somebody else is doing, and sometimes the client wants certain changes.

Other PR Jobs

Many public relations agencies hire specialists to work in particular areas. Lots of agencies have a speechwriter, often a former reporter, who ghostwrites op-eds (opinion and editorial pieces) or speeches for clients in order to help raise their visibility. A specialist in investor relations would help a client enhance its image

3:00 The caffeine from the morning coffee is wearing out. Run downstairs for more.

3:15 Go to a meeting with the assistant account executive. One of her jobs is to evaluate every new competitive television commercial. She writes up an analysis, and I need to approve it before it goes out. Creative calls twice during the meeting to ask a couple of questions for two new campaigns. Meeting is interrupted by a phone call from a client that needs to cut its budget.

4:15 On the phone with the media department to talk about changes to our media plan due to budget cuts. After I'm done talking to media, one of the account executives I supervise stops by, and we discuss a problem he's having with a client.

4:45 Finally, some time to work on my projects. Write a letter to a client, then work on a comparative-advertising deck (industry-speak for a presentation). A client wants to know when comparative advertising is effective and when it isn't. I do all the writing and organizing of the deck, but the research department supplies the necessary background information.

7:30 Pass up a media party celebrating the launch of a new magazine. Instead, I go to the gym. It's how I deal with the stress of work.

What are your career aspirations?

I don't know. Sometimes, I think I'd like to go back to school and work on the client side. Other days, I think that would be completely boring, and I want to work my way up to management level and one day run my own agency. And other days, I think I want to quit altogether and do something for the good of society—maybe join the Peace Corps.

What kinds of people do well in this business?

To be a good assistant account executive or account executive, you need to be very detail oriented, have good follow-through skills, and keep track of things well. Once you move on, it's marketing sense and your ability to devise strategies—it's a completely different job for an account supervisor versus an assistant account executive. Also a sense of always being able to please your client; that's important too.

What do you really like about your job?

The creative environment; the many young, smart people; the fast pace of it—in advertising, every day your job is different. Even if you only work on one brand, you're always coming up with new ideas, new creative strategies, new problems to solve. The money—it can be very, very lucrative, which just begins at the account supervisor level. I love marketing: I love writing strategies and solving problems for my clients. And I like the fact that it's deadline oriented. I work well under deadline conditions; they keep me on my toes.

What do you dislike?

Every now and then, when I'm feeling a lot of stress, I look around and say, So what? If this problem doesn't get solved, what really happens? Corporate America makes $5 less this week—it's just not that important. That's my biggest issue, that my job isn't contributing a whole lot to the world. Also it's hard not to be able to have a life—if I get a phone call from a client at 6 P.M., I stay until what the client wants is done. For junior people, they're working sixty-hour weeks and making $25,000, which isn't even cost of living in New York. Oh, one more thing: I don't like dealing with creative egos, that's for sure.

What is the biggest misconception about this job?

It's the depiction on *Melrose Place* that it's glamorous. Also, the image that you're always doing fun things and entertaining clients. That's not the job.

How can someone get a job like yours?

By starting out at an entry-level position, putting the time in, learning at the assistant account executive level how to be a good account executive. Then moving onto the account executive level, be a big-picture strategic thinker and learn how to be a good supervisor.

among investors or perhaps help it raise additional capital. Labor relations, public affairs, media relations management, corporate reputation management, consumer products marketing, and crisis communications are other common specialties. Salary range: $50,000 to $100,000 or more.

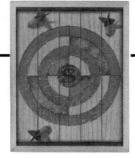

GETTING HIRED

Advertising isn't easy to get into. Most people start out at the entry level and jump agencies as they move up—insiders say that it may even be essential to move from agency to agency in order to get to work on new clients. Once you pick your area—creative, account management, media—it can be difficult to change, unless you want to go back to the entry level. Public relations agencies are more likely to hire somebody with several years of experience outside PR, but that depends on the experience. Proof that you can juggle lots of projects, write well, can work under deadline, understand media, and can serve a client will help you land a job. If you're interested in getting into this industry, keep these things in mind:

- Many advertising agencies only hire people into the industry at the entry-level. If you're in college and you know you want to enter the industry, see if you can get some work experience. (Every year a huge number of internships in advertising and public relations are available.) If you've done an internship, you'll have a definite leg up on others trying to land a spot.

- Before an advertising interview, look at some magazines and watch television. Pick a couple of campaigns that you like and be able to explain why you think they're good. Think about how they target a particular audience and what they do well.

- In creative, you'll need to present your book, a portfolio of projects you've helped design or write copy for. If you don't have one but want to break into the industry, then make one. Create some ads or concepts on your own ("on spec," in the industry parlance). Your book must demonstrate your design ability or your writing ability and marketing sense.

- Advertising and PR are all about selling products; to get hired, you need to sell your abilities. If you can't communicate why you're better than all the other people who want the job, then you probably don't belong in the industry at all.

Aerospace and Defense

I n 1989, millions watched as the sledgehammers flew and the Berlin Wall crumbled. The Cold War was over; history had been made. But some people were not rejoicing at this turn of events—among them, you can be sure, those at the top of the nation's aerospace and defense firms. For them, the breakup of the USSR meant that the gravy train of U.S. government defense spending was squealing to a halt; indeed, between 1990 and 1996, annual Department of Defense arms spending plummeted from $81 billion to just $42 billion.

But that wasn't the only bad news. At about the same time as the fall of communism, the industry was wracked by recession, and foreign companies began mounting big-time competition to American firms like Boeing and Lockheed. In response, the American aerospace and defense industry began cutting costs and strengthening market position, slashing the industry workforce and consolidating left and right. (Among those to join forces: Northrop with Grumman, Lockheed with Martin Marietta, and Boeing with McDonnell Douglas.) At the same time, the industry stepped up its sales of defense products to foreign governments and speeded diversification into new commercial markets—often using technology originally developed for aerospace and defense purposes. Hughes, for example, used satellite technology to develop DirecTV, while

REAL PEOPLE PROFILE

OLIVIA KESSEL

OCCUPATION: Flight test engineer for F/A-18 fighter planes

YEARS IN BUSINESS: 6

AGE: 36

EDUCATION: BS in management information science, BA in Spanish, BS in general business, Louisiana Tech University

HOURS PER WEEK: 40, 9:00 A.M. to 5:00 P.M.; 1 hour for lunch

SIZE OF COMPANY: 750

CERTIFICATION: None

ANNUAL SALARY: $45,000

How did you get your job?

I do systems testing on Navy F/A-18 fighter planes. I found the job over the Internet through a military placement–assistance program on the base. Since I was a reservist, I had access. I called the number and the interviewer passed my name onto a recruiter, who looked at my résumé. After a brief phone interview, I was hired.

Describe a typical day.

7:00 Get to work. Check e-mail and voice messages. Most calls are from support people at contractors that actually create the software we test.

8:00 Go to the lab for testing. The pilot did a flight test yesterday and found a problem: Every time he presses a button to bring up a map the right side of his display goes black. I try to duplicate the problem in the lab and then write up a flight card and have the pilot duplicate the problem himself.

10:30 Operational flight program (OFP) from a new software cycle comes in. I write test procedures to get ready for the testing feature. Integrate all systems together.

11:30 Team meeting. Talk about new OFPs and budgets.

12:30 Go out for lunch.

1:30 Back to flight procedures. Go to the library to do some research.

2:30 Time for a test flight. Go to the briefing room and brief the pilots, going through the flight cards and telling them what I want them to do.

3:30 Preparation for flight time. I go to flight line and monitor the pilot via radio. If the pilot has a question, I can answer it.

4:00 Actual flight. I come back to office. Check e-mail and messages.

5:00 Pilot lands.

5:30 Debriefing time. Discuss any problems. Talk through each flight card.

6:00 Put off writing reports for the test flight till first thing tomorrow. Go home.

AlliedSignal used satellite technology to develop commercial applications of global positioning system (GPS) technology.

Now, almost a decade after the end of the Cold War, the industry is significantly smaller than it was back in its heyday—and that translates to more competition for fewer jobs. The aerospace industry used to employ more than a million people; now it employs around 700,000. That's an enormous drop, but look at it this way: 700,000 is still an awful lot of people. And total aerospace and defense revenues topped $120 billion in 1997. Make no mistake about it, the aerospace and defense industry remains immense. It designs, manufactures, and services everything from commercial planes to jet fighters to single-prop private planes and traffic helicopters, from satellites to the space shuttle to mission control software, from radar systems to rocket-guidance systems, from missiles and submarines to aircraft carriers. We're talking big here.

What does all this mean for the job seeker? Well, this is still an industry in transition. An upswing in commercial aircraft orders, the growth of the use of satellites for communications and entertainment, and increases in defense spending have those in the industry smiling. But upon closer inspection, one can see that those are guarded smiles. After all, 1998's global economic downturn might

What are your career aspirations?

I really like what I'm doing. It's fun. Rather than going to upper management I'd like to be a senior engineer, learning more systems and doing research for business development.

What kinds of people do well in this business?

Those who are flexible and who can accept a lot of change. Somebody who can be innovative enough to help change things that aren't working. A lot of this stuff is predictable, but you need to be able to adapt when things aren't. People who are detail oriented and organized. People who are good at technical writing. Ex-military personnel and ex-pilots are in demand because they are familiar with the work environment and the culture.

What do you really like about your job?

I like working with the fleet. And I like the hands-on aspect of starting up an airplane: being able to lift a canopy and start it up without anybody watching me is fun. I also get to

support my country by making sure that airplanes are safe for people who fly them. That gives me a lot of satisfaction.

What do you dislike?

Writing test procedures. And, you know what? There's politics involved too. Because getting funding is really difficult. You have to fight Washington to get funding. You also have to fight with the contractors to get them to improve their products within the constraints of the budget.

What is the biggest misconception about your job?

That I get to fly the planes.

Looking back on your career or job search, what do you wish you would have done differently?

For what I do I'm pretty much on target. I actually lucked out because my military background helped me out. I would try to continue to increase my technical knowledge on basic aircraft information. It takes two years before you get comfortable doing this job.

How can someone get a job like yours?

Be in an engineering discipline and take courses in understanding systems integration and testing. It doesn't have to be aircraft. As long as you can do SI in satellites or tanks or whatever. Meet people in the military and civilians who build aircraft. There's a big market for what I do in the private sector: you can double or triple your salary there. Keep your focus broad when you do your résumé. Emphasize general skills while at the same time tailoring it to the specific job. That will encourage employers to hire you because they will see that you are broad enough to do different things. Keep the language generic. Emphasize the skills you've developed, not the detailed duties.

lead to reduced defense spending by governments, as well as softer demand for commercial planes. And then there's the fact that the commercial aircraft industry is currently at the peak of production. Already, the industry is responding to these pressures by reorganizing and consolidating product lines, and by—what else—cutting jobs. Northrop Grumman, for example, plans to cut 8,400 jobs between 1998 and 2000, while Raytheon plans to let 14,000 workers go between 1997 and 1999, and Boeing is getting rid of between 18,000 and 28,000 positions during the same period.

Still, aerospace and defense firms continue to publish thousands and thousands of help-wanted ads. Being so large, the aerospace and defense industry offers a wealth of opportunities to technically minded candidates, with electrical engineers at the top of the list, a host of other engineering types trailing behind, and those with computer science degrees bringing up the rear. Whether the industry turns the corner and starts to grow once again remains to be seen. Until then, aerospace and defense may not offer the job security it once did—and it may not be the place to get rich—but it remains an industry with plenty of opportunities on the cutting edge of technology applications.

The aerospace and defense industry is interesting in that it serves both military markets (missiles, tanks, transport helicopters, and so on) and commercial markets (jumbo and corporate jets, virtual-reality games based on flight-simulation technology). Though the industry includes many smaller companies—makers of airplane cabinetry, for example—the biggest employers are the big guys: the Boeings, Raytheons, and Lockheed Martins of the world. The industry is a large and complex one, with many firms knee-deep in various market segments, and as a result, the breakdown that follows is somewhat arbitrary.

Commercial Aircraft and General Aviation

This market segment makes airplanes and helicopters and the parts they're made of. The big daddy here is Boeing, maker of the 747 and other commercial jet planes, with 1997 revenues of some $45.8 billion and nearly 240,000 employees—and a wealth of jobs for summer interns, college and advanced-degree graduates, and experienced industry people. Only Europe's Airbus challenges Boeing in sales of large passenger jets. Other members of the commercial aircraft and general aviation segment include corporate-jet manufacturers such as Gulfstream Aerospace and Bombardier, the Canadian company that makes Lear jets; industry giant Textron's subsidiary Cessna; and helicopter makers such as Bell, also a subsidiary of Textron.

Military Aircraft

These are the makers of our military's birds of prey, such as the F-15 Eagle jet fighter, made by Boeing; the F-16 Falcon and the F-117 stealth fighter, both made by Lockheed Martin; and bombers such as Northrop Grumman's B-2 stealth bomber. Also included here are makers of other military aircraft, such as transport planes and attack and transport helicopters.

Missiles and Space

The big players here depend on U.S.- and foreign-government spending for the bulk of their revenues. Forces in this segment include Raytheon, which makes missiles including the Sidewinder, the Stinger, the Maverick, and the Tomahawk; Lockheed Martin, maker of the Trident II missile and provider of management services for NASA operations; and Boeing, the primary contractor of the NASA space shuttle and international space station programs. As more and more satellites soar into orbit, launching has become another big part of this segment; France's Arianespace is the world leader here.

Ground Defense

These are the makers of the tanks and transport vehicles purchased by the military. Perhaps the most important member of this group is General Dynamics, maker of the M1 Abrams tank and other armored vehicles.

Satellites, Electronics, and Communications

In all likelihood, this is the segment of the future for the aerospace and defense industry—an area whose commercial-client demand is sure to grow as countries around the world become more technologically intertwined. More and more, individuals and companies are dependent on satellite-based technologies—for everything from cell phone communications to accurate weather forecasts to auto-dashboard global positioning systems. This segment also includes technologies like infrared, radar, and sonar, as well as avionics (the systems that planes and helicopters depend on to take off, fly, and land safely), missile-guidance and -control systems, lasers (such as the Airborne Laser System—designed to destroy missiles in flight—on which Boeing is the main contractor), and information systems (for example, mission control in Houston and aircraft-modeling systems at Boeing). Big players in satellites, electronics, and communications include Litton, Raytheon, and Honeywell.

Shipbuilding

The role of this market segment is pretty obvious: to build and maintain seagoing vessels, including surface ships like destroyers and aircraft carriers, as well as submarines. Included in this group are Newport News Shipbuilding (the sole maker of U.S. nuclear aircraft carriers), Avondale Industries, General Dynamics (maker of nuclear submarines, among other things), Litton Industries (maker of the Aegis destroyer), and National Steel and Shipbuilding.

What's Great

Shh! Top Secret!

For those into Tom Clancy or sci-fi novels, there can be something sexy about the aerospace and defense industry. This is, after all, where they developed the Star Wars defense system and the stealth bomber and where people are currently working on the international space station. For those lucky enough to land the right job, this is indeed an industry in which you'll work on exciting cutting-edge-of-technology projects.

Take Off Your Coat and Stay Awhile

Despite recent reports that extensive layoffs will continue, people in aerospace and defense have more job security than those in most industries. One big reason for this: The projects that companies here take on are big and complex and come with long-term contracts. As long as the contract for the project you're working on continues, so will your job. And the hours aren't bad, either; while your friends in other industries are whining about their hellacious work schedules, you'll be getting home for a six o'clock dinner every night during your forty-hour workweek.

This Is Not Your Father's Aerospace and Defense Industry

The industry still relies heavily on government spending, but today the emphasis is on finding ways to break into consumer markets—often by developing new applications for aerospace and defense technologies. NASA, in fact, has a goal of finding at least one non-aerospace and defense use for each new technology it develops. This is still an industry full of slow-moving, behemoth organizations—but this is bound to change, however slowly, as the move into faster-paced consumer markets continues.

REAL PEOPLE PROFILE

RICH KUHN

OCCUPATION:
Dynamic analyst at a large (or multibillion dollar) aerospace company

YEARS IN BUSINESS: 1½

AGE: 27

EDUCATION: BE, mechanical engineering, and ME, aerospace engineering, George Washington University

HOURS PER WEEK:
40, 7:00 A.M. to 4:00 P.M.; 1 hour for lunch

SIZE OF COMPANY: 120,000

CERTIFICATION: None

ANNUAL SALARY:
$50,000

How did you get your job?

I knew somebody. Someone from my master's program was working at my company and got my résumé to the right people. Pretty much everybody I know here got in that way. I also had real-world experience in my GWU master's program, where I did work with NASA at Langley, Virginia. I recommend that program and others like it. It gave me tremendous exposure to the industry, great experience working with NASA, and it has an excellent reputation when it comes to getting a job.

Describe a typical day.

7:00   Arrive at office, check e-mail and voice mail, and respond to important messages.

8:00   Contact the other people on the dynamic-analysis team I manage, to see how things stand on the parts of our projects that they're responsible for, to make sure we're all on the same page.

9:00   Start computer modeling of screws used in missiles, testing for responses to varying levels of vibration. Spend time getting rid of bugs I thought we'd gotten rid of last week.

11:00   Call testing facility to check on the testing of another missile part, which I'm done doing computer modeling on, and which is now being tested in the real world instead of virtually. Receive and analyze the results of the first round of tests.

11:30   Receive phone call from the program office; they want to know why we're behind schedule on the screw testing, and I tell them about the computer bugs.

12:00   Lunch in the cafeteria.

1:30   Go to the testing facility to observe thermal tests on yet another missile part I'm involved with.

3:00   A bit more modeling on the screws, then an end-of-the-day e-mail check.

4:00   Homeward bound.

What's to Hate

The Cutting Edge Is Dull

Despite what you might think about the industry, most of the work in it does not concern breakthrough technologies. Rather, you're more likely to be working with technologies that were cutting-edge in the '80s or even as far back as the '70s. For one thing, it costs too much to update technology for most projects for most companies to use the highest of high tech. For another, if they're using technologies that get the job done, companies don't see the need to change. If you want to work with the latest technological toys, it might be best to look elsewhere.

What are your career aspirations?

To get involved with a smaller company where I can develop, build, and prove ideas—an environment bordering on the academic world, where you're experimenting on something new all the time. Eventually, I'd also like to get my PhD—but I'm a bit burnt out on school right now.

What kinds of people do well in this business?

Beyond having technical skills, people in this industry have to have good communications skills. If you can't communicate an idea, after all, then it's a wasted idea. And there are political aspects to the job. To get things done, it's important to be able to communicate.

What do you really like about your job?

Nothing right now. My company is in a serious state of disorder. It's consolidating, and as a result, all the best, most-challenging work we used to get is going to a facility in another part of the country.

What do you dislike?

This can be a hard industry to work in right now. There are a lot of miserable people out there—good engineers in locations that just happened to get shut down. Half the people I went to school with, I'd say, are in that kind of situation, and many of them are pretty pissed off and frustrated. Also, engineering environments can be kind of closed-minded and almost too logical; it can be hard to find people you get along with socially. That's not always the case, of course, but not everyone I work with is my best friend. Finally, older engineers can be pretty conservative about change. That's being washed out of the industry now, though; more companies are adopting what's called a West Coast management philosophy, which places more emphasis on what employees think. Pratt and Whitney, for example, is supposed to treat its people really well.

What is the biggest misconception about this job?

Kids just out of school sometimes look at the industry as being cutting-edge, a place where they can go to change the world. That can be true for the very best, most-motivated people, but most of the industry isn't using breakthrough technology. Most of the industry uses older, proven technology, because why change it if it works? Another misconception is that engineers are highly paid. If you're out to make a lot of money, I don't think engineering is for you; it's an honest living, but you're not going to be a millionaire.

How can someone get a job like yours?

Get a master's degree in engineering from a good program. I hate to say it, but people with undergraduate degrees don't get the same respect, salaries, or career opportunities in the industry.

Like Turning Around an Aircraft Carrier

These are huge companies we're talking about here. Boeing has almost 250,000 employees; Lockheed Martin has almost 175,000. And these huge companies are working, in most cases, on huge, long-term contracts. Government contracts, for products that need to be tested, tested once more, and then tested yet again. People in the industry claim that this is often not a dynamic place to work. There's plenty of bureaucracy—and plenty of old-timers dead-set against doing things in new ways. If you're looking to work someplace where things happen quickly, where markets change daily and new products come down the pipeline every week, then you're looking to work in another industry, not aerospace and defense.

Odor-Free Industry

Engineers are smart. Engineers had to study hard to become engineers. Engineers design our cities, our roadways, and our machines. But there's one thing that engineers are not, especially in the aerospace and defense industry: highly compensated. The pay is pretty high for newcomers—low-40s or so for undergrad hires, low-50s or so for ME-degree holders—but the pay curve flattens out fairly quickly. Money can't be your big motivation in this industry. If one of your career goals is to get stinking rich, you'd best think about going elsewhere to acquire your odor.

KEY JOBS

Most of the jobs in the aerospace and defense industry are filled by engineers. In general, engineering hires with an undergraduate degree will start in the low- to mid-40s and earn into the mid-50s in the early stages of their career. Those with an ME will start in the low- to mid-50s and earn up to $65,000, and those with a PhD will start at around $60,000 and earn up to $75,000 or so. The job descriptions in aerospace and defense are nearly countless. There are so many products being made here, after all, and so many different jobs to do to get them made. As a result, the job titles and descriptions that follow constitute a very general guide to industry opportunities.

Design Engineer

People in these positions design, develop, test, and implement everything from the smallest parts of ships or aircraft to the ships or aircraft themselves. Included here are aerospace engineers (who design planes and rockets and the parts they consist of, including landing gear, wing flaps, doors, and engines), electrical engineers (who design electrical systems for planes, ships, and other industry products), and materials engineers (who design the materials used in industry products). These positions invariably include copious amounts of computer modeling and will concentrate on designing small portions of whole systems or vehicles (the locking systems of emergency exit doors rather than the entire 747, for example) at the lower levels. Salary range: $40,000 to $75,000.

Avionics Engineer

These are the people who design the navigational systems for aircraft. Like all the other engineers in the industry, avionics engineers do a lot of computer-aided design and start off working on small sections of entire systems. These positions are filled by people with avionics and electrical engineering degrees. Salary range: $40,000 to $75,000.

Controls Engineer

A hot job in aerospace and defense right now, as aircraft become increasingly computer controlled, controls engineering involves the design of systems that interpret pilots' commands to the plane. Again, there is a lot of computer modeling involved here. These positions are filled by people with aerospace and electrical engineering degrees. Salary range: $40,000 to $75,000.

Environmental Engineer

This has become a hot field in the industry in recent years. People in these positions have a degree in environmental engineering and design everything from noise-abatement systems (like those walls around the local airport) to systems to dispose of the waste resulting from manufacturing processes. Salary range: $40,000 to $75,000.

Researcher

Research positions are filled by PhDs in physics, chemistry, mathematics, aerospace, and other hard sciences. People in these positions do basic research using computer modeling to test the aerodynamics, performance, and other aspects of proposed aerospace and defense products. Salary range: $60,000 to $75,000.

Software Engineer

Software engineers write and test the software used in guidance and navigational systems for planes, ships, missiles, satellites, and so on. Generally, these positions are filled by people with bachelor's degrees in electrical engineering or computer science. Salary range: $40,000 to $60,000.

Manufacturing Engineer

These engineers, usually mechanical engineers, design the tools and processes used in the manufacturing of industry products. Usually, people in these positions need to have managerial skills in addition to technical skills. Salary range: $40,000 to $75,000.

Technical Support Specialist

People in these positions test and maintain aerospace and defense products after they've been delivered to the customer, to ensure their reliability. Tech support specialists travel more than most other people in the industry, as they must visit client sites as part of the job. People in these positions usually have an engineering or other technical degree. Salary range: $40,000 to $60,000.

Instructor

Instructors train customers in the use of aerospace and defense products. These jobs usually require a college degree, an instructor's certificate, and a pilot's license or some other proof of experience and expertise with the product in question. Salary range: $30,000 to $45,000.

Purchasing Manager

This position is one of the less technical entrées into the aerospace and defense industry and is often filled by people with an undergraduate business degree or an MBA. Purchasing managers find and buy the parts and materials needed to build aerospace and defense products. Salary range: $30,000 to $45,000.

Market Analyst

People in these positions study the aerospace and defense industry and how their firm fits into it, forecast trends in the marketplace, and recommend business strategy. This position is usually filled by liberal arts or business undergrads and MBAs. Salary range: $30,000 to $50,000.

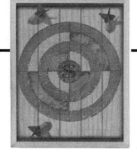

GETTING HIRED

If you're an engineer, you'll do better finding a job and getting ahead in the industry if you have a master's rather than an undergraduate degree. Master's degree holders receive better pay and better advancement opportunities than their undergraduate counterparts. And if you do go for your master's, make sure to do your thesis on a topic which relates to that aspect of the industry you want to get hired to work in when you apply for jobs. Another thing to consider: Many of the big players in the industry recruit on campus. This means of recruiting is usually limited to regions in which a given company is located. For example, Boeing recruits on the West Coast, particularly in the Pacific Northwest, but does not recruit in the rest of the country. With that in mind, here are a few things you can do to make your job hunt effective:

- Probably the best way to get a job in the aerospace and defense industry is to have connections. Does somebody you went to school with have a job in the industry? Contact her. Get your contacts to pass your résumé on to people in the area in which you want to work. Then get on the phone and set up a meeting to kick-start the job-application process.

- While you're doing that, you can also surf aerospace and defense industry websites. Most of the big companies have websites where you can check out recent news about the companies and get information on job openings in the United States and around the world.

- If you're a college sophomore or junior or are in the first year of your MBA program, and you're considering a career in aerospace and defense, check with the companies you're interested in to see if they offer summer internships. This can be a good way for you to learn more about the industry while making a positive impression on potential full-time employers.

Commercial Banking

Banking ain't what it used to be. For decades, banks profited by simply holding customers' money, charging them fees for writing checks and interest for borrowing more money. Jobs were well defined and stable, and promotion paths were clear and secure. Not anymore. Consolidation, competition, and technological change are shaking the industry to its core, forcing layoffs but also creating opportunity. Since 1995, over two hundred large and small banks have merged. Several of these and a handful of recently consolidated giants—Citigroup, Bank of America, Bank One—dominate the $486 billion banking industry. The new behemoths are entering new markets, while at the same time closing branches and replacing service personnel with online and other technologies. However, there are also growing numbers of nonbanks, such as MBNA and Capital One, which focus on credit cards and credit information; the transaction-processing and data services like First Data and Fiserv; and bill-payment-services marketers like MFSDC and Integrion.

In these turbulent times, what's the good news for job seekers? Opportunity. Banks remain in the business of profiting from other people's money, but now they need to do it in as many markets at home and abroad as possible, as aggressively as possible. Competition has forced banks to move quickly and more creatively into mortgage lending, securities and derivatives trading, and transactions

BELINDA JAIME

OCCUPATION:
Branch service manager

YEARS IN BUSINESS: 15

AGE: 40

EDUCATION: BS in psychology degree from a South American university

HOURS PER WEEK: 40 to 50, 8:30 A.M. to 5:30 P.M.; 1 hour for lunch

SIZE OF COMPANY: Small regional bank, recently acquired by a large one

CERTIFICATION: None

ANNUAL SALARY: $33,000

How did you get your job?

I came to the U.S. twenty years ago with a BS in psychology. I didn't speak English well enough to get a job in my field, so I took English courses. The first job I got was as a teller in a small bank that merged with another bank (which has just recently merged with a much bigger bank). I worked my way up from teller to branch sales and service manager. Then, in the current consolidation, the two jobs were split. The bank manager now handles most of the sales, and I'm in charge of customer service. But in many ways it's a change in name only. I'm still involved in every area of banking.

Describe a typical day.

8:30   Arrive at work. The first thing I have to do is make sure there's enough staff. Somebody is always calling in sick, especially on Fridays, when it's crazy around here. The next important job is to check the cash supply.

9:00   My morning is usually spent putting out all kinds of fires. Top of the list is to explain as carefully as possible to a customer why he doesn't qualify for a loan—and what he might be able to do to change that. When I first came to the U.S., I didn't have any money either. I'm much more sympathetic than some bankers might be; I try to make it easier for people to work within the system we have set up.

9:30   Calm down a customer who is angry because the computer balance for his checking account doesn't match the balance in his passbook. As it turns out, he left out an item in his checkbook reconciliation. But

very occasionally, the fault is ours, so it's always worth walking customers through their debits and credits.

10:00 A customer's husband has just died and the titles on several accounts need changing. This is a very routine chore, but it takes quite a bit longer because of the circumstances. Sometimes you can move people along a little faster and sometimes you can't.

10:30 Meet with the bank manager about the agenda for a staff meeting this afternoon.

11:00 More phone calls, more fires. Help a new bank representative with several calls he's unsure how to manage.

12:00 Lunch with my mother, who lives nearby. (I don't do this every day, but it's much more difficult for older people coming to this country to adjust and I remain very close to my family.)

1:15   Meet with two employees. One is wearing a miniskirt and an inappropriate blouse. The other hadn't done his homework and had misinformed a customer about the fee for one of our investment products. No one likes these meetings, least of all me.

2:30   Check with head teller to make sure all the deposits were sent through and that we're all caught up on the processing of ATM deposit envelopes.

3:00   Run a check on all the wire transfers, domestic and international. There are so many of them, and this is an area where mistakes can get made very easily. If I didn't do this every day and catch a lot of the problems early, we could spend all our time just resending wire transfers.

3:20 Interruption. A customer wants a printout of her account transactions for a mortgage company. One of the customer representatives can give it to her, but she demands to get it from me. (This is someone I worked with very closely last month to make a mortgage possible, so I stop what I'm doing and print it for her.)

3:40 A customer has deposited a check and insists that he can't wait for it to clear. He needs to make a withdrawal now. We do the necessary paperwork to make this possible.

4:00 Hold a staff meeting to inform everyone that I've hired a new head teller who will start next week. We then review sales and service performances and talk about how close we are to meeting sales goals. We had a good month last month. I try to make sure everyone gets the credit they deserve.

5:30 Head for home. I enjoy the half hour of complete quiet—no one asking me any questions!—before an evening with my noisy family begins.

What are your career aspirations?

I'd like to be in charge of an entire branch, maybe a larger one than the one I help to run now. I'm not sure if the current merger is going to make this more or less likely, but I'd like as much responsibility as the bank is willing to give me.

What kinds of people do well in this business?

People with a sense of responsibility and commitment. You also need to be able to establish good relations with customers and employees. And you need to be goal oriented. We have to meet quotas in loans and new accounts. If you've worked hard with someone on one loan—say, a car loan or a personal loan—it's much easier to sell them on some of the other bank products. It's important to establish the trust first, though.

What do you really like about your job?

Dealing with people. I really do enjoy relating to people and their problems. I can't imagine myself doing paperwork in an office all day. We have these marketing centers where people solicit customers all day. I would die doing something like that.

What do you dislike?

Sometimes you go the extra mile for the customer and there's no recognition for it, either from the customer or from the company. With all the mergers currently going on in our bank and others as well, most of us just don't have much self-confidence about our jobs anymore.

What is the biggest misconception about this job?

That it's slow-paced. I do everything and I'm constantly learning new things, especially about technology. We're always being bombarded with changes, and these changes sometimes affect morale. The pressure is worse than ever here. Customer service doesn't bring a whole lot of new dollars to the bank and our resources are really limited. A growing number of

our customer service and salespeople are part-timers, and they just don't have the commitment and focus of a career person. That makes managing them more difficult.

How can someone get a job like yours?

Banks have all kinds of training programs. I've trained many, many college kids for branch management positions. They rotate through different departments and learn the business. And though banks are trying hard to replace customer reps and branch staff with telephone and online assistance, this only works some of the time. It's an uncertain period to be going into banking at all, but it will never become completely automated—and the parts that do become automated are never the parts that are really interesting or fun.

processing. The demand for people who understand technology, the full gamut of financial services, and how to market to new customers is intense. The *New York Times* recently reported that banks and other financial firms need to fill close to 400,000 job openings in information technology. Almost as pressing are banks' needs for retooled sales and marketing staff, developers of new products, mortgage and securities experts, and credit analysts. These numbers will only increase in the next decade.

Banking and bank-related work are a good fit if you know something about finance and you like software development; if you're interested in marketing and sales; if you're a business school grad and you want a solid career start; if you're not a B-school grad but you're looking for work experience the equivalent of an MBA; if you're fluent in Spanish, Japanese, or another language and you want to live overseas for a few years; or if you just want the know-how to eventually start your own business. One thing about banking skills: They are extremely useful and portable. So even if you join a bank that gets gobbled up by a competitor and you end up a merger casualty, you can usually transfer your expertise somewhere else with relative ease.

How It Breaks Down

The most important distinction to keep in mind as a job seeker is between regional banks and the big global ones. Here we've broken down the industry by type of banking, rather than size of player, because banks are increasingly offering new services to their array of traditional ones.

Consumer or Retail Banking

This is what most people think of when they think of banking: A small to midsize branch with tellers and platform officers—the men and women in suits sitting at the nice wooden desks with pen sets—to handle customers' day-to-day needs. Although thousands of small community banks, credit unions, and savings institutions still exist, employment opportunities are increasingly coming from a few mega-players such as Citibank, Chase Manhattan, Bank of America, and Bank One, most of which seem hell-bent on building national—and even international—banking operations. (Indeed, some experts predict that fifty banks will control 80 percent of the industry by the year 2000.) One complicating factor in this picture is that the banks mentioned above, in addition to extending their consumer-banking operations, have added to their portfolios by strengthening their investment-banking and asset-management capabilities, among others. So, if you want to work at a Citibank branch, make sure that you're applying to the right part of the organization.

Business or Corporate Banking

Many of the players in this group are the same ones in the consumer-banking business; others you'll find on Wall Street, not Main Street. At the highest level, the larger players (Bankers Trust, Bank of New York, and J.P. Morgan being three names to add to the list of mega-players above) provide a wide range of advisory and transaction-management services to corporate clients. Depending on which institution and activity area you join, the work can resemble branch banking or investment banking.

Securities and Investments

Traditionally, this field has been the domain of a few Wall Street firms. However, as federal regulations have eased, many of the biggest commercial banks, including Bank of America, Citibank, Chase, J.P. Morgan, and others have aggressively added investment-banking and asset-management activities to their portfolios. For people interested in corporate finance, securities underwriting, and asset management, many of these firms offer an attractive option. However, the hiring for these positions will frequently be done separately from that for corporate and consumer banking.

Nontraditional Options

Increasingly, a number of nonbank entities are offering opportunities to people interested in financial services. Players include credit card companies like American Express, MasterCard, and Visa, credit card issuers like Capital One and First USA, and credit-reporting agencies such as TRW. Although people at these firms are still in the money business, the specific jobs vary greatly, perhaps more widely than the jobs at the traditional banks do. In particular, given the volume of transactions that many of these organizations handle, there are excellent opportunities for people with strong technical skills.

What's Great

The Three Ps

Banking's Three Ps are pay, portability, and promotions. As the line between investment and commercial banking continues to blur, commercial banks are increasingly having to match Wall Street salaries. And, regardless of whether you join the commercial or investment banking ranks, you'll pick up skills that you can easily take with you to other jobs in finance.

Opportunity Abounds

No longer does a position with a branch bank confine you to twenty years of reviewing loan applications before you get that VP title. Now, provided you don't get downsized, you have a huge variety of opportunities: you could do anything from handling corporate loans to hard-core computer programming to running a credit card–marketing program; you name it. The one prerequisite: a tolerance for the ambiguity and dislocation that accompanies the type of change this industry is experiencing.

Prima Donnas Need Not Apply

If you're just not the I-banking type and your selling style is less brutal than what most brokerages seem to be seeking, banking may be where you belong instead—unless, of course, you want to join the investment-banking operations of one of these players. An MBA is helpful but not a prerequisite to future success. Your degree, graduate or undergraduate, doesn't have to be a highly prestigious one. You still need to be smart, detail oriented, good with numbers and people, and resilient in the face of fairly constant change, but otherwise, most banks aren't high-stress, difficult places to work. And it's not against the rules to be nice to your colleagues.

How Do You Feel About Change?

Mergers, competition, and evolving technology mean fewer jobs and more uncertainty. Even as you read this, big banks are plotting and negotiating for the next big stock swap. They have to in order to survive. There was a time when all you had to do to keep your job at a bank was remain faithful and stroke the boss. These days, however, even faithful and competent sycophants are getting pink slips. When it comes to putting your career on the edge, banking is not Silicon Valley. But no one would mistake it for the civil service, either.

The Great Banking-Services Robbery

Brokerages, corporations, and insurance firms have snatched bank products and successfully made off with them. Fidelity, AT&T, Ford, and the rock group Kiss now market credit cards. Some mutual fund companies allow customers to write checks and take out loans against their accounts. Banks no longer have payment processing, mortgages, or ATMs to themselves either. No matter what area of banking you're interested in, remember that brokerages and virtually every other type of financial institution are embarking upon an unstated mission—to make the banking job you want obsolete. Just so you know.

Bank on Longer Hours

Once upon a time, banking was a nine-to-five job. But increasingly, bankers' hours are coming to resemble those of brokers and consumer-product marketers. What's more, as brokerages, securities firms, and insurance companies move into banking, their take-no-prisoners culture could mean longer work hours still. Banking may still be better than a lot of jobs for semi-fast-track moms and as-yet undiscovered Broadway stars, but your seat on the 5:04 now belongs to someone else.

KEY JOBS

The jobs available at different commercial banks vary significantly according to the scope of their operations. Mega-banks offer a huge variety of positions, from hard-core programming spots to investment banking and trading. Small and regional banks tend to have a smaller range of more-traditional positions (loan officer, teller, credit analyst, and so on).

Loan Officer

Many a bank executive has started in this job. Many will continue to do so. Loan officers determine, based on the bank's criteria and an ever-improving intuition and instinct, who gets loans and who does not. There's a fair amount of schmoozing in this job, either at the local chamber of commerce and Rotary or overseas in emerging markets. If you prefer to crunch numbers in private and deal with people only occasionally, this isn't the job for you. But an accounting whiz with sales skills and diplomacy will thrive. Salary range: $30,000 to $35,000.

Branch Manager

This is a great way to learn the industry. A merger could temporarily derail your career; but the risk may be worth it if you want to learn all there is to know about banking. This is a bit like the principal of an elementary school. You cannot be an imperious executive. But if you manage operations well and take good care of your upper management, staff, and customers, everyone will be happy to reward you. Many of these people have been promoted from a position as a loan officer. Salary range: $35,000 to $80,000 or more.

Bank Teller

This is the front line in the banking world—and possibly the position most likely to feel the shock waves from banking consolidation and automation. In addition to having extensive customer contact, tellers have to have a good feel for numbers, a willingness to handle large amounts of cash, and an attention to detail. There are more than 500,000 tellers in the United States; most work nine to five, and many work part-time. A college degree is not required for this position—and you almost certainly won't save enough to afford one! Salary range: According to the Bureau of Labor Statistics, full-time tellers in the United States in 1996 earned a median salary of about $16,000. On the high end this could go up to $25,000 or $30,000.

Programmer

Financial institutions have a huge need for programmers and people with technical skills: Citibank boasts that it has more software programmers than Microsoft does. Specific responsibilities can range from managing network systems to coding applications for a wide variety of transaction-oriented processes to modeling bank functions such as loan approvals and risk management. Positions usually require specific platform experience or programming knowledge. Salary range: $30,000 to $100,000.

Sales

Here's another relatively sure prospect for the uncertain future. Banks are competing with brokerages, investment banks, and mutual funds, all of which offer more obvious and alluring opportunities in sales. If you seem to have a talent for this and you'd like a chance to be a big fish earlier than all the B-school hotshots, then a bank might be just the pond for you. There is also a rising demand for salespeople who understand product development and investment managers (brokers). An undergraduate degree in finance, business, or economics gets you in the door. An MBA gets you a second interview. Salary range: $30,000 to $100,000 or more (commissions and new business you bring in can add substantially to these figures).

Trust Officer

Give this area a shot if you have a flair for financial counseling and if you like hobnobbing with high-net-worth individuals (folks with serious money). The job involves helping clients with trust services, estate planning, taxes, investing, and probate law. Warning: Sooner or later you'll find yourself in the middle of family

RON VICUNEZ

OCCUPATION:
Computer programmer for
a large regional bank

YEARS IN BUSINESS: 1

AGE: 33

EDUCATION: AA in
computer science; various
technical courses from several
institutes and programs

HOURS PER WEEK:
45, 8:30 A.M. to 5:30 P.M.;
1 hour for lunch

SIZE OF COMPANY: 17,000

CERTIFICATION: A range of
certifications for various software and systems

ANNUAL SALARY:
$42,000

How did you get your job?

After I got out of the Navy, I worked odd jobs like being a used car sales-man while taking technical courses and getting different certifications. I got a job programming for a small design firm and stayed there for about a year before beginning my search for something more stable. I actually applied for this job online, took some tests, including a two-hour exam on Visual Basic, and then had two rounds of interviews. They called me back and I got the job.

Describe a typical day.

8:30 Arrive and check my e-mail.

9:00 In our group, programmers work in teams of three so we usually try to meet briefly before the day begins to discuss what we've got ahead of us.

10:00 The biggest part of my job is making sure that the people who bank from home, and cor-porate bankers, can access the system with no trouble. My first task each day is to see that the system is responding quickly and efficiently. I also have to check for unauthorized users. If there are no problems, then I move on to the customer ser-vice enhancements we're working on.

11:00 Spend some time with a pro-gram to install dial-up net-working on customers' computers. This is a program-ming job, but one that's very closely connected to our cus-tomers. If they don't like or want the new features we're developing, we need to pay attention and make changes in what we're doing. Right now I'm immersed in some of these new changes.

12:00 Lunch, usually in the employee cafeteria with team members. We talk mostly about work. All of the guys are real computer nerds, the only difference being that some really look like nerds and others do not.

1:00 More work on the dial-up net-working program. It takes almost as long to make a few changes as it does to develop something from scratch. Because it's a bank, everything has to be checked and checked again and then checked a few more times.

2:00 Shift my attention to a Y2K problem one of my team mem-

squabbles, jealousies, disinheritances, and lawsuits. This job requires diplomacy, tact, deference, and a better, more current understanding of tax law than most attorneys need. Salary range: $35,000 to $100,000.

GETTING HIRED

Many roads lead into the commercial banking world. At the bottom end, you can apply to your local branch for a number of different positions. At the corpo-rate level, the large banks hire hundreds of people from college and graduate pro-grams each year; they hire even more from industry, especially for positions requiring certain types of knowledge or experience: programming, credit analysis, marketing, and so on. Many of the largest players also have extensive job listings

bers is working on. He and I are actually working on it together. We discuss our progress and write up what still needs doing. Banks not only need perfect QA (quality assurance), but also clear timelines and progress updates.

3:00 Back to the dial-up networking program. The current task is to teach the application to recognize passwords and numbers. Lots of experimentation at this point.

5:30 Off to the parking lot and the Baby Benz for the trip home.

What are your career aspirations?

In five years, I'd like to be involved only in developing new applications for customers. I think that's possible. Maybe even sooner than five years. My current work gets boring sometimes, and I need more of a challenge. I really have to resist the temptation to change jobs too much, though. It's tempting and very easy because people like me are in such demand right now. I can make a lot more money by changing jobs, but first I think I have to see if this place can take me where I want to go. I think it probably can.

What kinds of people do well in this business?

People who play follow-the-leader seem to do pretty well. I can do that because I'm used to it from my Navy days, but how well that works for me in the long run I'm not sure yet. Most conversations are work related, and you can't really kid around or even talk about politics. Our city recently had a referendum on a new tax to pay for a professional baseball stadium. The bank supported the tax, but hardly anybody at work wanted to talk about how they felt about it.

What do you really like about your job?

The hours are somewhat flexible. I can work ten hours a day for four days if I want to. I also like not sitting at a desk all day, although I hate coming back to a cubicle. Guys on my level don't have to wear a coat and tie, although some wear just a tie. I don't.

What do you dislike?

The corporate culture. It's pretty straitlaced and I am not crazy about that. But I'm getting used to it. People are strictly business. There is very little interaction on a lighthearted or even semi-personal level. But the culture isn't overbearing or intimidating,

and the bank encourages and rewards creativity and teamwork. My supervisor is more of a banking type than any of the people on my level. He wears a jacket and tie and deals with the senior executives in the bank. I don't have much official contact with them.

What is the biggest misconception about your job?

I think many noncomputer people think that you have to be a brainiac to have this job, but you don't. Most of the stuff I do, at least right now, is pretty basic in terms of what programmers do. Hopefully, that will change.

How can someone get a job like yours?

People come here from all backgrounds. Some of the top programmers have a college degree and some don't. People learn about openings from others in the field or through the Internet. The important thing is how well you do on the technical tests. A degree may influence your promotion, but you can usually get a job if you show that you know your stuff.

on their websites and solicit electronic résumés. If you want to get a foot in this industry, keep these things in mind:

- In banking, most jobs will relate in some way to convincing people to part with their money (checking, savings, investing) or to take yours (credit, loans) and pay you surcharges for the privilege of doing either. Financial skills are only part of the job. To excel, you need some serious interpersonal skills as well.

- Bankers' hours ain't what they used to be. Increasingly, these firms are looking for talented, competitive individuals with the desire to work hard to beat out the competition. Expect an extensive interview process. At banks, you have to talk to lots and lots of people before you get hired. And then you have to talk to some more just so they can all be in complete agreement on what a wonderful addition you'll be to the bank and its customers.

- Commercial banking remains a relatively conservative industry. To make a positive impression on your interviewer, wear a suit. Don't wear patterned stockings. Address no one by his or her first name, not even in California, not even on casual Friday. And smile. No matter how much your brand-new dress shoes are pinching your feet, smile and have a warm handshake ready.

- Especially for corporate jobs, you'll be expected to have some knowledge of the change going on in the financial services sector—and an opinion about it. Also, you'll want to keep an eye on the business section of the newspaper—at least while you're interviewing—to make sure that you catch the headline about your potential employer merging with another firm.

Computer Hardware

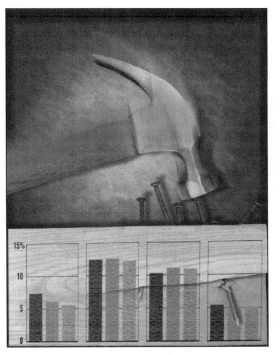

Raise your hand if you still use a typewriter. Didn't think so. Despite the occasional slump in computer sales, computers are here to stay, and the Internet boom will continue to bring more first-time computer users into the consumer market. Meanwhile, business applications—including software that runs on corporate intranets—will continue to increase demand for business computers and the services needed to support them. Consider that worldwide shipment of PCs for the second quarter of 1998 exceeded 21.1 million units, a 14 percent increase over the second quarter of 1997. This means lots of new opportunities in the computer hardware industry, not only for engineers and others with technical skills but also for people with marketing, sales, and product-management backgrounds.

Computer manufacturers face stiff competition. The similar (often, for all intents and purposes, identical) specifications across different manufacturers' products make it difficult for companies to distinguish themselves on technical merit alone. The challenge to computer makers in all market segments, then, is to create brand identity and loyalty by offering unparalleled customer service, made-to-order computers (especially for purchases over the Internet and by mail-order), and other perks that customers want. The competition stems in part from

REAL PEOPLE PROFILE

CYNTHIA O'LEARY

OCCUPATION: International marketing manager

YEARS IN BUSINESS: 6

AGE: 28

EDUCATION: BS in communications and economics, University of Pennsylvania

HOURS PER WEEK: 55, 9:00 A.M. to 8:00 P.M.; 1 hour for lunch

SIZE OF COMPANY: 26,000

CERTIFICATION: None

ANNUAL SALARY: $90,000

How did you get your job?

I was working as a marketing programs manager for a hardware company that got acquired by my current employer. After the purchase, our marketing team was invited to propose what our new role would be, and we proposed international marketing. The current company really gave us a lot of say in how we would fit in after the sale.

Describe a typical day.

9:00 Time to attack a large inbox of e-mail messages. A couple dozen from Asia and several from our distributors in Europe. Time to plan another trip to Hong Kong—probably next month.

11:00 Attend a project meeting concerning a conference next month in London with one of our partners in the manufacturing sector. Develop plan for putting out press releases with enough lead time.

12:00 Back at my desk—a few more e-mails to answer before lunch. Send tentative information about next Asia trip to company's travel office.

12:30 Impromptu "touch base" meeting with marketing director about latest figures of units shipped. Make note to check these against the same period for last year.

1:15 Grab lunch in the company cafeteria. Get caught up with some friends in marketing communications.

2:15 Review three-month schedule of upcoming public relations events overseas. Schedule project meeting for next week to discuss deliverables needed. More e-mail to answer, including some requests for information from the Japanese press.

3:00 Marketing staff meeting to begin discussing strategy for next six to nine months.

5:00 Meet individually with other marketing staff members to discuss follow-up to staff meeting.

6:30 Write a couple e-mails to Europe to inquire about visits to marketing partners in the next month.

7:00 Out the door and off to yoga class.

the clone vendors—Acer, AST, and Micron, to name a few—who have put pressure on major brands such as Compaq, Dell, IBM, Gateway, and HP. In response, these top vendors have been forced not only to cut prices but also to focus on distribution and brand image to lure customers back. With the Internet providing new ways of moving various types of data—including voice and video—look for the lines between computers and telephones and televisions to blur. Also, the runaway success of the PalmPilot personal digital assistant (PDA) suggests that the hand-held market has finally come of age.

While job seekers with technical expertise and a computer science degree attract the most opportunities and the sweetest compensation packages, the growth of the industry will create opportunities for individuals with good people skills, a strong customer-service bias, and the ability to communicate complex ideas in plain English. If sales and marketing interest you, give computer hardware a close look—but be prepared to get up to speed on the technical side of the hardware when you join this competitive but potentially very lucrative field.

What are your career aspirations?

I'd like to be a director or a senior-level manager overseeing a marketing group at a high-tech company. I wouldn't mind keeping the international focus, though I'd like to move back into partner marketing and the marketing side of business development. I'd also consider going back to more of a start-up environment.

What kinds of people do well in this business?

People who adapt quickly to change. Unlike more traditional brand-management settings, high-tech marketing has no set way of doing marketing. The technology changes so quickly that you can't rely on what's worked in the past. So people who are more comfortable with set ways of doing things aren't going to cut it. It's also important in this field to multitask well. Working at a large company, you'll also find that everything you do is part of a team effort. There is little work that is truly individual, and you have to be comfortable getting approval for most things.

What do you really like about your job?

I like the international aspect of the work. It's a challenge to understand how to market in different cultures, and I enjoy this learning process.

What do you dislike?

I don't like the bureaucracy of a large company. For instance, we are in the midst of large reorganization, and it's been a long, slow process with a fair amount of confusion. Also, there's a lot more politics at a large company, and it sometimes seems like you spend half of your time marketing yourself internally.

What is the biggest misconception about this job?

A lot of people rule themselves out of a high-tech career because they lack a high-tech background. But not all jobs require an in-depth understanding of the intricacies of high tech, and there's a great deal of on-the-job learning.

How can someone get a job like yours?

This depends on the type of marketing you're interested in. If you want to be a generalist—which includes PR, marketing, and advertising—you can get in at an entry-level position in something like PR and then expand your work and skills. It's often a good idea to start in a smaller company, where you get more hands-on experience and where you get exposed to different types of marketing. Of course, you need to be prepared for the fact that small companies have much less structure than large companies. Anyone interested in high-tech marketing needs to keep up with the industry—this includes reading up on what companies are doing and understanding the history of the industry. You should also familiarize yourself with the Internet and how marketing works on the Web. You also need strong skills in writing, presenting, and listening.

Important note: Although all hardware makers require some in-house software developers, the environment is often quite different from the software industry. Most companies in this industry are noticeably more hierarchical and rulebound, though you can still expect a relatively casual work environment.

It's no surprise that most of the action in computer hardware is happening in Silicon Valley and the San Francisco Bay Area. But also bear in mind that some of the big players are spread out across the United States. Compaq is based in Houston, and Dell is just outside of Austin. There's also the Research Triangle (Raleigh-Durham–Chapel Hill) region of North Carolina, home to IBM's largest hardware lab. Gateway is in South Dakota, Micron is in Idaho, and AST and a number of Japanese companies are in Southern California. If you're looking for international work experience, you may be surprised to learn that Japanese and Asian companies aren't really threatening U.S. companies—for now at least. However, domestic computer manufacturers actively market themselves internationally, so a job in the States could still have you filling up your passport quickly.

For job seekers, the most meaningful way to segment the industry is by the type of computer system the company makes. Other differentiating factors for firms within these segments include industry and application focus and sales-and-distribution methodology: mail-order, Internet, or retail.

Servers

If you work on an office network, you probably use a server every day. Servers sit at the hub of a network of users—called clients—and provide a centralized location for storing files and executing precarious computing tasks. As servers have grown faster and more powerful, they have all but replaced their predecessor, the mainframe. Although some institutions—banks, hospitals, government departments—still use mainframes, mainframe sales continue to lose steam. The major server operating systems are UNIX and Windows NT, and people entering the industry usually specialize in one or the other. Key players in the UNIX market are Sun Microsystems, IBM, and Hewlett-Packard. Hewlett-Packard, IBM, and Compaq are big names in the Windows NT market, though companies like Dell and Gateway—largely known for their position in the PC market—have begun vying for the server market with powerful, lower-cost machines.

Individual User Systems (PCs and Workstations)

This broad market segment encompasses both the business and home markets. Workstations are high end—often multiprocessor—machines used by engineers, graphics professionals, and other power users. PCs are standard equipment for business users (workers who do word processing, run large spreadsheets, work with simple graphics) and casual users who might use their machine for nothing more than accessing the Internet and running basic applications. One of the real booms in the PC market in recent years has been the advent of highly successful mail-order manufacturers like Dell and Gateway. Most companies are also extending their direct-sales model to the Internet (where they are doing over $1 billion a year in business). Major players in the PC and workstation market are numerous: Compaq, IBM, Toshiba, and Hewlett-Packard are a few. Ever since the hugely successful rollout of Windows 95, the PC market has seen increased domination by the Windows operating system. Apple continues to put out high-powered PCs that run MacOS, and both Sun and Silicon Graphics make Unix workstations. But these companies' customer bases—while still fiercely loyal—are shrinking, and the increased popularity of Windows and Windows NT will inevitably make non-Windows systems seem like niche products.

Others to Watch

Look for continued growth in machines that don't look like computers, but take advantage of chip technology to integrate digital appliances into more parts of users' lives. Companies like WebTV (purchased in 1997 by Microsoft) are targeting noncomputer users who want Internet access by producing easy-to-use TV-top boxes. Telephones with e-mail access are also coming to market, and with more companies developing powerful software for hand-held PDAs, this industry segment should thrive in coming years.

What's Great

The Technology Revolution

Computers have long touched almost every aspect of our lives. But with the growth of the Internet, computers have moved far beyond being just productivity tools. More than ever, computers are at the heart of how we interact with other people, how we learn, and how we are entertained. The breakneck pace of the industry—and the fierce competition for market share among the big players—may not be for everybody, but if you find the right niche, the computer hardware industry promises an exciting work environment in an extremely hot industry.

The New Gold Rush

One of the industry's biggest draws is money. For many people, working in the computer industry—and watching as your stock options become more and more valuable—is a modern-day version of the American dream. Keep in mind that individuals with programming experience or other specialized technical skills are best positioned to command the most attractive compensation packages.

A Better Mouse

In homes and businesses alike, computers are tackling an increasingly complex list of tasks. The name of this game is speed, and computer companies survive by always seeking ways to make their machines more efficient. One of the thrills of working in this industry is consistently pushing the envelope of what's possible and establishing products that keep your company on the cutting edge.

What's to Hate

New Technology, Old Management Style

Because of the change-before-your-eyes pace of product development, it's easy to forget that the computer industry is still a capital-intensive manufacturing sector. This, in turn, can breed bigger bureaucracy and hierarchical decision making. So while the industry itself is somewhat trendy and cutting-edge, the companies themselves can be marked by very clear hierarchies, rigid organizational structures, and decision-making processes that favor a few high-level shot callers.

Learning to Love CPU Cycles

The way we use computers is going through one of its most exciting periods, but the computer hardware industry is (and has always been) a highly quantitative field primarily concerned with an endless array of specifications. If you aren't fascinated with how these machines work, the work can seem rather dry—not just for technical staff, but also for marketing professionals, whose work partly involves translating specs and other technical data into more accessible language.

The Boy's Club

Even though women have made tremendous headway in technology careers across the board, the computer hardware industry is still a place that feels male

REAL PEOPLE PROFILE

ROBERT TYLER

OCCUPATION:
Senior hardware systems architecture engineer

YEARS IN BUSINESS: 14

AGE: 39

EDUCATION: BS and MS in mechanical engineering, University of Michigan

HOURS PER WEEK:
45 to 50, 7:30 A.M. to 5:30 P.M.; 1 hour for lunch

SIZE OF COMPANY: More than 100,000 employees in United States and over 200,000 worldwide

CERTIFICATION: None

ANNUAL SALARY:
$83,000, including bonuses

How did you get your job?

I joined this company right out of school, and my job search was pretty standard. My graduate degree helped me to get an on-site interview, and the company had jobs that matched my skills. I began as an associate engineer and worked my way up to my current position.

Describe a typical day.

6:00   Grab a workout at employee fitness center.

7:45   Arrive at office, review e-mail, read technology news websites.

8:30   Meet with project team (three other engineers and two programmers) over coffee in the cafeteria. Informally set goals for the day.

9:15   Work with team in lab; discuss problems with parts we've received from some other technology vendors.

11:30   Lunch with the team.

12:30   Review and respond to e-mail, telephone calls. Management wants a quick update on the current project.

1:00   More time in the lab, get some progress updates from team members.

3:30   Spend some time in office reviewing and revising planning schedules.

4:45   Check e-mail once more, then head home for dinner and time with the family.

---

dominated. The gender breakdown on the marketing side of companies is evening out. But, according to one insider's estimate, men still account for 95 percent of the technical workforce. With a growing number of women now in high-profile positions in high tech, look for this gender imbalance to decrease—but it's not going to happen overnight.

KEY JOBS

The job outlook for computer manufacturers—as for the high-tech industry in general—is quite good overall. Although people with technical backgrounds will have an easier time with their job search, people without technical degrees can also find work. The following are a few representative positions in the industry:

Junior Engineer

This entry-level position is the foot soldier of engineering. You're not so much coming up with ideas as implementing solutions developed by your superiors. Still, this is an important first rung to more-specialized, higher-paying engineering positions. This job category can also include software programming, which involves writing the code built into the hardware system. Salary range: $40,000 to $60,000.

What are your career aspirations?

I don't foresee any big changes. I made the decision early in my career to take a technical track, rather than a management track, so I'm pretty happy where I am. At this stage in my life, I'm more family oriented than career oriented, and on the career front I'll be satisfied if I continue to enhance my skills and seek new challenges within my current line of work.

What kinds of people do really well at this business?

Working in a large technology company requires patience and relentlessness in getting things done. If you feel like a project is not going on the right track, you need to be vocal, but in a tactful way. It's also important to have a broad range of skills, be easy to get along with, and avoid being pigeonholed into one type of work. Most importantly, people who thrive in this industry are those who are constantly looking to enhance their skills.

What do you really like about your job?

I like the hours, because they allow me to have a life outside of work. I also enjoy the people I work with and the fact that I find the different projects I work on to be very interesting.

What do you dislike?

There's some frustration around a certain lack of executive focus. Even though I work in a division that produces $25 to $30 billion in revenue, we can't always get the executive support and interest that we need to keep projects moving along quickly. We'll often hit milestones in the production process only to find that executives don't have the time to give us feedback.

What is the biggest misconception about this job?

Most people don't realize the amount of teamwork involved in what we do. I'll often show interviewees around the place, and they expect to find a bunch of solitary workers. In fact, it takes the integrated contributions of 150 people to get a project through development.

How can someone get a job like yours?

There are two keys to getting a senior-level engineering position like mine. First, be sure to keep your skills at the highest level while constantly looking for ways to broaden your skills throughout your career. Second, establish a reputation for getting things done. A solid work ethic will open up a lot of doors for you.

Engineer

The middle ground between junior engineer and system architect, this position encompasses about 95 percent of the engineering workforce. Systems engineers have previous experience and tend to be categorized by a specific focus area. Salary range: $55,000 to $100,000.

Systems Engineer

This position typically is filled by an engineer who combines technical expertise and strong people skills. Systems engineers, who must know the technology inside out, assist the sales staff in managing the relationship with the potential buyer. Sometimes an SE is paired with an individual salesperson, sometimes with a team of salespeople. Salary range: $60,000 to $120,000.

Technical Support

The technical support staff fields the never-ending barrage of questions from businesses or consumers who recently purchased a product. With computer companies trying to use top-flight customer service to set themselves apart from the pack, tech-support positions are becoming increasingly important. A technical background helps in this position but is not a condition for employment.

Patience and the ability to soothe the confused matter far more. Salary range: $25,000 to $50,000.

Technical Writer

This is an excellent way for those of you with nontech backgrounds to break into the computer industry. Technical writers are responsible for translating technical concepts into readable prose for user manuals and other types of documentation. Salary range: $28,000 to $40,000.

Marketing Communications Assistant

This position is suitable for those with strong writing, communication, and people skills. You'll help with events, public relations tasks, and press conferences, and coordinate the publicity materials in various media including online and print. After gaining a few years' experience, you might move on to a sales or marketing associate position. Salary range: $30,000 to $50,000.

Product Manager

As a product manager, you're a key player in coming up with product ideas and working with engineers to make them reality. This position requires some grasp of technical matters, the ability to build consensus and teamwork, and a knack for spotting—and anticipating—market trends. Again, most of these jobs require an MBA or comparable experience. Salary range: $50,000 to $90,000.

Financial Analyst

Financial analysis in computer hardware companies can take many forms: numerical analysis for production planning, industrial operations management, or general finance and accounting. In some cases, analysts evaluate other companies as potential merger or acquisition targets. Depending on how the analyst position is defined, an MBA may be necessary. Salary range: $50,000 to $70,000.

Sales Associate

The demands of this job vary widely depending on whether you sell PCs, large servers, or mainframes, and which markets you're selling to. In some instances, significant travel is required; in others, comparatively little. You'll always have to learn, quickly and completely, your product's technical specifications, but training and support are usually provided. Salary range: $30,000 to $40,000 base, with commissions up to $45,000 to $60,000 or more.

GETTING HIRED

Your job search in the computer hardware industry will vary widely depending on the type of technical expertise you have. There are basically two types of job seekers in high tech—technical people and everybody else (or, depending on whom you ask, marketing people and everybody else).

- If you want to be a marketer, you'll have to present yourself as a quick thinker, a good communicator, and someone who has a real affinity for or interest in the technology world. An ability to translate technospeak into English may also be a real plus, depending on the position.

- For technical people, employers want to see tangible related experience (or, for recent grads, a degree or relevant coursework in computer science or electrical engineering), strong analytical skills, and some affinity for the rigid structure of most computer companies.

- Whatever avenue you take into the world of computer hardware, you'll do well to come across as someone who is excited and energized by change. Employers also look for self-starters with the ability to handle multiple tasks simultaneously. Despite the rigidity of computer hardware companies' management structures, you're not going to get a lot of hand-holding on the job. You'll need to impress upon your potential employer that you can take a project and run with it.

Consumer Electronics

Think about it: 98 percent of all U.S. households have a color TV, 70 percent have a cordless phone, 52 percent a CD player, and 30 percent a camcorder. Now think about the engineers, designers, marketers, salespeople, customer service reps, and finance gurus who design, manufacture, and market the PalmPilots, Game Boys, DiscMans, StarTAC cell phones, and other electronic gadgets we use every day. A job in consumer electronics puts the technology that shapes our culture—how we work, play, and communicate—in your hands. For technically oriented job seekers, the trend toward interactive products means high demand for both software developers and hardware experts. If you're a people person—if you can sell product, write marketing copy, or help a confused consumer understand a complex product— consumer electronics companies have a place for you, too.

According to the Consumer Electronics Manufacturing Association (CEMA), total factory sales of consumer electronics increased 5 percent in 1998, to an estimated $76 billion—and annual sales growth is expected to average 5 or 6 percent through 2002. What's driving this slow but steady growth? New products created by a convergence of digital technologies. For the past fifty years, the various frequencies, bits, and analog signals that powered our radios, computers, and

REAL PEOPLE PROFILE

NANCY KIPPLINGER

OCCUPATION: Marketing manager for handheld computer products

YEARS IN BUSINESS: 5

AGE: 35

EDUCATION: BA in history, UNC–Chapel Hill; MBA, Stanford University, with coursework in mechanical engineering

HOURS PER WEEK: 60, 8:00 A.M. to 7:00 P.M.; working lunch

SIZE OF COMPANY: 400

CERTIFICATION: None

ANNUAL SALARY: $90,000 including bonus

How did you get your job?

I called up the VP of marketing. First I told him that I was an early adopter of the company's product, and that I loved it. Then I detailed an unpleasant customer service experience I'd had with the company and suggested a way they could fix it. After we'd talked for a little while, I asked whether they had any job openings. He referred me to one of his colleagues who had an opening. I interviewed and got the job.

Describe a typical day.

8:00 Arrive at work. Respond to e-mails and voice mails.

9:30 Have a team meeting to go over the online marketing strategy for a new accessory product. Decide that we need to get more feedback on the effectiveness of the banner ads and links currently in place before we roll out any new spots.

11:30 Return e-mails and voice mails that came in during the meeting. Software programmer has questions on how two new features on the product should

work together. Plan to sit down face-to-face this afternoon to go over it in detail.

12:15 Run to a lunch meeting at the corporate cafeteria. Discuss two new hiring needs with the recruiting manager. Glad to find she already has some candidates in mind.

1:30 Back at desk. Time to focus on the product update report I'm presenting at tomorrow's departmental meeting. The engineers have hit a snag since last month's meeting, so I need to revise the schedule and let the sales group know.

3:30 The software programmer is already knocking on my cube. Grab a hard copy of the specs and head to a meeting room where we won't be interrupted.

4:30 Sit down at desk again to go through voice and e-mails from this afternoon. Try to reply to each e-mail as I read it so my inbox doesn't overflow completely.

TVs also isolated these products. Now that we have digital technology, though, we have a common currency that lets these products communicate by capturing and transmitting data, images, and sounds using the digital code (zeroes and ones) found in computers. For example, a digital TV can download pictures from a digital camera and then send them over the Internet to another digital TV (or PC). Soon, everything plugged in or battery operated will become "smart," using a microprocessor and software to communicate digitally with other products.

For job seekers, this convergence of technologies is important because it is expanding the employer landscape. Big, established consumer electronics (CE) manufacturers, such as Royal Philips Electronics and Sony Corp., are competing and collaborating with computer and communications companies like Microsoft and 3Com to develop new digital products like cable set-top Internet boxes and multimedia-enabled personal digital assistants (PDAs). Small, entrepreneurial companies like Softbook, WebTV, Audible, and Diamond Multimedia are entering the race with innovative digital technologies like Internet audio and MP3 players. These companies are all competing for employees—and competition equals better compensation, mobility, and opportunity for job seekers.

5:30 Print out product update report and read through one more time. Ask assistant to make final changes and copies for tomorrow's meeting.

6:00 Go through mail, picking out the trade mags that I need to read.

7:00 Head home, trade mags in hand. I need to get up to speed on the current news for tomorrow.

What are your career aspirations?

I'd like to be in charge of a bigger product group or an entire division. Eventually I'd like to be running a whole company.

What kinds of people do well in this business?

Product marketing requires people who can multitask and prioritize. You constantly have to synthesize a lot of information. It's also important to have good communications skills; you often need to lead groups that include people who don't report directly to you.

What do you really like about your job?

I like the variability in the work. I get to work with both software and hardware, which is fun for me since I'm very interested in the engineering side of things. Also, marketing requires that you work with people from all different disciplines, from engineers to ad execs and sales. I really enjoy that diversity. And leading a team to bring a product to market and then seeing the customer reaction is very rewarding.

What do you dislike?

I don't like it when I lose control of the product development process because of other factors in the company. When you are so intimately involved with every detail, it's hard to let go for what can seem like arbitrary, external reasons. Also, decisions are sometimes made in an indirect way that can be frustrating.

What is the biggest misconception about your job?

I can't really think of any big misconceptions people have about product managers.

How can someone get a job like yours?

If someone wants to be a product marketer I would suggest that they start with a product they are passionate about. Choose a couple products and start networking to find out everything you can about the company. A technology or marketing background is also helpful. Also, check out the company's online job listings; they are a good place to start.

You can earn your stripes at a multinational corporation like Samsung or Mitsubishi, where big money is backing big products like high-definition television (HDTV) and smart phones (a combined wireless phone/PDA). Or you can try your hand at a young start-up like Play Inc., maker of the SpaceCam, a videophone that lets you record, broadcast, and receive live video on your PC. So before you start your job search, think about whether you like the structure and resources (and bureaucracy) that a big organization will have or whether you prefer the flexibility and cutting-edge spirit (and bare-bones budget) of a new company.

Job seekers should also keep in mind that consumer electronics are global brands, so many companies have opportunities for international positions and travel, and foreign language skills are often highly desirable. (In fact, the three largest manufacturers are foreign-based—Sony and Matsushita in Japan, Philips in the Netherlands.) And in the United States, though there is some concentration of consumer electronics jobs on the East and West Coasts, the industry is sprawled across the country. Many of the large companies have multiple offices to choose from, with each location housing a different product line or corporate function.

The consumer electronics industry includes manufacturers of all shapes and sizes. The largest are multinational conglomerates with over 100,000 employees and interests in many different industries. The smallest often have only one office with less than 50 employees focused on one product. In the middle are manufacturers that offer a range of products within a certain category, such as speakers and audio accessories. Because companies of all sizes can make similar products (for example, Diamond Multimedia's MP3 player competes with Samsung's), industry observers usually break down the market by product category rather than company size.

Video

These days, all eyes are on video. As the switch is made from analog to digital technology, the market is quickly expanding beyond traditional TVs, VCRs, and camcorders to include digital TVs, digital versatile disc (DVD) players, home theater systems, home satellite systems, and set-top Internet access devices. Key players include Matsushita (Panasonic), Philips (Magnavox), Sony, Thompson (RCA), TiVo, and WebTV.

Audio

Vinyl may be the latest retro resurgence, but it can't stop the digital wave that's taking the audio market by storm. Consumers can now choose from CDs, DVDs, MiniDiscs, and MP3s (a computer file format that lets you download music from the Internet) to get digital-quality sound. The proliferation of digital formats is also driving new demand for upgraded home theater systems, multimedia PCs, car stereos, and portable players. Key players include Bose (speakers), Diamond Multimedia (Rio), Harman International, Sony (MiniDisc), and Toshiba.

Mobile and Wireless

Mobile electronics and wireless technology have transformed communication. Better technology and lower prices have turned high-end products like cell phones and pagers into commodities sold out of streetside kiosks. And broad market demand is fueling the race to develop the next generation of phones, pagers, and PDAs, which will use digital cellular, digital personal communication service (PCS), and wireless modems to interconnect. High-end car audio, security, navigation, and multimedia-systems manufacturers are also taking advantage of the new digital technologies and making inroads in the mass market. Key players include 3Com (PalmPilot), Magellan (GPS), Nokia, Philips, and Clarion (AutoPC)

Multimedia

Multimedia products create an interactive experience for the user by combining sound, graphics, text, and video. The personal computer is the main carrier of multimedia products, although the digital TV will also offer a multimedia experience. Again, digital is the word to watch. For PC users, DVD-ROMs offer better speed and storage capabilities than CD-ROMs. Digital cameras save digitized images in a memory cache, rather than on film. Software plug-ins, which can be downloaded from the Internet, let users experience streaming audio and video applications on their PCs. And new video game consoles let players interact while playing games that include robust graphics and sound. Key players include Canon (PowerShot), Creative Labs (DVD-ROM, SoundBlaster), Nintendo (Game Boy, Game Boy Camera), Sega (Saturn), and Sony (PlayStation).

Integrated Home Systems

Picture this: While sitting at your computer at work, you pull up the website for your home, check out the live video feed to make sure your new puppy isn't devouring the muffins you forgot to put back in the cupboard this morning, click a link to preheat the oven for dinner, and turn up the thermostat to warm the house. This is the smart home. Smart homes are powered by integrated home systems—electronic products that are networked together and connected to the rest of the world via the Internet or wireless technology. Key players in this fledgling market include IBM (Home Director), RCA (Home Control), and X–10 (ActiveHome).

What's Great

Cool Stuff

Working in the consumer electronics industry is a gadget lover's dream come true. Whether you're in engineering or sales, you'll have the inside scoop on this year's hottest product and next year's new technology. You may even like bringing your work home with you—especially if it means doing a little market research on the competitor's home theater system or beta testing a new video-game console.

Agents of Change

The world was different before TV. It was different before radio, before cell phones, and before CD players. And it will change again with the advent of smart homes, smart cars, and smart phones. By changing the way people communicate, share information, and entertain themselves, consumer electronic products become a part of the culture. For the people who create these products, it's a powerful feeling to see your work shaping how people interact and communicate every day.

Mobility

The consumer electronics industry is big and diverse; behemoth conglomerates and tiny start-ups coexist on almost every continent. But all of these companies use similar technology to develop similar products that are targeted to similar consumers. For the job seeker, this means that the skills you develop at one company will be valuable at many others. Once you have a few years of experience, you can move almost anywhere with a good chance of finding a consumer electronics company that needs your services.

Headache Technology

Engineers spend a lot of time debugging, and though they catch most of the glitches, it's difficult to catch them all. At the same time, today's level of competition has shortened design cycles and reduced testing time. So when a bug doesn't raise its ugly head till it's comfortably entrenched in several million living rooms, headaches arise not just in the engineering lab, but in marketing, sales, and, especially, customer service.

Luxury Industry

Let's face it, a new gadget is not exactly a life-or-death purchase; it's a luxury. This means that the consumer electronics industry is inherently tied to the strength of the overall economy, both domestically and abroad. If consumers' disposable income dries up (or there is a threat that it might), most consumers will be quick to realize which products they truly need—food, medicine, housing—and which they merely want. The resulting slowdown in sales can trigger layoffs at big and small manufacturers alike.

Cog in a Very Big Wheel

The top executives in this industry don't spend all their time thinking about consumer electronics. For Hitachi, Matsushita, Mitsubishi, Philips, Sony, Samsung, and others, the consumer electronics divisions of their company are just small parts of empires that can include cars, movies, turbines, missiles, and nuclear power plants. At these enormous conglomerates, the view from the bottom of the corporate ladder can be daunting, and your work may sometimes be lost in the crowd.

KEY JOBS

Inventing, designing, building, manufacturing, distributing, and selling consumer electronics is a big business that requires lots of people with lots of different skills. On the technical side, engineers and product designers will find a multitude of opportunities in hardware, software, and systems. On the business side, marketers, customer service professionals, and operations specialists are in particular demand.

Software Engineer

Manufacturers of digital television systems, home automation systems, video games, personal digital assistants, and other products need software engineers to write the code that makes these products work. Most positions require a BS in computer science or electrical engineering; experience in real-time, embedded-software development is helpful. Salary range: $35,000 to $65,000.

Hardware Engineer

Electrical engineers design the products and their components and are involved with everything from layout and prototyping to manufacturing and quality control. People in these positions have a BS or master's in electrical engineering, mechanical engineering, or computer science. Salary range: $35,000 to $60,000.

Senior Engineer

Once they've put in time in the trenches, engineers can move into managerial roles, such as leading a project team or division as the head architect of a particular product. These senior roles combine technical expertise with a wider range of responsibilities including team building, budget and resource management, long-range planning, and coordinating with other divisions. These people have strong organizational, communication, and leadership skills in addition to several years of experience and the requisite engineering degrees (BS required, master's or PhD preferred). Salary range: $60,000 to $110,000.

Marketer

Marketers are the people who convince consumers to buy CE products—which, let's face it, in most cases they don't *really* need. Responsibilities can include pricing strategy, distribution, promotion, advertising, and public relations. Marketers analyze market trends, prepare sales forecasts, and manage inventory levels. Some also coordinate trade show preparation. Entry-level positions often require a BS in business or marketing, while product-management positions usually require an MBA. Candidates should have strong analytical, business-planning, and presentation skills, plus good creative judgement. Salary range: $35,000 to $200,000.

Operations Specialist

Operations specialists plan, organize, and direct the purchasing, manufacturing, and distribution of consumer electronic products and components based on sales forecasts and orders. Responsibilities may include quality control, inventory control, product testing, import/export management, transportation management, and warehouse or plant management. Many of the larger consumer electronics manufacturers have plants overseas, so foreign language skills, travel, and even relocation may be required. A BS or engineering degree is usually required and strong analytical, organization, and negotiation skills are helpful. Salary range: $20,000 to $70,000.

Product and Technical Support

Support specialists are the primary contact for customers on issues ranging from product usage and product recommendations to troubleshooting support and parts and repair management. Requirements usually include a high level of telephone and customer service skills and a high school diploma; a college degree and electronics or technology training may also be required. Salary range: $25,000 to $35,000.

Sales Representative

Salespeople manage an account base of chains and specialty stores that retail consumer electronic products. Responsibilities include ensuring that products are merchandised properly and in working condition, conducting training for store

REAL PEOPLE PROFILE

HEATHER MICHAELS

OCCUPATION:
Content account manager

YEARS IN BUSINESS: 2

AGE: 28

EDUCATION: BA in German literature and international relations, Smith College

HOURS PER WEEK:
40 to 50, 9:00 A.M. to 6:00 P.M.; 30 minutes for lunch

SIZE OF COMPANY: 800

CERTIFICATION: None

ANNUAL SALARY:
$50,000 to $60,000, depending on bonus

How did you get your job?

I managed content and e-commerce partnerships for an Internet/TV provider. A friend I used to work with called me. She was working here and knew that the company was hiring. So I sent in my résumé, interviewed, and got the job.

Describe a typical day.

9:00   Settle in and listen to voice mail. When my ear gets tired and my stomach starts grumbling, head over to the free juice machine for a smoothie. A bowl of cereal and I'm set to go.

10:00   Now that voice mails are done, I start in on the e-mails. My manager has set up a conference call with a new e-commerce client for two o'clock this afternoon. Spend some time outlining the promotions I think will be effective for them.

11:30   Customer-care department calls. They've received a number of calls about a bug on my biggest client's site. Check out the bug for myself and then call the client to discuss.

12:30   Skip the company cafeteria today and head out to the deli down the street to try to get some reading done.

1:15   Back at desk to finish up some more data on our latest promotion strategies for the two o'clock call. Then head to the conference room to quickly debrief with my manager about the client's expectations.

2:00   Our contact at the client is the VP of marketing. We discuss how our product can promote their e-commerce business most effectively. We have a new affinity program that would allow them to develop tighter relationships with their customers. They are very interested and want to include some international markets as well. We patch in the legal department to make sure that's within the bounds of their contract.

4:00   Sit down at desk to return e-mails that have been piling up

---

personnel, and advising on sales promotions and advertising. Salespeople need good presentation and communication skills to articulate a brand's value versus competing products. Salary range: $25,000 to $35,000 plus commission.

GETTING HIRED

So you're ready to find the job of your dreams in the consumer electronics industry. How should you get started? Here are a few tips to keep in mind:

- Start with a brand or product category that you're familiar with. Employers are looking for people who can create demand for their products, and you'll find it easier if you're excited—even passionate—about a given product. But don't forget to research the company you're interviewing with as a whole, including its other products and its competition.

- Keep your eye on campus-recruiting schedules. Many of the larger employers, such as Sony and Philips, recruit on college and graduate-school campuses for

this afternoon. Check out the bug from this morning to make sure its been fixed.

5:15   Pull together performance reports for a client visit tomorrow. Make sure the laptop has the new versions loaded so it's ready to go for the demo.

6:15   Head for the door.

What are your career aspirations?

I'd like to be a consultant for start-up companies, especially in the e-commerce sector. I'd like to use my expertise to help them with their marketing and business plans. I'd also like to be a founding member of a new start-up. Now *that* would be fun.

What kinds of people do well in this business?

In a sales or business development group for a consumer electronics product, you have to be able to think on your feet, give good product demonstrations, and answer difficult questions. You need strong analytical skills to recognize business development opportunities and figure out how to show partners the benefits they'll get from our product and services. It's also really important to be confident and organized.

What do you really like about your job?

I like working with high-profile companies. Its exciting to be involved with creating the news and reading about it in the newspapers. We have a really hot product that is part of a major change in the TV industry. That means there's something new every day.

What do you dislike?

Well, I've been with the company since it was a start-up. We've grown really quickly and now it's not as easy to get things done. You have to go through more people to get decisions made. There's just more politics. I guess that happens to most companies like ours.

What is the biggest misconception about this job?

Even though we work with really cool products, there's still a lot of nitty-gritty work to be done, just like at any other company. Plus, with new technology, things don't always work the first time. There are a lot of surprises that you have to deal with.

How can someone get a job like yours?

It really helps to know people; internal recommendations always carry a lot of weight. But if you don't have the skills already or you don't know the people, then I would just try to get my foot in the door anywhere in the company. Once you're in, most companies are very supportive of letting you try different groups. So, get into the industry, build the skills you need, and then you'll have a lot of flexibility to move around.

a wide range of positions. For technical positions, you can find many consumer electronic manufacturers represented at career fairs.

- Experienced and entry-level candidates alike should use any and all of their industry contacts to get a foot in the door. At smaller companies in particular, networking is the name of the game. So search out the people you know to see if they know anyone who knows the people in the know at the company you know you want to work for.

- Think about whether you want to go big or small. The training programs at large companies can be invaluable; you'll be steeped in the marketing strategy, technology, and operational structure that created a recognized brand and successful product. If you think you can handle the bureaucracy that a multinational corporation sometimes has in exchange for some good experience and credentials, the big names aren't a bad place to start. A word to the wise: Even if a small company is the first to market with a new technology, a big competitor can squash that advantage with just a few shakes of its marketing muscle. Call it the Microsoft effect. So do your research.

Consumer Products

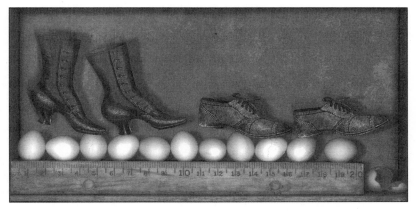

In case you're unclear on this—and most people are—"consumer products" is one of those elastic phrases that can include any of the jars, boxes, cans, or tubes on your kitchen and bathroom shelves. Or it can expand to include pretty much everything you charged on your Visa card last year. For the purposes of this overview, we've limited our discussion to food, beverages, toiletries and cosmetics, and small appliances. (Apparel, entertainment products, autos, and other consumer durables are covered in other industry profiles.) Even this slice of the consumer goods pie is huge. Consider these statistics for 1997: U.S. consumers purchased more than $400 billion worth of goods from supermarkets; the soft-drink market had a retail value of more than $50 billion; and the small-appliance industry was worth more than $270 billion.

Clearly, there are a lot of people dedicated to loading our shopping carts with Cheerios, Charmin, Drano, Coca-Cola, and any other product you can imagine. Career opportunities are available to job seekers interested in everything from market research to manufacturing to product development. However, the glory in this business is mostly reserved for those who hold the marketing spots. If you manage to land a marketing job at a leading firm, such as Procter & Gamble,

REAL PEOPLE PROFILE

SALLY CORRIN

OCCUPATION: Research scientist

YEARS IN BUSINESS: 7

AGE: 34

EDUCATION: BS in chemical engineering and biology, Duke University

HOURS PER WEEK: 45, 7:30 A.M. to 4:30 P.M.; 1 hour for lunch

SIZE OF COMPANY: 12,500

CERTIFICATION: None

ANNUAL SALARY: $75,000, plus a 5 percent annual bonus

How did you get your job?

Through my college placement office initially and then for my current job, I went through headhunters and their referrals. I did a fair amount of personal research on my own for both companies, but I didn't have any friends or contacts at either. At least for me—and maybe for product development in general—the networking just wasn't as necessary as it is for other areas and industries.

Describe a typical day.

7:30   Check e-mail. I actually do this constantly throughout the day. It's something of an addiction.

8:00   Touch base with other team members—mostly other scientists and a section manager who's the boss.

8:30   Attend first meeting. These actually go on throughout the day and generally last about an hour. This one includes four scientists and we're discussing timetables for projects and giving progress reports on our own work.

9:30   Check e-mail and make a few phone calls.

9:45   Much larger meeting with operations and marketing to discuss manufacturing issues. I lead this meeting as the project representative from R&D.

11:00   Write up summary reports for meetings and spend some time formulating a new project with a computer simulation. Most of my formulating is done on a computer, not in the lab. I try to research my ingredients and plan my lab time as thoroughly as possible in advance.

12:00   Lunch with friends in the cafeteria. Even when I'm really busy, I always try to take a break midday and not just grab a sandwich at my desk.

12:30   Lab time to test my ingredients and my latest formulations. Some of the senior scientists who have been immersed in these products for years are around today and available to answer questions. This does a lot to speed up my work.

3:30   Check e-mail. Tie up lots of loose ends. Begin preparing for a big meeting at the end of the week to follow up on the manufacturing issues raised today.

Coca-Cola, or Kellogg, you'll gain a wealth of important skills. Not only will you learn how to sell anything to anybody in ruthlessly competitive markets, but you'll also get the chance to run your own little business (with minimal risk and lots of resources). If you choose to remain in the industry for a long time—and many people do—you can spend time overseas, try out new products and categories, and ultimately move into general management.

Although you'll probably lead a less glamorous life than any of your pals in banking or consulting, this is an industry in which you can have real profit-and-loss responsibility, earn a very comfortable salary, and get home from the office while there's still daylight, at least during summer. One other important note: Once you've mastered your marketing skills, you'll have an excellent and desirable background for starting or moving to an entrepreneurial firm.

4:45 Off to the gym well before the crowds arrive at six and seven o'clock. It's early to bed and early to rise, but also early to leave at the end of the day.

What are your career aspirations?

There are actually two choices open to me. I can become a very high-level scientist, a real expert in one area, or I can go into R&D management, becoming a liaison with marketing and market research. For the latter, there's a real shift away from lab work and a focus instead on budgets and finance. The hours are longer and there's considerably more stress—and money. Here, the women who want to combine a family with work tend to opt for the senior scientist route—you can work three days and still have a lot of responsibility. But until that's a pressing issue for me, I think I will probably work toward a managerial position in R&D.

What kinds of people do well in this business?

You need a lot of initiative and a genuine interest in science. By that I mean scientific concepts and how things work, not just how to mix things together to come up with something new. (That's just cooking, frankly.) You also have to understand consumers and how they might react to new products. A shampoo or body lotion that works just fine but has a really strange color or fragrance is not going to sell. You can never get too far into your own idea and too far removed from what real people are going to buy.

What do you really like about your job?

It's fun to roll up your sleeves and really get your hands dirty. And it's a real thrill after all the work to see the product you helped to invent up there on the shelf. You can call up your friends and say, "Hey, go check out what I just made!" That part is really great.

What do you dislike?

Projects are always subject to the whims of marketing. Stuff gets canceled abruptly after weeks of really hard work. And the failure rate is also very high. It can get quite discouraging at times. Some people would also say it's too far removed from "real" science, but I don't actually feel that way.

What is the biggest misconception about this job?

I thought it was going to be just like school, but it really isn't. It's more common sense than anything else. There's very little from the formal scientific training I had in school that's actually directly applicable to my current job.

How can someone get a job like yours?

Probably the best ways are through college placement if you're just starting out or through headhunters at the higher levels. Obviously knowing people within the company is also very useful. This is one of those jobs that depend on ability, not anything qualitative and hard to pin down. You can either do the work and do it well or you can't.

All in all, this is a relatively stable industry. Yes, competition is ferocious for price and shelf space, brand loyalty ain't what it used to be, and a spate of mergers and acquisitions in recent years has resulted in a smaller group of larger giants. But General Mills is not planning to merge with P&G any time soon, and Coca-Cola and Pepsi seem content to vie for market share in perpetuity. Even companies with a fairly narrow focus, such as Clorox, appear to flourish and grow. As you've perhaps inferred by now, this is not an industry with a lot of boutique enterprises and garage entrepreneurs. Which is not to say that cute little mail-order pickle-and-jam companies don't crop up every now and then and make a serious go of it. They do. These places aren't where the majority of the jobs are, however. Or at least not until Williams-Sonoma takes them over.

We've divided the industry into four groups: beverages, food, toiletries and cosmetics, and small appliances. Most firms tend to offer products that fit primarily into one of these groups, although they may have a smattering of brands that cross the lines. (Did you know that Clorox makes bleach, Combat roach killer, and Hidden Valley dressing?) Whatever the product category they fall under, most companies are similar in organizational structure, emphasis on brand management, and approach to business.

Beverages

Intensely competitive, hugely reliant on advertising, and with annual growth of about 5 percent, this is a mature industry. Different segments of the beverage world include beer (Adolph Coors, Anheuser-Busch, Philip Morris, Miller, Stroh's), soft drinks (Coca-Cola, PepsiCo, Cadbury-Schweppes, National Beverage), and juices (Tropicana is owned by Seagram, Minute Maid by Coca-Cola). These companies do recruit on-campus, but they also pull experienced people from other firms in the consumer products industry.

Food

There may be a little less consolidation in the food industry than in beverages, but this is also a mature and competitive industry with single-digit growth. Most of the packaged goods that fill our plates from morning till night come from a handful of big-league corporate players. Some are household names; Campbell Soup, Dole, General Mills, H.J. Heinz, and Kellogg have spent enormous sums of money to tattoo their names onto your brain. Other big players, such as Philip Morris (Kraft) and ConAgra (Hunt's, Healthy Choice, and Wesson) are better known for sub-brands they own. Many of these firms have strong training programs for people interested in marketing.

Toiletries and Cosmetics

Baby boomers aren't getting any younger and vanity will outlast us all, making this a solid category for the foreseeable future, despite its mere 6 percent growth last year. At three and one-half times the size of its nearest competitor, Procter & Gamble is the Godzilla of this world—and indeed the consumer products world in general. Other players include Avon Products, Clorox, Colgate-Palmolive, Revlon, Gillette, Kimberly-Clark (Huggies, Kotex, and Kleenex), and Johnson & Johnson. If you're not necessarily a business person but think you might enjoy an active, well-funded R&D environment, these companies are great places to begin.

Small Appliances

This is an amalgam of companies in various industries. More people are building and buying homes, and forecasters don't expect the trend to slow. So tools, kitchen gadgets, air-conditioners, chain saws, and anything else Saturday shoppers enjoy pausing over in the hardware store are selling well, and the future looks rosy for this $270 billion segment of the industry. Nevertheless, this is also a relatively mature industry, and the brand system is not as strong as it is for the other categories mentioned above. Players here include Black & Decker, Sunbeam, Sears, and Snap-On.

Run a Business

People in marketing positions cite this as the number one attraction. Because each product is run like its own business, the person in charge, usually the brand manager, has a ton of autonomy and ownership—as well as responsibility for the bottom line. As one insider puts it, "The difference between what I do and what consultants do is that I deal directly with running the business, not just providing a service to a client."

See the Results

Whether it's Alpo dog food or Touch of Butter, everybody will understand what you do (and you'll get plenty of samples to share with friends). But beyond that, consumer products work provides immediate feedback on your effort: the market is your ultimate report card. Do a good job, and you'll nail your competition to the wall. Fail and your product (and your reputation) will get flushed down the can.

Have a Life

The hours are much easier than in consulting, investment banking, law firms, and other notorious sweatshops. You'll have more time to exercise, eat right, and sleep well. In general, a job in consumer products is much easier to combine with family life, and the cost of living in cities where many of these firms are headquartered makes it possible to buy a nice house early in your career. Often, companies have excellent loan or grant programs to help employees pay for that house, or a child's college tuition. But remember, it may also be a lifestyle choice. As one insider puts it, "You'll be glad you have a family—some of these places aren't exactly meant for party-prone bachelors or bachelorettes."

What's to Hate

Pushing Product

How excited can you or anyone else really get about flogging breakfast cereal or spending many lab hours formulating a new detergent? And there's a decent chance that you'll get put on something much less sexy than Cheerios sometime in your career. Sure, it might make you feel better to promote a cholesterol-lowering pharmaceutical and a fiber-rich health-nut brand, but this is not about saving lives, it's about pushing product.

Lag Time

This is a mature industry with stable growth. Growth often comes at the expense of other companies' market share, making the rivalries intense. Moreover, many firms lack the shoot-from-the-hip mentality and go-for-broke tolerance of risk that pervades, say, the Internet world. Translation? Bureaucracy rules. Insiders often complain about the time they spend selling their ideas to people inside the company rather than outside. In the process, many a great idea has gotten lost going up and down the ladder.

Marketing Drives This Bus

Let's face it, marketing is what this industry is all about. Even if you're the hottest research chemist or operations specialist around, you'll still have to get the marketing folks to sign off on your brilliant ideas. And, as people-oriented as the marketing staff may be, they won't always see eye-to-eye with you. Because this is consumer products we're talking about, the consumers' fickle needs and wants (or marketing's perceptions of them) will drive the direction of the company, and you'll be obliged to go along for the ride.

KEY JOBS

Most of the jobs described below require an undergraduate degree or an MBA. Senior management positions in marketing, operations, R&D, and other departments tend to be filled from within the company (or at least, from within the industry). This is a hierarchical business and though merit and hard work count for a lot, even the wunderkinds have to do time before they're promoted.

Customer Service

This is as entry-level as you can get at any major consumer products company; customer service representatives are on the front lines with the consumer all day, every day. Tasks can include everything from registering complaints to hearing praise, entering orders to solving a crisis with a distributor or shipping company. Many CS folks use this position as a launch pad for a career in marketing—arguably, there are few better ways to really get to know the product and the customer. To thrive in this job, you have to be a people person with a lot of energy. Salary range: $20,000 to $35,000.

Marketing Assistant or Analyst

If you've just graduated from college, these are the trenches which prepare you for product management and brand management. Some of the work here is administrative, but your ideas are welcome and the brand management team will depend on your organizational ability as much as your knowledge of the target customer. An MBA will typically start as an assistant brand manager for a few years before being put in charge of shepherding all the product pieces to market. In either case, you can expect a lot of poring over sales and merchandising figures, Nielsen ratings, and premiums. Compensation varies widely depending on the company and its location, as well as where you went to school and your relevant experience. Salary range: $25,000 to $70,000.

Product or Brand Manager

Conjure up your gloomiest images of what shopping was like in the Soviet Union. This is the fate product managers work to save us from. They create the catchy new names and novel packaging. They ask prospective customers how to make products even more irresistible. Then they scramble like mad for prominent display space, ad dollars, and their marketing director's active support. You either work your way up the ladder to these jobs or start at this rung with an MBA. Very important reminder: Headhunters really love successful product managers. Salary range: $45,000 to $100,000 or more.

Market Researcher

To do this job, you don't really have to wear glasses and ask silly questions—you do have to have a strong interest in the psychology of customer behavior and an ability to coax this information out of prospective purchasers. Tools of the trade include focus groups, one-on-one interviews, Nielsen data, and quantitative surveys. People can enter these positions from undergraduate, MBA, or industry backgrounds. Salary range: $30,000 to $100,000.

Research Scientist

Academic appointments for chemists and biologists are hard to come by these days and often don't pay enough to support a family. Formulating and developing new products—whether shampoo or frozen dinners—is a compromise many scientists find less difficult and more interesting than they had imagined. You don't need a head for numbers, but you do need a better sense of consumers and markets than most lab technicians have. "Just because you think purple cereal with pink speckles would be really fun to develop doesn't mean people will buy it," says one scientist. Salary range: $45,000 to $55,000.

Sales

You still see them from time to time, personable young people trundling from small retailer to small retailer promoting their wares. Sales is generally the easiest place to enter the company without experience. Those who become successful at this work are usually stronger on personality and gumption than on higher education. Generally, the bigger the accounts you work on, the more money you can make. At the senior level, the earning potential far surpasses that of a brand manager—and you won't have the MBA debt to worry about either. Salary range: $25,000 to $100,00, not including commissions, which can significantly increase take-home pay.

Logistics or Manufacturing Engineer

And now for something completely different. Logistics engineers are the folks who figure out the popular but complex just-in-time manufacturing—the approach to scheduling which allows retailers to receive factory orders when they need them, not weeks or months in advance. If you have strong organizational and computer skills—plus patience and diplomacy—you'd be good at this work. But no matter how carefully you think you've calibrated just-in-time, every now and again human fallibility will intrude, and according to one insider, "just-in-time becomes just-in-time-to-catch-hell-and-worse." Salary range: $45,000 to $60,000 or more.

Manufacturing or Finance Manager

Because of the just-in-time inventory pressures, manufacturing and production plants also increasingly need MBAs with creative financing skills to help solve problems, assess profitability, and acquire new businesses. In some companies, these finance analysts and managers actually have equal and occasionally even greater authority than marketers. They aren't responsible for the presentations to senior management or the coordination with advertising, but they make many of the important recommendations and decisions that direct the course of new product development. Salary range: $50,000 to $60,000 and up.

REAL PEOPLE PROFILE

MICHAEL CHAVEZ

OCCUPATION:
Marketing associate

YEARS IN BUSINESS: 3

AGE: 32

EDUCATION: BA in economics, Rutgers; MBA, Wharton School of Business

HOURS PER WEEK:
45 to 50, 8:00 A.M. to 6:30 P.M.; 1 hour for lunch

SIZE OF COMPANY: 200,000

CERTIFICATION: None

ANNUAL SALARY:
$75,000, plus an annual bonus of 5 percent

How did you get your job?

Two ways actually. This is a very big food and beverage company, but one surprisingly difficult to find an opening in. I work in a great location—Southern California—and a lot of people would like to work here. So first, I found out through a head-hunter that there were openings available. Second, I followed up with a classmate from business school who I knew worked here already. It was actually the combination of the two that got me the job I have now.

Describe a typical day.

8:00   Arrive at my desk and have a cup of tea.

8:10   Make phone calls to set up meetings and confirm appointments with team members or management for project reviews. Lots of internal selling and pushing a product through the system in this job.

8:30   Have a meeting for one of my three projects. This one includes most of the cross-functional team: market research, promotions, finance, operations, R&D, and manufacturing. Although my manager attends, I lead the meeting. Our first task is to review the brand's monthly volume performance. From there, we'll address key issues on the business side.

9:20   Have a meeting for my second project. In this one, we're renovating a brand—one of my favorite things to do. We're a bit farther along on this one so now we're focusing on working with manufacturing to produce some prototypes.

10:30 Meet with my manager. We review the morning's meetings and come to a consensus on what the next steps should be. We also discuss who will lead the various initiatives currently under way.

11:30 Quickly write up the most important points to emerge from these various meetings. Make copies for cross-functional team and senior management.

12:00 Conference call with one of our plants. More notes to write up and distribute.

12:15 Down to the cafeteria for a welcome break. Almost everyone eats there. You can eat outside on the patio, and it's hard to spend more than $5. The food is good, and it's nice to have a moment with colleagues that is more social than it is work.

1:00   A few more phone calls; most are work related, but a few are household catch-up calls as well.

1:30   This is the time I try to set aside to get some real work done. I usually block out approximately one hour per project—to write a marketing plan, finish a senior-management presentation, do some analysis with sales data or Nielsen ratings, work with models and Excel, and figure out ways to push the project through the system a little more efficiently. Meetings in the morning and very focused work in the afternoon provide a nice balance. The day flows well.

4:00   Off to a focus group. These don't happen all the time, but they really are helpful. I love listening to people talk about brands. In this part of the world (Southern California), they're also pretty sophisticated and articulate. This first group is kids just out of school.

6:00   Adults for this next round. The facilitator has been taking lots of notes and so has the ad agency. As always, what we thought they'd say isn't what they're saying. Focus groups keep you honest.

7:00   Time to call it a day. In addition to interesting people, this area has lots to offer after hours. You can actually have a life in this job and probably have a lot more to offer the job itself as a result.

What are your career aspirations?

I'd like to do what I'm doing now at a higher level in four to five years—though helping to manage a midsize company may be more appropriate over the long term. I'd like to stick with marketing and be managing a much larger portfolio. I enjoy the food business and other consumer products as well. I don't see myself in high tech, though obviously it's where a lot of people end up after a job like my current one.

What kinds of people do well in this business?

Cheerful. Jump-starting. Lots of enthusiasm. Bright people who can motivate others. We all hear too much about teams and teamwork but they really are important. You have to be able to work with so many different types. People need very different incentives and it's not easy to get them rallied behind a common goal. You also have to be organized. There's constantly a lot of stuff going on. Little things—why is volume not up this month? You have to be able to drop everything and answer that immediately. You have to be flexible and not let the constant interruptions really affect you.

What do you really like about your job?

Working with different types of people and putting on different functional hats in addition to marketing—finance, operations, market research—it makes the job more dynamic. But the people are what really matter. They're very energetic. Friendly. The kind of people you like to hang out with as well as work with. There's a little dating here, but actually not a lot. Maybe more so than in other places I've worked since most of us are the same age and have the same lifestyle.

What do you dislike?

The layers. All the bureaucracy, though most of senior management is very approachable. The VPs will walk around the floor, and you can walk into their office and just shoot the breeze. Layers are more of a problem when you're trying to get things through the system. It really just depends on the project. Typically, you have to sell all the way up to general manager—four levels above me. But you don't have to do it all by yourself, and you can often do two at once. And if you've done all your homework and you cover all the major points, you usually sail through. It just takes a lot of time.

What is the biggest misconception about this job?

That we're so underpaid. A lot of good people stay away. Obviously, consulting and banking command higher salaries, but I think we actually make more per hour. Most people start appreciating their free time later, once they've paid off their student loans. But you can do that in these jobs as well. The other big misconception is that this is advertising or promotions. People actually ask me, "Oh, do you design the coupons?" There are marketing jobs that could be defined that way, I suppose, but not

this one. In fact, the more appropriate name for this job really is brand management.

How can someone get a job like yours?

It's very hard without an MBA if you go to a big company. And unfortunately, there aren't a lot of companies, large or small, recruiting from undergraduate programs. Marketing assistants are usually the new MBAs. My company recruits at the big schools and takes some write-ins, but for the latter it's pretty difficult to land a job without heavy work experience or impressive contacts. If you're a minority and you don't have impressive contacts, you may be able to get an interview through the various conferences and minority programs. There was a black MBA conference last year in Dallas, and there's the national Hispanic MBA conference as well. Scholarship programs are also available.

GETTING HIRED

The hiring process in many consumer products companies, like their approach to marketing, tends to be relatively structured. One firm we spoke with boasted about having followed the same process for decades. Most hire some people from college campuses into marketing, sales, engineering, and other positions. Once on board, new college hires often go through a rigorous training program designed to fill their heads with the standard operating procedures for their firm. In addition to entry-level hires, many firms also scout for candidates with industry experience. However, compared to fields such as advertising, movement among firms seems to be less common.

Many firms have somewhat quirky selection procedures. For example, General Mills administers a creativity test to some candidates; P&G has its candidates complete a problem-solving test, colloquially known as the P&GMAT. Despite the quirks, however, the competition to land a spot at a top company is intense. The biggest players are well known, they offer great training programs, and they hire a relatively small number of talented candidates. If you're set on landing a job at a consumer products company, keep these things in mind:

- Because turnover in the industry is low, growth is stable, and most firms hire a relatively small number of candidates each year, the competition for positions is very strong. To get a job, you'll have to have a solid educational background, good people skills, and evidence of your leadership capabilities.

- No one in consumer products is interested in hearing why you might deign to work for them for a brief period while en route to something far more glamorous and well paid. Many of the top people in the industry have been with the same company since graduating.

- Be prepared to demonstrate your interest in the consumer products world. For marketing positions, you'll likely be asked to explain a favorite product promotion strategy; even for other positions, you'll probably be expected to know what products the company produces, who the competition is, and why it's not as good.

Consumer Software

Like almost every other aspect of technology just now, consumer software is growing and a good place to look for work. According to International Data Corporation, worldwide sales of packaged software in 1997 were about $120 billion, of which about $30 billion came from sales of personal-computer packaged software and $5 billion from home-use products. Moreover, the industry has enjoyed a 12 percent annual growth rate throughout the 1990s. For the purposes of this profile, we will focus primarily on application software—the programs designed to do word processing, build spreadsheets, manage finances, learn a foreign language, set up a home office, or build a website. Although businesses and consumers are key purchasers of these applications, both groups are essentially end users seeking to enhance personal productivity. Not surprisingly, companies that sell consumer software are intensely focused on the needs and desires of customers. Probably the quickest way to talk yourself out of a job in this segment is to make the technology seem more important than the end user.

A number of industry trends are worth noting before you begin your job search. First, the Internet's impact on software development has been substantial. Many consumer software applications now include some sort of Internet tie-in, like online checking integrated into a personal finance package or the multiplayer Net version of a CD-ROM game. Developers increasingly need to be able to

REAL PEOPLE PROFILE

JANE SCANLON

OCCUPATION: Producer for a software publishing company

YEARS IN BUSINESS: 8

AGE: 32

EDUCATION: Wellesley; MA in education, Harvard University

HOURS PER WEEK: 60, 9:30 A.M. to 7:30 P.M.; 30 minutes for lunch

SIZE OF COMPANY: 2,000

CERTIFICATION: None

ANNUAL SALARY: $80,000, plus bonus

How did you get your job?

I came to the educational software field with a directly relevant practical and educational background. Prior to getting a master's degree in education (with a specialization in technology), I worked in educational television. During graduate school, I interned with a software company and after getting my degree did freelance work for software publishers. I joined this company as a learning specialist after hearing about the job from a woman I'd attended grad school with.

Describe a typical day.

9:30 Arrive at work later to avoid the worst of the rush hour traffic. Grab some hot tea and review my usual websites for news—either general or specifically related to software and education.

9:45 Dig into the mountain of e-mail waiting to be answered. The director of marketing wants an advance look at the features we anticipate for next spring's product release. An "advance look" is going to require a lot of preparation and a well-choreographed presentation. Start all the many, many wheels necessary for setting this in motion.

11:00 Review production schedule. Make changes and note in capital letters that some of the educational activities for the new CD–ROM are still under

discussion. If I don't remind people at every phase of production that certain issues are still open, some fairly serious "misunderstandings" can occur. I also have to flag all the other areas which are affected. The ripple effect of even just two or three missing pieces is always more significant than anyone thinks.

11:30 Make the rounds to check in with staff. One of the educational specialists has some ideas for building out the activities on the product. She'll drive one of next week's staff brainstorming sessions.

12:15 Work on performance review for one of the senior artists. Send e-mail to set up review meeting for later in the week.

1:15 Grab lunch at desk. Check out the "Circuits" section in the *New York Times* for article on trends in game software.

1:45 Go to a meeting for everyone on the team to check in on production schedule. Hammer out key deadlines and responsibilities.

2:30 Observe the beginning of a testing session with kids trying out one of our new product prototypes.

3:00 Quick break to grab coffee before design meeting.

3:15 Design meeting with artists, engineers, and educational

include both disk and Internet design in the work they do. The Internet also promises a new and dramatically cheaper way of distributing software to consumers. Online distribution does an end run around the expensive questions of shelf space and also the cost of shipping catalogs to mail-order users. The largest companies have dibs on valuable retail shelf space. And mail-order distributors offer customers even more titles and price options than the retail outlets. The Internet gives all players, even start-ups, another way of bringing a product to market. Individuals with a background in online marketing and e-commerce will find lots of opportunities, particularly with smaller software companies.

specialists to discuss activities for product. One of the specialists suggests ways to involve a slightly older group of users. Engineers agree to report back next week with potential ways of integrating the activity into the product.

5:15   Back at desk. Another queue of e-mails to answer. Leave voice mail for the vice president to firm up budget for current project. Remind him (nicely) that several key elements can't move forward until he signs off on the money.

6:15   Check websites of competitors to see about any upcoming product releases.

6:30   Impromptu meeting with associate producer to discuss casting options for upcoming CD–ROM and when to schedule the recording sessions.

7:30   Last check of e-mail—two more messages, but they can wait until the morning. Out to the car to face the evening commute.

What are your career aspirations?

If I stay in this industry for the next three to five years, I'd like to be working as a director for a small company or overseeing an entire brand for a large software company.

What kinds of people do well in this business?

People that succeed in educational software usually have their heart in their work. It's important to really believe in the value of educational software and to have an educational sensibility. You should also be flexible. Things are always changing: what you're assigned to can change, products get canceled, the market changes, and so on. Also, there are no set working schedules, so you get used to coordinating activities of people who come and go at different times. Other important attributes are creativity, strong communication skills, and effective time management.

What do you really like about your job?

I like that I get to wrap my brain around a bunch of different things every day. This job brings a lot of variety and complexity, and I get to use my analytical skills. I also enjoy working on vastly different levels of the process (everything from overall design to HR decisions), being in the field of education, and spending my time with lots of creative types.

What do you dislike?

Sometimes I'm not too crazy about the administrative/managerial aspects of my job—for instance, situations where I come across like the bad guy for sticking to the company's party

line. It can also be difficult trying to stay five steps ahead of everybody, which is definitely part of my job.

What's the biggest misconception about this job?

People oversimplify what we do. Sometimes the perception is that you come up with an idea and produce it—end of story. But the development process is extremely complex, and it involves a lot of strategic thinking. The field is also intensely competitive.

How can someone get a job like yours?

My advice would be to get into the industry in whatever capacity you can. Learn as much as you can about this industry by doing, rather than just by studying. Industry savvy and hands-on experience go a long way in this field, and you should seek out positions that expand your skills set. As for becoming a producer specifically, I believe that the best producers are naturally good at managing and organizing both people and schedules. Too many details and periodic crises are just all in a day's work.

One other key industry trend: the battle for market share. Unlike computer hardware, which has essentially become a commodity business, the software business offers huge rewards to the companies that can establish—and retain—a leadership position for particular types of applications. Microsoft has been the most successful and most feared practitioner of this, but other examples, such as Intuit in the personal finance arena, also exist. The implications for job seekers? Think about the competitive positioning of your prospective employer and whether you prefer to work for an underdog or an industry leader.

Most of the new activity in consumer software is happening in Silicon Valley and the San Francisco Bay Area. But you also might check out opportunities in other tech-friendly areas: Boston (The Learning Company and Lotus are in Cambridge), Seattle (suburban Redmond is home to Microsoft), and New York City's flourishing Silicon Alley. If you're looking for international work experience, give consumer software a close look. Foreign markets are the next big thing for software companies, who are now focusing their sights on China, Japan, Southeast Asia, Germany, and the U.K. Note, however, that these opportunities are usually limited to sales and marketing, and even in these areas, culture and language differences are such that local talent usually takes precedence.

How It Breaks Down

It's possible to divide the industry most broadly according to the setting in which the software is used—in other words, personal versus home office. But industry observers more commonly segment the market based on the type of work an application does. Primary market segments include:

Education

Educational software helps your kids learn to read, teaches you about geography or a foreign language, or stimulates logical thinking, and so on. This category also comprises children's educational games, the nascent electronic-book industry, teaching resources, and music instruction. Key players: The Learning Company, Cendant Corporation, and Disney.

Finance

Financial software includes applications for small business and personal accounting, personal finance, and tax preparation. Key players: Intuit (maker of Quicken), Block Financial (the Kiplinger titles), Microsoft.

Games

A highly competitive and extremely broad market segment, this includes role-playing software, auto and flight simulation, sports, strategy games such as chess, and children's games. Key players: Electronic Arts, GT Interactive, Hasbro Interactive. Also, note that there are many small, thriving studios that use the bigger players for distribution and marketing, as well as big-name individual designers— Sid Meyer, Ron Martinez, Will Wright, Jim Gasperini—who will work for game companies on a project-by-project basis.

Personal Productivity

With more people setting up home offices, this is a market segment with real growth potential. Personal productivity includes desktop publishing, word processing, career development, hobbies, health and nutrition, legal, personal improvement, travel (including airline-tracking packages), and others. Key players: Adobe (PageMaker, PhotoShop, Illustrator), Microsoft (Word, PowerPoint, Excel, Office), Symantec (Norton Utilities). Note: All these packages are obviously aimed equally at corporate markets as well, but home offices are on the rise—marketing, pricing, and functionality may be tailored somewhat differently for various audiences in the future.

Reference

Homes, schools, and businesses are getting rid of old bound reference collections in favor of CD-ROM reference tools that offer portability, lightning-fast searches, and interactive media. This market segment includes encyclopedias, dictionaries, atlases, Internet guides, and zip code directories. Key players: Microsoft, Grolier Interactive.

What's Great

The Right Stuff

Partly because it's a very hot industry (and partly because of the long hours typically asked of workers), consumer software attracts an abundance of young and energetic people. Software company employees are quick to point out that they feel inspired and challenged by the intelligence and acumen of their peers. Also, there is a strong team ethic that infuses many software companies, with employees sharing a common passion for making a great product.

Your Opinion Counts

Because software development is less capital intensive than many types of manufacturing, it's more likely that members of the development team will have a hand in making decisions about what goes into the product. Software workers enjoy the sense that they can have a direct impact on product features and cost. And often there is lots of room for creativity in determining how to position a product in the market.

Follow the Money

Microsoft is famous for the wealth it has created (more than two thousand millionaires and six billionaires so far). But while it's the most famous, it's not alone. Even small software companies—and their employees—can reap huge financial rewards from a big hit. Keep in mind, of course, that there are a lot more people out there with stock options that didn't make them rich. Nevertheless, the opportunity is there. And, at more successful companies, employees can receive annual bonuses that are 10 to 15 percent of salary.

What's to Hate

Too Much of a Good Thing

Even software workers who are passionate about their work note that burnout is a real problem. As one industry veteran put it, "Companies feel that every extra day a product is in development is a day of lost market share." So sixty- to eighty-hour weeks can be the norm. And the short development cycles mean that you are almost always looking ahead to the next deadline—which may only be a few weeks or months away.

No Terra Firma

Some of the most exciting aspects of the industry—its dynamism and fast pace—also mean that there is very little stability in the field. Company priorities (and prosperity) change quickly, and this year's big hit doesn't guarantee a company's long-term stability. (Broderbund was recently bought by The Learning Company despite the runaway success of Myst; Maxis, of Sim City fame, suffered the same fate with Electronic Arts.) Some attribute this to the fickle market; critics claim that software companies, big and small, often lack clear decision-making hierarchies and road maps for getting things done.

Watch Out for Gender Bias

The high-tech industry in general clearly needs to work on attracting a more equitable gender balance to its ranks. Not that there hasn't been progress. In software companies' marketing and technical-support areas, women and men are present in about equal numbers. But engineers are almost always men, and women often note that the industry can still seem somewhat male dominated.

KEY JOBS

Software Engineer

Software engineers are programmers who write the code that makes the software products run. Tasks include implementing and debugging the software. Senior software engineers do some of these same things, but also make higher-level design decisions. Software companies typically fill this position with individuals who have a computer science degree or equivalent programming experience. There's a huge demand for engineers, and this is unlikely to change in the coming years. Salary range: software engineer: $40,000 to $90,000; senior software engineer: $65,000 to $120,000 or more.

Product Specialist

As a product specialist you master a specific area within the software development process and attend to relevant projects. For instance, you might take on the area of customer service and help develop customer-service procedures for titles published by your company. This is a common starting point for recent college grads. Salary range: $40,000 to $75,000.

Graphic Artist

Some of the happiest people in this business are the visual developers. The tools and techniques are constantly changing and improving—and though you have to report to the same project or product manager the programmers do, you're often allowed much more leeway and creativity. Customers also understand and pay a lot of attention to the graphics, and if they like yours, you have an enviable career ahead of you. It's not fine art, but most artists would agree it's the most interesting turn commercial design has taken in decades. Salary range: $35,000 to $60,000.

Designer or Content Developer

This role has several titles and in the past was often shared by the project manager, senior programmers, and others on the development team. But usually now one person is in charge of the user experience and logic flow—how all the text, graphics, sound, and other information fit together. Like a magazine with a very good art director, well-designed content feels natural, inviting, and easily understandable. Software companies are increasingly willing to spend time and money finding just the right writer, artist, or interface expert with significant technical experience for this slot. Salary range: $55,000 to $80,000.

Technical Support Specialist

Tech-support people staff the phones and answer questions from consumers who recently purchased the product. If you don't have a tech background, this is a great way to break into the industry, and recent college grads from various backgrounds (and with excellent people skills) can do very well in this area of the company. Salary range: $30,000 to $45,000.

Technical Writer

If you have a strong writing background and an aptitude for technology, this could be the job for you. Computer science and economics majors with a flair for writing might also take a look at this position. Technical writers produce materials that support the software products—like product documentation and marketing white papers. Salary range: $30,000 to $65,000.

Product Manager or Project Manager

Product managers take the software title from conception through development to the finished product. You define the features that the product will encompass and work with teams of designers, engineers, writers, and quality-assurance testers. Product managers typically hold MBAs or have extensive experience in the software field. Salary range: $55,000 to $90,000, with more-senior product managers (with about three to five years' experience) making $70,000 to $110,000.

Software Architect or Designer

This senior-level position requires someone with a comprehensive grasp of software design and an understanding of industry trends. Software architects make key decisions about how to put together products and typically oversee a vast array of titles and a large staff. Salary range: $70,000 to $120,000 and up.

GETTING HIRED

As you embark on a job search in the software industry, you should decide first whether you prefer smaller companies, including the many new start-ups that surface each week, or larger industry players. Small companies offer far less in the way of organizational structure and office systems, and you'll often be fending for yourself on the administrative front. You'll almost certainly have a smaller salary, but if you're lucky, a potentially much more generous stock package. At

REAL PEOPLE PROFILE

BARNETT JAMIESON

OCCUPATION:
Director of marketing for a software company

YEARS IN BUSINESS: 5

AGE: 35

EDUCATION: BA in chemistry and MBA, Stanford University

HOURS PER WEEK:
70, 8:00 A.M. to 6:00 P.M., some weekend work; 45 minutes for lunch

SIZE OF COMPANY: 3,500

CERTIFICATION: None

ANNUAL SALARY:
$170,000, plus stock options

How did you get your job?

Right after business school, I worked for five years in management consulting, including a fair amount of marketing work. When I decided to leave consulting, I realized that I wanted to be inside a company whose customers cared about the product. So I joined this company as an assistant product manager. This was a bit strange for someone five years out of business school, but I was very committed to making this change. After three months as an assistant product manager, I was promoted to product manager, overseeing an extension of our product line. The company was growing quickly, and nine months later I was made a group product manager, where I oversaw launches of new products. I did this for two and a half years, worked on the international side as director of new-business development in Europe for about a year, and then took my current position.

Describe a typical day.

8:00   Arrive at work. Spend a few minutes scanning the business page for high-tech news. A couple dozen e-mails to return, including one from a manager seeking clarification on follow-up to yesterday's staff meeting.

9:15   Leave a voice mail for the entire staff with final agenda details for the product-plan-

ning meeting later in the morning. Return a few voice mails that have already popped up this morning.

9:30   Another e-mail to return—an urgent one from senior management seeking input on the past performance of our ad agency.

9:45   Final preparation for morning staff meeting.

10:00   Staff meeting to discuss branding for a new product under development. Managers review market-research data and propose ideas for key product features to highlight in marketing plan.

12:15   Staff meeting breaks up; huddle with senior product managers to clarify follow-up steps.

12:45   Lunch break. Squeeze in a quick two-mile run in the corporate park surrounding the office. Grab a salad in cafeteria and head back to the office.

1:45   More e-mails to answer. The engineers have a couple of questions about some of the features we're going to offer with the product-upgrade release.

2:15   Make the rounds to my staff, touching base with product managers and associate product

larger software companies, your job will likely be more narrowly defined, but you'll also have a much greater sense of security that your company will be around in a year or two. If you need some degree of structure in your work, the larger firm is the better bet, though this also means a more settled and very possibly less dynamic work environment. Whatever your preference, here are some tips on landing a job:

■ If you're applying for a technical position, you will almost certainly be asked to write some code as part of your interview. You'll also impress your interviewer if you can discuss previous programming you've done—especially if it relates to the type of application you'll likely be working on.

managers on their current projects.

3:00 Work on performance reviews for a marketing assistant and a product manager, both coming up on two years with the company.

3:30 Meet with senior product manager and art director to discuss packaging for upcoming product release. The art director presents a couple of prototypes, and the senior product manager agrees to take the lead on driving the next stage of development.

5:00 Post-meeting conference with senior product manager to agree on follow-up to packaging meeting.

5:30 A few more e-mails to answer. Also, return voice mails from an account manager at ad agency.

6:00 Out the door—after a quick glance at stock quote website for latest from Nasdaq.

What are your career aspirations?

Working with people who care about the product is very important to me. So, a few years down the road, I'd still like to be leading a team of marketing people working on a product that customers are passionate about.

What kinds of people do well in this business?

People who have a "can do" attitude regardless of the many hurdles that get in their way. Also, people who are capable of getting things done by persuasion—rather than by sheer authority—and by moving a group of people in a single direction. It's also important to be bright and have the ability to change direction quickly.

What do you really like about your job?

I like that in consumer software you can make a product that has a direct impact on customers' lives, and we do get a lot of consumer feedback. I also like the creative aspects of the marketing process, like advertising and packaging, and the chance to work with a whole team of people.

What do you dislike?

One result of our company's growth is that it's harder to get things done quickly. You need to get more buy-in before moving forward.

What is the biggest misconception about this job?

There are two related misconceptions, and they're really two sides of the same coin. People who come to consumer software from technical backgrounds expect the industry to be mostly technological work, and

they're surprised to find out how much emphasis is placed on consumer marketing. On the other hand, people from consumer marketing backgrounds expect software marketing to be just like traditional consumer marketing, and they're surprised to find out the extent to which technical considerations figure in the process. Basically, consumer software marketing is split about 50–50 between technical work and marketing work, and many people outside the industry don't realize this.

How can someone get a job like yours?

My advice would be to get an MBA from a top school and then start working your way up. There are certain skills that you want to develop: an aptitude for strategic planning and big-picture thinking, management and team-leadership skills, and sound marketing skills—running an ad campaign, running a direct-mail campaign. When you come out of business school and enter the software industry, you face a key choice: Do you go with a more established company with good training and lots of structure, but less growth potential? Or do you go with a newer company with less structure but more potential for growth? My personal preference is to look for the growth potential, but this isn't for everyone.

- Whether you're applying for a technical or a business position, you should know the products of the company to which you're applying. It's even better if you can offer suggestions about how you'd improve the product from a user's standpoint, and how that would give the product a stronger position against the competing products on the market.

- Be enthusiastic and energetic. Remember, this is an industry in which ten- to twelve-hour days are the norm, and product launches kick off the next product-development cycle. Your interviewers know that success on the job depends on dedicated work by all members of the team.

Education

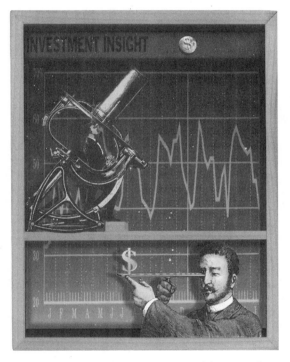

Education is a field that everyone feels he or she understands. After all, we all went to school, didn't we? We all remember that wonderful teacher or professor who changed the way we look at the world—and unfortunately, we all remember that idiot who was just punching the clock, wasting our time, day in and day out. But few of us realize just how vast this field is. Get this: Education in the United States is a $660 billion industry that employs 6.5 million people. And those aren't all teachers; everyone from the guidance counselor to the administrator, from the school nurse to the librarian, from the district locksmith to the bus driver to the investment fund manager is an essential part of the system.

There are two basic categories of schools in the United States. Public schools receive the bulk of their operating funds from the local, state, and federal governments—in other words, from your tax dollars. As a result, these schools—from PS 182 to UCLA—are accountable to the public. When we go to the polls to vote—be it for president, governor, or school district officials—the candidates' educational policy is often one of the criteria we use to make our decisions.

Private schools are not funded by taxes; they're funded by tuition fees and private donations. As a result, they're not accountable to the public; who attends

REAL PEOPLE PROFILE

BETH KIM

OCCUPATION: Sixth-grade humanities teacher

YEARS IN BUSINESS: 4

AGE: 27

EDUCATION: BA in comparative literature, Chico State University

HOURS PER WEEK: 60, 7:30 A.M. to 5:30 P.M.; 30 minutes for lunch

SIZE OF SCHOOL: 900 students

CERTIFICATION: Teaching credentials from UC Berkeley

ANNUAL SALARY: $34,000

How did you get your job?

Just going by word of mouth, going into the principal's office and letting him know who I was. I'd also tutored there a few years ago, before my credential.

Describe a typical day.

7:40   Begin prep work (photocopying and so on).

8:30   My first humanities core class; it goes until 10:20.

10:35   The students have a break until 10:35. After their break, I teach a 45-minute reading period.

11:30   Do more prep work.

12:15   My students and I have a lunch period—but we don't always eat together.

1:10   Teach the same humanities core class to another group.

3:15   One day a week after school we have an hour-long staff meeting. Another day, I stay after and work with the kids on their homework. The other three days I'm there until about 5:30 grading papers and the like. That means I'm home by about six. I don't generally take home work during the week, but I grade a lot of papers over the weekend. Today I have to call a student's parent who may come in as a guest speaker. She lived in Italy for a number of years and has a lot of slides on Italian art and architecture.

What are your career aspirations?

I think I'd still want to be in a classroom in some capacity. I could also see doing some consulting, maybe working with new teachers, maybe teacher training or some kind of corporate teaching as well as being a regular classroom teacher. I wouldn't want to give that up.

What kinds of people do well in this business?

I think, the kind of people who need to feel like their job means something beyond the money; people who really need to feel like it matters whether or not they show up at work. And obviously, people who love kids, who are very patient, and who have a sense of humor.

What do you really like about your job?

I really like the creativity and just being so independent, never having anyone really looking over your shoulder telling what you can and can't do, but at the same time being able to work with others and collaborate. I like being appreciated so much by the kids and their parents. And the vacation. And just feeling like you're doing something that means something. It doesn't pay much, but teaching has one of the highest job satisfaction ratings.

What do you dislike?

I dislike how hard I have to work: the hours and all the meetings. The number of kids we have to work with. And the pay. I would also say, how disrespected you feel by the administration in districts, by the bureaucracy. You're often not treated like a professional by the people who are supposed to be advocating for you.

What is the biggest misconception about your job?

That it's easy, especially at lower grade levels. It's a different kind of hard work.

How can someone get a job like yours?

You need the credential if you want to teach in a public school. It costs money, but you make up for it in pay and benefits when you land a job. You really need to network when you look for a teaching job. Have anyone you know ask everyone they know if they've heard about an open position. The easiest way to get in is if a position opens up suddenly—the person got sick, quit, whatever. If you can find something like that, you can scoot right in.

these schools (and how much they pay), who teaches at them (and what they teach), and who runs them are all privately made decisions.

Recently, however, the lines between public and private schooling have begun to blur in response to criticism of American students' standardized test scores and the sorry financial and physical state of schools in some parts of the United States. In some places, private entities are awarded charters to operate public schools (for example, the Edison Project and the Hope Academies). Some local governments give vouchers to parents for them to use to send their children to private schools. Some public schools even raise funds by selling ad space on school grounds to corporations.

The jury's out on whether any of these actions can improve educational institutions. Regardless, this is a huge field with opportunities aplenty for job seekers. In most cases, if you want to teach K–12 or work in other positions that include student contact, you'll have to get certification. If you don't have your credential, though, don't despair. You might still be able to land a job in a troubled (that is, under-funded, inner-city) school district or through Teach for America, which hires college grads for two-year urban- and rural-district stints. You can also work at a private school; many hire recent grads. If you teach in an urban district or at a private school, be prepared to earn a meager salary; suburban public schools generally offer the best K–12 salaries. At the college level, you'll probably have to have at least a master's in your academic specialty. But the big bummer for would-be college-level teachers is that jobs are scarce and that you may have to move to Oklahoma or Alaska to do the work you want to do. (No offense to those of you in Oklahoma and Alaska—it's just that for most folks, those places are far away.)

How It Breaks Down

K–12

In this segment there are about 85,000 public schools and 26,000 private schools in the United States. In terms of enrollment, there are some 46 million public-school students, and almost 6 million private-school students. The structure of schools in this segment is shifting toward bigger middle schools, with many of these now handling students from the fifth through the eighth grade. Another big trend: growing class sizes. There are a lot of opportunities for job seekers in K–12 education, but be forewarned: Public-school teachers usually earn significantly more than private-school teachers (about $35,000 versus about $22,000).

Higher Education

This segment includes community colleges, large universities known for their research programs, and everything in between, public and private. As in the K–12 segment, the public schools do a major share of the hiring. Higher education provides a host of opportunities in a number of positions rarely found in the K–12 segment: investment manager, alumni fundraiser, financial-aid officer, admissions officer, buildings and grounds manager, and the like. Higher education is the place to look if you're as interested in doing research and publishing in your field as you are in teaching. This segment also includes non-degree-granting teaching institutions like the University of California at Berkeley Extension Program; if you have expertise in a given field but lack academic credentials, you may be more likely to find at least part-time work at these institutions than at a college or university.

Education-Oriented Businesses

Education-oriented businesses teach subjects that fall outside the scope of traditional schools. Thus you have Kaplan-owned SCORE! to help kids improve grades, as well as Kaplan proper and the Princeton Review to prepare students for the SAT, the GMAT, and other exams. Foreign-language schools also fit into this category, as do a plethora of business, computer, self-help, and other education companies. While such organizations prefer experienced hires, many will train new hires or expect them to learn on the job. Lots of college grads get jobs in these types of schools to get a taste of teaching and possibly move on to more-traditional schools after getting a master's or a teaching certificate, but others make a career out of this type of teaching. Downsides for job seekers include low pay, little job security, and few chances for advancement.

What's Great

Doing Good Is Doing Right

There's a lot that's wrong in our society: crime, apathy, and so on. As a teacher, you'll take pride in knowing that you're doing more to fight our problems than almost anyone else—by attacking them at their roots. If your students move on to the next level with the confidence that they can learn, achieve, and make a positive difference, they'll be less likely to drop out and became a drain on society and more likely to lead lives in which they make things better.

Can't Touch Me

Job security is high in many areas of the education field. Many teachers at both the K–12 and higher-education levels enjoy the benefits of tenure, which protects their jobs unless they screw up in the most egregious way. If you do well early in your career and get tenure, you may not get rich, but you'll be set for life in terms of having a career.

Continuing Education

For those who love to learn, a higher-education faculty job can be a dream come true. You'll be expected to continue your learning by keeping up with advances in your field. In many positions, you'll also be expected—even required—to continue your research. (We've all heard the phrase "Publish or perish.") In addition, your school will send you hither and yon to academic conferences and give you sabbaticals during which you can focus on research. And there are always those summer vacations.

What's to Hate

Life on a Budget

You're never going to get rich as a teacher. Oh, there may be some professors who make $250,000 a year—but they're generally already businessmen or writers at the pinnacle of their profession. Unless you're the same, prepare yourself for life in the middle class. You can advance in your career, but at every level you're not going to make much more than $60,000 a year. And there'll be no corporate-style perks—no free dinners or cab rides home if you work late and no stock options.

Busting at the Seams

We've all heard the news: There's a crisis with a capital C in American education. This means a lack of money for supplies (in poorer areas, for basics such as toilet paper—it can be that bad) and large class sizes. The job of teaching in many places may indeed be more difficult today than it ever was. The flip side, of course, is that there may be more opportunity to help kids than ever.

Not This Again

If you teach at the secondary-school or higher-education level, prepare yourself for some yawns. You'll be expected at department meetings, where there may or may not be topics of substance to discuss. And often, you'll find yourself teaching the same course every year. This might be great during the second and third years, when you can improve on areas of your lectures that were weak the previous year, but after that, things might get dull at times. No matter how much you tweak the curriculum, you'll still be lecturing about the same topics—and even *Paradise Lost* can get old after a while.

KEY JOBS

Elementary School Teacher

People in these positions have a huge impact on their students' lives. The obvious part of the job is the time spent in the classroom, writing letters on the blackboard or helping students construct model cities out of milk cartons. But that is just the beginning of the work here. Teachers also have a lot of out-of-the-classroom work to do: grading papers, collecting those empty milk cartons, composing class plans, and the like. There is also night school or summer school to consider, for those who wish to improve their credentials and make a bigger salary. Salary range: $18,000 to $50,000.

Middle School, Junior High School, or High School Teacher

The job description here is similar to that for the elementary school teacher; the big difference is that rather than teaching a number of subjects and seeing the same students all day, every day, you'll be teaching a single subject to a number of different classes. You'll also be dealing with students who are no longer children but are on the verge of adulthood—and with all the hormonal trouble that can mean. Salary range: $18,000 to $55,000.

College or University Faculty Member

Most often, you need a PhD to work in this capacity. The time spent lecturing in front of class is just a fragment of the total number of hours you can plan on working; you'll also be conducting research, writing books or articles, attending department meetings, and attending academic conferences. The beauty of this career is that it will support your pursuit of your academic passion. Salary range: $30,000 to $100,000 and up.

REAL PEOPLE PROFILE

SHEILA MARQUETTE

OCCUPATION:
Reading teacher

YEARS IN BUSINESS: 1

AGE: 27

EDUCATION: BA, psychology and elementary education, State University of New York; MS, education and reading, State University of New York

HOURS PER WEEK:
50, 8:00 A.M. to 6:00 P.M.; 1 hour for lunch

SIZE OF SCHOOL:
800 students; 60 teachers

CERTIFICATION: New York State reading certificate; New York State elementary education certificate

ANNUAL SALARY:
$41,000

How did you get your job?

I have a relative in the school district I work for. Last year the district received a reading-education grant, and my relative told me about positions that were created as a result. The district hired me part-time to teach first-graders, to try to hook them on reading. At the end of the year, I interviewed for a full-time job teaching reading to grades one through six, and I was hired. I pull children who need reading help out of their classes and teach them in small groups, and I teach entire classes of students reading strategies—everything from letter recognition for the youngest students to recognizing central themes for more advanced students.

Describe a typical day.

8:00   Arrive at school. Catch up on paperwork.

8:30   Meet with a fourth-grade teacher to discuss the progress of a girl in her class who meets with me in a small group three times a week.

8:45   Call a parent of one of my second-graders to try to figure out ways to encourage the boy to do more reading at home.

9:00   Teach reading strategies to a second-grade class. Today we're working on underlining the details of a story to help with comprehension.

10:00   Administer a practice test to fourth-grade class. This year, New York is testing fourth-graders' reading skills in the spring.

11:00   Third-grade class. Today we're working on predicting or anticipating what will happen next in a story.

12:00   Lunch with a couple of second-grade teachers in the cafeteria.

1:00   Corrective reading session with a small group of first-graders who have been slow picking up reading skills. Today we're working on matching letters to sounds.

2:00   Another fourth-grade test-prep class.

3:00   The students go home for the day, and I begin prepping materials I'll use in my classes tomorrow—including a couple of colorful graphic aids to illustrate the main characters and their roles in a story I'll be reading with my third-graders.

4:00   Check in with a school psychologist about a fourth-grade boy who's reading at a second-grade level, to find out if his home situation is improving at all.

5:00   Speak with a school speech therapist about a few of my students.

6:00   Head for home.

Student Services

This includes everyone from (at the K–12 level) the guidance counselor, the school nurse, and the attendance officer to (at the higher education level) the admissions officer and the financial-aid officer to (at both) the maintenance worker and the librarian. Salary range: $18,000 to $80,000.

What are your career aspirations?

I would really like to learn more about teaching techniques and resources that are out there. The other reading teacher here, who's more experienced than I am, can read with a student and almost immediately pinpoint his or her problem issues; I want to get as good as she is at doing that—to master being a reading teacher. Someday, I might also want to do something administrative in addition to teaching reading.

What kinds of people do well in this business?

Of course, you've got to like kids. You've also got to be friendly, to be able to work with everybody and anybody, because there are a lot of different personalities among all the teachers you'll be dealing with. You've got to be flexible, because your schedule will be juggled to make sure kids get to reading class whenever there are events upsetting the normal daily schedule, such as when there's a school assembly or during the holidays. You've got to be organized, because you'll be dealing with so many different topics and grade levels every day. You've got to be very patient—for instance, when you're teaching a fourth-grader who can't sound out words and all you want to do is tell them what the words are. You need to be sensitive, as well, especially with the older kids who've been pulled out of their classes for corrective reading instruction; they are very aware that they are behind their classmates and can get very emotional as a result. And you must be enthusiastic, to make reading extra-fun for the kids.

What do you really like about your job?

For one thing, I get to work with kids at all different ages and reading levels. Also, I teach only reading, which means I get to go deeper into a single subject, to master it, rather than just dipping into a whole slew of subjects. And I work with teachers from all grades; teachers tend to form cliques by grade, excluding those who teach other grades, but that doesn't apply to me. Most importantly, I get to help kids learn; they get so excited when they "get" something, and I love to see that.

What do you dislike?

Some teachers don't view corrective reading as an important program, and I don't like that. I don't like that my classes can get canceled whenever there's a school play or a band concert or a class trip; things like speech and reading get pushed aside when this happens, and the kids progress more slowly as a result. I teach first-grade students every day, but see the other kids just a few times a week, and I think the program would be more effective if I saw every student every day. I also don't like the way people—other teachers, in addition to people outside education—sometimes view teaching as a nothing job. Sometimes people turn their noses up when I tell them what I do, and I hate that. I can't honestly complain about anything else. Some people might complain about the money, but right now for me the money is fine.

What is the biggest misconception about this job?

It's not easy. Lots of people, including other teachers, think it is. But there's so much work that goes into it; in particular, nobody ever sees how much there is to do on the administrative and paperwork side of the job.

How can someone get a job like yours?

Get a degree in reading—I'm not sure whether a master's is required or not—because a degree in elementary education is not enough. And get the necessary certification. Then keep your eye on the classifieds and work your connections as hard as you can.

Administrator

These positions include everyone from the high-school vice principal and the school-district superintendent to (at the higher-education level) the provost, the president, and the dean. These are the people responsible for maintaining and improving the intellectual and financial conditions of the institutions they represent. Advanced degrees and significant work experience are a must for many of these positions. Salary range: $30,000 to $100,000 or more.

Substitute Teacher

So, you want to be a teacher but you can't find a job? You can always start as a substitute. Subs are at the bottom of the totem pole in terms of salary and respect, but they are essential to the smooth functioning of any K–12 school. As an elementary school sub, you'll be as much a babysitter as anything else, but from middle school on up, you'll actually be teaching—that is, if the teacher you're subbing for left you a class plan. Salary range: $65 to $100 per day.

GETTING HIRED

Most jobs in education require a BA. For a public-school K–12 job, you'll also need certification in all likelihood. Certification requirements vary by state, but generally, you'll needs a basic-skills certificate in the state in which you want to work. Elementary-school teachers need a multiple-subject certificate, secondary-school teachers need a single-subject credential in the subject they want to teach, administrators need an administrative certificate (and often a teaching certificate, as well), and student-services workers need a services credential. In contrast, many private schools require only a BA degree for teachers, although most look for prior teaching experience.

At the higher-education level, you can sometimes find work at a community or city college with just a master's degree in the subject you want to teach (some community colleges require only a community college teaching credential), but even here most faculty jobs will be filled by PhDs. At the college and university level, there may be work for MAs (for instructors and for those working toward a PhD). But if you want to work at a prestigious school or in one of the more desirable locations in the country, you'd better have gotten your PhD at one of the top schools in your field.

Aside from acquiring the various pieces of paper that employers will want to see, there are a few things you can do to make your job search as effective as possible:

- Network as much as possible; jobs are often filled by word of mouth, so ask friends in the teaching business to keep an ear to the ground for you.

- Show your enthusiasm in interviews. There are plenty of reasons to become jaded in this business; a true passion for teaching will be about the only thing that will get you past the rough spots. No employer wants a cynical or uncaring teacher on staff.

- Be flexible. This is a competitive field, so consider taking a less-than-ideal job with the knowledge that the experience you gain will help you find a better job more easily in the future.

Energy and Utilities

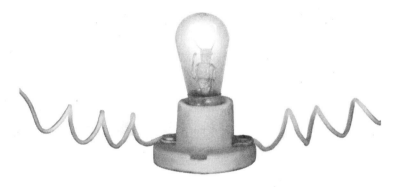

Do you hear a giant sucking sound? It's probably the United States devouring down the lion's share of the world's energy supply. With only 5 percent of the world's population, the United States manages to consume about 30 percent of global energy output. That might not be great news for the environment, but it does spell big business for the country's energy and utilities industry. (Usually energy and utilities are considered closely related but still distinct industries, but we're lumping them together.) How big? This is an industry that has annual revenues of nearly $700 billion—and in which demand will double by 2020, according to the World Energy Council.

But all is not rosy in the energy and utilities industry. For Big Oil, it's a textbook case of supply outstripping demand. 1998's global economic crisis slowed demand for energy, especially oil, significantly. Yet oil-producing nations haven't cut production in kind; the once invincible Organization of the Petroleum Exporting Countries (OPEC) has suffered from internal rifts, and Mexico and Venezuela, both facing shaky domestic economies, have balked at production cuts. In early 1999, oil prices dropped below $10 per barrel—the lowest level since before the great oil crises of the 1970s. That's meant a lot of sleepless nights in the bedroom

REAL PEOPLE PROFILE

CHRISTINA ROBERTS

OCCUPATION: Process engineer at an oil refinery

YEARS IN BUSINESS: 7

AGE: 27

EDUCATION: BS in chemical engineering, UC Berkeley

HOURS PER WEEK: 40, 8:00 A.M. to 6:00 P.M.; 1 hour for lunch

SIZE OF COMPANY: 40,000

CERTIFICATION: None

ANNUAL SALARY: $63,000

How did you get your job?

That was the easy part. My university had a great recruiting program. I met with recruiters, was invited to a site visit, and was offered the job. I'd been a co-op student, which meant I worked one semester, then attended school one semester, then worked one semester, and so forth; I worked as a chemical researcher with Los Alamos National Laboratories, where I did the things chemical researchers do: mixing and synthesizing chemicals. The experience wasn't directly related to petroleum refining, but it may have helped me get the job.

Describe a typical day.

8:00 Check e-mail and voice mail. Read the records of the workers in the refinery, which are called turnovers, and which document the work that has been completed during each shift, as well as any potential problems. This is a big part of my job and the only thing that I have to do every single day.

9:00 Go down to the plant and check on current conditions: temperature, pressure, flow rate. Talk with the operators on duty to make sure things are running smoothly.

10:00 Work on a couple of reports: a weekly report for the refinery crew, which concerns day-to-day operations, and a monthly report for management.

11:30 Go out for pizza at a local restaurant with a few other engineers.

12:30 Prepare report for the refinery crew detailing production needs, highlighting changes since the last report.

1:00 Attend a meeting about a special project for upgrading a piece of equipment—the operating well—in the refinery.

2:00 Attend a meeting in which engineers discuss long-term planning for the refinery with an eye on keeping it running efficiently. We discuss both maintenance and safety issues.

3:00 Meet with an expert on heat exchange to get his input on our facility's operations.

communities of so-called Oil Patch cities like Houston and New Orleans, with oil equipment and services companies taking a particularly hard hit. Job seekers face a particularly tough market as major companies such as British Petroleum and Amoco merge specifically so they can trim their workforces. But don't throw away your geology or petroleum engineering degree yet; the industry recovered from a similar slump in the 1980s, and it's bound to do the same now, since the world's thirst for energy will only grow in the future. In addition, the natural gas and coal industries haven't been affected to the same extent as oil and still offer opportunities to new employees.

Meanwhile, the utilities segment of the industry is undergoing its own enormous upheavals. Following the successful deregulation of the airline, telecommunications, and natural gas industries, the government turned its attention to America's power utilities, which turn oil, coal, uranium, and natural gas into electricity, then deliver it to your door. The result: The passage in 1992 of the National

4:00   Visit the refinery for a second time to make sure the day's operations are running smoothly.

5:00   Finish some paperwork.

6:00   Head home.

What are your career aspirations?

I'm trying to figure out if I want to stay in a strictly technical environment, where I've been for the last seven years. Because my company is so large, there are lots of opportunities for engineers to enter the business or management side. A natural progression might be to start managing other engineers, then possibly take on a more business-related management position. But for the moment I'm happy working in the plant and trying to figure out ways to optimize its operations.

What kinds of people do well in this business?

You have to be able to communicate, which can be challenging for some engineering types. In fact, I'd say about 75 percent of my job is com-munications. And I have to interact with vastly different personalities, from engineers and business people to the operators who run and maintain the plant on a daily basis.

What do you really like about your job?

I like the hands-on aspect of the job. You're in the plant with all the pipes and valves, and you interact with so many different kinds of people. I actually have to wear a hard hat and fire-retardant clothing whenever I'm inside the plant.

What do you dislike?

Sometimes I don't see where I have an impact, whereas if the company were smaller, I'd feel like I was affecting the bottom line. Of course, I am, but I don't always feel that way.

What is the biggest misconception about your job?

You'd be surprised how much attention is paid to safety and the environment. When I first started working here, I hesitated to tell people I worked for an oil company because of the misconceptions there are about Big Bad Oil. Sometimes people are critical, but I consider them hypocrites. Also, you might not realize how much of the job is about communications; it's not just sitting at a desk solving problems in your head.

How can someone get a job like yours?

Grades matter a lot for engineers, and I've heard of some companies having a 3.0 or 3.2 GPA cut-off. Also, communication matters a great deal, and recruiters are going to figure out your communication abilities during the interview process, so practice if you need to. Otherwise, getting an engineering job in the energy industry is much like getting a job in any other industry. Find someone you know in a company and ask them to pass on your résumé. Best of all, find an internship and for three months prove you can do a great job. Not everyone can, so if you do, you'll stand out.

Energy Policy Act, which set the stage for the break-up of the old utility monopolies. Federal and state governments are now opening power lines to competition in much the same way as they opened AT&T's phone lines to competition in the 1980s. So far, changes have come slowly, but the evolution of this segment is likely to accelerate. That means utilities will lose the rock-solid stability that made them the investment of choice for widows, orphans, and retirees.

But it also means brand-new opportunities for people looking to work in the industry. With competition comes the need for expanded marketing and PR departments. In addition, many utilities, suddenly free to diversify their business interests, have plans to enter the telecommunications industry, with the Southern Company and American Electric Power leading the way. Such seismic shifts in the industry are sure to open up new opportunities for young, ambitious employees, as formerly stuffy, hierarchical organizations are forced to entertain new ideas.

America's energy companies are clustered in the Oil Patch region of Louisiana and East Texas, though many have major offices in Los Angeles and other coastal cities. Engineers and management types at these companies often do stints overseas; Exxon alone has a presence in some one hundred countries. Outside the United States, London offers the most opportunities. By contrast, utilities are generally more local in nature than energy companies, usually doing business in a single city or region—though with deregulation, this is beginning to change.

Integrated Oil Companies

We have John D. Rockefeller and his Standard Oil Company to thank for the vertical integration of the world's largest oil and energy companies. His empire has long since been dispersed, but its legacy remains in the form of giants like Chevron, Exxon, and Mobil, which are involved in every phase of petroleum production and sales—from the extraction of crude oil through refining and shipping all the way up to gas pump. Unfortunately, recruiters at Big Oil companies are currently following a "don't call us, we'll call you" policy; these companies are reeling in the face of plummeting oil prices, and even the most stable among them are laying off workers.

Equipment and Service Companies

Companies like Schlumberger, Baker Hughes, and Halliburton provide the stuff that makes it possible for the oil, coal, and gas companies to extract those products from Mother Earth. A once-booming business, energy equipment and services have taken a hard hit due to over-production, and only top-notch job-seekers stand a chance in the current difficult market. While the largest companies will certainly survive, boutique concerns such as Dawson Geophysical (a technology expert) and Global Marine (a contract driller) are more vulnerable.

Coal and Natural Gas Companies

Coal and natural gas are increasingly in demand as developing countries wire themselves for electricity. That's good news for those looking to enter these sectors. While Big Oil is increasingly involved in the natural gas business, there are still specialists such as Consolidated Natural Gas, NorAm Energy, and Columbia Energy Group. Since the deregulation of the natural gas industry in 1978, third-party suppliers such as Enron are also growing rapidly. And while coal mining may seem an old-fashioned line of work, business in this sector is still good today. With nearly $20 billion in annual revenues and mines in the Appalachian, Plains, and Rocky Mountain states, the U.S. coal industry is the world's largest.

Utilities

The job of the United States' more than three thousand utilities is to deliver electric power to individual homes and businesses. Major players include the Southern Company (the nation's largest investor-owned utility) as well as regional giants such as Pacific Gas and Electric in California and Boston Edison in Massachusetts. The balance of the industry comprises federal agencies such as the Tennessee Valley Authority; local, publicly owned utilities, which are usually run by municipal or state agencies; and rural electric cooperatives, which serve small communities on a nonprofit basis. While electricity prices have been somewhat depressed in recent years, demand is rising, and utilities offer opportunities for everyone from the linesmen who maintain power grids to the electrical engineers who design them.

Nonutilities

Though they're in the business of electric power generation and distribution, nonutilities serve large individual clients (read: utility companies that need extra electricity to meet demand) as opposed to entire cities or regions. Though they only account for about 10 percent of power generation, nonutilities represent the fastest-growing sector of the industry. In the wake of deregulation, smaller-scale generators are freer to sell energy to big distributors, and small, efficient producers can be quite profitable. Though nonutilities lack the guaranteed business of utilities, they can be attractive to job seekers in search of more-creative challenges.

What's Great

Meet a Need

Unless we collectively forgo the sports utility vehicle in favor of the horse and buggy, the energy and utilities industry is here for the long haul. Work in this industry and you'll help provide a product that's absolutely indispensable to modern life—one that powers hospitals, runs factories, heats homes, and cooks food. And if the world's energy demands double over the next two decades as expected, profits are likely to follow suit.

Change Is Good

Deregulation has the utilities scrambling to compete. That's good news for young, resourceful employees, who can now make a difference in organizations that were once barely discernible from state bureaucracies. "People are really beginning to see how their work ties in with a company's end goals," says one insider. "We're looking for employees who can think independently, even in entry-level positions." Utilities are also expanding into new businesses from trading energy to providing telecommunications products, and that spells good news for job seekers who combine technological expertise with business acumen.

High-Tech Heaven

Everyone in the energy business recognizes the need for innovation. "Even Big Oil knows the future is limited unless they expand into new areas," says one insider. Companies are constantly seeking to use technology to cut costs and increase efficiency. And many—especially integrated oil companies—are rich enough to support cutting-edge research into alternative fuels and other exciting projects that could transform the way the world powers itself. If you're interested in the practical application of your technological skills, this may be the industry for you.

You're the Problem

While in the United States we're still debating whether global warming exists, the rest of the world knows it does. If you work for a natural gas company, you can go to sleep with a relatively clean conscience. But if you're pushing oil or coal, or electricity produced with these polluters, you might find yourself tossing and turning at night—and listening with a fake smile as strangers at cocktail parties let you know just what they think about your line of work.

Drop in the Bucket

Historically, energy companies have tended toward vastness; the same goes for utilities. After all, you cannot wire a city and meet its energy needs with a dozen people on your staff. With size comes a feeling of security, but also the frustration of bureaucratic inertia. "Energy companies are so large and have so many organizational layers that it's frustrating when you actually want to get something done," says an insider.

Social Darwinism

Once upon a time, energy and utilities employees punched a clock, did their work, and received a paycheck. Today, that's changing, as competition forces companies to cut costs and increase efficiency. Some might like this new dynamism, but as a result of it, competition among employees can be fierce and job security is on the decline. According to an insider, "To succeed you must be good. Without the right set of skills, you can expect a lonely and short career." If you need to feel warm and fuzzy about your work, look elsewhere.

KEY JOBS

Electrical Engineer or Gas Engineer

These are the people who design or maintain power plants or natural gas delivery systems or ensure the smooth operation of the complex grid that connects power plants and individual homes and businesses. A BS in electrical or gas engineering is generally required. New grads can expect to begin by performing technical support and analysis. More experienced engineers can move on to project planning and management, where duties range from cost analysis to the evaluation of new products and technologies. Salary range: $50,000 to $90,000.

Mechanical Engineer, Civil Engineer, or Architect

These engineers design and oversee industry construction projects—the offshore oil rigs, dams, and coal mines built by energy and utilities companies. A BS in engineering or architecture is a minimum requirement. Recent grads handle the nitty-gritty of design and structural analysis; experienced people move on to project planning and management, where duties range from the planning of future projects to management and cost analysis once work is under way. Salary range: $50,000 to $120,000.

Computer Systems or Telecommunications Specialist

Jobs range from technical support and troubleshooting for existing systems to the planning, purchasing, and implementation of new systems. The best positions require at least a BS in computer science or a related field, with strong communications skills and project management experience being big pluses. Salary range: $40,000 to $120,000.

Petroleum Engineer or Geologist

These are the people responsible for the discovery and development of new oil deposits. Geologists, geophysicists, and geology engineers form the team that figures out where and how deep to drill; petroleum engineers handle the drilling itself, plus the production, processing, and transport of the extracted crude. Minimum requirements include a BS in petroleum engineering or a geology-related field; a higher technical or business-related degree will help you move from technology support positions into project management. Salary range: $45,000 to $120,000.

Chemical Engineer

These are the people responsible from turning the raw materials into salable products—for example, the transformation of crude oil into gasoline. Recent grads with a BS in chemical engineering provide support for day-to-day operations; experienced chemical engineers can expect to participate in project management as well as the planning and development of future projects. Salary range: $50,000 to $100,000.

Project Manager

For candidates who combine technical training with excellent business and communication skills, project management is the way to go. Stress levels can be high, but so are the pay and the sense of accomplishment that comes with the work. These jobs require at least a BS in engineering, as well as an MBA or an excellent industry track record. Salary range: $90,000 to $200,000.

Lobbyist

The utilities industry is still in limbo, half-regulated and half-deregulated. That means that lobbying and public relations are key to determining the future of the industry. Candidates with JDs are particularly attractive for these positions, though excellent communication and people skills and lobbying experience are often sufficient to get the job. Salary range: up to $150,000.

Marketer or Public Relations Specialist

Marketing people have to have a solid understanding of the client's energy needs, and of the utility or energy company's ability to meet them. Once again, candidates who combine technical and marketing backgrounds have the edge. Salary range: $30,000 to $100,000.

REAL PEOPLE PROFILE

MARVIN FREDERICKS

OCCUPATION:
President of a renewable-energy consulting firm

YEARS IN BUSINESS: 10

AGE: 45

EDUCATION: BS in mechanical engineering, Rensselaer Polytechnic Institute; MS in nuclear engineering, MIT; PhD in mechanical engineering, Stanford University

HOURS PER WEEK:
50, 8 A.M. to 7 P.M.; 1 hour for lunch

SIZE OF COMPANY: 5

CERTIFICATION: None

ANNUAL SALARY:
$75,000 to $100,000

How did you get your job?

I founded my company because I saw there was a niche that wasn't being filled. I'd worked for the Department of Energy, and I'd made a lot of governmental contacts. I approached people to offer my services, and I also found people approaching me. When you start your own business, you depend to a great degree on your professional reputation. But I also have to keep a high profile by attending industry-related events.

Describe a typical day.

8:00 Make a pot of Peet's coffee, which I import from California, and try to resist the temptations in our local bakery. I sit down and check e-mails and phone messages to see if there's any urgent business to conduct, then start putting in calls to Europe because of the time difference. A lot of my clients are European.

10:00 I meet with the office director to review the previous day's work and plan the day ahead. Then I'll often take a walk around the office and chat with the employees to see how they're doing and how their projects are coming along.

10:30 At this point, I start working on my own projects, which can include a wide variety of activities: thinking; drafting marketing plans for clean energy providers; conducting strategic analyses of companies and industries; integrating research into concept-oriented draft reports; talking to clients.

12:00 Either I meet clients for a business lunch, or I stay in the office and eat a salad and read the *Wall Street Journal*, which is a great paper—except for the editorial page.

1:00 Meet with business manager to go over expenses, payroll, and other financial and office management issues.

2:00 Get back to work on my own projects, with frequent interruptions by the telephone. Generally I'll stay at my desk like that until 7 P.M.

7:00 I work in Washington, which is rife with evening meetings and receptions. In my business, it's essential to be visible at events

Trade Representative

Traditionally, people in these positions handled the sales of oil and other energy products in the futures markets. These days, electricity is becoming as much a commodity as oil; as a result, utilities now offer these types of positions as well. Candidates should have degrees in engineering or business and marketing, plus proven negotiation or communication skills. People with both technology and MBA degrees can expect to do particularly well. Salary range: $50,000 to $150,000.

that are related to energy and particularly renewable energy sources, so very often, I'll leave the office and head to one of these events.

What are your career aspirations?

I want to continue to find a way to make renewable energy a major source for the world's total energy needs. I really believe it's possible, and can even make economic sense, but it takes a lot of work to get these ideas accepted. Petroleum engineers own the road and they don't want to move over.

What kinds of people do well in this business?

People who have a background in engineering do well, though people who are simply bright and clear-thinking can do very well too. I've had English majors work for me very successfully. We're interested in making things happen. It's great to understand the technology, but we're not directly involved with building things. So basically, these projects take smart people who can think creatively and write and communicate well.

What do you really like about your job?

This is a really exciting time to be in this industry. New technologies are threatening the status quo, and enormous changes are coming, which is great for people in my line of work.

What do you dislike?

It's a struggle to bring clean technology to a business setting. It can be a shock to see how much things are stacked in favor of waste. And I don't like the bidding process. Sometimes, I know I can do a project better than anyone else, but I won't get it. And bidding is a costly process—it takes considerable time and money. Unfortunately, clients frequently go for the lowest bidder even though they won't do the best job. That's because the client doesn't know what a quality job is, and sometimes the client doesn't even want a quality job.

What is the biggest misconception about your job?

Well, there are a lot of misconceptions about renewable energy generally. People think you've got your head in the clouds. They also don't realize the time, thought, and effort that must

go into solving a client's problem or to make a renewable energy source a commercially viable product.

How can someone get a job like yours?

This is a great time for someone to get involved in the renewable energy sector. The energy industry is being cracked open, and today there's room for new types of people—sociologists, marketing people, everything up to, and maybe even including, poets. If you want to impress recruiters—and move ahead in the industry—you need to understand how the industry is changing. Show that you have vision, expertise, and a variety of skills. Show that you can combine technical expertise with business acumen.

GETTING HIRED

The first thing to do before you apply for a job is study the changes that are rapidly transforming energy and utilities companies; if you do, you'll be better prepared to ride the wave of change washing over the industry. And recruiters will be impressed with your knowledge, especially because they're looking for people who understand how their work affects a company's bottom line. Here are some other tips for your job search:

- Highlight your technical expertise. Energy and utilities companies are highly dependent on advanced technology, and they need people who can design, build, and maintain technology systems. As a result, companies are willing to hire and train people with proven technical aptitude, even if it's not with the same technology you're being hired to use.

- Work on your communication skills. Even engineers and technical people must be able to communicate with their fellow workers; in fact, one insider estimates 50 percent of a new engineer's work involves communications—and an experienced engineer with project management duties sees the proportion increase to 90 percent. Recruiters know this, and they'll be watching how well you listen and communicate.

- Play up your business acumen. "All our employees need to be aware of our company's business drivers," says a headhunter for a large utility company. Even if you're in a specialized field, recruiters will be impressed if you understand what makes a company profitable and how your work adds to the bottom line. You'll also want to emphasize your leadership skills. As the market tightens for certain engineering positions, recruiters can afford to be pickier. High grades are great, but if you can demonstrate leadership and project management skills, a company is more likely to consider you for the long term.

- Network, network, network. Call any contacts you might have to demonstrate your strong desire to work for a particular company. If you're a student, participate in on-campus recruiting. Most big energy and utilities companies come to campuses, so take advantage of their presence.

Enterprise Resource Planning

I f you've been keeping up with the business media, you probably have at least a vague idea of what the term ERP refers to. For the rest of you, just trying to pronounce it might cause someone nearby to ask you what you had for lunch. But ERP (enterprise resource planning) is a booming industry that offers a lot of opportunities for job seekers excited about technology and the role it can play in business. Right now, it's one of the hottest areas in high tech. According to International Data Corp., the ERP market was worth $14 billion in 1997 and will be worth twice that by 2001. This in spite of the slump that some analysts say will hit the industry around 2000 as companies delay ERP software implementation and upgrades to see how the Year 2000 problem shakes out.

At its broadest, ERP is the segment of the software industry that helps large and midsize companies automate basic business functions and integrate data from different departments to streamline the manufacturing process or consolidate all the information about a company's employees. It can even link a company to its suppliers and distributors to form a seamless flow of information about supply and demand called supply chain management.

REAL PEOPLE PROFILE

CANDACE PARK

OCCUPATION: Software development engineer

YEARS IN BUSINESS: 3

AGE: 25

EDUCATION: BS in Industrial Engineering, UC Berkeley

HOURS PER WEEK: 50, 10:00 A.M. to 8:00 P.M.; 30 minutes for lunch

SIZE OF COMPANY: 6,000

CERTIFICATION: None

ANNUAL SALARY: $60,000, including bonus

What do you do?

Basically, I do programming. I develop business software for companies to handle day-to-day business problems. I work in a team, and I concentrate on one small area of a module, adding new functionalities on top of existing ones. To do this I need to know when and how to present a field—a space that holds one piece of information like a person's name or Social Security Number, for example—and how the end user will interact with it. This is all done in the context of a database—a bunch of tables that store data within a server. Based on your business requirements you can design these tables to relate to others in different ways. Once I have one table, I want to make sure I don't duplicate info across tables. The underlying premise is this: When you store data it's meaningless until you create an application to make use of it. Our job is to know what our customers want to do with their data and to enable them to do it.

How did you get your job?

I passed my résumé into a job fair knowing very little about the enterprise resource planning (ERP) industry. When I got called, I couldn't even remember having submitted my résumé. They offered me an internship, which I really enjoyed. Later, I

asked my manager about full-time work, and he offered me a job. I never had to interview formally for the position.

Describe a typical day.

8:30 Leave home. Hey, at least I'm coming into the office; a lot of designers will probably be working at home today.

9:30 Arrive at the office, pour myself some coffee, and grab a bagel and a half for breakfast. Start munching as I set up my laptop. I also log on to my desktop computer for e-mail. No voice mail today.

9:45 Respond to e-mails, none of which are very important. Except one from the support center. A customer called in with a problem. The support person couldn't figure out what was going on so he forwarded it to me. Right off the bat, I can see it's a user problem that a more-experienced support person would have known how to handle. I e-mail him with the answer, nicely.

10:00 Start working. Like a lot of people in my group, I like to split my day between projects I'm working on and fires that have to be put out. Mornings I

This means that the ERP world is very different from its cousin, the consumer software (sometimes called "packaged software") market. Consumer software often sells for less than $100 and can be installed by the user with little trouble. ERP, on the other hand, costs six or, more likely, seven figures for companies to purchase and takes as long as a year for trained professionals to install and customize. Companies take months to determine an ERP budget, decide what they need it to do, and which vendor is going to be able to meet those needs, resulting in a lengthy sales cycle. According to one insider, ERP vendors sell a relationship as much as a product: "Companies choose the people they like best, not the best product."

Opportunities for job seekers exist in several areas. Software vendors such as SAP and PeopleSoft are hungry for technical, sales, and service talent. Likewise, big-name consulting firms such as Andersen Consulting and Ernst & Young are

usually spend on my own projects, knowing that by lunchtime someone will have run into a snag and will be coming to me for an answer. Right now we're in the design phase for the next release. I'm working on a prototype to make it easier for customers to place purchase orders to their vendors over the Internet. It's kind of exciting to be working on Web-related stuff—it's the future of business.

1:00 Grab a sandwich with a coworker.

1:30 Get back to work on a bug that came through the support center yesterday.

3:30 A developer from the team that supports developers comes to me with a bug of his own. I gladly take a look at the problem and give him a few hints.

7:45 Back to my own bug. Finally figure out what the problem is. Now is a good stopping point. I'll do the actual fix after lunch tomorrow. On the way out of the office I chat with the only other developer who's still here this late.

8:40 Get home, eat dinner, and watch TV.

What are your career aspirations?

I will probably eventually try to move into a management or consultant type of role. I still like development, but I don't see myself doing it full-time ten years from know. And you never know, there may be other opportunities that pop up that will interest me.

What kinds of people do well in this business?

You have to have a very intuitive mind. You've got to understand business processes. Some people with a technical background have problems with that. You also have to be detail oriented and hard working. You're doing programming, so you have to know technology and keep up to date on new trends.

What do you really like about your job?

I love the flexibility and the work environment. But the main thing for me is that there's always something new to learn.

What do you dislike?

Sometimes you get really bogged down in detail, searching out bugs. You can get lost in the details and forget the big picture. That's why I'm

interested in management. And near the release date, the hours get really long—up to sixty or seventy hours per week. The job is very demanding, which is why I can't see doing this when I have a family. Also the knowledge I have can become obsolete in two or three years. I worry a little each year that the new crop of graduates will have fresher knowledge and lower salary requirements than me.

What is the biggest misconception about your job?

People think we get paid so much, but it's not really a lot considering how much we work. And that doesn't even include the seminars, classes, and research we have to do to keep up with technology.

How can someone get a job like yours?

I think all they need to do is check out companies' websites and apply online to positions they are interested in. Some people think that networking is all-important, but I think if you have a solid résumé, it's not.

eagerly seeking people with technical skills to help with a wealth of implementation work. At the very least, job seekers will need to be comfortable working with software and figuring out how to use it to solve business problems. But according to insiders, you'll also have to be able to deal with people in potentially stressful situations. Understanding your clients and their business problems and making them feel confident that spending several hundred thousand—or several hundred million—dollars on your software will be an effective and relatively pain-free solution is crucial. To understand how difficult that can be, consider the following statistic from a 1996 Standish Group survey: 40 percent of large IT implementations fail.

Although this is still a hot industry, insiders point to intense competition among vendors as a sign that the industry is maturing. They also suggest that you watch out for continued consolidation among the various players. Currently, the emphasis on new products and markets is shifting to one of providing services to clients. ERP vendors have found that the service business can bring in three to seven times software-licensing fees. Such services include training users, taking on the maintenance of a client's system, and most lucratively, implementing and customizing the software, though all the major vendors rely on information technology consulting firms to do the bulk of the work.

ERP software companies are located all over the country, though the biggest players are located on the West Coast and in New England. Two giants, SAP and Baan, have world headquarters in Europe. Though roughly 80 percent of ERP implementations are located in North America and Europe, opportunities exist all over the world, with Asia in particular being an area of great potential growth. Great opportunities to work abroad exist for people comfortable with foreign languages and business customs.

How It Breaks Down

Most observers break down the industry according to size as follows:

Tier One Players

International Data Corp. estimates that Baan, Oracle, PeopleSoft, and SAP now own 55 percent of the market and that that figure will increase to 80 percent in 2003. The Big Four are full-service multinational vendors that create software suites—covering everything from payroll to manufacturing and distribution to company financials—tailored for specific industries. Increasingly, they implement the software, train users, and maintain and upgrade systems.

Tier Two Players

These smaller players tend to focus on one functional area—HR, for example—and tailor the product for only a few industries, though some have the same scope as the Big Four, just with much less market share. J.D. Edwards, a software-suite vendor that is the reason why the Big Four is sometimes called the Big Five, and Manugistics, a supply chain management specialist, are examples of solid Tier Two companies that may be able to weather the storm ahead.

Tier Three Players

These are primarily startups that tend to focus on niche areas of the ERP market, hoping to fill needs that the Big Four have overlooked. Approaches vary: for example, Convoy develops software that complements that of ERP heavyweight PeopleSoft, while Employease spars with PeopleSoft in the human resources ring. A lot of Tier Three players focus on e-commerce and other Web-related technologies, so if you want a true cutting-edge start-up experience, this is the area to research.

Consulting Firms

Apart from the vendors, there are also the partners—Big Five consulting and accounting firms (Arthur Andersen, Deloitte & Touche, Ernst & Young, KPMG Peat Marwick, and PricewaterhouseCoopers) and other consulting firms that help implement and integrate ERP software with clients' preexisting, or legacy, systems. Implementation is where the big bucks in ERP are, because it takes months for consultants to customize software to the end users' needs. While the Big Four vendors are starting to eat the Big Five's lunch, there's still plenty of food on the buffet table for all.

What's Great

Surfing the Next Wave

One advantage ERP has over consumer software is that businesses require more-sophisticated products. Opportunities to learn a lot about technology and business abound, no matter what job you have. One insider says, "You get a chance to see the way businesses are run. We've pretty much figured out how to solve most business problems. The biggest challenge will be adapting new technologies to what we already know. When the next wave of technology comes, [as someone with ERP experience] you'll be ready."

Money in the Bank

Okay, it's not I-banking, but ERP pays well. And you can have a life. Better still, once you've worked several years, you can start to make as much as 50 percent of your base salary in incentive bonuses. Experienced consultants earn well over six figures, and according to one insider, "There are people here [in sales] who are millionaires." Stock options are a standard—and often very lucrative—part of compensation.

You're Not Alone

Those who like to work in teams will find that to be the rule rather than the exception in ERP. Many core functions, whether sales, development, or implementation tend to be done in a team setting of coworkers, clients, and staff at partner companies.

What's to Hate

Trains and Boats and Planes

Salespeople and especially consultants will find the travel onerous. Salespeople might make three or four presentations a week in a region of the United States. Consultants will usually be on the client site four or five days a week, so it's extremely difficult to have a routine home life.

Service with a Smile

This is a service industry. Salespeople will have a tough time finding the decision makers in a company; especially in the middle market, executives may be leery of investing hundreds of thousands of dollars in technology when their company has been doing just fine without it for years. At the implementation level, consultants will often run into opposition from employees who may resent having to essentially relearn their jobs to accommodate what they consider alien technology.

REAL PEOPLE PROFILE

PHIL SFORZINI

OCCUPATION:
Technology consultant

YEARS IN BUSINESS: 1½

AGE: 25

EDUCATION: BS in business administration, Cal Poly

HOURS PER WEEK:
40 to 50, 8:00 A.M. to 7:00 P.M.; 1 hour for lunch

SIZE OF COMPANY: 6,000

CERTIFICATION: None

ANNUAL SALARY:
$95,000, including bonus

How did you get your job?

Through the university résumé bank. I submitted my name, résumé, and career objective to the electrical engineering career planning office. Companies like the one I'm now at buy the résumés from my school and contact the students who match their needs.

Describe a typical day.

7:30   Grab a bagel and OJ in my hotel lobby.

8:00   Get to client site, a large state university, set up laptop, log on to client's network, check e-mail.

8:15   Start working on modifications to the transfer credit module. This is part of a larger student administration implementation.

8:50   Get a couple of modification requests from the project coordinator, in this case a university employee. Answer his e-mail and then walk over to one of the users.

9:00   Meet with the user to discuss the specifications for the modification. I need to know exactly what he wants the modifications to do before I start working. The priority isn't

too high, so we decide I can do it next week.

10:30   Go back to my desk and continue working on the transfer credit module.

12:00   Go get Chinese take-out and bring it back to the office. Eat it with a couple of coworkers and a partner consultant.

12:50   Check e-mail again. Nothing urgent.

1:00   Get an urgent call from a user; she must have been waiting for me to get back from lunch. I delivered a modification to her last week. It's been completed and signed off on by my manager, but it needs some minor tweaking. I hightail it over to her office and we go over the changes. I tell her that it won't take long. First thing in the morning, it'll be done. She says it needs to be done today if possible.

2:30   I get back to my desk and go to the development database to make the changes. I migrate it to the test database and call the user to ask her if the changes are acceptable.

4:30   She calls me back with the green light, so I get my man-

Here Today, Gone Tomorrow

You can expect a major shakeout in the industry as it consolidates. Job security at some of the smaller companies will be iffy, and even the Big Four can't necessarily guarantee lifetime employment. Baan, for example, was forced in 1998 to cut staff by 20 percent as a result of—get this—too many poorly integrated acquisitions. The silver lining in this cloud is that in ERP, experience is everything—so getting laid off by one company will not preclude you from getting a job elsewhere if you know your stuff.

ager to sign off on it. Then I have it migrated to the production database, which means that it's now live. Whew!

5:00 Get back to work on my transfer credit module.

6:00 Go to a meeting with the implementation team, five of us in all. We discuss technical and functional issues related to the project and the client. Things are going fairly smoothly. Looks like we're on target for the deadline, maybe even a little ahead of schedule. One consultant has a problem with a foreign address field, so another consultant helps him out, and we break up the meeting.

7:00 Go back to my desk to finish up some loose ends on the transfer credit module.

7:30 Rough out my work plan for tomorrow and check e-mail one last time.

8:20 Go out to dinner with a coworker.

What are your career aspirations?

I would like to get a strong foundation in technology and possibly be a project manager or move into a sales position in maybe four or five years. At that point I'd like to find a small company and be a part in creating a product myself. By my thirties, I think I will have enough experience to help grow a technology company.

What kinds of people do well in this business?

Energetic and personable. You've got to be able to communicate well—both expressing yourself and understanding what other people say. I know that sounds generic, but if you don't understand what the users are talking about, then it's going to take twice as long to get the job done.

What do you really like about your job?

I like the travel. I like dealing with people, learning new technology, and being able to build something and see the client benefit from that. I get satisfaction out of seeing the user's job made easier.

What do you dislike?

Travel. Too many things to learn and not enough time to learn it all. I want to better myself, but there's so much to learn. But I don't think I really hate anything about my job or I wouldn't be doing it. I do miss my family during the week—it's lonely on the road.

What is the biggest misconception about your job?

We're not computer nerds. We're just a new generation of computer advocates. We're not nerds. I snowboard. I'm not a nerd. My fiancée would agree.

How can someone get a job like yours?

Be aggressive. Learn the skills that are needed, the basics: databases, SQL. Market yourself with in-demand e-business, Internet, and database skills. I think networking is the biggest thing in this industry. Interview on-campus with as many companies as possible. But stay in contact even if they don't hire you. Down the road they may realize that they need your skill set. Keep in contact with your former classmates and coworkers. The greatest thing for a weak résumé is a good network of contacts in the industry.

KEY JOBS

Jobs fall into two general areas: technical and nontechnical, or business. About 80 percent of the jobs in this industry are on the technical side. Salary levels listed are base salaries only; compensation generally exceeds the base. And don't forget those magic options! "Compensation in this sector has a lot to do with stocks," says an insider. Performance bonuses are also common.

Software Developer

Software developers write the code that makes the software products run. Tasks include designing, testing, and debugging the software. ERP vendors typically hire people with technical degrees and significant programming experience, though the dearth of qualified candidates has resulted in vendors' recruiting people right out of college and training them intensively. There's a huge demand for engineers, and this is unlikely to change in the near future. Salary range: software developer, $40,000 to $90,000; senior software developer, $65,000 to $120,000 or more.

Implementation Consultant

Consultants are the shock troops with the technical and business know-how to implement the software and customize it to fit a client's particular business needs. Most work is done on client sites, working in close contact with clients in projects that can last from a few months to more than a year. Salary range: $40,000 to $60,000 to start; senior consultants make well into six figures.

Technical Support Specialist

Tech-support people staff the phones and answer questions from users who are having trouble with their software. If you have a nontech background, this is a great way to break into the industry, and recent college grads from various backgrounds (and with excellent people skills) can do very well in this area. Salary range: $30,000 to $45,000.

Technical Writer

If you have strong writing skills and you're not allergic to business or computers, technical writing can be a great way to get started in ERP. Technical writers produce materials that support the software products—like product documentation and marketing white papers. Salary range: $30,000 to $65,000.

Sales Manager

Sales in ERP is a little different than sales in other industries, particularly consumer software. Although you will need to keep very focused on customer needs and wants, the dollars involved mean that the sales cycle is longer, more technical, and may often involve custom solutions. In-depth knowledge of both the product and the client's business issues are essential, so experience with ERP software and lots of sales experience are usually prerequisites. Salary range: $45,000 to $80,000 base pay; meeting quotas will earn you your base pay figure again in bonus, and exceeding quotas will earn you multiples of your salary.

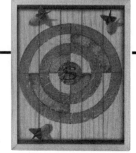

GETTING HIRED

Companies in this industry hire new and experienced employees alike. Although some companies will be seeking people who have very specific technical or sales skills, others will be willing to bring relatively inexperienced people on board and train them (this is especially true of the consulting firms). In any case, you will need to demonstrate that, if not a techie geek, you at least enjoy using and improving computer software. Technology is constantly changing, so adaptability is also crucial. Finally, if you don't have a wealth of technical expertise, but do know a functional area very well (such as accounting, payroll, or material resource planning), be sure to play up your experience. After all, to be successful, ERP software must really solve the problems of lots of people who don't have computer science degrees. Here are a few other tips that may help you with your search:

- Interviewers will delve into any technical or functional experience you have. Be prepared to talk in-depth about any experience you put on your résumé; you will be asked about it. If, for example, you claim to have extensive exposure to Oracle's database during an interview with another Big Four company, you can bet an ex-Oracle employee will be called in to verify your claims.

- No matter what position you're applying for, you should know the company's products well. Experience using ERP software—even that of a rival company—can help you land a job even if you have few other qualifications, so do your research and play up any experience you have.

- Remember that in midst of all the business and technical issues that ERP encompasses there are human beings. People skills are very important in this customer-oriented business, whether you're a salesperson, a support person, or a consultant. Just about the only position that doesn't require people skills is software development, but even there you tend to work on teams, so you can't be completely lacking in social graces.

Entertainment and Sports

So, you want to be in pictures? Or in sports, music, or television? By now, you've presumably made peace with the fact that you're not going to be one of the brand names—the next Michael Jordan or Madonna or Jerry Seinfeld—but you think you might enjoy helping manage or promote or legally protect them. Sports alone is estimated to be a $180-billion business, sprinting along at 5 percent annual growth. Entertainment covers even more ground—film, music, network TV, cable—and though stats are harder to pinpoint, *Fortune* pegs revenues at over $58 billion for the top conglomerates last year and total return for investors hovers near 46 percent.

Trends? Watch for unexpected employers such as NYNEX, Microsoft, and Intel. The 1996 Telecommunications Act lifted an important ban on utility companies developing new media content, and the convergence of digital TV and computers is a reality, despite the woes of high-definition TV. Recorded music revenues may be down, and the future of VCRs and videocassettes remains uncertain, but leisure time and discretionary dollars aren't shrinking. This is a healthy sector of the economy and a good place to look for work—particularly if you live in L.A., New York, or a city with popular big-name teams.

LEE RHEINGOLD

OCCUPATION: Director of development at a movie studio

YEARS IN BUSINESS: 3

AGE: 33

EDUCATION: BA in political science, American University; JD, Georgetown University

HOURS PER WEEK: 50, 9:00 A.M. to 7:00 P.M.; working lunch

SIZE OF COMPANY: 15

CERTIFICATION: none

ANNUAL SALARY: $50,000

How did you get your job?

It's all about connections. I knew one or two people in the film business and I was very thorough and persistent about tracking down every one of their suggestions and leads. In my case, it helped having a law degree, but I certainly wouldn't say it was essential—especially for my current job. It just made me a little different and a potentially more valuable employee.

Describe a typical day:

9:00   Get to work and immediately dive into the mail—both online and the stuff that still comes in envelopes. In my work, a lot still comes in very heavy packages.

10:15   The worst of the mountain has been at least opened if not responded to, and I can now focus for a while on the trades—*Variety* and *HR*—and then some of the financial press as well.

10:30   Start making some calls to other development directors. This is maybe the most important part of the job. Sometimes it can take up almost the entire day. What's everyone else looking at and thinking about? Should I take a look at it too? What's hot, what's not? Gossip matters in any industry, but in this one, sometimes it seems like it's *all* that matters.

1:00   Lunch with an agent and a writer. More gossip. Not anything I don't know already. I'm not sure I'm going to work with these two, but it's important to keep options open.

3:00   Start reading a promising script. Constant interruptions from phone calls.

4:00   Meet with a writer. Hand her over to a staff member to finish the business we've started. I try not to spend too much time in meetings if I can help it.

It's also an industry that encourages mobility, and the increasing overlap between entertainment and sports—Time Warner, Disney, ABC, and News Corp all now own sports teams—means that your contacts in the industry matter even more. Agents, personal managers, and studio executives usually got their start as lowly assistants, but unless your dad knows Ted Turner or someone at Sony or Paramount, don't count on landing even an entry-level slot easily. For those of you with a business and technical background, work is more readily available, and for the rest of you, these are useful areas to develop and learn more about.

Whether you're just starting out or you enter the business with a specific expertise, your contributions are generally limited to contracts, spreadsheets, and dazzling promotional copy, but you often actually come to know the stars you serve over time. One legal assistant recalls being on tour with two famous jazz musicians. Part of her job was to wake them up every afternoon and make sure they got to rehearsal on time. "It wasn't easy,"she admits, "but, you know, when I went back a few years later to work for a firm which did no entertainment [law], it was just so boring." The culture in these milieus is one of anticorporate, studied casualness. There are still uniforms—in the music biz, it's an ever-changing array of baseball caps and jackets; in film, it's tasseled Italian loafers—but they're invariably more relaxed than what anyone else in finance or law wears to work. The people? Well, there's no people like show people, and the sports

4:45 Go back to the script. Make a few notes and then a few calls. Why isn't everyone else all over this? Who else has seen it? Who else likes it?

6:00 Focus my undivided attention on script. Definitely has potential. Take it home with me for a second look, outside the office, away from the phones.

7:00 Catch the train home.

What are your career aspirations?

To be an executive for one of the big studios.

What kinds of people do well in this business?

People who are willing to make their job their life. You really do have to live, eat, and breathe this stuff. If you're looking for something which doesn't intrude too much on your personal life, this is the wrong line of work to get into.

What do you really like about your job?

The feeling of incredible accomplishment when you get to see a film you helped to develop actually made. It doesn't even have to be all that great a film, but the fact that you found it and made something out of it is really great. You also get to meet a lot of very interesting people, all of whom want to be doing the same thing.

What do you dislike?

Sometimes the workload can be daunting and this is not always a sane business. It attracts some very insecure and at times even cruel people. That aspect I really don't like at all.

What's the biggest misconception about this job?

That this profession is in any way similar to any other job out there. It isn't. It's a very distinct kind of work and you have to learn all the ways in which it's different if you're going to survive and succeed. There are certain things you can say and certain things you can't. There are certain things you *have* to say. And since everyone knows everyone else, you have to be careful. Outsiders think it's so glamorous and somehow easy because—what the hell?—it's just movies.

How can someone get a job like yours?

You have to use any connection you have in the film business to get introduced to as many people as possible. And then use them to introduce you to others. It's not as hard as it sounds. Most people here started out not knowing anyone either so they're more willing to help you out than they might be in other industries.

world has even more pep. This is a high-energy crowd. Even if your job is to pore over Nielsen ratings all day, it's probably more fun to do it with these folks than elsewhere.

How It Breaks Down

Despite the blurring lines between sports, music, movies, cable, and publishing—and the media behemoths that preside over them all—these various forms of entertainment are distinct domains. And though at Time Warner you could conceivably enjoy a career that includes working for the Atlanta Braves, Home Box Office, Six Flags theme parks, and the Atlantic record label, most people choose one area and stick with it. These worlds are closely knit, and who you know and who you owe—and who owes you—counts for a great deal, particularly when you're looking for work.

Film

In the days of celluloid movie factories, the major studios controlled the project from the earliest script draft to the opening night at Radio City. Most films were completed in under a month and cost as little as $200,000 to produce. Today there are six major entertainment companies: News Corp, Time Warner, Seagrams, Sony, Viacom, and Walt Disney. Known as the Big Six, they all have their roots in the original MGM, Warner Brothers, Paramount, and other Hollywood back lots. But the modern studios control Hollywood in a different way now: They solicit projects, provide the financing, and make the deals with thousands of smaller production companies. The indies (independents) remain only marginally profitable—and are often owned by one of the Big Six. (Miramax and Fine Line, for example, are actually Disney and Time Warner subsidiaries, respectively.)

To make a movie can now take years, and a cast of thousands—on and off the set—is involved. The costs are invariably staggering (up to $100 million for a special-effects blockbuster), so the promotional blitz before the opening weekend and the synergistic selling of toys, video games, and apparel often have to be that much more pervasive and intense. But as soon as the studio green lights a project, the jobs begin. These are usually short-term contracts or per diem arrangements, but there are still a hundred applicants for even the most menial slots. One insider says, "Everyone's ambivalent and everyone just keeps coming back for more."

Music

To get a job here, you'll have to follow a path almost as long and complex as that from the first stirrings of a tune in a musician's head to the final song you hear every time you turn on the radio. Like most movies, music is often created by committee and the whim of the record label. But the artists retain more control throughout. At least, some do; the Billboard charts always seem to have room for Menudo, the Monkees, Milli Vanilli, and other packaged products. The important support jobs in this process are cover art production, promotional video production, marketing and sales, and publicity—and then more publicity, and then different publicity for radio, clubs, and both the mall stores and anti-mall stores such as Tower Records and Virgin Records. Heads up, lawyers and anyone interested in copyright and licensing: Perhaps the biggest growth area right now is in publishing rights. Whoever owns the rights to songs used in big national ad campaigns stands a good chance of making even more than the record company or the artist.

Sony is currently the acknowledged leader in the business. Other top music companies are Time Warner (Atlantic), EMI (Virgin, Capitol), Philips Electronics (PolyGram, A&M), and Bertelsmann (Arista, RCA). The marked increase in website music sales may change this lineup in the near future, however. If you're interested in marketing to an online audience or the challenge of developing better online audio, these are also great job areas to explore in music right now. So are MiniDiscs and DVDs, as well as videodisc technologies, which are growing apace and are seen as the next replacement candidate for CDs.

Television

The old news in TV is the emergence of cable, especially in terms of ad revenues, and the surprising success of Fox TV, the only new network to date that has threatened the supremacy of CBS, NBC, and ABC. The more interesting and pertinent news for job seekers is the slow but inexorable digital convergence of PC technology, the Internet, and TV, and also the 1996 Telecommunications Act, which allows phone companies and power utilities, among others, to create and distribute entertainment content. The new law also lifted the restrictions on how many stations one company can own, and suddenly many more large corporations now own big pieces of TV's revenues. The good news is that you no longer are limited to the very narrow range of dreary PA jobs that used to be the entrée into TV. You can go work for Pacific Telesis (NYNEX and SBC) or Intel or Compaq or pretty much anywhere that has a digital TV or convergence development group. You'll learn a lot of technology that will be outdated and unusable in six months, but you'll also be on top of three industries, earn more than most people starting out in TV, and have an enviable flexibility and list of contacts for whatever emerges next.

Sports

Okay, we can either be sentimental about this—the O'Malley family sold the Dodgers to Rupert Murdoch's News Corp, no one plays on grass anymore, licensing is more important than the game—or we can just talk about job opportunities. Back when both the O'Malleys and the Dodgers were still in Brooklyn, most of the players had to have day jobs because the pay was so low. And there certainly wasn't any lucrative ancillary employment in marketing, promotion, sports medicine, and managing athletes and events. Now there is, and your options extend well beyond one team or sport. You can work for the William Morris Agency, IMG, or Worldwide Entertainment & Sports and help plan events and the colossal revenue-sharing deals. You can work for Nike, Reebok, Adidas, or a growing host of sportswear manufacturers on endorsements and sponsorships that range from farm clubs to the Olympics. You can earn almost as much as a good pitcher if your legal skills include licensing and contract negotiation. And if you still want grass, coaching jobs are always available—from Little League to college teams—and increasingly contracts and benefits are generous for those who improve team performance.

What's Great

Decreasing Those Six Degrees of Separation

If you get off on proximity to the famous and infamous (and, admit it, no one's completely immune), the entertainment business offers unparalleled access to the great and near great. Whether you are climbing the executive ladder at one of the Big Six film studios or answering the phone for a top sports license lawyer, you're likely to enjoy fairly regular celebrity encounters. If you work for record companies and recording studios, you play host to talent even more frequently, insiders report.

Onward and Upward

Film, TV, and music are industries in which you can move from one job to another with relative ease, depending on whom you know or have worked with previously. You might start out as a secretary in the marketing department of a major studio and become, surprisingly quickly, a development executive—if you've put in your schmooze time. Or you could work for a few years in development and then go off on your own, writing and selling your own projects to the contacts you made in your old job. These are milieus where people reinvent themselves constantly; you can, too.

REAL PEOPLE PROFILE

CATHERINE NAZDEN

OCCUPATION:
Music label publicist

YEARS IN BUSINESS: 5

AGE: 27

EDUCATION: BA in communications, minor in business, San Diego State University

HOURS PER WEEK:
55 to 60, 9:30 A.M. to
8:00 P.M.; 1 hour for lunch

SIZE OF COMPANY: 17

CERTIFICATION: None

ANNUAL SALARY:
$46,000

How did you get your job?

I began as a summer intern and then continued to work on a part-time basis when I went back to school. My first big promotion was when they made me the receptionist! This doesn't sound like much of a promotion, but in this business receptionists wield a lot of power. To get in to see anyone, you have to be nice to the receptionist. I then moved up to an assistant's job in publicity, and after working on tours for a while, I was made a national publicist.

Describe a typical day.

9:30 Get to work and chat with coworkers for short while. This is a very informal office, not a lot of politics or back stabbing. I think this is unusual, though. In general, the music business is pretty competitive.

10:00 Browse through e-mail. Nothing that can't wait.

10:20 Glance at the trade papers and then plunge into some of the more mass-market publications to see what labels and artists are getting coverage, what kind, and how much.

11:35 Begin calling around to journalists and pitching them story ideas over the phone. This is not my favorite part of the job—almost no one has time to listen to even a short pitch. But most of the artists and bands I'm helping publicize really are great, so these are good stories.

12:00 Return to e-mail for a while and make some calls or write letters to managers and labels.

1:00 Lunch (lettuce leaves and matchstick vegetables) with a young artist and manager to go over interview schedule and set up photo shoots. Make a mental note to remind these two often of upcoming events. Both look preoccupied with other issues. This is also not my favorite part of my job.

2:00 Write up several press releases and edit the first drafts that the person who has my old job prepared. Try to be a better teacher (and more patient!) than my former boss was.

Being Part of the Buzz

No matter how jaded entertainment professionals become, they still enjoy being part of the show. You help make *Monday Night Football* happen or the next disaster movie even more memorable in the public imagination than *Titanic*. You know all the inside skinny long before it hits the supermarket checkout tabloids.

What's to Hate

Vicarious Chills

Living your life in the shadow of others' real and imagined greatness has its limits. Not surprisingly, most stars are all too human. However luridly the supermarket tabloids paint these peoples' lives, the reality is often more banal, more comic, and far more tragic by turns. The money involved in the top tiers of sports, film, music, and TV is directly proportional to the egos, childish behavior, and levels of serious neurosis you might expect. The thrills are fun to share; the chilling underside of these worlds is not.

3:30 Review schedules for other artists. Uh-oh . . . trouble ahead. Not enough time between the various events. Luckily it's not too late to make changes. This is supposed to be the tour publicist's job, but until you've been on tours and listened to enough bitter complaints from the artists, you really have no idea how much time anything takes.

4:30 Press release packages ready to be sent out. Final check to make sure everything is in order.

5:00 Fun brainstorming session with other publicists. Some good new ideas emerge.

6:30 Time to do some more careful reading of the trades, make notes, and browse some new websites. The Web is becoming increasingly important, and we need to pay more attention to publicity in this area.

7:45 Write up a to-do list for tomorrow. Time to call it a day. Well, maybe just one last e-mail and then I'm off. . . .

What are your career aspirations?

I'd like to continue to grow in the music industry and learn more about all the areas of the business. I'm not sure ultimately what I'd most like to do, but I think this is where I want to stay.

What kinds of people do well in this business?

Workaholics who are genuinely interested in helping bands and artists advance. You have to really like music—listening to it and putting up with all the personalities as well. There are a lot of "personalities" in this business, believe me.

What do you really like about your job?

I like working with lots of different people—managers, label executives, journalists, travel agents—and I really enjoy helping artists advance their career. A good publicist can make all the difference for someone.

What do you dislike?

The long hours. Sometimes it just seems like I'll never get to the bottom of the pile on my desk.

What is the biggest misconception about this job?

That all of us publicists just hang out with rock stars all day—like we have nothing better to do with our time or theirs.

How can someone get a job like yours?

Definitely sign up for an internship, any internship. This isn't a closed world exactly, but the sooner you find a place inside it and learn how things are done, the more choices you'll have. If you work hard, you'll get ahead pretty quickly—but you do need to work very hard.

Enormous Changes at the Last Minute

If you saw *The Player,* you already know what we mean. This is a topsy-turvy world where today's gopher is tomorrow's studio head. And vice versa. These sudden shifts invariably affect whole armies of people. So if you were in line for a big promotion and had picked out the perfect Jaguar, don't do anything hasty. Next month your Camry may be repossessed. Likewise, a project you've poured your heart and soul into may crash and burn, even after shooting has begun, if the folks in the front office decide the budget's out of control.

One Step from Glory

This is the real path in the entertainment business. Not the temper tantrums, not the temporary dips in fame and fortune, but the vast numbers of very talented individuals who never get the lucky break. These aren't the hangers-on, the wanna-be's, the vicarious thrill-seekers. Every facet of entertainment has far too many never-gonna-be's, and after a while even the most hard-hearted and cynical in the business have moments of hating the unfairness of it all.

KEY JOBS

Marketing and Promotion

These are perhaps the most transferable of all skill sets in this business. Vast and constant infusions of market analysis, research, writing, graphics, and well-organized planning and distribution support every important sports event, hit song, new TV show, and box-office gamble. Being an account executive or marketing manager is also great training for whatever senior executive role you may ultimately want to play in one of these entertainment engines. The gas they all run on is marketing and promotion. Learn how to do it effectively and well, and you'll always have work. Salary range: $40,000 to $110,000.

Assistant to a Producer

No, the salary listed below is not a typo. And, yes, people really do kill for these jobs. They're the tried-and-true way in, and most of the titans in music, TV, and film began this way, too. This is diverse work—from answering phones, handling correspondence, and setting up and canceling appointments to picking up dry cleaning, fetching take-out food, and taking the kids to their therapy sessions. For the biggest and best, you're on call 24-7; midrange producers only need you sixty hours, five or six days a week. Salary: $300 per week.

PA (Production Assistant)

First to arrive on the film or TV set, last to leave, rotten pay, no respect. Often you wear a walkie-talkie. Always you're running, not walking, to resolve the latest crisis. You stop traffic for shoots, find lost props, make sure the OJ and Calistoga water are chilled, and do a lot of driving. This is viewed as invaluable experience. Some survive to become producers; many go into another line of work. Salary range: Nothing (well, lots of free food and drink) to $300 per week. You'll earn much more—about $150 per day—if you're in TV-commercial production.

Publicist

This is another time-honored route for all you would-be sports-show hosts, screenwriters, and TV scriptwriters. Your job is to coax stars into interviews and multi-city junkets they want no part of and to prepare elaborate press kits with info tidbits available nowhere else. If you're ingratiating, highly efficient, and a very good writer, this is an easier, better-paid job than any of the assistant slots above. Salary range: $1,200 to $2,500 per week.

Script Reader

Sounds like there are a lot of people out there writing screenplays, treatments, and TV pilots? One insider likens it to "a slush pile the size of Greenland—most of it unimaginably awful." For around $50 first readers write up a lengthy synopsis and either pass it on to the second reader or send out a polite "no hope" letter. These used to be ill-paying but comfy studio jobs for the unusually patient and forgiving. No more. Now it's freelance work, and lots of would-be writers line up to do it (because they can get close to both the second readers and the development office to learn over time what they're most likely to buy). Salary range: Wretched to marginally adequate. (There are $40,000-per-year reader's jobs out there at some talent agencies, but you usually get to them by working freelance first.)

Writer

Whether you land a coveted screen or script or TV talk show gig, this is not writing in the publishing sense. This is not your creative vision; it's the actor's whim, the director's divine right, and the producer's executive fiat. You'll spend a lot of all-nighters hammering out rewrites, only to find them changed again or forgotten in a day or two. Cynics succeed; the sensitive don't. Salary range: $35,000 to $50,000; often much less for an independent or documentary, and occasionally much more.

Artist, Illustrator, or Computer Artist

Lines are becoming increasingly fuzzy in this category, but whether you're working on a storyboard or an animation or publicity materials, with a chewed-on pencil or a laser pen, there's ample opportunity for earn-and-learn jobs here. The ultimate goal is to become the art director or production designer and dream up magnificent sets and choreograph the special effects. Expect long hours and low pay, but also in many cases more autonomy and creativity than other entry-level jobs in entertainment or sports. Salary range: $25,000 to $50,000.

Special Effects

This is the industrial magic that's responsible for the dinosaurs in *Jurassic Park,* the fires, the fog, the terrifying explosions, the cute animatronics—basically anything that isn't human or stationary. One insider says, "You have to start pestering places like Lucas Ranch for an internship when you're very young. And you have to be relentless." Engineers have a better shot at this exclusive community than most; otherwise, many of the specialties (blood and glass, for example) are reportedly handed down from parent to child. Salary range: $25,000 to $30,000 for an apprentice or intern to the mid–six figures for an experienced professional.

GETTING HIRED

Mostly this depends on being in the right place at the right time and who you know. That said, here are several tips from insiders:

- Don't be too proud to start at the bottom. Whether it's sports marketing, record-label production, or a TV shoot, you're ready and able to do whatever it takes to learn the business. If this involves fulfilling lunch orders and playing messenger, then that's your job for a while. The talent takes up all the available prima donna space in these industries.

- Even the business types need to be flexible and willing to assume responsibility in areas usually outside their domain. Emphasize your organizational skills. In the final analysis, all these productions—ball games, music events, TV shows, movies—require a fanatical attention to detail. If you can remember everything on the to-do list with phones ringing, priorities changing, and a forecast for heavy rain, you're the one who they'll all want to hire.

- De-emphasize your need to be in control. Unfortunately, most detail-oriented people are not particularly great at letting chips fall where they may. Quite often in this business they fall helter-skelter, and the show, whatever form it may take, must go on. Making the best of a bad situation is key to your long-term success.

Health Care

Health care is now a product. And though this line of work probably interests you because of its humanitarian and service aspects, the industry as a whole—hospitals, nursing homes, home health care, specialized clinics, and "nontraditional" options such as homeopathic treatment—is all business these days. According to the most recent government figures available, Americans spent over $1 trillion on health care in 1997—more than 13 percent of the entire U.S. gross national product. Moreover, the U.S. Bureau of Labor & Statistics predicts that health care will be the fastest-growing sector in the economy in the next five to eight years, with 4.2 million new jobs forecast.

The magnitude of these numbers, as well as their rapid growth, has created a volatile environment in the industry. Even though Bill Clinton's proposed overhaul of the health care system toppled under its own weight, the powerful underlying forces have brought significant change. One key trend is the emphasis on reducing costs. As payers (primarily insurance companies, HMOs, and the government) have reduced their reimbursements for various medical services, health care providers have become much more careful about disbursing services. This also has meant that the financial opportunities that once existed for people in the field (especially doctors) are less attractive today. Critics also contend that cost reduction has had a negative impact on the quality of the health care we receive.

A second, related trend is the increasing importance of effective management to successful health care institutions. For example, Hospital Corporation of America (now Columbia/HCA Healthcare), which was started in the late '60s, was among the first health care networks to use a business model aimed blatantly at increasing revenues. By turning patients into customers and disease treatments into product lines, many hospitals have become profitable. Not surprisingly, they've also become embroiled in a series of mergers and acquisitions. In 1996 and 1997, there were close to 1,400 mergers, and hospital ownership in some cases changed almost daily. The frenzy has abated somewhat, but job cuts have not. This remains a period of flux and uncertainty for anyone associated with hospitals.

So, what's the good news? Growth! There are an abundance of opportunities for people interested in health care—whether or not you have an MD (or even a bachelor's). Some of the biggest growth opportunities are expected to be for personal and home care aides (171,000 openings, up 85 percent from 1996 to 2006), home health aides and nurses (378,000 new jobs, up 76 percent), physical therapists and their assistants (147,000 new jobs, up almost 80 percent). The government even predicts continued opportunity growth for physicians, despite the current state of oversupply. To qualify for some positions in this industry (including doctor, nurse, tech, and others) you may need technical training.

How It Breaks Down

Hospitals

Still usually the biggest employers despite mergers and the increased outsourcing of medical records, housekeeping, lab testing, and clinical services like orthopedics and radiology. The huge networks such as Columbia and Tenet still need a steady supply of doctors, nurses, administrators, medical technicians, therapists, and other support staff. In areas where competition from HMOs is mounting and cost cutting is a priority, former staff may move outside the immediate confines of a hospital, but close and important links remain—particularly for any type of surgery or specialized treatment like chemotherapy.

HMOs

Health maintenance organizations are something of a hybrid between a hospital and an insurance company. Some of the largest ones actually have their own medical staff and facilities at which they treat patients; smaller ones may just access networks of private providers and hospitals. This segment offers jobs in medicine as well as management—particularly if you understand IT and data system development. As a job seeker, you should know that HMOs have been the catalyst for many of the efficient business practices imposed on all aspects of health care in recent years. Be aware, though, that this is a difficult period of transition for most of these institutions. Mergers, poor earnings, and a host of internal problems have eliminated some jobs and made competition for others far more competitive. Kaiser, Humana, Group Health Cooperative, and Pacificare (one of the leading Medicare HMOs) are a few of the better-known players.

Specialty Providers

As hospitals have attempted to cut costs, they have turned to firms that can provide specialized services at lower cost. These include everything from nursing homes (Beverly Enterprises) to home infusion therapy providers (Apria Health-care) to diabetes treatment providers (American Healthcorp), and strong growth is expected for all. Clinics that focus on special treatments such as chemotherapy, MRIs and other scanning techniques, and physical therapy for the handicapped are also proliferating. Most are small and locally run, but Gambro and Fresenius Medical Care are two enormous service companies that focus on this type of care; more will undoubtedly emerge as their popularity increases.

Home Care

Technology has recently done much to improve efficiency and reduce costs for both patients and home-care staff. Today, nurses and health care workers can administer complex treatments, previously only available in hospitals or clinics, to the elderly and severely disabled in their own homes. And because almost all hospitals and HMOs now release patients before they are self-sufficient, home care is often the most viable choice. Olsten's Home Health Care is the biggest and best known of a growing number of agencies for registered nurses, home aides, technicians, and specialized therapists. A whopping 119 percent growth in home health care is expected by 2005. Most jobs in this sector don't require much training, just deep reserves of patience and kindness. But the pay is terrible—often under $10 an hour—and the work is arduous. The rewards? Hours are extremely flexible, and most of your patients recover.

What's Great

Feels Good to Make Others Feel Good

Even if your medical career has only extended as far as plumping pillows and soothing a fevered brow, you can probably sense why the many dedicated, self-less people in this industry continue to do the menial, tiring work they do for little money and recognition. Recent studies have shown that HMO technicians and doctors rate their job satisfaction significantly lower than the nurses, aides, and therapists who care for the sick for much less compensation.

Need Flexibility?

One former teacher recalls arriving in a small town in Florida with no prospect of finding work in the local schools. Finally, in desperation she took a part-time job at a nursing home and discovered a whole new career. "I really love my work," she says. "I make my own hours and I'm earning very good money [after five years of experience]." Many people fall into this work by accident and then continue because they can balance the demands of family, schoolwork, or other commitments with more ease and many more emotional rewards than with most other part-time work available.

Goodbye, Rusty Saw

The advances in medical technology over the last thirty years have been truly phenomenal. Patients who were once read their last rites are now routinely patched up and returned to healthy, productive lives—often with procedures that can be handled on an outpatient basis. Whether or not you're a researcher at heart, being part of the medical revolution can be immensely rewarding and intellectually stimulating.

REAL PEOPLE PROFILE

MARIA O'CONNELL

OCCUPATION:
Psychiatric nurse

YEARS IN BUSINESS: 5

AGE: 42

EDUCATION: BS in nursing, studying toward MSN with a psychiatric specialty

HOURS PER WEEK: 32 (part-time), 7:30 A.M. to 3:30 P.M.; 30 minutes for lunch

SIZE OF COMPANY: 3,500-bed community hospital

CERTIFICATION: Registered nurse (RN) training

ANNUAL SALARY: $35,000 (would be $44,000 if I worked full-time)

How did you get your job?

Actually I got it via my clinical rotation when I was getting my BS. I was really interested in psych anyway, and the manager there at the time said, "If you want a job here when you're done, you've got one." So I left obstetrics, which is where I used to work, and did this instead. I just loved it. I found it infinitely more interesting. People also stayed longer when I started five years ago, and it felt like you did effect some change. I've always liked talking to people. There aren't too many other places you're actually allowed to talk. In other parts of nursing, it's very task oriented. I was always getting yelled at in OB for sitting around chatting with the patients. Now I'm justified in doing this.

Describe a typical day.

7:30 I arrive on the job. The first thing I have to do is listen to the evening shift and night shift reports. This gives us the highlights of what's happening in the unit. I always listen to both. Often people just sleep at night. Evening is visiting hours with family and friends. As you can imagine, if something is going to happen, that's when it does. The whole process takes about 40 minutes.

8:15 Out to the unit. We start the day with the five million meds you have to give. The insurance companies these days won't tolerate patients not under psychotropic medication. The whole process takes about an hour, sometimes longer. Whereas medical nurses administer medication to people in bed, we deal with patients all over the place. It's a locked unit, but they can wander

around doing anything they want. So, first we get the meds out and organized—that's complicated enough—and then *into* patients. The most difficult are usually the elderly ones who are in a holding pattern before going off to a nursing home. They won't swallow and sometimes you can't force them to.

9:30 In addition, there are just all the usual issues of a unit. Doctors call in changes for the med orders and they have to be recorded. Often people are physically sick as well and you have to deal with that. Crazy people do very crazy things to themselves, especially the suicide attempts. Then there's the throwing stuff and biting people. They have tantrums because they didn't get a sesame bagel. Often as not, nursing is scientific waitressing.

10:00 Hustle everyone down the hall to group therapy. The response to this is everything from "Yes, okay" to "Screw you" to violent resistance. On a good day, when everyone actually goes off without too much bother, you take a deep breath, drink a cup of coffee, and make a few phone calls. Sometimes, though, you can't because someone is acting out and has to be put in constraints. That doesn't happen often, but there's always something. On paper, we're allowed extra staff in these instances but of course there never are any extra people actually available. So we just cope.

12:00 We try to take 30 minutes for lunch. If you can believe it, we don't get paid for lunch. We work 7:30 to 4:00 in an acute unit, but no lunch. We cover for each other. Always. You have to have lunch. Big push for more meds and food around this time. A fair number of people are anorexic and bulemic so you have to be on top of that. Then there's your basic sociopath and those who are detoxing from alcohol and cocaine. None of these people are fun to feed. Ages range from thirteen to ninety, though I'd say it's weighted more toward adolescence. They seem to do the most damage. This is a big-city hospital so it's a complete mix of classes and backgrounds.

3:00 There's usually another group activity in afternoon. Alcohol detox patients need a lot of special attention around now. Though those people take a lot of intensive physical care—regular nursing care—all the time.

3:15 Crawl to end of day. I have to write up something about everyone and work on their charts. The closest observation is for the suicide cases. You need a heightened sense with them, and you can't ever let your guard down. I actually don't know how in the world I do this. It looks so horrible on the outside looking in, but that's not really the problem. I'm just totally burned out. I don't think I would be if they were able to stay here longer. We would all feel then we could do something for them.

What are your career aspirations?

I really would love to work in an outpatient setting with people who do not need to be contained. I'd love to be doing group therapy. Once I get the degree and take another licensing certificate (CS–P), I'll be a clinical nurse specialist and all this may be possible. It would be so much simpler to be out of Acute. I'm also interested in helping people in disaster zones. Not even necessarily working with the victims but working instead with the fire fighters or emergency engineers.

What kinds of people do well in this business?

People who are enormously flexible and can tolerate a lot of chaos. I have always felt being a mother makes me a better nurse and being a nurse makes me a better person. This work is pretty much like taking care of a lot of babies—the really bad parts that no one ever remembers or talks about. You don't meet a lot of twenty-six–year-old psych nurses. They're just not experienced enough to handle it. The really good ones are around fifty.

What do you really like about your job?

I like the day-to-day contact with people. Being right there in the moment. And I like talking to them. I do feel some of them get better. Some even write us letters or come back and visit! One actually sent us a two-hundred-dollar gift basket. She's one of those frequent fliers. "You guys are my family" was what she wrote in the note.

What do you dislike?

I dislike the whole thrust of corporate business in hospitals and health care. No, let me state that more strongly, I hate that we are supposed to think of sick people as "customers." This is actually taking something very impor-tant away from them, not letting them be patients anymore. Being a customer implies choice. These people have no choice. I absolutely loathe and detest what is happening—and it's going to get worse. It's all about money. I know that's wrong. You know that's wrong. So why are we allowing this to happen?

What is the biggest misconception about your job?

People think it's not really nursing and that somehow it's easier because you're not really dealing with blood and guts or any of the technology. Actually that makes it all the harder, because there's no machinery in our work to back us up. And as I said before, plenty of psych patients are in very bad physical shape when they arrive in our unit. People also probably don't understand how important the teamwork is. All we've got is each other. No "gainsharing" here. It's about helping, working, giving. It will never be about earning more money.

How can someone get a job like yours?

You'll need some solid psych experience. Even though I actually had very little, I did have a whole semester's rotation and I already had a strong interest in it. Most people don't come out of school and go into this kind of work. They can't. You need all the regular training as well. People do crazy things when they're crazy, and you have to be prepared for that.

Care for Profit?

Most people pursue a career in health care because of their desire to help people in need. Increasingly, however, the business of health care has come between patients and providers. "At my hospital we are supposed to call the patients 'customers,'" says one insider. "I keep telling my boss this is not Lord & Taylor!" "All I can say is it stinks, and corporate America has no business in the system," says another. Lots of strong emotions emerge in this discussion, and it's not an easy or happy time in the health care industry. The higher you go, the more bruising and difficult the politics and economics become.

The 15-Minute Consultation

With or without the able assistance of a PA or nurse practitioner, this is how much time most physicians are allocated per patient these days. Think about it. If a patient showed up with searing leg pains, and two previous doctors apparently weren't able to help, how would you feel about giving yet another cursory inspection and diagnosis? Everyone's complaints, no matter how seemingly routine, deserve focus and attention. Most health care professionals feel this even more strongly than their patients do. Physician practice management groups (PPMs) are proliferating and becoming increasingly vocal in their angry opposition to the heavy, restrictive hand of managed care. This is a problem which will likely get worse before it gets better.

Survival of the Fattest

Insiders acknowledge that the poor receive a different standard of health care. Some would argue that for the richest nation in the world to be without a federally subsidized health program, particularly for the indigent, is unconscionable. Others insist that a rigorous level of medical excellence can only be maintained as a well-run, competitive business. It's troubling to everyone, though, that those most vulnerable to both chronic and emergency illness are those with fewer and fewer available recourses to competent health care.

KEY JOBS

Physician

Doctors have long been at the peak of the health care pyramid. Although most medical students today will tell you that the industry has changed for the worse and that they'll be lucky to be able to pay back their school loans, physicians still get the most pay and respect in health care. But they also study the hardest; in most cases, a doctor must complete seven years of graduate school and residency before being certified to practice medicine and often more if he or she wishes to specialize. There are currently more than half a million physicians in the United States, of which about one-third are primary-care physicians. Most of the rest have some sort of specialty: surgery, neurology, anesthesiology, radiology, and so on. The demands of the work, the pay, and the lifestyle vary considerably from one specialty to another. Salary range: as low as $32,000 for residents and up to $180,000 for many practicing physicians.

Registered Nurse (RN)

This is a good news/bad news scenario. Most RNs easily find jobs after they've completed their master's work, but more often than not these days they're in outpatient centers, clinics, and home care, not hospitals. Pressures on hospitals to reduce costs have led to replacement of RNs with medical assistants, licensed practical nurses, and UAPs (unlicensed assistive personnel). Salary range: $45,000 to $170,000 (median approximately $50,000 to $55,000).

Licensed Practical Nurse (LPN)

These nurses work under the supervision of RNs and physicians, and though many are taking over for RNs in hospitals, here too your job prospects are much brighter in nursing homes, home health care services, medical centers, and ambulatory surgi-centers. Physicians' offices are also popular, particularly as more and more become outpatient clinics for orthopedics and other specialties. Salary range: $400 to $700 per week.

Nurse Practitioner (NP)

This is a good career choice for those of you who have a master's degree and training in pediatrics or family health but can't afford or don't want to go to medical school. In many states, NPs can prescribe medicine and are increasingly allowed primary-care status for basic health problems. Oxford Health and Columbia-Presbyterian Hospital pioneered these new responsibilities for NPs in the New York area and HMOs elsewhere are following suit. Salary range: physician's rates for primary care; $50,000 to $80,000 otherwise.

Medical Technician

Another good career choice, particularly for those of you with IT and other computer skills. There's brisk demand everywhere in the country, particularly the West Coast and Rockies, and in every type of facility—hospitals, medical labs, and anywhere else special tests such as electroencephalographs, MRIs, and CAT scans are administered. Budget cuts may come and go, but as is the case with so many other aspects of modern life, technical expertise commands its own price. Moreover, this is knowledge based on experience, not academic credentials; many technicians have only high-school or college degrees, plus several years of specialized training. Salary range: $35,000 and up, with the best pay being in nuclear medicine technology.

Physical Therapist

As the general population ages and athletes continue to get injured, physical therapy becomes ever more popular a field. One unexpected drawback is that PT master's programs are in such demand that, according to one insider, "those interested in PT should start early, because it may take a few attempts to be accepted into a program—and you need to have a master's to get a job." For communities where managed care predominates, home care and nursing homes are better long-term bets; their focus is on the benefit, not the cost, of physical therapy for their patients. Salary range: $45,00 to $100,000 or more for those in private practice. PT assistants can expect to make between $26,000 to $40,000.

REAL PEOPLE PROFILE

IAN BETTS

OCCUPATION:
Postdoctoral fellow in molecular biology

YEARS IN BUSINESS: 7

AGE: 36

EDUCATION: BA in molecular biology, Yale; MD, Emory University

HOURS PER WEEK:
70, 9:00 A.M. to 8:30 P.M.; 1 hour for lunch

SIZE OF COMPANY:
15 people in my lab

CERTIFICATION: California state medical license, Board Certification in neurology

ANNUAL SALARY:
$65,000

How did you get your job?

I got it through my residency. My current adviser was recommended to me by my previous advisors. I'm employed by a large state university, but my funding comes through the National Institute of Health. Originally, I was paid through grants that my adviser had, so I was making half what I make now.

Describe a typical day.

9:00 Arrive at the office. Get samples that I set up last night: bacteria carrying pieces of a gene that I'm interested in.

9:15 Start preparing the samples. They are in suspension, so I use a centrifuge to isolate the bacteria.

9:30 Start isolating DNA through chemical processes.

10:30 Set up an enzyme digest analysis of the DNA. This takes an hour, so I can either do some reading or get something to eat. I do both.

11:30 Set up a gel electophoreses to separate the fragments of the DNA. I have some more free time now, so I grab an Odwalla and do a bit more reading.

1:00 Look at the results of the gel. Decide whether or not I'm going to use it for an experi-

ment in the next couple of days.

1:05 Go to the medical center cafeteria to get some lunch with some colleagues.

2:00 Go over to the radiology department to look at the film of an MRI test that was conducted on a patient with a stroke. Talk with the radiologist about the results of the test. Then I call the patient and inform him of the results of the test and whether or not we need to do more tests.

3:00 Set up buffering solutions for a new experiment. This entails dissolving the components in water and measuring the pH components with a pH meter.

4:00 Go to a visiting researcher's lecture on genes related to Alzheimer's disease.

5:00 Spend some time talking to people about the lecture and about our projects.

5:30 Do an experiment to identify the function of the genes I've isolated. I'm working on proteins, called transporters, which transport small molecules across membranes. To determine whether the transporter works on a particular molecule, I take radioactively labeled molecules

Health Care Managers

These are the jobs where an MBA comes in handy and a background in cost cutting, marketing, and information management will give you an edge over the competition. Lots of people want these jobs, and though industry observers predict that the number of managerial slots in hospitals and HMOs will shrink to perhaps half their current number, the need for qualified executive staff in home health care, nursing homes, and clinics is expected to more than make up the difference. Salary range: $55,000 on up. Experienced managers with an impressive track record in meeting and maintaining strict budgets can earn well over six figures.

and see whether or not the molecule is transported across membranes that have the protein in them. This includes incubation of the molecule with the radioactive molecule, washing the samples with buffer, and using a scintillation counter to measure the amount of radioactivity within the membrane. We do this under several different conditions, and it can take up to three hours.

8:30 Look over the results to decide whether they're positive or negative and then decide whether to repeat the experiment. Write results down in my notebook and do a little research on my computer.

9:00 Go home and eat dinner.

What are your career aspirations?

To get a faculty position at a university medical center, to continue to see patients, and to act as an adviser to grad students and postdoctoral fellows in a lab that I would run.

What kinds of people do well in this business?

You have to be relatively independent, disciplined, and willing to make a lot of personal sacrifices, mainly in terms of time. There are also financial sacrifices: I could have been making over $100,000 right out of med school as opposed to the $25,000 that I was making. I'd like to say that intelligence is also critical, but I don't know how important it is beyond having the smarts to get into and finish medical school. Working hard and being careful are just as important. Communication and writing skills are essential because in getting publications and grants you have to be able to present your research and get people to support it. You also need reasonably good interactions with people to get lab space and funding.

What do you really like about your job?

The things that are best about it are that I do have some independence and that the environment encourages scientific creativity. A big plus is that what I'm doing may actually affect people's health and well-being. That's the reason I went to med school in the first place. Also, though I'm comfortable with my career path so far, I'm not locked into anything yet. People have left where I am now to go into private practice, pharmaceutical companies, or law school, and I have friends who are working in intellectual property law and at a biotech startup. I don't feel locked in to what I'm doing because biotechnology is still a growing industry.

What do you dislike?

The uncertainty with regard to the long term. My future will depend on getting funding every five years. The other thing is limitations on where I work, since I have to work in a major medical center. That limits me to about 150 places in the country. Also, the daily time commitment is a bit more than I'm comfortable with right now.

What is the biggest misconception about your job?

I think it's the amount of effort and work that goes into what we do. It's underestimated. People think that if you have government funding, you work thirty hours a week and are overpaid. Also, it takes six months to a year—not one experiment—to get enough information to publish an article.

How can someone get a job like yours?

The biggest hurdle is to get a grad degree, either a PhD in biochemistry or biology or an MD. After that, you should be able to get into this field fairly easily if you want to.

Home Health Care Aides

This encompasses a wide spectrum from the high-school student with minimal training who shops, cleans, and cooks part-time for an elderly or infirm patient to a full-time nurse who can perform many of the procedures available in a hospital and be on call twenty-four hours a day. Many states now require brief training and some form of certification for all such workers, but these regulations are difficult to enforce. This is where the jobs will be as the population ages and hospital facilities become less available, especially for long-term care. But bathing, dressing, feeding, and administering to the disabled and the very ill is difficult work. And not surprisingly, the biggest growth is at the bottom end of the pay scale.

Salary range: $6 to $10 per hour—lowest for those without formal training or state certification—up to $25 to $50 per hour for aides with a BS in nursing.

Medical Secretaries

Mergers, budget cuts, financial and insurance misdeeds—none of these nor any of the other more permanent changes in the health care industry seem to have much effect on the patient souls who answer the phones, juggle all the canceled and emergency appointments, and comfort the tearful and frightened. Network-computer and sophisticated record-keeping skills are necessary these days, but these workers are an essential part of every doctor's office, clinic, outpatient center, and hospital. As with secretarial positions in other industries, training is usually done on the job, though classes in computers and administrative duties will give you a leg up on the competition. Salary range: $25,000 to $40,000.

GETTING HIRED

Much depends on what aspect of this diverse and changing industry you choose to pursue. For anything involving a high level of medical or technical skill, you're going to need a lot of training and equal amounts of personal dedication. For the growing home care sector, training is less important than stamina, patience, and an empathy for the sick and elderly. Here are some things to consider before starting your job search:

- Many health care professionals now see an MBA as a vital career boost, and combined degrees in business and pharmacology or business and nursing are becoming quite common. A facility with technology is also a big plus on your résumé, and a CS or EE degree coupled with some aspect of medical training will be an increasingly useful job-hunting tool.

- Whether you're caring for the ill directly or managing an office or business that looks after their needs, your bedside manner matters. This is not an industry for the impatient, the abrasive, or the weak stomached. You may be working in front of a computer terminal all day and see very few patients, but to be happy and succeed over the long term the sight of blood shouldn't make you feel faint.

- You'll want to think carefully about what you want out of a job. Talking to people in the field will not only help alert you to jobs no one else knows about, it will also help you choose the right type of workplace so you can avoid early burnout.

Insurance

Okay, let's be candid. Hot it's not. If you want glamour, sizzle, and prestige to impress your friends and family with, insurance is the wrong game to get into. But like taxes, insurance is something we all have to pay, and it's not going away. Alas, there's no such thing as genuine job security these days, but insurance comes closer than most and, unlike other industries, the more it changes, the more it stays the same. If you're a good claims adjuster, you'll still be good and eminently employable twenty years from now. Ultimately this is a business based on understanding human behavior and betting both for and against it. Insurance is also expanding fast. It has to. Banks are increasingly allowed to sell and underwrite a wide variety of insurance products. So are mutual funds. The demise of the traditional fee-for-service plans that Blue Cross/Blue Shield offers in favor of set-fee HMO plans has changed the landscape even more. This means if you're interested in risk management and derivatives, AIG and other large life insurers have new departments you need to know about. Want to work abroad? Lots of opportunity in insurance. Europe and Canada are still a focus for claims processing and investment and actuarial services, but Asian markets—particularly Japan, Taiwan, and South Korea—are heating up even faster. If cultural differences are

REAL PEOPLE PROFILE

PAUL SUMMERS

OCCUPATION: Business consultant for a large insurance company, marketing mutual funds

YEARS IN BUSINESS: 1

AGE: 29

EDUCATION: MBA

CERTIFICATION: Series 6 license

SIZE OF COMPANY: 25,000 employees

HOURS PER WEEK: 50 to 55, 7:45 A.M. to 6:30 P.M., plus reading on weekends; 30 minutes for lunch

ANNUAL SALARY:
$70,000, with $15,000–$18,000 plus relocation expenses for signing bonus and $5,000 year-end bonus

How did you get your job?

I was recruited on campus at business school.

Describe a typical day.

6:30 Pull in to the office parking lot and head straight to the company gym for a workout before the real work begins.

7:45 Sit down at my desk with the *Wall Street Journal* and check out our mutual funds' performance. Look over sales numbers.

8:00 Head to a meeting with the director and the six other members of the mutual funds team to brainstorm, share news and ideas.

8:45 Begin making phone calls to potential distributors and clients, record keepers, and institutional brokers.

10:00 Lead a meeting with a task force on product market feasibility studies.

10:45 Sit down to work on marketing literature, put together materials for our newsletter.

12:00 Go down to the cafeteria, *Wall Street Journal* in hand, to grab a sandwich and read.

12:30 Another meeting, this time with the service group.

1:30 Work on material for a presentation next week in New York. Look over PowerPoint documents prepared by assistants.

3:30 One-on-one meeting with the director of mutual funds to discuss strategic issues.

4:30 Return phone calls, set up meetings, write thank you notes, make plans, and tie-up loose ends.

6:30 Quitting time, head back home.

something you understand and you speak a foreign language, you're someone insurance companies will want to talk to.

How It Breaks Down

As you can see, insurance comes in a variety of flavors: life and health are fairly self-explanatory. They're benefits packages which you pay a premium to enjoy. Property and casualty insurance differs in that the focus is on liabilities and the insurance protects owners of cars, homes, and businesses against loss, damage, or injury. It all boils down to risk and how to minimize the likelihood and cost of that risk. The jobs tend to fall into two general categories: selling insurance against everyone's worst fears and managing expectations and the harsh realities of those worst fears. Here's what else you need to know:

What are your career aspirations?

I hope to be running a business unit within this company—hopefully a new unit with high-growth possibilities. I like the idea of building a business within the business.

What kind of people do really well in this business?

This may sound contradictory for the reputedly stodgy insurance industry, but the people who rise to the top are the ones able to make quick decisions, get other people to buy in to their ideas, and then implement their ideas quickly. Energetic people with high initiative will really make an impact.

What do you really like about your job?

The mutual funds business is relatively new to the insurance industry, so even though we're part of a large company, what I actually do is a lot like running a small start-up business. I can take ownership of an idea or project, and I have lots of flexibility and freedom to make decisions. Also, the rotational program I am on is great general management experience. I like both finance and marketing but I'm still unsure exactly where I want to direct my career. This is a chance to gain exposure to both areas. And the quality of life is very good; you can do finance without living in New York and working obscene hours, and you can do internal consulting without living out of a suitcase.

What do you dislike?

There is still a stigma attached to the insurance industry, as many people continue to view it as slow and dull. Certainly it isn't as glamorous to work for an insurance company as it is to work for a Wall Street firm. Also, many of my single colleagues find it particularly difficult to deal with the location—after all, Hartford is not quite as cosmopolitan as New York or San Francisco—but for people with families, the location could be an advantage.

What is the biggest misconception about your job?

The opportunities in insurance are more exciting than people think.

There is a lot of work which is very comparable to that done by management consultants and investment banks, and because of the insurance stigma and the lack of glamour, not as many people want these jobs. The insurance companies still need new talent, though—particularly MBAs—so they're likely to offer great opportunities for immediate advancement in order to attract people away from competition. Insurance is in many ways a better place for people who are looking to start a career, as opposed to just making a quick buck.

How can someone get a job like yours?

Many of the positions are filled through on-campus recruiting at target schools, but the companies are certainly open to qualified people with business training. Anyone who is interested could contact the human resources department.

Life Insurance

Slow growth in terms of life insurance products, but a host of interesting sidelines are emerging—such as securities, real estate, foreign markets—as mergers continue apace within this industry. Expect at least some of those future mergers to be with banks and securities firms. Help wanted: certified financial planners and information systems experts.

Health Insurance

A bit uncertain. The population is aging and baby-boomers are going to need more, not less of this stuff, in the years ahead. Insurers that are running the large managed-care networks are your best bet for the long term, but if you're keen on creating new market niches (for example, disability and annuities are hot prospects right now), look into more-established, multiline firms that want to keep old customers and win new ones.

Property and Casualty Insurance

Heating up while falling apart. Competition is fierce. Rates are going down. Only the strong will survive as weaker companies continue to tank and even the more secure ones sell off this line. Find a firm committed to an aggressive market-share strategy and join the fray. If you were worried about insurance being a tad dull and not as lucrative as Wall Street, think again.

What's Great

The Trend's Your Friend

Baby boomers aren't getting any younger, which means that however uncertain the current climate may be, insurance has a happier future. Life insurance, long-term care, and retirement investment are all growth areas which will only improve in the years ahead. Commercial insurance, such as product liability and employee benefits, is also in demand, and its potential is equally promising.

Get Met, Get a Life

Insurance people work hard for their money, but no one expects them to work the hours investment bankers and high-tech start-ups endure. If you have a family or simply other interests you like to pursue, most jobs in this industry allow you a fair amount of flexibility and your weekends off.

Tech Mecca

Information systems specialists will find more work than they can handle— LANs, AI, CASE (computer-aided software engineering tools), client/server systems, image processing, pen-based computers (for all those on-site sales), and a host of other needs. Got an innovative idea? Many of the big firms would love to give you some bucks to develop it for them.

Not Just Actuarial Tables

Interested in direct marketing? Want to learn more about derivatives and financial planning? These are hot and getting hotter right now; and even at a fairly junior level, you probably won't have to work under a lot of layers of bureaucracy. Environmental claims are another important growth option for those of you with a science/social policy bent. Interested in training? Insurance needs you. In fact, just about anything you can think of that isn't actuarial is a possible option in this industry.

What's to Hate

The Incredible Shrinking Insurance Business

Computerization, consolidation, and competition. Watch your back. No job is safe right now. If you're not replaced by a "systems environment," you'll be replaced by the takeover company's bigger, better department. Or your whole division will be outsourced to some outfit in South Carolina. Too long a commute and who knows if their contract will be renewed (probably not). Layoffs are common, and a recent CIGNA case sets an unhappy precedent for those of you who thought legal recourse might insure better severance packages or out-placement help.

How Do You Feel About Org Charts?

Okay, so the industry's somewhat in disarray at the moment. This does not mean chaos reigns anywhere inside these august firms. There's a right way and a wrong way to do things. If you aren't copying at least six people on the memo you're formulating re: wasted Xerox paper, you'll be called on the carpet and asked why not. The times they may be a-changin' but most insurance companies make banks look loose. If you have a problem with bureaucracy, this is going to be a tough fit.

Equity Is Not an Option

At least not at most places. Remember that amazing idea you had? The one your department head thought was so great he found special money in his budget for you to develop with a team and on your own? Well, it's not really yours. So don't get any silly intellectual-property ideas in your head that it might be. This is work-for-hire, and both the work and the hire are easily replaceable. Just so you know.

No Aid for AIDS

The dark side of risk management is that most health insurance companies don't reimburse and won't insure anyone who's HIV-positive. Apparently there's too much pain (and tests and long-term hospitalizations) and not enough gain (well, let's be frank: zero gain) to make it worth anyone's loss ratio. This is also true for numerous other life-threatening diseases. Grapple with your conscience now. Your interviewers aren't interested in debating this one with you. They've got a business to run.

KEY JOBS

Actuary

Do you like to play the odds or do you prefer to set them? In actuary, your job will be to predict the risk to insure people, property, and businesses. Mathematics and statistics will help you make these decisions. You'll also need to know general social trends and laws that affect risk. Most actuaries have college degrees. Many have advanced degrees. Salary range: $35,000 to $70,000 to start, depending on skill set.

Agent or Broker

Think of being an agent and broker as giving advice for a living. You'll tell others how they can best protect their valuables. Then you'll sell them a policy. Knowledge of insurance contracts is essential. A college degree is not a requirement to be an agent, but many agents are college grads. Salary range: $22,000 to $27,000 to start, plus substantial commissions.

REAL PEOPLE PROFILE

FRANK BASCOME

OCCUPATION:
Health and life insurance broker

YEARS IN BUSINESS: 5

AGE: 35

EDUCATION: BA in political science, U.C. Berkeley; Master's in urban planning, New York University

HOURS PER WEEK:
40, 8:30 A.M. to 5:30 P.M.; 45 minutes for lunch

SIZE OF COMPANY: 3, including me

CERTIFICATION: Licensed financial planner, Series 7; licensed life and health insurance agent in California and New York

ANNUAL SALARY:
$112,000

How did you get your job?

My father was in the business and when he decided to retire, I took it over from him. I used to work in New York for a real-estate developer, but family ultimately brought us back. The real-estate market was in one of its slumps, and though real estate and insurance don't appear to have much in common, both require constant dealings with government and large bureaucracies. It wasn't too hard a transition.

Describe a typical day.

8:30 Settle in with coffee and the morning mail. Sort through the bills and premiums. Two piles: money out and money in.

9:30 Chamber of Commerce calls to confirm my speaking engagement next Tuesday. I sign up to help with a big human resources effort they're sponsoring and a financial-planning seminar. (Some of my best referrals come from the Chamber so I'm happy to volunteer a fair amount of my time.)

9:40 Mrs. Sosovitz, age sixty-seven, calls in very upset about a four-hundred-dollar lab charge on her bill. I explain (again) that the lab is just copying her; she's not responsible for paying this charge.

9:50 Check in with the L.A. AHU (Association of Health Underwriters), another one of my community resources. AHUs around the country have done a lot of research relevant to the Chamber's HR project. Agree to speak at a Small Business conference next month.

10:30 Meet with prospective clients. They've completed their census reports for all their full-time employees and are ready to discuss carriers. One of the principals likes Aetna but we show him other, less-expensive options with better customer-satisfaction records.

12:00 Break for a quick lunch and a meeting with my assistant. She's had a long morning of soothing agitated clients. If you can't deal with a daily onslaught of other people's anxiety, this isn't the business to be in.

1:00 Catch up on employee benefits reading for CEBS course. Spend some time reviewing SEPP (Simplified Employee Pension Plans).

2:00 Send out follow-up letters to several prospects who expressed interest last week.

2:30 Send out fourth and final notice to a client who has let

Claims Adjuster

These folks negotiate claims when people lose something by theft, fire, flood, whatever. You'll need to be good with people, because your job is to be fair to those the company insures, while being fair to the company, too. A college degree is not a requirement to be an adjuster, but many agents are college grads. Salary range: $25,000 to $30,000 to start; worker's compensation claims adjusters are in demand and start at $35,000 to $40,000.

his premium lapse. This business operates on a fairly simple premise: no premium, no policy. As long as there's always new business, it's hard to lose money.

3:00 Handle client calls so my assistant can have the afternoon off for a class. (She's also learning more about pension planning.) Mrs. Sosovitz calls two more times. Check in with my contacts at Kaiser and two other local carriers to confirm resolution of several problems last week.

5:30 Out the door to a CEBS class and then home to my family. Unlike most of my old friends in New York, I have time with my wife and kids.

What are your career aspirations?

One of the reasons I took the Series 7 exam was to diversify beyond life and health insurance. I'd like to move into pension and estate planning for customers. I'd also enjoy an ombudsman role for the new legislation and regulation coming out of Sacramento. There are an increasing number of options for individuals, families, and small businesses—but very few underwriters really understand what they are.

What kinds of people do well in this business?

This may sound surprising, but it's a good job for entrepreneurs or someone interested in running a small business. There's no big capital investment, very little overhead, no billing or inventory. You have to like helping people and be willing to make a commitment to your local community. You also have to know something about sales—many people start out as "captive" agents for the big insurance companies—but it's much more business development than just selling a product.

What do you really like about your job?

Three things: the freedom, the freedom, and the freedom. It used to be hard for me to take a vacation; now it's almost too easy.

What do you dislike?

It's hard to stay focused. The learning curve has flattened out, which is why I'm trying to get into pension planning. I'm also unsure about the long-term prospects for life and health. Legislation is being introduced around the country to regulate "guaranteed insurance." This would mean very little incentive to buy a policy until you get sick—which would effectively defeat the need for us and put us out of business.

What is the biggest misconception about this job?

People think it's just a sales job. They have this image of being chained to a desk making endless cold calls. Or of spending days on the road twisting people's arms to buy more insurance, more, more . . . .

How can someone get a job like yours?

In order to be licensed in most states, you have to be certified, and the easiest way to do that is to be sponsored by a large insurance company. For life insurance, most people start out as captive agents for one of the big carriers. And most people who end up in health insurance do so via the life route. You need to learn about prospecting—not just how to use the phone book. You should definitely join a professional organization such as the National Association of Health Underwriters or a more local chapter. NAHU and CAHU's websites are also useful for someone who just wants information.

Service Representative or Account Manager

The service rep is the liaison between the agent who sells the policy and the company that writes the policy. You'll need to know your company's products and work well with others. A college degree is also usually required. Salary range: $25,000 to $35,000.

Loss-Control Specialist

Loss-control specialists try to prevent accidents and losses from happening by scouting out, say, the shop floor. Knowledge of safety management or engineering and a college degree are generally prerequisites for this sort of job. Salary range: $25,000 to $30,000 to start.

Risk Manager

Large corporations like Intel and Procter & Gamble hire risk managers to help them figure out how to save money. Risk managers advise upper management on the best type of insurance to buy or on how the workplace can be made safer. They also help manage employee benefit plans. Most risk managers have advanced degrees or several years of work experience. Salary range: $70,000 to $100,000 to start.

Underwriter

The underwriter's central question is a variation of Hamlet's: To insure or not to insure this applicant? The applicant's exposure to risk generally determines the type of policy offered, and the price. A college degree is a must. Salary range: $30,000 to $35,000 to start.

Information Technology

This isn't the sort of job you think of when you think insurance, but every big insurer needs IT experts to manage its databases of information. If you like computers and figuring out the best ways to work with the huge networks and vast information that insurance companies invariably develop, here's a job for you. A technical degree is a plus but not essential. Salary range: $35,000 to $70,000 to start.

GETTING HIRED

- Know why you want to work in insurance. And when you interview, show that you're personable. Agents, claims adjusters, service reps, and risk managers all deal with a wide array of different people, and they've got to be able to get along well with all of them. Tact is an important quality, and it's important to be assertive, too. If you get a tough question, don't back down.

- It's no accident that ads for insurance companies feature families prominently and objects, such as rocks, that represent strength and permanence. Insurance is all about security—and more than securing investments, valuables, and lives against the unexpected catastrophe. It's about security of mind. If you are good at putting people at ease, you're well suited to represent an insurance agency.

- Insurance is also about your company's security. Aetna, Prudential, State Farm, and other well-known insurers didn't get big by insuring everybody; they got big by carefully calculating risks and making sensible bets. Caution is an inherent part of this business. Risk managers get paid to figure out how to prevent accidents and save money on claims; in actuary, you need to slice numbers thin to pick good bets and bad bets. Underwriters match policies to people, based on these bets. But never think you're playing against the odds to win: insurance companies sell security of mind, and they profit when more people buy into it than collect.

Internet and New Media

The rapid growth of the World Wide Web has ushered in a new era in the age-old marriage of technology and media. In 1995, fewer than 3 percent of all U.S. households regularly accessed the Internet. Today, more than 20 percent are online, and with the introduction of WebTV, many more are signing up. In response, an entire industry has sprung up to venture forth into the space of possibility that the Web represents. Internet-based companies are doing a stunningly wide variety of things online—selling products, producing newspaper- and magazine-style publications, providing traditional services like travel agencies and stock brokerages, creating search engines, recruiting employees, building brands, and developing online game networks, to name a few. Add to this all the companies that underpin and service these endeavors—the online ad agencies, Internet Service Providers (ISPs), and innumerable consultants—and you get a sense of just how broad this industry is.

Despite the diversity, it's possible to speak of the industry as a whole. It's very young, as are most of the employees. (Some of the most successful firms have had to hire "grown-ups"—business types over forty with track records—but they don't quite fit in and they know it.) The culture is casual. People interact almost exclusively on a first-name basis, and they almost never wear suits. It's also

REAL PEOPLE PROFILE

RUBY GONZALEZ

OCCUPATION: Website producer at an Internet company

YEARS IN BUSINESS: 2

AGE: 27

EDUCATION: BA in art history, University of Georgia

HOURS PER WEEK: 50, 8:00 A.M. to 6:30 P.M.; 30 minutes for lunch

SIZE OF COMPANY: 52

CERTIFICATION: None

ANNUAL SALARY: $45,000, plus stock options

How did you get your job?

When I came to work here, there were only a few people in the company, so they wanted someone who could do a lot of different things—administration, operations, and marketing—and who could learn on the fly and grow with the company. So I basically showed that I had project-management skills and that I was smart and easily adaptable. As the company has grown, the projects that have come my way have become more complex, I've assumed more responsibility, and my salary has increased.

Describe a typical day.

8:30 Come in, fire up both computers (one Mac, one PC). Deal with twenty-seven e-mails spread across three accounts—the CEO has a new idea for the site, an engineer wants to push back the work schedule on our commerce overhaul, a friend is having a dinner party, and so on.

9:00 Meet with a designer and a copywriter to make sure they're on track in their work on our upcoming home-page redesign.

10:15 Walk down to the bay and back. It's a clear, cold day.

10:30 Interview a candidate for a design position we have. (We're hiring so fast these days that interviewing is like a part of life.) She's done some good work, but I'm not sure she can handle the pace here.

11:30 Put together a quarterly report for one of our strategic partners. Analyze impressions, click-throughs, and sales for the traffic that came from its site to ours. (Actually, dealing with partnerships is not in my job description anymore, but I'm maintaining some of the relationships while the guy who's taken over that responsibility gets up to speed.)

12:45 Tuna sandwich in South Park.

1:10 Surf our competitors' sites, see if they're up to anything new. Nothing earth-shattering today.

2:00 Run some numbers through Excel to try and figure out the data from our most recent online business development.

4:00 Meet with the engineer who's on the commerce overhaul. Tell him we can't push back the launch date. Agree five minutes later to push back the launch date by a week.

extremely demanding—ten-hour days are the norm. The face of the industry changes constantly and dramatically, which makes for a ton of possibility and excitement and an equal amount of stress and uncertainty: today's pip-squeak may be tomorrow's giant, and today's giant may end up on tomorrow's trash heap. And most companies are awash in cash—many tech stocks are still high (and possibly going higher) and venture capital is flowing freely—but they're also short on profits, with many major players predicting losses through 1999.

The outlook for the job seeker mirrors the outlook for the industry as a whole: high levels of both excitement and risk. Those who choose careers here will have unique opportunities to create an industry as they build their careers. But they'll also face less stability than peers who enter more-established traditional industries. Investors are growing increasingly anxious to see returns on their new-media investments. If the speculative cash bubble bursts before the industry

5:00 Write a long e-mail to the CEO detailing my ideas for integrating the e-commerce overhaul and the website redesign. Add a note explaining my analysis of the data from the recent promotion

5:45 Spend a while thinking through some long-term strategic issues. Sometimes it doesn't seem like we'll ever be profitable.

6:15 Do some beta testing of the e-commerce overhaul. Find some bugs; have an idea to improve the interface. E-mail the relevant engineer.

7:00 Shut down. Out the door.

What are your career aspirations?

I used to think I'd like to stick it out and then move into a senior management role. But I think I'd rather get a PhD in art history and teach at a liberal arts college.

What kinds of people do well in this business?

Outgoing people who communicate well. At this company, everybody knows the big picture: marketing people have ideas about what engineering should be doing, and engineers have ideas about what marketing should be doing. If you're not outgoing or don't communicate well you'll having a hard time getting in this loop. You'll also need initiative and flexibility to handle the lack of structure; there won't always be someone to tell you what to do, and things can change quickly. And it's definitely fast-paced and high-stress, so you need to cope well with stress.

What do you really like about your job?

I like that I can go barefoot in the office; it's a very warm, human environment. I like that the management structure is egalitarian with a strong sense of mutual trust. And the people I work with are very smart and dynamic, and I am constantly learning.

What do you dislike?

In such a volatile industry, there's a realistic chance that any small company will go out of business. That means that there are times when things get pretty bleak and very stressful. And sometimes I feel like this whole company is extraneous, that what we're doing doesn't matter.

What is the biggest misconception about your job?

That everyone makes a million dollars. Most people don't.

How can someone get a job like yours?

As the Web matures, we're seeing more candidates with previous Web experience. So any Web experience—including internships—is valuable. But it's definitely not a prerequisite. More important is that a person be a good fit—comfortable with an egalitarian, unstructured work environment and a frequently changing job description. Beyond that, one thing that differentiates candidates is their knowledge of our company and our competitors. A candidate who has spent a few hours surfing our site and our competitors' sites and who comes in with a few thoughtful things to say about the landscape is way ahead of most of the candidates who come through here.

becomes widely profitable, lots of companies will go out of business, and lots of people will lose their jobs. And even if profitability comes before the money men bolt, it's only a matter of time before the industry consolidates, which will also mean fewer jobs. For the time being, though, companies are hiring like mad, and new media—particularly in the context of the Web—remains a charmed space where anything seems possible.

How It Breaks Down

The industry is a baggy monster that resists classification. The following breakdown is not a definitive taxonomy but rather a chance for the uninitiated to make some sense of this rapidly changing landscape.

Publishers

Online publications make money by selling advertising or subscriptions or both. Most of the players are losing money, and widespread profitability seems unlikely in the near future. Many players in this field are online ventures of already-established media brands. Some examples include the *Wall Street Journal Interactive Edition* (www.wsj.com), a subscription-based version of the leading business newspaper; Pathfinder (www.pathfinder.com), Time Warner's supersite featuring online versions of the publishing giant's most popular magazines; ESPN.com (www.espn.com), an extension of the sports cable channel; and ZDNet (www.zdnet.com), an online information site from high-tech publisher Ziff-Davis. There are also a number of important players whose primary presence is online. A few examples are WetFeet.com (www.WetFeet.com), the leading publisher of company and industry information for job seekers and the creator of this guide; CNet (www.cnet.com), which provides news and information on the online world; TheStreet (www.thestreet.com), a magazine for investors; and City-Search (www.citysearch.com), which is actually a cluster of publications, each devoted to life (restaurants, movies, community-service opportunities, and so on) in a given city.

Vendors

Vendors make money by selling goods or services. Though many sellers are consistently losing money, the segment as a whole seems far closer to profitability than the online publications do. The best-known online seller of goods is Amazon.com (www.amazon.com). Mail-order companies with websites—Lands' End (www.landsend.com), for example—fall into this category, as does Music Boulevard, (www.musicblvd.com), a seller of CDs. Other sellers provide services. E*Trade (www.etrade.com) and Charles Schwab (www.schwab.com) act as stockbrokers, and Travelocity (www.travelocity.com) acts as a travel agent.

Aggregators and Portals

Most of the busiest sites on the Web fall into this category. Search engines—which account for five of the ten busiest websites—are aggregators (so named because they offer a huge aggregation of links to other websites). Portals (also referred to as gateways or start pages) are sites that are designed to serve as home base for Web surfers. Both Netscape (www.netscape.com) and America Online (www.aol.com) feature home pages designed to serve as Internet portals. Not surprisingly, Microsoft has followed suit with Microsoft Internet Start (home.microsoft.com). In a move that typifies the fluidity and opportunism of this industry, the leading search engines are working hard to position themselves as gateways, and vice versa. All of these sites make their money from banner advertising (think billboards on your computer screen) or increasingly, through alliances with companies that pay a lot of money to be the gateway or aggregator's "preferred provider" of travel services or greeting cards or what have you. Although most of the companies in this niche are losing money, many of the major players seem poised to make the break into profitability.

Communities

Online communities serve as centers for people who share special interests. GeoCities (www.geocities.com) is one of the largest, hosting a number of communities with interests as varied as fashion, golf, and government. Other examples of community sites include BabyCenter (www.babycenter.com), a site for parents; Bolt (www.bolt.com), a site for teens; iVillage (www.ivillage.com), a site for women; PlanetOut (www.planetout.com), a site for gays and lesbians; and Tripod (www.tripod.com), a site for college students. All of these sites encourage users to sign up for free memberships by offering access to chat, newsletters, and bulletin boards; some offer members the opportunity to construct Web pages, which then reside in the community's site and serve as a draw for more members. Like most other Web ventures, these sites make money from advertising and alliances, and most aren't profitable.

Consulting and Support

This sprawling category encompasses all of the companies that have sprung up to support and enable the industry. Unlike the other industry segments, this one is filled with profitable—often highly profitable—businesses, mostly Internet service providers (ISPs), companies that allow users to get online. The ISP world is still divided between large players like America Online and smaller local players. Most of the major phone companies are also competing as ISPs. This segment also includes online advertising firms such as CKS (www.cks.com) and DoubleClick (www.doubleclick.com) as well as the myriad consulting firms that work as designers and developers. Two of the better-known design and development firms are Organic (www.organic.com) and Studio Archetype (www.studioarchetype.com).

What's Great

As You Like It

Go barefoot in the office. Dye your hair purple. Don't bother to learn anyone's last name. The culture of this industry is casual and fun, and insiders wouldn't have it any other way.

To Boldly Go . . .

The Web is being invented day by day, by the people who work in the industry. Have an idea for something that hasn't been tried before? Chances are good that if you make a compelling case, you'll get a shot at making your idea a reality. This is true not only for design and technical ideas; new business models are constantly being tested as well. Five years ago the Web barely existed in the public consciousness; what it will look like five years from now is up to the people who work in the field now.

Movin' On Up

The explosive growth of the Internet has meant explosive growth for many Web-based companies. This has in turn been a boon for many employees, as their careers grow along with the industry. This growth, combined with the entrepreneurial nature of most new-media companies, means that many people in the field can move rapidly into positions of higher pay and greater responsibility. For a lucky few whose companies really take off, it also means a quick bundle of cash when it comes time to redeem those stock options.

Life on Internet Time

Things in this field change very, very quickly. While this can be exciting, it can also leave insiders frazzled and frustrated. That project you've been working on every day for two months? Passé, and it never even got launched. Enjoy what you're doing right now? Too bad, the company's business model just changed, and it's time to do something else. Don't know the first thing about your new assignment? That's okay; you've got the weekend to learn.

Planning to Take Over the World

The vast opportunity that new media presents draws incredibly ambitious people to the field. While there are obvious benefits to this, it also means that there's a decent chance that you'll be working for a twenty-five-year-old with an ego the size of cyberspace for whom no measure of success is ever enough. Be prepared.

What, Me Worry?

Times are great in new media right now—sort of. Companies are awash in cash, but most of the cash is from investors, not customers. The vast majority of Web-based companies (and Web-based divisions of traditional companies) are not profitable. This is obviously not a sustainable situation. Industry experts are predicting a major wave of consolidation, which means that many companies will be acquired (good news for those with equity), and many more will go out of business.

KEY JOBS

New media is the ultimate "create your own title" industry. It's also a place where "significant experience required" means having worked in some element of the business for about two years. Although base salaries in this industry are often lower than those in other, more-traditional industries, many firms do offer employees stock options (potentially worth a bundle, but in many cases not worth the paper they're printed on).

Project Manager

The project manager (aka producer or product manager) acts to make sure that the various pieces of a multimedia puzzle—a website or a CD-ROM—are on track. This means making sure that the creative, technical, and business people are all in synch. Or as one job listing puts it, the producer "manages product from concept to final release, maintains product vision, and upholds business objectives." A project manager usually has substantial experience on the business or design side of things. Salary range: $35,000 to $75,000.

Ad Sales Rep

This entry-level position is a business basic, much like an ad sales rep at a newspaper or magazine. It is a good entrée into the online world for anyone who enjoys making deals and working with people—the business end of things. As with most sales jobs, the pressure to deliver can be intense. Salary range: $25,000 to $35,000, with substantial bonuses based on sales.

Marketing Associate or Marketing Director

In these positions, you'll conceive and execute advertising campaigns in the virtual and physical worlds. You'll also build a site's brand. Titles vary quite a bit in marketing, but the general idea is to drive people to a company's website. A college degree and good communications skills should be enough to land you a job in online marketing. Any previous marketing experience is helpful. Salary range: $30,000 to $80,000.

Business Development

Alliances and partnerships between and among sites are one of the driving features of online business. Business development folks identify possible partners, then negotiate and close deals and maintain relationships. MBAs tend to fit well in business development. Salary range: $60,000 to $120,000.

Technical Producer

This entry-level tech position is a good place for anyone interested in working on the technical side but who doesn't have a technical degree. Technical producers need to know HTML and Java Script and how to work with Java applets. Salary range: $30,000 to $40,000.

Webmaster

As the name would suggest, webmasters run websites. The nuts and bolts of this will naturally vary dramatically, depending on the nature of the website. Webmasters are typically required to have a few years of experience and to know HTML. CGI (Common Gateway Interface) is also a common requirement, and for more complex sites, knowledge of Java or specific databases is often necessary. Salary range: $40,000 to $90,000.

Engineer

This is the midlevel technical position. Engineers write code. They typically need to be experienced in Java, Perl, and C, and need to be familiar with database-connectivity issues. Positions at this level typically require two or three years of technical Web experience. Salary range: $40,000 to $90,000.

System Architect or Information Architect

These are the gurus who build and maintain the most complex systems in the business. They typically have ten years of experience working with databases or building applications. As the salary range indicates, these are the elite of the industry. Salary range: $90,00 to $175,000.

REAL PEOPLE PROFILE

TUCKER LAWRENCE

OCCUPATION: Website editor for an online general information and news feature service

YEARS IN BUSINESS: 1½ years

AGE: 26

EDUCATION: BS in economics from Harvard University

HOURS PER WEEK: 50 to 60, 10:30 A.M. to 8:00 P.M.; working lunch

SIZE OF COMPANY: 50

CERTIFICATION: None

ANNUAL SALARY: $38,000

How did you get your job?

Before this job, I worked as a desk assistant for two years for a major TV news show. I was looking for something in nonprofit, and while I was researching on the Web, I came across some openings at the company I work for in Yahoo's "Good Works" section.

Describe a typical day.

10:00 First, of course, I check e-mail. There are usually thirty to forty messages overnight. I read them all and answer the urgent ones. The rest I get back to throughout the day. I also check my to-do list from the night before and attend to whatever's at the top of the list.

11:00 Next, I go to my browser to check that the features that were supposed to be posted, have been. If not, I have to immediately find out from production and QA why not. Most material is supposed to be updated at midnight every night.

11:30 Start answering e-mails from freelance writers. The ones I've been working with for a while pitch their own story ideas; the newer ones I usually assign the material and direct a bit more closely.

12:00 Put together status reports for features in all my various sections in preparation for this afternoon's big production meeting.

12:30 Go for a quick walk with another editor and someone from Tech. Grab a bite to eat and talk about how to handle a project everyone hates.

1:15 Browsing other sites. I'm always on the lookout for good writers and nice design ideas.

2:05 Brief conversation with a writer while waiting for the meeting to begin. This is his third draft, and the story is almost ready. Usually writers submit copy via e-mail, and I send back comments the same way. But sometimes the editing work is done by phone. Either way, the piece is generally in good shape by the time the final draft is handed in. I have to do some editing, but not a lot.

3:00 More e-mail and lots more online comments for pending features.

5:00 Two features are almost ready to post. Put them into HTML

Production Artist

The foot-in-the-door design position. Production artists typically take a design that someone else has created in one medium and transfer it to another—for example, taking a hand-drawn design and replicating it in Photoshop. A college degree is not normally required for this position; vocational training or experience in another area of design—most often graphic design—is often sufficient. Salary range: $25,000 to $35,000.

to see how they look in our template. Big surprise—we have space problems. Yank them back to fiddle with both the text and the graphics. They look better, but still not quite right. Call over one of the designers. She has some good suggestions. Try again.

6:30 Write up a to-do list for tomorrow. Check to make sure all my e-mails got taken care of. Nope, there's one left over from the day before, a contract issue that needs to be resolved. Make a phone call, find the legal boilerplate, type in the new information and send it off. Okay, time to call it a day.

What are your career aspirations?

I'd like to move up to become a senior producer and creative director of a website. I'm interested in creating the overall tone, optimally for a career site.

What kinds of people do well in this business?

People who love teamwork. Your coworkers become your friends in this business. You need a sense of humor and the ability to turn around mate-rial really fast. If you need a slower, more-careful pace, Web development probably wouldn't work for you. If you're going to do anything in business, it really helps to have a serious interest in finance and economics. The only way to make this very dry material readable is to really understand it. If people ask me, I usually tell them to take as many courses as they can and keep up with the finance magazines. *Inc.* and *Worth* are two that I find particularly useful for the work I do.

What do you really like about your job?

This will sound unimportant, but I really like not having to dress up every day. It's a very informal atmosphere with nice people. We used to have a bowling league; now we have a soccer team. A couple times a month, someone in the office gives a party. It's a great chance to talk, gossip, and dance.

What do you dislike?

Having to turn on a dime. Everyone is still trying to figure out what works on the Web. No one is sure and no one is really making any money yet. So the solution seems to be to change the tone and then change it again within a month. It's also hard not having enough manpower to manage three or four sections. We're getting to the end of our ropes. Ultimately the content suffers, and I don't want to stop caring about my sections.

What is the biggest misconception about this job?

Anyone who thinks this would be a career with money. It is not the path to glory. And it's not easy. Even if someone buys you out—not often the case—very few people get rich doing this.

How can someone get a job like yours?

First, you have to love being on the Web and show an interest in the medium. Internships are always good, even the unpaid ones. You also need to think in terms of graphics and presentation, not just text. In TV, I learned quick turnaround. Whether or not we were ready, the show always went on at 6:30. So, of course, I think that TV news is great preparation for this. Mostly, we advertise our openings through Silicon Alley websites in New York since we're also on the East Coast.

Art Director or Lead Designer

Experienced designers work as art directors conceiving and executing designs. They typically have a bachelor's degree in a design-related field and a few years of experience working as designers, though not necessarily in new media. Salary range: $45,000 to $65,000.

Creative Director

The creative director takes a strategic role in the company, determining how to best represent a company. It's very much a people-oriented job, involving development of high-level concepts for design projects. It also involves working with clients, pitching designs, and understanding client needs. Creative directors usually have several years of design experience. Salary range: $50,000 to $90,000.

GETTING HIRED

It's no surprise that job seekers with technical skills are in high demand in this field. Knowledge of HTML and CGI is the bare minimum for programmers. Experience working with databases or writing in PERL is a big plus. Another language that's good for programmers to know well is English—unlike some of their counterparts in the software industry, most Web programmers need to work closely with nontechnical people, and solid communications skills are crucial. Finally, insiders tell us that examples of your work are far more powerful than anything else. If you haven't done any Web work, spend a few hours writing a sample page using CGI and find some place to put it online before you go looking for a job in this field.

For designers, Photoshop is the industry standard; to work as a new media designer, you need to know it. You should also know HTML or be proficient with a design-oriented HTML authoring tool such as Macromedia's Dreamweaver. Knowledge of Illustrator is a plus. You should also keep up with technology. Know what this week's versions of Internet Explorer and Netscape Navigator support—and what they don't. And as one creative director told us, "If a designer can interface well with programmers, that's a big plus." This means that the more technically literate you are, the better. This includes understanding jargon and being familiar with Internet protocols such as FTP. More generally, being excited about technology and the possibilities it brings to design is essential.

More than any other field right now, the Internet and new media offer wide-open opportunities to a wide variety of people. A college degree is not necessarily a prerequisite, but a genuine interest in the field is. Experience or a specific skill will make it easier for you to get a job, but they're not always essential. After all, there aren't many places to learn the necessary skills, and experience is often measured in months rather than years. Still, companies won't take just anybody. Here are a few things you can do to make sure you connect with the job you want:

- Impress your interviewer with your knowledge of and interest in the industry in general and the company in particular. If you're interviewing with a company whose website is central to its business, spend a lot of time surfing it and those of competitors. Be ready to discuss your opinions about these sites and have a few specific ideas for improving the site of the company you want to work for.

- Consider doing some volunteer work to gain some skills—and valuable contacts in the industry. Find a small business or nonprofit organization and offer to help it build, design, or maintain a site.

- Don't forget to demonstrate that you'd fit well in the industry—that you are flexible, deal well with chaos, work hard, and get along well with people.

Investment Banking

Investment banking is about gambling in a pinstripe suit. Most people think it's about money—and given that the top firms in the bulge bracket posted revenues of more than $23 billion in 1997 and that even the small I-banks cleared $3 to 4 billion on average, you could be forgiven for making this assumption. But the thrill for most traders and anyone dealing in the hugely popular domain of derivatives is the risk, not the reward.

Two things you need to know about jobs in I-banking: (1) these jobs pay a lot, with year-end bonuses that can match your salary; and (2) bonus or no bonus, you are going to work very, very hard. This is a rite of passage, a macho cultural totem. No one is exempt, and no one, particularly anyone who's already paid dues, is much interested in a crusade for change. "Investment banking is the last bastion of conformity," says one recruiter. "Once you accept this, you'll be able to understand it better. But the big salaries and bonuses aren't ultimately what defines these jobs. The recruiters at the top banks who each fall receive more than eight thousand MBA and undergrad résumés for only eighty to one hundred openings will tell you they're looking for excellence and leadership—in academics, athletics, the armed services, and even the arts. If you care as much about security as you do about securities, you won't be happy here. But if you always got straight As, have a Type-A personality, and are turned on by the thought of

REAL PEOPLE PROFILE

RITA JONES

OCCUPATION: Corporate-finance analyst for a big investment bank

YEARS IN BUSINESS: 2

AGE: 24

EDUCATION: BS in economics, Dartmouth College

HOURS PER WEEK: 70 to 80, 9:00 A.M. to 10:00 P.M., 7 days a week; working lunch

SIZE OF COMPANY: 5,000

CERTIFICATION: None

ANNUAL SALARY: $45,000 is the base. The bonus depends on your performance and the firm's performance—anywhere from $25,000 to $50,000.

How did you get your job?

I got my job through on-campus recruiting. I sent in my résumé; it was prescreened, and I got an interview on campus, and then a second-round interview in New York. Then I got an offer.

Describe a typical day.

8:00   I get to my desk and have a bagel and coffee while I listen to voice mail. There is already a message from someone in equity capital asking for a particular analysis. I start organizing materials right away.

9:00   I start putting together a skeleton of the information required and check it out with a couple of associates to make sure I am on the right track before I start filling in the gaps.

12:45 I run down to the cafeteria and grab a sandwich, which I bring back to my desk.

1:00   No time wasted on lunch, I am back to work. I spend the afternoon finalizing my data and preparing to send it off to our client. Afterwards, I discuss the presentation that my colleagues and I will be making to the client's CEO.

6:30   We go down the street for a quick dinner at a local pizza place. (Even investment bankers have to stop working for a moment or two to maintain sanity, and it helps to get out of the office for a half hour.)

7:00   Come back to the office and crunch a few more numbers, then spend some time looking over what I've done to make sense of it all.

10:00 Stumble home to bed.

What are your career aspirations?

Next year I am going back to business school. When I am done with that, I think I'd like to start up a company of my own. Right now I am gaining an excellent understanding of what makes some businesses work while other businesses don't, and I hope to put that to use in my own future.

What kinds of people do well in this business?

People with a lot of focus. And people who are not afraid to work hard. There is no substitute for hard work.

What do you really like about your job?

I like the excitement of working with really big clients—companies that everyone has heard of, and which play a part in many people's lives. It's fun to be a part of something that affects so many people. It's also a real rush to open the *Wall Street Journal* and read about a big deal that you had a hand in.

What do you dislike?

I hate not ever being able to make plans in advance. You can't plan two days ahead—much less two weeks ahead—to do anything on your own time, because you never know what demands will be put upon you at work.

What is the biggest misconception about this job?

People tend to think that I-bankers are aggressive and unfriendly. While we may be a little obsessed at times, we're not mean. Since coming here, I have made some of my best friends ever. People help each other and stick up for each other and are generally supportive.

How can someone get a job like yours?

Start early. Call up companies that interest you in August or September for jobs starting the following summer. Get your résumés out early and find out who you'll need to talk to in the upcoming months. Of course, it helps to be from a university where the firms you want to work for actively recruit, but even if they don't, you can get a job by getting in touch with the company and showing them your determination. Call back repeatedly. Someone is bound to remember you eventually.

closing deals, investment banking is probably one of the few jobs that won't bore you.

Investment banking covers a lot of turf. Its central role is as intermediary between the issuers of securities and the investing public. I-banks buy and sell large blocks of stocks and bonds, and they make their money off the spread between their purchase price and the public offering price. If the issuer of the securities is a client, I-banks also make money counseling the company, helping with the financing for its initial public offering (IPO), pegging the price during its early distribution (so that an eager pool of ready investors is always available), and providing follow-up after the IPO.

Investment banks also help mastermind and underwrite mergers and acquisitions, leveraged buyouts, public financing, and asset management. They offer these services to successful start-ups; large corporations; local, federal, and foreign governments; nonprofit institutions; and very wealthy individuals. As a result of the mergers, the easing of the Depression-era Glass-Steagall Act restraints, and the need to stay competitive, many I-banks have also folded retail consumer brokerage and commercial banking into their offerings. But their real focus remains the big money for the big players. Not surprisingly, the power of this industry rests in the lofty aeries above Wall Street and Midtown in New York City. Other hot spots include London, Los Angeles, Chicago, and increasingly, San Francisco and Silicon Valley. These are the headquarters. Even the smaller firms also compete in London, Frankfurt, Tokyo, Hong Kong, and other foreign markets twenty-four hours a day.

How It Breaks Down

The Bulge Bracket

There's not a clear and uniformly accepted definition of this group, but it basically means the biggest of the full-service investment banks. This is the group that matters most in investment banking, and admission into its ranks counts—on your résumé, in the deals, in how the markets move all over the world. Merrill Lynch, Morgan Stanley Dean Witter, Goldman Sachs, Salomon Smith Barney, and Lehman Brothers hold, for the moment, top spots in this bracket. A whole host of others, such as Donaldson, Lufkin & Jenrette; Credit Suisse First Boston; J.P. Morgan; and Bear Stearns, are sometimes included and sometimes not. This is a touchy subject. When in doubt, be it an interview or casual encounter, save yourself the agony and the hours of protest and just include everyone who ever appears anywhere in a tombstone in the bulge. (But when it comes time to decide on where you want to hang your hat, consult your WetFeet Insider Guides on these firms before you make your choice.)

Boutiques and Regional Firms

Obviously the investment banking world extends beyond New York and the bulge bracket. In fact, there are hundreds of firms that fall into this category, and increasingly, the stronger and more specialized ones are challenging the Goliaths in technology, agribusiness, public finance, and other specializations. For example, Hambrecht & Quist and NationsBanc Montgomery Securities, both in San Francisco, enjoy impressive underwriting connections and leverage in Silicon Valley that even Morgan Stanley Dean Witter's Menlo Park office has a tough time competing against. It's even harder to get jobs at these firms than in the bulge bracket, because they don't hire the same quantities of new blood every year. For the boutiques, the regionals, and the niche firms like Allen & Co. (entertainment and media) or Lazard Freres (media, France), your contacts and industry knowledge will usually count for more than your degree.

The European Invasion

The Japanese tried this strategy in the '80s; now it's the big European banks' turn to buy up I-banks in order to capitalize on an American bull market. ING Barings in the UK bought Furman Selz, Swiss Bank Corp. bought Warburg, Credit Suisse took over First Boston, and Germany's mighty Deutsche Bank created Deutsche Morgan Grenfell. Too soon to tell whether this strategy is going to pay off for the European parents—and job seekers should proceed with caution. Insiders at some of these other firms report that the bicultural undercurrents are important—and tough to grasp if you didn't grow up in a similar milieu. These hybrids tend to offer more responsibility and a little less structure up front to incoming associates and analysts, but less job security overall.

The Expansion Teams

As we mentioned above, everyone in financial services wants in on this game. The profits are higher than in their bread-and-butter business, the rewards in the current capital markets outweigh the risk, and of course, if they don't do it, they won't remain competitive. Moreover, many of these players are pumping lots of money into creating their investment-banking reputations and are hungry for talent. Several years of experience in these ranks (with generally more independence and managerial involvement than the I-banks) will position you nicely for a move downtown later on. Or you may well decide—as many others have—that investment banking at a slight remove from Wall Street has significant advantages and that you're better off as big fish in a small pond.

What's Great

Well, First the Obvious

Where else are you going to earn close to six figures—and often more—in your mid-twenties? Maybe as a consultant or as an associate for a big Wall Street law firm, but certainly nowhere else. (And consultants and lawyers don't move up your same steep salary curve after the first two years.) Nothing wrong with wanting to pay off all that school debt and make some sound investments early in life. Even in some of the high-rent locales where I-banks operate, you'll be able to save a significant chunk of your earnings.

Doin' Deals

Many bankers mention their love for the business of high finance. It's an exciting, fast-paced world with periods of great intensity. Often, the specific deals you'll work on—whether you're on the trading floor or in CorpFin—are the lead stories in the *Wall Street Journal.* Moreover, as one insider says, "You get to be a player in multi-million-dollar transactions; your analysis helps the CEOs make major decisions that have a huge impact on that company's bottom line and potentially a substantial impact on the economy."

Friends in High Places

It's a long life and this is a hand-picked, unabashedly elitist bunch. You never know when it's going to prove helpful to know someone important. One insider says, "I guess this is what the freshman class at Harvard feels like every year. I never went to those kinds of schools so I don't really know, but I know what this feels like—very exclusive." This has its drawbacks, obviously, but another insider says, "Basically, people are people. You soon find out, despite the names and the pedigrees, who's a nice guy to work with and who's not." Keep in touch with the nice ones.

Earn and Learn

Insiders agree that there is no better way to learn about finance and the inner workings of Wall Street, corporations, and the global economy. When you read in the *Journal* that Company X is making a semi-hostile bid for Company Y, that's you behind the headlines busily churning out spreadsheet models to help Company X decide how much it should pay, what the return on investment will likely be, and whether it should acquire or merge. These skills will help you in the future, regardless of your career path in business.

What's to Hate

Well, First the Obvious . . .

Has anyone seen my social life? I seem to have misplaced it. As an analyst or associate, expect to work eighty- to one-hundred-hour weeks during the crunch periods, and receive phone calls at 4 A.M. or cancel vacations if a crunch suddenly arises. Even on the slow days, someone invariably needs a project completed before flying out at eight o'clock the next morning—a project that didn't exist several hours ago. Your first several years in I-banking require a lot of stamina, patience, and hours. If you don't have them to spare, don't worry—we have lots of other career options for you!

The Politics and the Personalities

If you don't know what "Type A" means before you go to work at an I-bank, you'll quickly learn. Only the strong survive these very assertive (you can read that any way you want) personalities and the heated competition for the crowded rungs higher up the ladder. Although many I-bankers do enjoy the company of their colleagues, note the adjectives they use to describe each other. In our experience, brilliant, hard-working, and tough are far more common than nice, friendly, or sensitive.

Wearying Work

Yes, it's great experience. Yes, you'll learn a lot. But let's be serious. Updating comps (comparable company analyses) or even researching them can get dull. Running spreadsheet models for the zillionth time is even more tedious. None hold a candle to wrestling with a jammed copier at 2 A.M. For the people at the bottom of the totem pole, most of the work, most of the time, falls under the heading of Paying Your Dues. Pay them and you too will use your brain to optimal advantage again.

What Goes Up . . .

That's right, will inevitably come down. Asia, Russia, and Latin America will remain unstable; our own economy may well be overvalued and less sturdy than it appears. As one veteran puts it, "One of the most dangerous phrases on Wall Street is 'This time it's different.' It seldom is." Consider yourself warned. The world will always need I-bankers in good times and in bad (debt is a beast and someone has to manage it), but the bad times are hard on everyone.

KEY JOBS

Jobs in investment banks are divided into four areas: corporate finance, sales, trading, and research. Movement between areas isn't unheard of, but because doing your time and moving up the ranks in one area is the quickest way to make a ton of money, most people stay put.

Corporate Finance

Think of corporate finance as financial consulting to businesses. Specific activities range from underwriting the sale of equity or debt for a corporate client to providing advice on mergers and acquisitions, foreign exchange, economic and market trends, and specific financial strategies. When most people refer to investment banking, this is what they mean. CorpFin (as it is known internally) analysts work eighty-hour weeks to help prepare (that is, proofread and Xerox) pitch books to compete against other banks for prospective clients. They run endless financial models and help prepare (again, proofread and Xerox) due diligence on target companies. After two or three years, they're bustled off to B-school. MBAs are brought in at the associate level, where they help underwrite equity (stocks) and fixed-income (bond) offerings, write sections of pitch books, and sit in on client meetings—mostly taking notes—and help devise financial strategies. They also supervise teams of analysts. After three or four years, they move up to vice president; after another three to five years they make it to managing director. Salary range: $45,000 to $75,000, including bonuses, for analysts; $100,000 to $170,000, including bonuses, for associates; and $200,000 to $300,000 or more, including bonuses, for VPs.

Sales

Some firms only hire MBAs for sales jobs. Other firms don't even ask about your education. In either case, the bottom line is how well can you sell the new debt and equity issues CorpFin unloads on your desk—and how quickly you can translate news events or a market shift into transactions for your clients. These jobs are usually much less hierarchical than the banking side. Your sales volume and asset growth are what matter. Salary range: $40,000, with a $5,000-plus signing bonus for undergrads; MBAs start at $70,000 to $85,000, with a signing bonus of up to $20,000. Year-end bonuses fluctuate; they can be as high as 80 to 100 percent of base pay.

Trading

When Hollywood directors want to portray the rough, unruly underside of Wall Street, they wheel the cameras onto a trading floor. This is as close to the money as you can get. Trading also commands respect because it's tougher, riskier, and more intense than any other job in finance. Traders manage the firm's risk and make markets by setting the prices—based on supply and demand—for the securities CorpFin has underwritten. Like sales, but more so, you're tied to your desk and phones while the markets are open—but you get to leave after the closing bell. Beginners fetch endless take-out food and run other thankless errands; more seasoned traders scream and yell when their markets heat up and do the crossword puzzle the rest of the time. Not for the genteel or the faint of heart. A few traders even grow up to be CEO. Why? Because they know more about the markets and the money than anyone else in banking. Salary range: similar to that in sales.

Research Analyst

Research departments are generally divided into fixed income (debt) and equity. Both do quantitative research (corporate-financing strategies, product development, and pricing models), economic research (forecasts for U.S. and international markets, interest rates, currencies), and individual company coverage. An equity analyst usually focuses on a particular sector—software, oil and gas, health care. You move up in this profession by consistently predicting the movement of specific company stocks. The best analysts are ranked annually by *Institutional Investor* magazine. Their buy, sell, and hold recommendations, wield enormous clout, and competition among firms for the top analysts can be intense. Salary range: For the few undergrads and MBAs hired, starting salaries and signing bonuses are often slightly higher than the rest of investment banking. Senior analysts earn six figures and up (way up). Their bonuses and periodic raises are closely tied to the accuracy of their quarterly earnings projections.

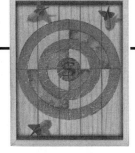

GETTING HIRED

Investment banking is a career that is most commonly entered from the bottom—although there is quite a bit of movement among the players once you're in the industry. Most of the large players in this industry have extensive on-campus recruiting programs that bring on dozens or even hundreds of bright, young BAs and MBAs each year. In part, it's because these people have strong backs and will work for cheap (by I-banking standards at least). Occasionally, people with extensive industry experience or a strong finance background may join a firm midcareer. However, you'll have to start producing quickly and be willing to bust your butt until you've proven your capabilities if you want to remain. If this sounds like the field for you, think about the following:

- You'll need to exude enthusiasm for all things financial. If you don't have the requisite fire in your belly, you're not going to survive those 4 A.M. proofreading marathons or even half a day on a busy trading floor.

- Gentlemen, your suit needs to be navy, your shirt white or light blue, and your tie as expensive and dull as possible. Don't wear anything Armani till after you get hired. Ladies, please remember the dollar rule, which states that

REAL PEOPLE PROFILE

KEN THOMPSON

OCCUPATION:
Equity trader

YEARS IN BUSINESS: 7

AGE: 34

EDUCATION: BA in philosophy, Brown University; MBA, Wharton School of Business

HOURS PER WEEK:
60, 6:00 A.M. to 6:00 P.M.;
15 minutes for lunch

SIZE OF COMPANY: 25,000

CERTIFICATION: Series 7, 63, and 3 licensing

ANNUAL SALARY:
$75,000, plus $35,000 bonus

How did you get your job?

I got my job through on-campus recruiting.

Describe a typical day.

6:00   Get to my desk with a bagel in hand and update any overnight orders. It is best to prepare and update early for all of the day's activity.

9:30   Throughout the morning, I monitor stock activity and make sure position runs are correct. I am glued to the computer screen.

11:00   Disseminate information learned during the morning with my coworkers.

12:45   I run down to the corner deli and grab a sandwich.

1:00   No time wasted on lunch—it's back to work.

1:30   The afternoon has a meeting with upper management on tap.

2:00   I usually trade ADRs until 4:30, taking and leaving orders for people in London.

5:00   Prep people for NYSE open at 9:30.

6:00   Time to relax.

What are your career aspirations?

I would really like to stay in the equity business. I have many options, such as becoming a buy-side trader or working on a hedge fund. Who knows?

What kinds of people do well in this business?

Aggressive people who have no trouble making decisions. Those with a thick skin will excel in this business.

What do you really like about your job?

Every day is a different day. I love the international aspect and the fact that this is a growing business. It is an exciting time to be mixed into all of the growth prospects.

What do you dislike?

It is a tough business, very lively.

What is the biggest misconception about your job?

I can't think of any.

How can someone get a job like yours?

It helps to know people to get your foot in the door. If you can prove your focus and dedication, you can really increase your opportunities in the company. Having an MBA is one way to show you are a hard worker.

your navy hemlines should be no higher than the width of one-dollar bill above your knees. If it's a straight, narrow skirt, make sure you measure sitting down.

- The recruiters and VPs who are interviewing you for these jobs actually like the idea that investment banking is the last bastion of conformity. It's all about fitting into a culture.

- I-banks want team players who are committed to winning, to being the best—and to moral rigor. Lest anyone forget, these are not your billions we are investing here.

Journalism and Publishing

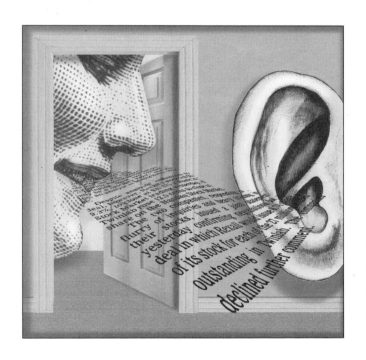

Once upon a time, English and history majors flocked to publishing. It was the one industry in which you could start at the bottom without any business experience and—through your sheer love of the printed word, your willingness to endure low pay and long hours, and your dedication to the craft—make a name and a legitimate career for yourself. Those opportunities still exist. However, rapid technological change is altering the face of this most noble of industries.

At the macro level, big publishing companies or firms (Random House, Simon & Schuster, Bantam Doubleday) are being gobbled up or traded around by even bigger media firms (Advance Publications, Bertelsmann, News Corp., and Time Warner, for example). Publishers across the board are keeping a careful eye on the economics of their businesses, making people with solid business backgrounds more attractive as hires. Finally, players in all corners are tremendously excited about—and at the same time, fearful of—the impact of the Internet on the future of the printed word. Although publishing is still a $130 billion a year business and revenues are growing in all segments (magazines, books, and newspapers), pundits are predicting that the end of the printed word as we know it is drawing nigh.

REAL PEOPLE PROFILE

ELSA GALESPRY

OCCUPATION: Freelance copyeditor

YEARS IN BUSINESS: 8

AGE: 29

EDUCATION: GED

HOURS PER WEEK: 40, 10:00 A.M. to 6:00 P.M.; 30 minutes for lunch

SIZE OF COMPANY: 1 (I'm a freelancer)

CERTIFICATION: None

ANNUAL SALARY: $35,000

How did you get your job?

I got into the business by working as a typesetter. I got to know some people at the company who were in the editorial side of affairs, and, because they knew me, they were willing to give me a chance in copyediting. Until very recently, every job I ever got in this industry was through personal contacts.

Describe a typical day.

10:00 I come into the office (at a national publication—I'm filling in for a copyeditor who's taking a sabbatical) and have a coffee, then look at the newspaper and wait. We are at the mercy of the writers, because we can't begin our work until they've finished their work.

11:30 An article arrives at my desk. I spend an hour going over it, checking for grammatical correctness, consistency, and sense. I make sure that all the figures add up and that everything holds together.

12:30 I eat my bag lunch and do a bit of the *New York Times* crossword. After that, I amuse myself at the computer by looking over pieces that will appear in the magazine at some future date.

1:45 There is a mad rush. A bunch of articles arrive all at once and I dive in on the work. This keeps me busy for several hours.

6:00 My official shift is over, but there is no going home until everything is done. I still have one more piece to finish.

6:25 I'm done. Time to go home.

What are your career aspirations?

I just want to find jobs that match my schedule and leave me time to pursue my other interests, like going to school and writing.

What kinds of people do well in this business?

Obviously you have to be good at spelling and grammar, for starters. You need to have a good memory and an eye for detail. It also helps if you have some natural interest and curiosity about the material you'll be working with.

What do you really like about your job?

I like getting things right. I like knowing that I have saved writers and other editors from embarrassment more than a few times. It's a real pleasure to work with writing and language because these are things I love, and it's nice to know that I am having some influence on how the published piece turns out. Also, the flexibility of the job is very important to me because it allows me time to pursue my other interests.

What do you dislike?

The sitting and waiting on other people can be enervating, especially when their tardiness causes you to have to stay late in order to meet a deadline. Sometimes the lack of control is frustrating too. You have almost no say about the content of an article. You could be working on an article that you think is terrible, but you have to just do the best you can with it anyway. There are times when you just have to work on a piece of junk in spite of your own feelings about the matter.

What is the biggest misconception about your job?

It seems not many people are aware that copyeditors exist, and those who are aware may overestimate the scope of our work. A copyeditor is not the same as an "Editor" editor. We work strictly with the copy, not the content. We don't get to decide what's written, we just make sure the copy is correct.

How can someone get a job like yours?

You could just send a résumé around to different publications and if any of them are interested, they'll call you. However, as I said before, personal connections have been very important to me in finding work. I would recommend looking for internships or other jobs in the publishing industry to get a foot in the door and make contacts.

What does this mean for job seekers? Publishing is still one of the bright and shining career options for humanities majors. There remain a large number of editorial positions in all the major media outlets. Moreover, the red-hot Internet has added a whole new layer of opportunity for people with technical, editorial, and creative skills. At the same time (to the horror of the more traditional editorial types), there is an abundance of high-profile marketing opportunities available throughout the industry. One publication, the *Los Angeles Times,* even went so far as to hire a former brand manager from General Mills as publisher. Depending on who you talk to, this is either a turning point in journalism or just business as usual. (Historians will note that the early Hearst and Pulitzer papers and even Ben Franklin's *Poor Richard's Almanack* made some notoriously dubious concessions to commerce.) Your view on this particular issue may help you navigate the various opportunities and players that exist.

How It Breaks Down

Journalism is the actual writing, photography, graphics, video, and other production work; publishing is the means by which all this information, plus books and other media, are distributed to viewers and readers. As recently as fifteen years ago, this was all much simpler. If you began life as a print reporter, you did not generally end up in TV or book publishing. If you covered hard news stories, you did not moonlight in PR and other promotional copy. It wasn't done, and no news editor would hire you if you did it openly. The mix is much more fluid now. And although a few old-school journalists decry these developments, this mix makes your job prospects more interesting than they once were.

Newspapers

Newspapers remain the biggest segment of the publishing world, accounting for nearly 40 percent of the industry's revenue. Although subscription rates have been in a long downward spiral, the industry continues to grow at about 5 percent per year. The big players here are Gannett, Knight-Ridder, Times Mirror, Dow Jones, the *New York Times,* and the *Washington Post.* But all of them also own substantial interests at this point in broadcasting, cable, and new-media technologies. And your local paper, the one that seems to be doing surprisingly well in terms of business and classified ads, is more often than not owned by one of the names above or a nonpublisher with dollars to invest in a going concern. For job seekers, this means that you have a lot more flexibility and options than you ever did before.

Magazines

This is an $11 billion industry expanding at about 4 percent each year, with top publishers such as Time Warner (*Time, People, Sports Illustrated*), McGraw-Hill (*Business Week*), and the *Washington Post (Newsweek)* leading in the *Fortune* rankings. *TV Guide* still outstrips them all in sales, and TV news programs' increasing reliance on the magazine format of lengthier features suggests the possibility of more links between the two media. Niche publications are a growing presence, too—they've been thriving for the past twenty years, and as the population ages, they're slated for even more impressive growth. If you're willing to focus on health, nutrition, estate planning, golf, and other subjects popular with retirees, you'll have a much easier time finding a job.

Book Publishing

Once a genteel profession known for its thoughtful editors choosing Great Books with pipe in hand, this is now a multibillion dollar business of pulp titles and blockbusters that accounts for about a fifth of the publishing industry pie. Nevertheless, it's still only growing at a sedate 3 percent annually, and jobs seem to be as hard to come by and ill-paid as ever on the lower rungs of the ladder. But move up a few levels and you may find a comfortable perch with a fair amount of job security. If you can ignore the clash of the titans overhead—Bertelsmann versus Viacom versus Time Warner—and just focus instead on the next hot title, you'll find the pace a good deal less stressful than online publishing or most journalism.

Online Information

This is the ever-expanding universe that no one yet knows how to define, how to make money in, or even how to feel about. Some of the emerging leaders such as America Online and Microsoft Network obviously pay a decent wage, but a significant part of the allure this medium seems to exert is that the old rules don't apply. CNet, one of the few with no outside buffers to hide its online losses in, took a $6.3 million hit last year. And though the Internet Advertising Bureau estimates ad revenues of almost $1 billion online, information sites only enjoy a tiny 7 percent of that income. But instead of discouraging all comers, these dismal prospects seem to actually hearten many. Americans have always adored frontiers, the more dangerous and uncertain the better.

What's Great

The Power of the Press

The pay may be lousy, the hours may be long, but even the cub reporter for a small local paper can break very big stories. And this is still a fairly honorable crowd. You'll usually get the credit you deserve for your scoop. Move on up to a bigger job at a more recognized publication and captains of industry and PR people earning three times your salary will actively seek to curry favor. Most journalists and publishers won't openly admit it, but their jobs are ego trips. The power you wield can be immense.

Say What You Mean and Mean What You Say

If you've been told ever since first grade that you have a problem with authority, you're too opinionated, too blunt, and too outspoken, this is the career for you. With the possible exception of sales and promotion, people in these jobs tend to be nonconformist and even downright eccentric at times. They're skeptical and tough, but they're also honest and fair, for the most part. No one minces words or pretties them up for the greater corporate benefit. (Of course, earnest beginners and senior management are regularly tempted to try, but as their efforts are usually met with such gleeful derision and scorn they invariably wish they hadn't.)

Work with Words

Sometimes it's tedious. Sometimes it's repetitive. But you won't find a lot of jobs out there that allow this much creative expression and diversity with money as compensation. Working with words—or words with pictures—is stimulating. Even working with people who work with words is stimulating. "This will sound a little corny," says one editor, "but I really think my job is exciting. I've been doing it for a long time and I still think it's really cool to be on top of the news all the time."

What's to Hate

Holier Than Thou

"Thou" refers to anyone unfortunate enough to work on the business side, in TV, or in public relations. In fact, thou probably includes any human not currently filing from a war zone or writing a blistering exposé of corporate malfeasance. Think of the worst snobs you know. Journalists and the lonely few still publishing worthy books are much worse than that. David Eisenhower once said, "Journalists are an interesting bunch, but nowhere near as interesting as they think they are." How high is your moral superiority quotient? It needs to be very high to survive in this crowd.

Faster! Faster!

The daily deadlines for newspapers are beginning to look positively leisured and calm compared to the exigencies of online copy demands. TV news upped the deadline ante years ago and radio and wire reporters have always had to write faster than they think, but now even "in-depth analysis" is done in twenty-five words—or 25 seconds—or less. If you like to reflect before putting pen to paper and you don't work well under pressure, even book publishing may be a bit too revved up for you these days. Minimal editorial ego also means being able to crank the stuff out. Poets are seriously miserable in these jobs.

Those Who Can, Do . . .

. . . those who can't, go into journalism and publishing. Chroniclers are by definition the ones who stand on the sidelines of life and observe. With the passage of time what they chronicle becomes history, but they are not the actual players. Sooner or later everyone in this industry, even the publisher, has to come to grips with the fact that he or she is not the one who matters in the story or book or show. Sportswriters can't ever play the games they cover; finance writers can't make killings in the market, even if the SEC suddenly decided this should be allowed. It's an active and bustling but ultimately passive role.

KEY JOBS

These titles and descriptions vary depending on the segment of the industry and the specific organization. And since the overall industry trend seems to be toward the incredible shrinking editorial staff, expect to see many of these jobs conflated soon if they haven't already been.

Editor

Lou Grant's time in the sun has come and gone. Editors now have to pay close attention to readership surveys, market trends, everything that's happening in new media in addition to the obligatory persecution of writers, graphic artists, and senior management. In large publishing organizations, editors usually preside over specific desks—national, foreign, finance, arts, new fiction, biography. In smaller houses and publications, they do it all—and a fair amount of the writing and layout as well. In the Internet world, these people are usually called producers, and they are responsible for supervising in-house and freelance writers and artists, and planning budgets and schedules. Salary range: $30,000 to $200,000.

Reporter

Jimmy Olsen and Lois Lane, by contrast, would find very little in their job description has changed. As one veteran says, "It's still the same old love—a fight for the story and glory." Reporters now often prefer to be called journalists and writers, and laptops frequently replace notebooks and stubby pencils. But it's still a lot of talking on the telephone, chasing ambulances and fire engines (or the equivalent), and writing feverishly to make a deadline. What makes it all worthwhile is the byline. Everyone else may only get to be famous for 15 minutes, but reporters get their name and, increasingly, their faces out there all the time. It used to be that anyone who wrote readable features for his or her high school paper could get a reporting job. Now many have graduate degrees in journalism or communications. Glamour quotient: very high. Work quotient: even higher. Salary range: $25,000 to $125,000.

Copyeditor or Proofreader

Chasing the commas and checking the facts is a bit like being a CPA. No one loves you. No one pays any attention to you. But without you, the paper, magazine, book, and online feature program goes out riddled with typos and errors. If you don't mind cleaning up after others, this is flexible, steady work. It's also one of the last truly democratic institutions in the industry: you take the copyediting test and you pass or you fail. Either you know the difference between restrictive and nonrestrictive clauses or you don't. You have an edge if you're also knowledgeable about a particular subject, but meticulous attention to detail is the only qualification necessary. Salary range: $10 to $75 per hour; the industry norm is $20 to $45 an hour.

Photographer or Graphic Artist

We know it's not fair to lump these two together, but we're going to assume that if you're interested in visual information, you understand all the differences between the two. Increasingly, this work is contracted out to freelancers. Job seekers who need a steady income: Your best bet may be to sign up with a reputable local agency. Once you have a good portfolio and can pick and choose your assignments, you may decide you prefer the diversity and freedom anyway. Salary range: $20,000 to $65,000.

Editorial Assistant

This is now the gateway in for those with fire in their belly, the pay-the-bills job for actors taking a break, the catch-all job for all the overflow from the copy desk and every other overworked, understaffed department. Editorial and desk assistants now have significantly more responsibility than they did in the past: if you want to grab for the brass ring, you're now actively encouraged to. It used to be a lifetime stigma, stamped somewhere on your forehead for every editor to see; it's now something of a badge of honor. Salary range: minimum wage or thereabouts.

Publisher

We now switch over to the business side, the world of dollars first, words second. Publishers make sure that enough ads are coming in, that enough book tours and *Oprah* appearances are scheduled, and that enough people are buying or watching or clicking to keep the editorial wheels turning. This is a thankless job, mostly because you get none of the credit and all of the blame. But it also offers a good deal of satisfaction to those who manage to turn a profit or rescue a failing venture. And amidst all the upheaval and change in the industry right now, publishers enjoy increasing amounts of leverage in editorial direction and development. Salary range: $50,000 to just about anything.

Ad Sales

The old model of selling space to anyone willing to pay, from local merchants to foreign tourist boards, in order to finance editorial operations is obviously changing. No one has figured out yet what logically should be taking its place, but in the meantime, the sales force continues to make cold calls, follow up on leads, and take clients out for nice dinners and golf games. Editorial likes nothing better than grumbling loudly and enviously about the expense-account perks, but they're hard won. This is discouraging and difficult work—only the most zealous survive and move up to the less-demanding plateaus of publishing. It's one of the only areas in this business where you don't need a college degree for an entry-level position; enthusiasm and the ability to persuade most of the people most of the time are the only musts. Salary range: $12,000 to $30,000, not including commissions.

Sales Rep

This is known in book publishing as being in the field. You trundle around to bookstores, colleges, and any other possible sales outlets for your wares. If you're lucky, you follow in the well-worn path of cordial relations established by your predecessors. The less fortunate find that their best orders are snatched up by competitors, and they spend all their time cultivating new and nonpaying customers. It's usually a three-year stint, and if you survive, you'll be welcomed back to headquarters and given a less difficult desk job. Anyone who has endured this rite of passage swears by it. "The only way to really know the customer," says one. "You can read all the [marketing] data you want, but being in the field is what really matters." Salary range: $12,000 to $30,000 before commissions.

Marketing and Promotion

This job varies from one segment of the industry to another. In magazines and newspapers the marketing staff's job is to get the publication into as many hands as possible. It may involve developing new subscription programs or checking out newsstands. In the book world, it may involve arranging book tours for your hot author. In the Internet world, it probably involves trying to get as many visitors as possible to your website. Despite grumbling from the hard-core editors, this job is increasingly important to the success of the publishing ventures in all segments of the industry. Salary range: $25,000 to $100,000.

REAL PEOPLE PROFILE

BOB LEHMAN

OCCUPATION: Reporter for a business magazine

YEARS IN BUSINESS: 5

AGE: 30

EDUCATION: BA in American studies, University of Virginia

HOURS PER WEEK: 50 to 60, 9:30 A.M. to 7:00 P.M.; 45 minutes for lunch

SIZE OF COMPANY: There are about 100 editorial employees at our magazine, which is owned by a large media conglomerate.

CERTIFICATION: None

ANNUAL SALARY: $43,000

How did you get your job?

I sent in my résumé blind, but that is pretty uncommon. Normally people are recruited by an editor, or they have contacts and they hear that a magazine is hiring before applying.

Describe a typical day.

9:30 Come in to my office and finish a cup of coffee while looking through all the newspapers. As I read, I'm thinking about the next great idea for a story.

10:15 I get on the phone and start tracking people down. I usually spend about one-third of my day making contacts and inter-viewing people for articles I'm working on.

12:30 Break for lunch.

1:15 I start reading through materi-als which I have gathered for a story which I am writing up for the next edition. At any given time I always have at least one story in the works. Sometimes I work on several at a time.

3:30 I start outlining the article. Tomorrow I will actually write it. I generally spend no more than three or four days a month actually writing because the magazine comes out biweekly and I rarely have more than one article in an issue.

5:00 I'm back on the phone, inter-viewing the CEO of a big firm on the West Coast.

6:00 I check on details for that trip to Chicago next week. Then I do a little more reading.

6:45 I call it quits for the day and head home.

What are your career aspirations?

That's a good question, actually. Most journalists eventually find themselves in a niche, and I'm still trying to figure out if business journalism is the niche I want to be in. I have also done some freelance writing, and I've found that I really enjoy food writing. I might like to do that more in the future. I also have a few good book ideas, which I might get around to writing some day.

What kinds of people do well in this business?

People who have natural curiosity about the world and a passionate interest in everything will thrive. You also need to have the ability to take in complicated subjects and boil them down to their essence so that you can explain them in a way which people will understand. And it helps to be fearless. If you have qualms about calling up strangers—some of them important and intimidating people—to ask impertinent questions, then you might have a tough time in this profession.

What do you really like about your job?

I love the access that I get to smart and important people. Because I am a journalist, I can call up the CEO of a multibillion dollar business and talk to him. I am always learning when I do research, and I get the satisfaction of teaching readers as well. Every now and again I'll get a letter from a reader who was really affected by something I wrote. It's nice to know that the things I write have been use-ful to people.

What do you dislike?

There is nothing particular to journal-ism that I can think of, but as with many jobs, there is always an element of politics and favoritism.

What is the biggest misconception about this job?

I don't know of any misconceptions about business journalists per se, but many people have a negative impres-sion of the media in general because of a few ugly incidents, like Princess Diana's death, in recent years.

How can someone get a job like yours?

Before you even begin, you've got to have a good collection of clips—stories you've already written—to demon-strate that you have the ability to do this kind of work. The best way to get an actual job is to make connections, through alumni or friends of friends— get to know anyone you can in the business.

GETTING HIRED

Traditionally, the tough part of breaking into journalism and publishing was the long apprenticeship period you'd have to survive. This still holds true on the editorial side for many traditional newspaper, magazine, and book publishers. However, the online world seems to be breaking the mold a bit, wooing people from the print world into the electronic arena with stock options, if not big paychecks. On the business side, many publishers are bringing in people with real business skills. Most of these spots still get filled on an ad-hoc basis with either entry-level or experienced people, but a few of the bigger players may have internships available for candidates coming out of college. If you'd like to land a spot in the industry, consider the following:

- The obvious criteria include enjoying reading, writing, and news. If you're on the business side, you should not only share these interests, but also be able to deal effectively with large egos and a lot of sanctimonious grief. For those applying for editorial slots, however, you too walk a fine line. One college text publisher is emphatic that he doesn't hire anyone with literary yearnings. "These are very mundane jobs," he says. "We work with teachers and students first and words second."

- Competence and calmness count for a lot in this business. So does modesty. Don't oversell yourself, even in ad sales. For all the changes, this is still a rather studious milieu. There's always too much work and not enough time.

- No need to tart up your résumé fonts or enclose your clips in an expensive-looking portfolio. You're only as good as your words, and visual distractions won't fool anyone in this business. Keep it short and simple. Less is almost always more.

Law

P ursuant to its mission as a purveyor of employment-related information, and subject to the disclaimers set forth herein, WetFeet.com (hereafter, the COMPANY) will describe the current state of the legal profession to you (hereafter, the JOB SEEKER). . . ." We've all seen this type of language, seemingly related only tenuously to English; we all know that it's the lawyers who speak it. But what exactly is the law? What do lawyers do?

Law is the means by which society regulates its own behavior. The intent of law is to create rules of conduct that are widely understood and respected and to create normalized processes for adjudicating disputes. Because law is considered to be a technical profession not easily comprehended by the untrained, individuals and companies hire professionals—lawyers—to represent them in these tasks. And although TV dramas might have you believe that you only need good looks and a fashionable wardrobe to succeed in the field, in reality you must complete three years of law school and pass a tough bar exam before you can practice law.

According to the 1992 economic census (the most recent one available), the legal industry was worth $101 billion in yearly revenues and employed 923,000 people. Many work for big corporate law firms or as in-house attorneys in

REAL PEOPLE PROFILE

JANE GLEASON

OCCUPATION: Family law attorney

YEARS IN BUSINESS: 5

AGE: 31

EDUCATION: BA in psychology and sociology, Dartmouth College; JD, Boston University

HOURS PER WEEK: 40, 9:00 A.M. to 6:00 P.M.; 30 minutes for lunch

SIZE OF COMPANY: 1 (I have my own practice.)

CERTIFICATION: Member of Massachusetts Bar

Annual salary: $36,000

How did you get your job?

I have a general practice with a focus in family law. My main focus is on child neglect and abuse cases. I decided it would be a nicer life working on my own than working for a big firm; I could choose the cases I want and schedule my time the way I want. So I decided to go out on my own. But I did it in a different way than others do—more slowly. Most people who leave a firm to go solo save their money, then quit and open shop. I was working at a firm and told them I wanted to go out on my own; they kept me onboard as I began taking on cases, until finally I had enough cases to stop working at the firm altogether. I got a lot of my cases at the beginning by taking court appointments, and I still like taking them. Some lawyers won't touch them, because of the low pay and the clients you're given, but getting a lot of cases this way helped me start my own practice.

Describe a typical day.

9:00   Arrive at the office; check e-mail and voice mail. A mother I'm representing in a custody battle with the state is among those who've left messages; I call her to update her on where her case stands.

10:00   Spend time talking to the other attorneys in a care and

protection case. I represent the child in this case, and I need to learn if there are any new developments from the attorneys representing the mother and the Department of Social Services.

11:00   Talk to the other side's attorney and my client's spouse to see if we can make any headway in a divorce proceeding.

11:30   Spend an hour and a half reading Department of Social Services case files, which are absolutely huge, on three of my other clients.

1:00   Call a psychotherapist to see if one of my clients who's been assigned to her is attending his sessions and, if so, how they're going. I'm trying to figure out if this therapist might make a good witness if this case goes to court, and what she might testify to.

1:30   Trip to the North Shore to visit an eleven-year-old boy who's my client. He lives in a residential facility, but has been transitioning to living at home (by spending weekends and some other days at home) and will be at home full-time in a month. I'm checking in with him to see how he feels about

corporations, while others hang out their own shingle and represent individuals or small companies in divorces, bankruptcies, and the like. Other lawyers work for the government, in various agencies or as district attorneys or public defenders. Still more work for advocacy groups such as the ACLU or the NAACP. There are even people who, although technically lawyers because they've gone to law school and passed the bar exam, do not practice law, working instead in business, banking, academia, or politics. There are also many high-caliber support people, known as paralegals, who do everything from word processing to legal research. Although popular wisdom has it that there are too many lawyers, the legal industry is a growing one; there are probably too few lawyers right now to handle the increasingly complex transactions of corporate America.

moving back home. Things are going well; he's happy about the move—but maybe even happier that I'm taking him to McDonald's for lunch.

4:00   Check back in at the office to see if there are any urgent messages. There aren't, so I do some billing paperwork.

5:00   Meet with new clients. I'm handling a big estate, which means a decent paycheck—but man, this is a complicated trust structure.

6:00   Trip to the supermarket to pick up the fixings for dinner, then on home.

What are your career aspirations?

To maintain and expand my solo practice. I'd like to make more money, and that means taking more private cases.

What kinds of people do well in this business?

To do well in a solo practice like mine, you've got to be disciplined and care a lot about society and individuals. You've also got to be good with people—patient, sympathetic—because you'll be dealing with people who are going through crises in their lives. For the same reason, because of the emotional nature of the cases, you need to be able to let things go when the day is over. And because you'll spend a lot of time arguing cases in court, you should have a professional demeanor and be able to speak well.

What do you really like about your job?

I like the daily contact with clients and other attorneys; many other attorneys have to sit and do research all day, and don't get to talk to people much. I also like the fact that I spend a lot of time in court, as well as the flexibility I have with my own practice. But more than anything else, I like knowing I'm doing something that's helping people and helping society.

What do you dislike?

I dislike the inconsistency. Some weeks or months, I won't have much work to do. During those times, I'm making less money than I want to—and because I work alone, there's nobody around to help ward off boredom when things are slow. Then five of my cases will explode in a single week, and I'll be swamped. I also get very frustrated at times with the system, and at the way some other lawyers operate, at some of the nastiness that can be involved.

What is the biggest misconception about your job?

That lawyers are snakes. The beauty of my job is that generally people who are in this area of law are in it because they care about people. I also dislike the way some other attorneys think of people like me—as though by doing family practice I'm somehow a lesser attorney, because I don't work downtown and wear fancy suits and don't do what they consider a more worthwhile area of the law, such as real estate or mergers and acquisitions.

How can someone get a job like yours?

Be disciplined. You also need to have the wherewithal to get cases. You can do this by advertising in bar association newsletters and through word of mouth. The more people you know, the better, in terms of getting referrals. This summer, in fact, I got my first golf course referral, from a guy I was teamed with during a round. You've got to be willing to put yourself out there.

While people enter law school for a variety of reasons, the vast majority of new graduates seek to land a partner-track position at a law firm. If they stay on track for anywhere from seven to ten years, they may be rewarded for their hard work and patience by being invited to join the lucrative partnership circle at their firm. Or they may not. However, in the meantime, they will likely make more than enough money to pay off the mountain of debt they incurred during their time in law school. They'll also be able to hone their legal skills to the point where they can pursue a variety of different options thereafter. In fact, many lawyers decide to leave firm life behind after two or three years, going to work for corporations, nonprofits, or government bodies, or just leaving the profession altogether.

Like doctors, lawyers come in many shapes, sizes, and specialties. Two main categories of private-sector lawyers are transactional (corporate) lawyers and litigators. Transactional lawyers deal with a wide range of business issues—corporate financing, contracts, acquisitions, bankruptcy, and others. The goal of this work is to get deals done and avoid future legal problems. Transaction-law centers include New York, Boston, Chicago, Los Angeles, and San Francisco and Silicon Valley. Litigators, in contrast, deal with legal problems after they occur. Litigators handle issues that could land their clients in court: breaches of contract, securities-law problems, rogue trading, class-action suits, antitrust actions, employment-related problems, white-collar crime, and the like. They are found in every city, but in New York and Washington especially. Other specialties include intellectual property, tax, real estate, labor and employment, environmental, personal injury, and family law, to name a few.

How It Breaks Down

Big-City Power Firms

There are about one hundred or so big-city power firms in the country. Typically, these firms offer clients a full range of services or nationally recognized expertise in a specific area. They have anywhere from 150 to over 2,000 attorneys on staff, often additional offices in other cities and countries, and a list of blue-chip clients that may spend millions of dollars on their services in a typical year. These firms typically pay the highest salaries and have highly competitive hiring processes that focus on top-ranked law schools around the country. They also require their associates to work long, hard hours and show exceptional brilliance in order to move up the partner track. Unfortunately, many now offer partnerships without equity in the firm, thus reducing the financial gains that were once a key perk of partnership. A number of these firms have had a poor record on ethnic and gender diversity, though that seems to be changing, albeit at a glacial rate. Although the turnover is quite high, even people who leave enjoy the luster of a well-known firm on their résumé. These firms are located in the major legal centers. A few of the well-known names include Cravath, Swaine & Moore; Davis Polk & Wardwell; Sullivan & Cromwell; and Paul, Weiss, Rifkind, Wharton & Garrison, all in New York; Covington & Burling and Wilmer, Cutler & Pickering in Washington, DC; Heller Ehrman White & McAuliffe; Morrison & Foerster; and Wilson Sonsini Goodrich & Rosati in San Francisco and Silicon Valley; and Baker & McKenzie in Chicago.

Regional and Specialized Firms

In addition to the big-city power firms there are a number of middle-tier firms that employ eighty to one hundred attorneys and provide legal services to local businesses and organizations: restaurants, hospitals, schools, insurance companies, department stores, mom-and-pop stores, start-ups, and public agencies. In some cases, these firms offer a relatively complete menu of services; in other cases, they may specialize in a certain type of client or practice (for example, intellectual property, employment, health, or environmental law). Often they include partners who left a big-city firm en masse, taking some clients with them. Regional firms offer slightly less pay than the big-city firms, but they typically grant equity partnerships after eight or ten years. They also give associates a lot more client contact as the clients are smaller companies, not huge corporations. Examples of regional players include Hanson, Bridgett, Marcus, Vlahos & Rudy in San Francisco; Farris, Mathews, Branan & Hellen in Memphis; Christiansen, Miller, Fink, Jacobs, Glaser, Weil & Shapiro in Los Angeles; and Glenn Rasmussen & Fogarty in Tampa.

Corporate In-House Counsel

The same companies that hire law firms already have their own cadres of in-house lawyers, which advise them on day-to-day business activities. Typically, but not always, companies prefer to hire transactional attorneys with three or more years of specialized experience in, for example, securities law or contracts. The salaries here are usually fairly competitive but the hours are far better. One other key difference is that there's only one client. So, if you're working for a company like General Motors, you might be working on a number of different types of issues (labor negotiations, hiring issues, contracts, a class-action lawsuit by an investor group), but they will all relate to General Motors.

Government Law

Federal, state, and local governments employ thousands of lawyers. One major employer is the Department of Justice, which hires lawyers to prosecute cases on behalf of the government. The most common entry point for those seeking to become a government attorney (or a judge, eventually) is as an Assistant U.S. Attorney (AUSA). These positions are appointments; in many cases, to get one, you must have connections as well as relevant legal experience. The executive branch also hires a lot of lawyers, primarily through the Office of White House Counsel. Other government jobs are available at the Equal Employment Opportunity Commission, the General Accounting Office, the Department of Labor, the Department of the Interior, the Department of Health and Human Services, the Department of Energy, the Solicitor General's Office, the Department of the Treasury, the Department of State, the Department of Housing and Urban Development, and the Department of Education. Opportunities also exist within the regulatory agencies, such as the Securities and Exchange Commission, and the Commodities Futures Exchange Commission—and in the military, in the Judge Advocate General Corps. A slight variation on government work is a judicial clerkship. A number of top graduating law students are hired each year by judges as law clerks. These clerkships, while not high-paying, provide aspiring attorneys with the opportunity to see the judicial process first-hand. Overall, the benefits of working in government law are job security and decent hours: you're not constantly worried about getting in as many billable hours as possible.

Public Defenders and Legal Aid

Public defenders are appointed by the court to defend those who don't have their own lawyers. Federal defenders are located in most major cities; the most important office is in Washington, D.C., but the offices in San Francisco and New York are also widely respected. In addition, states and counties provide publicly funded defense lawyers for those charged in nonfederal cases. Although the salaries for these positions are lower than those of most private-sector jobs, they are often not as low as people think. The jobs are, however, extremely difficult to get due to the competition for them. A cousin of the public defender is the legal-aid lawyer, who provides assistance to the indigent in civil cases. Funded primarily by the federal Legal Services Corporation and some states, salaries are quite low, but the work can be both frustrating and immensely satisfying.

Public Interest

Among the most prestigious jobs for lawyers are positions with impact—litigation advocacy organizations. These include the American Civil Liberties Union, the National Center for Youth Law, NOW, NARAL, the Lambda Legal Defense and Education Fund, MALDEF, the NAACP Legal Defense Fun, and the Environmental Defense Fund. Competition for these positions is fierce, and the pay is relatively low—with the exception of positions at environmental law organizations, which tend to be better funded. The advantage of these positions is that they're both intellectually stimulating and socially meaningful; however, the work usually consists of a lot of brief-writing and advocacy, with not much direct client service.

What's Great

Spending Change

If you play your cards right, you can make a good living as a lawyer. Most lawyers will never enter the ranks of the super-rich; but by the same token, they'll find it easier than most to buy a house or send their kids to the right college. After they pay off their own student loans, that is.

Security

Corporate lawyers have substantially more job security than the clients they work for. Once you've gotten your corporate job, you'll be much less likely to be fired during economic slowdowns than businesspeople or bankers; after all, legal advice is required as much during the down times as during the up. And lawyers are considered to be highly retrainable, so they find it easier to change firms (or careers) than many people in other industries.

You Really Like Me?

Recent bad press notwithstanding, lawyers get respect. Law is viewed by the public as a profession, not just a job. The words "lawyer," "attorney," and "JD" smack of tradition and mystique in a way that "manager" just doesn't.

What's to Hate

It Ain't *L.A. Law*

Private-litigation hell: You sit in a windowless room for twelve billable hours a day, dividing documents into piles marked "privileged" and "nonprivileged," while the paralegal sitting next to you does exactly the same thing. Corporate hell: You sit in a windowless room for twelve billable hours a day, reading documents and noting points that should be disclosed; every couple of days, you discuss your points with a senior associate or partner, who dismisses all of them as "immaterial." Even though you went through seven years of higher education to begin practicing law, you generally start at the bottom, doing the most tedious tasks.

Pickiness

Every company in the world wants employees who are detail oriented, but no employers are more detail oriented than lawyers. If you work at a major law firm, you'll be spending most of your waking hours with the most anally retentive 5 percent of the population. If you hate people correcting your grammar, syntax, typing, and spelling, you will be unhappy working as a lawyer.

The Hours

Don't worry; you'll earn your paycheck. A hundred thousand dollars a year can sound pretty good, but when you figure out your hourly pay, don't be surprised to find it just a tad above the minimum wage. (Okay, we're exaggerating—but not much.) If you're a corporate lawyer, expect to work far harder than just about anyone you know. And prepare to give up any dreams of having a personal life; you'll be on call almost all the time. Accept the likelihood you'll be canceling dates, giving away precious theater tickets, and postponing vacation plans. All this, and you might not even make partner.

KEY JOBS

Firm Associate

Associates do the bulk of the work in a law firm—from producing documents and doing due diligence to writing briefs and running deals. Because of the carrot of partnership dangling before them, people in these spots tend to work very long hours. A note for would-be litigators: It is extremely rare for associates in large firms ever to enter a courtroom; if you want to work in a big firm and want real-life litigation experience, do as much pro bono work as you can. Salary range: $55,000 to $150,000; more at the partner level.

In-House Associate Counsel

These are positions within companies' in-house legal departments. People in these positions advise the management of the company employing them on legal issues. The work can be a grind: studying the same type of transaction over and over. Or it can be very entertaining—for instance, a TV production company lawyer has to decide if there's anything legally objectionable in each day's talk-show broadcast. These spots are typically filled by attorneys with between three and six years' experience. Salary range: $50,000 to $300,000.

Public Defender

Public defenders are appointed by the court to conduct criminal defenses. They get a lot of courtroom experience early on and get paid better than most people think. But dealing with a lot of hopeless cases—and judges—can sour a young lawyer's idealism about the system very quickly. Salary range: $20,000 to $130,000.

REAL PEOPLE PROFILE

TONY BROWN

OCCUPATION:
Securities litigation attorney

YEARS IN BUSINESS: 5

AGE: 32

EDUCATION: BA in political science, Lehigh University; JD, New York Law School

HOURS PER WEEK:
50, 8:00 A.M. to 6:30 P.M.; 30 minutes for lunch

SIZE OF COMPANY: 6,700

CERTIFICATION: Member of New York Bar

ANNUAL SALARY:
$60,000

How did you get your job?

I work at a full-service brokerage firm doing securities litigation. I represent the firm in disputes between it and the customer. I got a job here through a friend while I was in law school. My current job stemmed from that, from having my foot in the door.

Describe a typical day.

8:00 Arrive at the office; check e-mail and voice mail.

8:30 Call a branch manager about a complaint lodged by a New Jersey housewife who lost money on a risky investment; order documents relating to the case.

9:00 Meet with my supervisor to discuss what I've learned about the case.

9:30 Review the investment history of a customer who has claimed he didn't understand the risk involved in investing in penny stocks. Learn that he lost $2,000 on another penny-stock investment two years ago;

his claim that he should be reimbursed for more-recent losses doesn't hold water.

10:30 Review the suitability of several customers to the stocks they claim they were convinced to buy unfairly.

11:00 Call a broker who's had complaints lodged against him in the past to learn his side of the story in the New Jersey housewife case.

11:30 Review published research reports about the company on which the New Jersey housewife lost money, as well as her investment history.

12:00 Call the New Jersey housewife about her complaint. She's a pretty green investor, and she sounds pretty believable.

1:00 Lunch: roast beef sandwich at the deli around the corner.

1:45 Call another customer to try to negotiate a settlement of his complaint against one of our brokers. We have a pretty strong case here; when the

Legal-Aid Lawyer

Legal-aid lawyers defend indigent clients in civil cases. Most of the people in these spots will have come from the more liberal part of their law-school class. While this position offers a lot of responsibility from the get-go, many legal-aid attorneys burn out on the job quickly, after representing too many unsavory defendants or seeing how cold or inefficient our legal system can be. Salary range: $22,000 to $90,000.

Assistant U.S. Attorney (AUSA)

This is one specific job you can get in the government. AUSAs work with law enforcement to put together federal cases against individuals or institutions. The jobs are fairly specialized; different AUSAs will work on, say, DEA cases, securities-law cases, and racketeering cases. Salary range: $40,000 to $130,000.

client refuses to negotiate, I advise him that his case will go to arbitration.

3:00 Meet with my supervisor to discuss the New Jersey housewife situation. Recommend that we settle with her and reprimand the broker who misled her.

4:00 Call the branch manager to advise him of where the firm stands on the New Jersey housewife complaint.

4:30 A bit of research on several other customer complaints.

5:30 Off to Penn Station, the Long Island Railroad, and home.

What are your career aspirations?

To move over to a corporate law firm.

What kinds of people do well in this business?

Energetic, organized, thorough people do well. The more cases you move across your desk, the better your career will go. You've got to be willing to speak to customers, follow up on details, and develop relationships with colleagues to help resolve cases. And as far as litigation is concerned, you've got to be competitive—you've got to want to win and be willing to put in the effort needed.

What do you really like about your job?

I like my autonomy. I approach cases the way I want, handle them the way I want. I can work at my own pace. I also like to see amicable resolutions to disputes, resolutions that are satisfying to all parties involved—though they're rare. And the hours of my job are pretty manageable.

What do you dislike?

There are moral issues that come into play that make me uncomfortable. For example, when I have to fight the eighty-year-old widow who's been convinced to invest in a risky stock by an unsavory broker who, even though he broke no securities laws, operated unfairly. Or vice versa—when I have to negotiate with a slippery customer who's taking advantage of the rules to get a settlement from us.

What is the biggest misconception about this job?

That we're here to defend the firm at all costs. We're here to get to the bottom of disputes, to resolve them—which can mean disciplining or firing a broker who's cheated and taken advantage of customers.

How can someone get a job like yours?

Go to law school and do really well. Get a job at a securities firm before or during law school. Network and play up your relevant experience.

Nonprofit Attorney

Lawyers in these positions are renowned for having the greatest job satisfaction—and among the lowest salaries. The responsibilities will vary greatly, but most focus on handling legal and financial issues for a charitable organization, many of which are trying to do good though low on funds and in organizational disarray. Salary range: $30,000 to $100,000.

Paralegal

This is a good way to check out the legal profession. Legal assistants, or paralegals, occupy a kind of glorified secretary position. Despite being college graduates, they do a lot of photocopying, proofreading, and filing. The hours are long, but these positions pay overtime. And if you're a star performer at a big firm, you may even find your law school education paid for. Salary range: $22,000 to $60,000.

GETTING HIRED

The best way to get a job at a top law firm is to have

- Top-25-percent grades (anything below the 50th percentile will be an obstacle, no matter how good your other credentials) from a top school. That said, law firms are pretty generous to those making a lateral move; experience will count more than grades at that point.

- Judicial clerkship experience, law-review experience, or meaningful work experience.

- Obvious characteristics such as intelligence, reliability, attention to detail, and people skills—also known as schmoozing.

- Professional demeanor. If leather and piercings are your bag, you should probably be thinking about another career.

Management Consulting

So, you want to be a consultant. Or, more likely, you think you'll spend a few years as a consultant and then move on to other things. You're not alone—there are more than 250,000 consultants in the United States. Consulting firms are traditionally among the largest employers of top MBAs and college graduates, and they are an attractive alternative career option for people who've toiled in industry for a number of years. Consulting is a high-paying, high-profile field that offers you the opportunity to take on a large degree of responsibility right out of school and quickly learn a great deal about the business world. It's also a profession that will send you to the corners of the country—and leave you there for days and weeks on end while you sort out the tough questions for a client that's paying your firm millions of dollars to get exactly the right solution.

In essence, consultants are hired advisers to corporations. They tackle a wide variety of business problems and provide solutions for their clients. Depending on the size and chosen strategy of the firm, these problems can be as straightforward as researching a new market, as technically challenging as designing and coding a large manufacturing control system, or as sophisticated as totally

REAL PEOPLE PROFILE

ANNA KAPOOR

OCCUPATION: Associate at a large consulting firm

YEARS IN BUSINESS: 3

AGE: 25

EDUCATION: BS in economics, Vanderbilt University

HOURS PER WEEK: 50, 8:00 A.M. to 6:00 P.M.; 1 hour for lunch

SIZE OF COMPANY: 1,500

CERTIFICATION: None

ANNUAL SALARY: $45,000

How did you get your job?

I was recruited on my college campus. As is the case with most management consulting firms, this was a highly competitive selection process.

Describe a typical day.

7:00 Get to the office. I'm working on a project for a retail client, a kid's clothing company. Status check on my team's deliverable, in this case, a presentation to the client's board of directors. Quiet time. What needs to be done to get the presentation done? I do this every day to plan my day out.

7:30 Try to chase down people on the client team to get some answers to questions I've come up with. Hope they get back to me by the end of the day. Want to find out what they are planning in terms of color coordinates for the next season. I let them know what I've learned about what competitors might be doing.

8:00 Personal e-mail time. My friends outside the company know that this is the best time to call me so we can chat.

9:00 Back to work. Review market data. This basically means crunching through the database of customer survey responses we constructed. We go beyond just reporting what

the client's best customers are like demographically. We find out what their shopping habits are and even more detailed information. For example, whether they are concerned more with price or with quality and whether they want a range of clothing for all ages of children or just for the under-seven crowd that is already the client's main focus.

12:00 Lunch with friends.

1:00 Have a case team meeting. The case is modular—meaning that we all work on different pieces—so we need to share information. One women is working on pricing, and I'm working on trends, so I tell her about an article that said that discount children's clothing is becoming more popular.

2:30 Before ending the meeting, we make sure other people out-side the office know what's going on via a conference call.

3:00 More e-mail.

3:20 Look at the masses of marketing materials and articles to figure out trends. Should the clients focus on babies more? If you want the client to narrow its customer base and still make more money, you have to do your research to show how this will happen. Spend some time doing research: current and pro-

rethinking the client's organization and strategy. One good thing about the advice business: companies always seem to want more. As evidence, the consulting industry has been on a sustained growth binge for well over a decade. Consulting firms of all sizes experienced growth in the 10- to 25-percent range in 1997, and the Bureau of Labor Statistics projects that the industry will continue to grow at more than 20 percent over the next decade. One other thing about the consulting business: The product really is the people, and firms compete on the basis of who's the smartest and the hardest working. As a result, each firm wants to hire the best and the brightest. If you're one of them—you probably know if you are or aren't—you'll have a good shot at landing one of these competitive jobs.

jected birthrate in the United States, average amount people spend on their own children's clothing versus those of friends and relatives, and potential competition from retailers ranging from discount stores to neighborhood boutiques.

6:00 Calls from client start to come in. Spend about half an hour talking with each person.

8:00 Go home.

What are your career aspirations?

I definitely want to stay in the business world. I'll probably remain with this firm for a couple more years. After that, I'll consider either staying in consulting or moving into a management position somewhere else in the business world. And at some point, of course, I'll get my MBA.

What kinds of people do well in this business?

You have to really be interested in business. This is not an academic group or a nonprofit (though occasionally we have clients in these areas). Our focus is on large business corporations. You also have to be a team player. If you prefer to work by yourself, this is the wrong job for you. Finally, you must have exceptional analytical skills, and not just in an academic way. In this profession, you need to be able to figure out what

your suggestions will mean for the client, which may require a more intuitive analysis.

What do you really like about your job?

I like the fact that I can make a significant impact on a large organization, even at a relatively young age. I also enjoy the challenges posed by the problems themselves—the variety alone of issues we have to deal with is interesting. And management consulting firms tend to hire top-notch individuals. It's exciting to work with so many bright people.

What do you dislike?

I travel anywhere from zero to three days a week, sometimes more. After a while, it can be extremely draining.

What is the biggest misconception about your job?

Three things come to mind, actually. First is the myth that consultants do everything in a vacuum. We work intensely with our clients in developing recommendations; we don't just sit around in our office writing up a report that will land on the client's desk when we're through. The second myth is that we don't stick around to see our suggestions implemented. We do provide our clients assistance through the implementation phase. The third misconception is that it's impossible to make an impact as a junior employee at the firm. If you

can make a compelling and meaningful analysis of a situation, you can have a substantial impact on the outcome of a case. Personally, I have even had the opportunity to manage a client team of twenty people to work on implementation of the recommendations that were made by our team. I don't sit in my office doing spreadsheets all day.

How can someone get a job like yours?

Logistically speaking, the most common way for an undergraduate at least is through on-campus recruiting. Prospective applicants can also contact the recruiting department of a firm directly if they're not on a campus where there is active recruiting. Once you've got the interview, the things that will actually get you hired are your analytical skills, your communication skills, and your presence. Demonstrated leadership potential is another quality they look for, so if you've held leadership positions in the past, it will be to your advantage—but you want to show them that you did more than just hold an office. Show your interviewer that you excelled at whatever you were doing. There is no cookie-cutter mold for a management consultant. There are lots of ways to demonstrate that you are a person with drive and potential.

How It Breaks Down

Even though there are thousands of consulting organizations across the country, these firms can be tough to get a handle on. Why? Most are privately held, work directly with other businesses rather than with your average consumer, and tend to be intensely private about the names of the clients they work with and the actual work they do. Nevertheless, if you want to get a job in the industry, you're going to have to know which firms do what and be able to say in clear and convincing terms why French vanilla is oh-so-much-better than vanilla with little specks of vanilla bean sprinkled throughout. To help you understand the consulting landscape, we've divided the industry into six different categories: the industry elite, the Big Five, boutiques, information technology (IT) consultancies, human resources specialists, and the independents. Most players in the industry can be put into one or more of these different categories.

Industry Elite

The rich and famous of the consulting world. These companies focus on providing cutting-edge strategy and operations advice to the top management of large corporations. They generally hire the best candidates from the best undergraduate, MBA, and other graduate programs. Slackers need not apply. Players in this group include A. T. Kearney, Bain & Co., Booz·Allen & Hamilton, The Boston Consulting Group, McKinsey & Co., Mercer Management Consulting, and Monitor Co., to name a few.

Big Five

The consulting operations of the Big Five accounting firms. Although these firms provide some of the same strategy and operations advice as the elite, they tend to have a stronger emphasis on implementation work, particularly in the IT world. The players are Andersen Consulting/Arthur Andersen, Deloitte & Touche, Ernst & Young, KPMG Peat Marwick, and PricewaterhouseCoopers.

Boutique

Firms that specialize along industry or functional lines. Although often smaller, these firms may have top reputations and do the same operations and strategy work the elite firms do, but with more of an industry focus. Representative players include APM (health care), CSC Planmetrics (energy and utility industry), Marakon Associates (strategy), Oliver Wyman (financial services), PRTM (high-tech operations), Strategic Decisions Group (decision analysis), Vertex Partners (strategy).

IT

Information systems (or information technology) specialists. One of the fastest-growing sectors of the consulting world (although not quite as meteoric as strategy consulting, according to Kennedy Information Group), these firms provide advice, implementation, and programming work on computer- and systems-related issues for clients. Representative players include American Management Systems, Computer Sciences Corp., Digital Equipment Corp., EDS, IBM, and the Big Five firms.

Human Resources

This area of consulting focuses on personnel issues such as employee-management and -evaluation systems, payroll and compensation programs, pensions, and other benefits programs. Representative firms include The Hay Group, Hewitt Associates, William M. Mercer, Towers Perrin, Watson Wyatt Worldwide. In addition, several of the Big Five firms have practices devoted to this area.

Independents

One-man or -woman shops. By sheer numbers, independent consultants far outnumber the larger firms—fully 45 percent of all consultants are reported to be independents. They typically have some sort of industry or functional specialty and get hired on a project basis. If you have an MBA and several years of useful and topical business experience, there's no reason not to hang out a shingle yourself.

What's Great

Battles of the Mind

By and large, people who work for consulting firms talk about how intellectually stimulating the work is: "The work is just phenomenal," says one. They enjoy the challenge of going into the ring to face some of the toughest, gnarliest, most-complex issues on the business roster and emerging victorious. As one consultant says, "Companies pay us so much that they make sure we work on things that are really critical to them."

Recession-Proof

Consulting has enjoyed a sustained growth binge over the last several decades. In good times, companies flush with cash want to hire consultants to help them make strategic decisions about growth. In hard times, clients come seeking advice about cutting costs and getting out of unprofitable businesses. In addition, consultants have been successful at taking on work that used to be done by staff that was laid off—no doubt as the result of a big reengineering project!

Payday!

Most consultants won't come right out and admit, but a key reason the industry remains so popular is that it pays well. Starting salaries can range from the low 40s to the mid-50s for people coming straight out of undergrad programs and hit six figures for twenty-six-year-old MBA grads. Even MBAs who'd rather be doing the entrepreneurial thing often opt to work in consulting for a few years in order to pay off their school loans before moving on to something else. Beyond the pay, the perks are generous—the only danger is that you may get accustomed to staying at the Ritz.

Just Like Me

As a consultant, you'll get to prolong that college experience. As one consultant told us, "People are universally bright, interesting, hard-working, and motivated." Most of the people you work with will be just like some of your favorite people from school—smart, attractive, friendly, full of energy. The only difference is that you'll probably be too busy to really spend much time socializing outside the office.

REAL PEOPLE PROFILE

PAUL CORDIER

OCCUPATION:
Senior consultant at a small consulting firm

YEARS IN BUSINESS: 2

AGE: 27

EDUCATION: BS in finance and marketing, Duke University; MBA, Harvard University

HOURS PER WEEK:
55 to 75, 7:00 A.M. to 10:00 P.M. at the worst, depending on travel

SIZE OF COMPANY: 100

CERTIFICATION: None

ANNUAL SALARY:
$95,000, plus $20,000 bonus

How did you get your job?

I got my job through on-campus recruiting. I knew from a previous internship at a large management consulting firm that I wanted to work for a smaller company, so I did research on about twenty different firms, then interviewed at about ten of them that came to our campus. I worked my way up to senior consultant, a step below the case manager on a case team. It's my job to help define the objectives of our analyses and the deliverables. I do a lot of coordinating and communicating with both the clients and the rest of the team and I delegate responsibilities to analysts and less-senior consultants.

Describe a typical day.

8:00   First thing in the morning, I check my e-mail and voice mail at home. After I hear my messages, I begin to plan my day.

9:00   I arrive at the office and begin to focus on producing deliverables for various clients. I often spend ten to twelve hours a day working on these.

10:30   The case team meets to discuss progress and objectives for our most important project.

12:00   I never spend more than a half an hour having lunch. Today I have Chinese takeout.

12:30   I am back in my office, working on a deliverable. In this case, it's a fairly in-depth marketing analysis. Frequently I am interrupted by phone calls. I send e-mail and voice mail to clients and case managers, answering their questions.

4:00   I talk with a client on the phone to do some preliminary data gathering before my trip to his site next week. When I'm through with this, I get back to work on the deliverables I've been working on since the morning.

6:00   I'm calling it quits for today, but before I leave, I spend some time thinking about deadlines and project goals. I send a few more e-mails out to some analysts on the team, delegating some number-crunching tasks to them.

What's to Hate

Dog's Life

Top complaints: the travel, the hours, and the difficulty of maintaining a personal life. But the consulting lifestyle, which often requires the consultant to log fifty to sixty hours per week and to be out of town for four days a week for months at a time, is hard to maintain over the long run, especially for people with families—or friends. Moreover, it will quickly become obvious that consulting is a service industry. "There are times when, even though you may have something planned, you just have to suck it up and stay at the office," says one insider.

IMHO (In My Humble Opinion)

If you like backseat driving, consulting is an excellent option. If you eventually feel like you want to grab the wheel and drive that car down the road yourself, it ain't gonna happen till you leave consulting. As an adviser, you'll always be advising.

What are your career aspirations?

I got into consulting because I wanted to stay on a fast-paced learning curve after I finished business school. Some day I hope to use what I have learned to start my own business, perhaps in low-tech manufacturing or in software or Internet services.

What kinds of people do well in this business?

You must have strong analytical skills. Quantitative skills especially are a big asset, as there is less of a need in consulting for purely qualitative analysis. You must like to learn and work hard, and be able to think fast. Above all, though, you need interpersonal skills—especially with clients—because in the end, this is a sales job. You have to be able to sell your ideas to clients, or all of the work that you did in formulating the ideas means nothing.

What do you really like about your job?

I like the challenge of facing a complex problem and solving it for people who have not been able to solve it for themselves. There is a lot of adrenaline—and stress—involved when you begin facing a problem that you don't necessarily know how to solve at the outset. Then, when you find the answer, it's extremely satisfying. Personally, I also enjoy the customer interaction a lot. Another thing I like about my firm specifically is that, because it's small, I was able to take on authority and responsibility more quickly than I could have at a larger firm.

What do you dislike?

The traveling gets old. My wife thinks so too.

What is the biggest misconception about this job?

Many people think it's more glamorous than it is. When you're a young guy who shows up at a client firm as a consultant wearing an expensive suit, people are either going to think, "What a stud" or "This jerk thinks he knows everything." Neither of these perceptions is really fair. When you get right down to it, consulting involves hard work and personal inconvenience. Despite what you may know about the established knowledge management principles that exist at some firms, most of the time these principles aren't effective when applied to an actual case. The individual consultants have to put in a lot of hours, do a lot of research, and spend a lot of time in a place they'd rather not be to come up with a proposal that will work—which isn't very glamorous.

How can someone get a job like yours?

Go to Harvard Business School. No, seriously, just get an MBA. That's the best way—the firms will come looking for you. Even if you don't have an MBA or any desire to obtain one, you can still get a job in consulting by going after the firms yourself. Right now the job market is so strong that consulting firms are hiring higher percentages of PhDs and JDs than ever before. Anyone who has had good academic results and who prepares well for the case interviews should stand a good chance of landing a job.

What Am I Living For?

Most people who go into consulting as a career believe that they do valuable, highly meaningful work. However, a common refrain among people who leave consulting is that the work isn't "real"; after all, no one really needs another org chart. One former consultant says, "I wanted to be making a difference in a smaller setting with real people."

KEY JOBS

As each firm has its favorite buzzwords, it also has unique terminology for its rank and file. While the titles may vary from firm to firm, the roles can basically be divided up as follows: analyst (also called research associate or staff consultant at some firms), consultant (or senior consultant), manager, and partner or VP. In addition, consulting firms hire a cadre of highly capable nonprofessional staff into administrative and support positions. (This is not a bad place to be if you've got skills on PowerPoint and you like to draw slides.)

Administrative Assistant

Most consulting firms have a fairly large pool of college-educated administrative assistants and support staff on board so that the consultants can keep focused on tasks that justify their billing rates of $200 per hour. In addition to performing standard support functions, many have specific roles (recruiting, office administration, or website maintenance, for example). Most firms also have a group of graphic designers on staff to prepare materials for presentations. Salary range: $25,000 to $50,000 or more.

Analyst, Research Associate, or Staff Consultant

This is the position at the bottom of the professional pyramid. The vast bulk of analysts are young, talented, and hungry college graduates. Many firms structure this position to last for two to three years, after which the analyst is expected to move on—perhaps to graduate school or another employer. (Some firms do allow people to progress up the management ladder without leaving the firm.) The work itself—as well as the hours—can be quite demanding. It often includes field research, data analysis, customer and competitor interviews, and client meetings. In IT, analysts may do heavy-duty programming. Salary range: $30,000 to $50,000.

Associate, Consultant, or Senior Consultant

This is the typical port of entry for newly minted MBAs (and increasingly for non-MBA graduate students as well). Senior consultants often perform research and analysis, formulate recommendations, and present findings to the client. Oh, and at many firms, they have to implement those great ideas, too. Although this is usually a tenure-track position, a fair number of consultants will leave the business after two or three years to pursue entrepreneurial or industry positions. Salary range: $65,000 to $130,000 or more with bonus.

Manager

After a few years, a senior consultant will move up to manager. As the title implies, this usually means leading a team of consultants and analysts toward project completion. Some firms may hire MBAs with significant work experience directly into the manager position, particularly in their IT practices. In addition to having more-rigorous responsibilities for managing the project team, the manager will typically be a primary point person for client interactions. Salary range: $85,000 to $150,000.

Partner or VP

Congratulations! You've forded the River Jordan of consulting and arrived at the Promised Land. Note that some firms further subdivide partners into junior and senior grade. And, if you aspire to it, there's always that chairman or CEO position. One primary and highly relevant difference is that a significant part of the partner's responsibility is to sell new work. Fortunately, as with other big-ticket sales jobs, the pay can be quite rewarding. Salary range: $250,000 to several million dollars at leading firms.

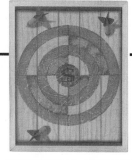

GETTING HIRED

There are two main routes into consulting. One goes directly from campus (undergrad and MBA, primarily) into entry-level positions (analyst or consultant). The other leads from industry into midlevel positions in specific practice groups (aerospace, energy, and financial services, for example), functions (marketing or supply chain management, for example), or technologies. If you're set on landing a consulting job, keep these things in mind:

- Competition for consulting spots is intense—major firms review hundreds of résumés for each hire they make. To stand out from the crowd, impressive schools, impressive grades, and a demonstration of significant work or leadership experience are almost essential.

- In addition to your bulletproof résumé, you'll need to show evidence of strong analytical skills—usually by acing a series of the notorious case interviews, in which recruiters ask you to analyze a hypothetical business problem—your raw intelligence, and your ability to work well with people.

- If you're applying for an IT consulting position, you may well be asked to write some code.

- In almost all cases, you will be screened for your fit with the firm. So, for the duration of your interviews at least, try very hard to scale back your most irritating habits.

- Remember, this is a very conservative industry. A pale blue résumé, white loafers, and off-color comments will certainly earn you a rejection letter.

Mutual Funds and Brokerage

f you're interested in mutual funds and brokerages, it's probably because you think where there's money, there are jobs. And you're right. The S&P Index, a broad-based measurement of the five hundred stocks with the largest capitalization, has slightly more than doubled in value in the past three years—that's three times faster than such an increase has historically taken. Mutual funds have experienced equally impressive growth—a cumulative return of 95.3 percent on the average diversified stock fund in the same period from '95 to early '98, according to Lipper Analytical Services.

Good reasons to pay attention to this industry. But why lump together two previously distinct areas of money management—securities brokerage and asset management? Principally because the way your parents invested is not how most people do it these days. Investment choices now include stocks, bonds, IRAs, and mutual funds; domestic versus global portfolios; and full-service versus discount brokerage services versus electronic trading. Brokerage firms (like Merrill Lynch, PaineWebber, Salomon Smith Barney, and discounters Charles Schwab and E*Trade) and mutual funds (like Fidelity, Vanguard, and Dreyfus) have invaded each other's turf in the ever-escalating financial-services war. Fidelity was

REAL PEOPLE PROFILE

STEVE PENN

OCCUPATION: Stock analyst in mutual funds

YEARS IN BUSINESS: 3

AGE: 32

EDUCATION: BA, economics, Colgate; MBA, finance, UCLA

HOURS PER WEEK: 50 to 60, 7:00 A.M. to 6:00 P.M.; 30 minutes for lunch

SIZE OF COMPANY: 6,400

CERTIFICATION: Series 7 license, Chartered Financial Analyst (CFA)

ANNUAL SALARY: $130,000, plus $65,000 bonus

How did you get your job?

Through on-campus recruiting at business school. I did my summer internship in I-banking and realized that that absolutely wasn't what I wanted to do due to the long hours and abrasive personalities. My second year I refocused on investment management. My employer was one of the few companies that recruited on campus, but also a leading company in the industry. I was handicapped because I had not focused on the industry in B-school. My background in business valuation and the fact I got along really well with the interviewer helped get me the job offer.

Describe a typical day.

7:00   Get to work. Review news and stocks movement online. Read *Barron's* and the *Journal*.

9:00   Attend a daily portfolio meeting with managers and the rest of the department. We exchange new ideas and announce rating changes.

9:30   Research individual companies by reviewing SEC documents and annual reports, and by talking to management, customers, and competitors. This is what I spend most of my day doing, though other things do come up.

11:00   Speak to sell-side analysts about individual companies.

11:30   Review prospectus for an IPO road show.

12:00   Attend IPO road show: have lunch and listen to the presentation.

1:00   Download historical financial data and do comparative valuation analysis.

1:30   Visit local operating office of a company in the investment portfolio. Meet with district manager. Try to get a sense of the culture and future prospects for the business.

3:30   Pitch new investment idea to portfolio manager.

4:00   Play nine holes of golf with a visiting sell-side analyst.

6:30   Go home and see the wife.

---

the first fund to offer a large discount-brokerage operation. Similarly, virtually every national and regional brokerage firm now offers its own family of funds, in addition to traditional offerings of external funds run by other firms like Fidelity, Eaton Vance, Nuveen, Putnam, and MFS.

In short, both brokerage and fund companies discovered a huge potential market out there for their offerings. Booming capital markets, an inexorable demographic bulge moving toward retirement, the inadequacy of social security benefits, and increased awareness in all age groups of the importance of meaningful retirement assets have led the surge. All this creates tremendous long-term career opportunities for today's job seekers. Competition for these openings is vigorous (some brokerages report as many as eighty applicants for every opening; funds can be even tougher), but there's a lot more money that will need to be invested in the years ahead, as personal incomes rise and retirement assets expand.

Whether you choose a brokerage firm or mutual fund, career growth and income can be excellent after your first three to five years. But those first few years of building a client base and learning the markets are hard—and with good reason. There's little patience in this industry for either mediocre or incompetent

What are your career aspirations?

Managing a small cap growth portfolio. Small cap businesses tend to be undervalued by Wall Street so there are a lot of hidden gems. I should be able to do this in the next two or three years, whenever a position opens up.

What kinds of people do well in this business?

Independent thinkers (people who follow trends will get you mediocre returns). You have to be analytical and inquisitive. You also need a good working knowledge of financial statement analysis, accounting rules, and so on.

What do you really like about your job?

Setting my own schedule—I'm given a lot of autonomy. There's no set agenda, and I decide what I want to work on each day. There are no clients per se, and there's no real "product" other than my investment opinion—you get paid for your thoughts. In contrast to people working in consulting and I-banking, I typically travel only when it's convenient for me and usually to industry conferences in attractive locations like Naples, Florida (in February). Additionally, since my firm manages over $200 billion in assets, I am able to deal directly with top management at companies and get access to sell-side research from virtually any Wall Street firm.

What do you dislike?

There is a little less people interaction than I would prefer. You're off on your own doing your independent research most of each day. You may consult with a coworker but there are not many group projects where you can interact with other people on a long-term basis.

What is the biggest misconception about your job?

Even in business school, I was surprised at how many people didn't know about this career as an option. I think it's an undiscovered job sector where you can make a good salary and still have a life.

How can someone get a job like yours?

Network extensively with people in the industry. It's a very closed community. Search alumni databases. Attend a top business school or take the CFA exam or both. Join the student investment fund to get contacts and get some hands-on experience. Bigger firms sponsor summer interns. There's a lot of operating leverage in the business, so there's no need to hire large numbers of people each year. There are therefore fewer positions in investment management than in consulting or I-banking.

performance resulting in slow or zero growth in client assets (and correspondingly in firm income from those assets). Turnover at some firms is periodically high, and fewer brokers or asset managers stay in the same place very long these days. You also have to be willing to be wrong. One investment adviser says, "When people ask me for my own forecasts, I have to remind them my accuracy rate is only 64 percent in simply predicting the past." Another is even more emphatic: "Never confuse brains with a bull market."

How It Breaks Down

Though we divide the industry up into brokerages and mutual funds, within the two segments there are significant differences among the players. You'll want to make sure you not only know which segment you're interested in but also what distinguishes the particular company with which you're interviewing from the competition.

REAL PEOPLE PROFILE

STEVEN WILLIAMS

OCCUPATION:
Investment broker for a large mutual fund company

YEARS IN BUSINESS: 4

AGE: 36

EDUCATION: BS in civil engineering, University of Southern California

HOURS PER WEEK:
50, 7:00 A.M. to 5 P.M.; working lunch

SIZE OF COMPANY: 12,000

CERTIFICATION: Series 7 and 63 licenses, state insurance license

ANNUAL SALARY:
$200,000, all from commissions

How did you get your job?

This is an amazing story. First of all, I never dreamed of doing this. My mother had the front desk job here when I was in high school. Through her, I got to know someone who was retiring. He was something of a mentor and kept dropping hints that I should go into the business. Well, after I'd spent five years as an officer in the Navy, I finally started listening to him. He retired shortly after I came on, and I took over for him. He has all the quotes and client database. I review information that Equity Research has sent me, and I look to see if the analysts have changed their opinion on any of my clients' stocks. Today there's a change from "buy" to "maintain" on GE, so I send out the word. In most cases, they just read it and put it away, but you never know who's going to need this.

Describe a typical day.

7:00 A couple of things are already printed out. I have a look at the media summary for the *Wall Street Journal, Investor's Daily,* and the local papers. Local details are just as important for a lot of my clients as world news.

8:00 Bond call comes in. Something in an account needs attention.

8:05 Lots more calls. There are a couple of tickets to write up.

Everything is automated now. We used to have to write a ticket and take it out to the wire operator. That changed about two years ago. But we're always automating things. Ultimately it's a good thing; it really does cut down on errors.

11:10 Talk to a reporter. Phone calls and office issues to resolve punctuate the interview, but we finally make it through.

1:00 Eat lunch at desk. Still interrupted by phone calls. Otherwise, I try to read a research report online since I'm currently recommending a stock and I really need to know this stuff in depth. Most of the time I just glance at these reports. I actually do most of my other work-related reading at home or early in the morning. I read *Forbes* first and foremost, then *Research* and *Registered Rep.*

1:30 I finish all my last trades before the market closes. I have an assistant who is registered (to trade) so she takes care of business for me if I'm away or really swamped. Mostly I like to deal with clients myself, though.

2:00 Today I have a client meeting scheduled. Usually I try to do these after the market closes so we won't be interrupted.

Brokerage

Brokers act as the intermediary between the buyer and seller in a securities transaction. The buyer and seller, not the brokerage firm, assume the risk. (If the firm acts as the principal or dealer, it deals from its own account and assumes the risk itself.) Brokers charge their clients a commission. A full-service firm such as Merrill Lynch or Morgan Stanley Dean Witter charges commissions up to several hundreds of dollars for transactions but offers extras such as tailored research, strategy and planning, and asset-management accounts—checking, credit (including lending on margin), and brokerage, all in one convenient package. A discount

4:00 Review all the notes I wrote to myself at this time yesterday. I am partially caught up. I write up a new list for tomorrow. Then I'm out the door.

What are your career aspirations?

I want to do exactly what I'm doing now for the rest of my career. I would like to retire early and live comfortably. Money isn't everything, but it helps. I really can't think of anything else I'd rather do—though I do want to continue to refine the process by which I do business now.

What kinds of people do well in this business?

This isn't rocket science. You have to be able to listen to clients' needs. Listen and really understand. Obviously you need some technical competency. That's actually now about a third of it. The rest is understanding sales. Understanding needs. And patience. Lots of patience.

What do you really like about your job?

Well, there's a great coffee machine in the back. I like the ability to control my own income. I also like that it's always different every day. And it doesn't really matter how the market performs. People always need advice. And I guess I like giving advice. Compensation is good. Excellent benefits.

Great 401(k). Good stock purchase. There's a lot to like actually.

What do you dislike?

I don't like some people's perception that I'm a bank teller. It was great inheriting the client list I did, but some people see me as a peddler. Others expect me to call every time I hear of a preferred stock. I'm not a used-car salesman.

What is the biggest misconception about this job?

Same as above really. Some people really do think we're gunslingers and gamblers. Another perception I don't like is that a broker is someone who handles your play money; all your real money is in CDs: "Here, take this $500 for a stock and double my money, please." Again, it's the idea this is somehow just gambling. The media have also created this idea that we're overpaid and you can do all your own investing without us. I'm not too afraid of losing my job to the Internet. Most people don't really trust it and want a second opinion. Right now it's a rising tide, but it won't always be, and though I don't live my life to say "I told you so," sooner or later people will need help. Everyone's overconfident. Everyone assumes you can't lose money. But guess what: You sure can if you don't know what you're doing!

How can someone get a job like yours?

Get to know the managers at several firms. Find the one you like. Go ahead. Put on a coat and tie and just go in and see them. It's all about who you know in this business. And who you're willing to get to know. It would certainly help to have sales experience. You need to come across as someone who speaks confidently and with a certain competence. You can't appear to crack under stress. Educational background doesn't matter. An MBA and CFP are not necessary. Sometimes people from the military do exceptionally well—my first ship captain from the Navy is in the same business in Florida and has done spectacularly well. But for others a corporate environment just doesn't work; they can't suck it in. You need an excellent work ethic. You have to know how to relate to people and you have to shoot straight.

broker generally just executes the orders and issues a confirmation. No frills. Even so, commissions range from eight dollars per order at E*Trade to upwards of thirty-five dollars per order at Schwab. Frills or no frills, to be authorized to trade on the various exchanges, you need to be a registered representative and licensed by the NASD (National Association of Securities Dealers). The New York Stock Exchange (the Big Board) and the pending merger of the American Stock Exchange and NASDAQ are the two largest, but the specialized markets for commodities, futures, and options and the foreign exchanges in London, Tokyo, Asia Pacific, Russia, and Latin America are growing in visibility and importance.

Mutual Funds

Whereas brokers act on investors' orders, mutual-fund managers raise cash from shareholders and then invest it in stocks, bonds, money-market securities, currencies, options, gold, or whatever else seems likely to make money. Mutual funds often have a specific investment focus—be it income, long-term growth, small cap, large cap, or foreign companies. And managers are restricted on what kinds of investments they can make. Compared to individual portfolios, funds hope to persuade investors they offer several advantages: professional money management; liquidity; and more diversification than most individuals can create or afford in a personal portfolio, particularly now that switching between funds is allowed.

All investors share equally in the gains and losses of a fund, and probably the most important factor in choosing one—whether to work for or invest in—is your tolerance for risk. Bull markets tend to make many funds look good, but a downward turn or a jump in interest rates can have a significant negative impact that may take longer to correct than the nimble independent investor's portfolio.

What's Great

Fat Wallets

Money attracts money. The best fund managers and brokers can make almost as much as I-bankers. The midlevel salaries are also competitive, and you'll be building quite a personal investment portfolio during office hours. One insider who has worked in both investment banking and asset management emphasized the overall value of this equation: "It offers the best compensation on a lifestyle-adjusted basis; that is, the most money for the hours worked, a reasonable travel schedule, and fairly interesting work."

Safer Throats

Your jugular is a little more protected at brokerages and mutual funds than in I-banking or consulting firms. Asset managers have a vested interest in nurturing talent they can trust to pursue long-range investment goals in an increasingly competitive environment. This is also a fairly independent business, built on personal relationships outside, rather than inside, the firms.

Job Flexibility

In the incredibly consolidating financial-services industry, funds and brokerages are now offering loans, mortgages, and other banklike services. This translates into a broader range of job categories, especially in the areas of financial sales and planning. Increasingly your skills in these areas will become interchangeable among commercial banks, investment banks, insurance firms, and other institutions that the financial services industry has yet to invent.

What's to Hate

Adieu, Downtime

The job-induced aging process doesn't quite match that of investment banking, but you still won't be able to have it all, especially during the early years of your career. As a new analyst, broker, researcher, data and meetings become your life. You'll have to choose whether you want to work out, eat right, or get a good night's sleep. You can't do them all.

Is This a Sales Call?

Prepare to be hated, hung up on, abused, and ignored. Cold calling is the most ego-battering, exhausting form of misery ever devised. But if you plan to sell and sell well, you'll probably have to suffer through this rite of initiation along with everyone else. It can last months or years, but it never lasts forever—and down the road, telemarketers who reach you at home in the middle of dinner will love you for being so nice to them.

Securities, Not Security

Remember that mutual funds and brokerage accounts aren't growing like crazy because the industry has suddenly unearthed the secret to attracting new customers. Nope, it's simply demographics. And the great flood of money from baby boomers won't last forever. It's only a matter of time before the market dips downward, perhaps sharply, and investors run for cover. Also, the consolidation in the financial industry is barely under way. All this could eventually mean deep job cuts, cramped mobility, and slower advancement for all but the very best.

KEY JOBS

Mutual Funds Portfolio Manager

This is the job everyone wants right now. The good managers are high priests. Flocks of journalists, investors, B-school profs, and wanna-be managers hang on their every pronouncement. But to do it well, you need discipline, patience, and guts, as well as uncommon analytical skills and a real feel for the markets. You pick the securities for the fund, plot the strategy, scan mounds of data to reshape and repick as necessary, and hew as closely to the fund's objective as possible. (At some firms portfolio managers do their own research and keep an eye on specific companies; at other firms, they rely on the work of the internal research staff.) You also have to promote the sucker exhaustively. And when it doesn't perform, guess who's responsible? Only the real hotshots get to be even assistant managers right out of college and B-school; to reach the pinnacle, count on many years in the ranks of investment advisory and money management. Insiders also point out that passing the SEC's Series 7 exam is necessary in order to be registered and that the Chartered Financial Analyst (CFA) designation is a huge plus for people planning on entering portfolio management. Salary range: $70,000 to $500,000, with a handful earning over $1 million.

Registered Rep or Account Executive

This is usually what brokers call themselves these days. And given the seismic shifts—technically, structurally, and psychologically—in the past two decades, a new job title is probably in order. If you work for a full-service brokerage firm, you need to be better, think smarter, and sound more knowledgeable than the discount option. A lot of handholding, a lot of the guilt and blame, and for the first three to five years, endless cold calls to disinterested strangers. (Investment advisory work is somewhat different in that you're generally working on customized reports for clients and focusing on the finer points of preinvestment quantitative analysis.) Salary range: as low as $21,000 for beginners before commissions to a more standard $140,000 once you're established. Bonuses can augment these figures significantly, particularly if you and your firm do well. The top 15 to 20 percent earn more than $250,000; an increasing number of these overachievers are in their thirties and forties.

Wholesaler

Brokers and many of their clients tend to like passive investments, and funds are ideal for this. But they may also want a little more involvement in fund information and details than Mr. and Mrs. J. Q. Public. Enter the wholesaler from mutual fund XYZ, ready to host a "client appreciation program." They market their funds to huge clients such as Merrill Lynch and Morgan Stanley Dean Witter, but also must focus on smaller brokers and independent financial advisers. This is nice work if you can get it, and most wholesalers do well. Salary range: $75,000 to $200,000 or $300,000, with liberal expense accounts for meals and seminars.

Analyst or Researcher

Here you delve into the "fundamentals," examining every single feature of a security to determine if it's really a buy. You specialize in a certain industry or an industry segment and come to know the companies that compete there inside out. Expect to give computer screens lots of quality time and to really get cozy with annual reports. If you don't like reading, accounting, crunching numbers, and more reading, you won't be happy here. But it's excellent training for more substantive and lucrative investment-advisory work or portfolio management. Top MBAs sometimes land plum industry assignments; everyone else has to cover trucking and footwear for a while before moving up to telecommunications, technology, and financial services. Salary range: $50,000 to $100,000, plus bonuses of like amounts or more.

Financial Planner

How is a one-income family going to pay for their kids' college education? How soon, if ever, can a graphic artist retire? Financial planners help people work out these and other difficult money problems. In some ways, this is a thankless job. Even wealthy people don't much enjoy tackling these issues head on, and everyone else actively dreads it. But if you sympathize with that anxiety and know a lot about tax law and different investment strategies, you can do quite well in this business. You can also do it alone with a fair amount of flexibility. Whether you decide to be independent or join a firm, many of these professionals now opt for a CFP (Certified Financial Planner) degree. Salary range: $60,000 to $120,000. The very best can earn over $250,000, typically working on a fee or commission basis.

Sales and Marketing

Why do four out of ten Americans now own stock? Why are many more thinking about yanking their money out of more-conservative investments and sticking them into a growth stock fund? Not just because the market indexes keep going up but also because sales and marketing reps for funds and brokerages are doing a bang-up job of persuading people this is where and how to make the most of their money. These jobs are similar to product management positions at consumer products companies, but the products are financial products. People in sales no longer focus on fund or investment. They need to be able to sell any one of a growing spectrum of financial products, depending on a customer's short- and long-term needs—and whatever his brother-in-law told him to do last week. Frustrating work, but if the long bull market continues, one well worth pursuing. This is also forecast as one of the strongest areas for jobs in the next five to ten years. Marketers focus on both the long-term picture and specific current product offerings. Who needs what and how much will they pay for it? Again, a rising tide floats all boats and this is a hot area to be in right now. Salary range: $40,000 to $100,000, not including bonuses, which can range into six figures.

Customer Service

Murphy's Law reigns supreme in this industry. If something can go wrong with other people's money, of course it will, regularly and often. So someone needs to be on top of what are euphemistically known as challenges and issues and make them disappear or at least diminish by the close of trading. And investors, especially the new ones, have endless questions. Even if the information they want is right there in front of them on the prospectus or in Section C of the *Wall Street Journal,* it's your job in customer service to "research" the right answers for them, quickly, capably, and cordially. Want to earn your spurs and make it to marketing or portfolio manager in the next few years? This is a great way to do so. No one knows more about the customer than you after a year of answering calls. Patience has its own rewards, particularly in this business. This is another area slated for growth in the next decade. Salary range: $40,000 to $65,000.

GETTING HIRED

Mutual fund companies and brokerage houses hire people from just out of school and from industry. Some of the larger players (Fidelity, Franklin, Merrill Lynch) have active campus-recruiting programs—they're particularly hungry for people with technical skills. Some of the smaller players lack a formal recruiting process, so you'll have to network to get your foot in the door. If you want to land a job in this industry, keep these things in mind:

- At mutual funds, teamwork is a core value. Don't give these people the idea that you need to be a star performer. Instead, convince them that you only want to help your team perform. If you're a gregarious loner and group activity is not what you do best, brokerage firms are where you should focus your job hunt.

- Selling stocks is easy in a bull market. But what happens when the market heads south? If you want to impress your interviewer, tell him or her how you'd help your team drum up sales for a complex and unpopular financial product at the bottom of a slump.

- Brokerages need to be persuaded you're a hard worker and a smart worker who doesn't give up easily. Sell yourself the way you'd sell a great stock.

Networking and Peripherals

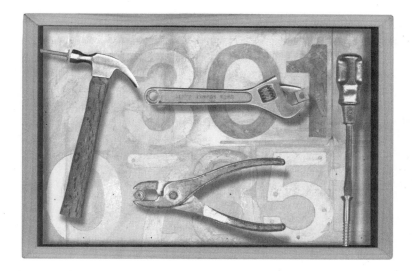

W e're all connected— currently by phone lines, but we're about to be linked via many more media as well, probably sooner than we think. Both peripherals and networks are playing a huge role in the new ways we connect, with networks in particular forecast to grow more than any other aspect of technology, according to the 1998 U.S. Industry & Trade Outlook. In other words, peripherals and networks together comprise a very good industry for job seekers. What exactly does this industry encompass? One insider describes it as "whatever you plug into the box, internally or externally: the modems, monitors, printers, scanners, Iomega Zip drives, microphones, speakers, video graphic cards, plus the networks—all the spaghetti that connects all the various boxes together."

Perhaps more than most other areas of software and hardware development, peripherals and networks serve two very different markets, and job seekers need to be aware of the distinction. One, the consumer and small-business market, buys peripherals such as printers, removable storage drives, mice and trackballs, modems, monitors, and, increasingly, low-end network devices. Major players here include Epson, Hewlett-Packard, Iomega, Canon. The second, a much more

REAL PEOPLE PROFILE

PAUL DRISCOLL

OCCUPATION: Manufacturing development engineer of packaging equipment

YEARS IN BUSINESS: 11

AGE: 34

EDUCATION: BS in electrical engineering, Purdue University

HOURS PER WEEK: 55 including travel, 8:30 A.M. to 6:00 P.M.; 1 hour for lunch

SIZE OF COMPANY: 91,000

CERTIFICATION: None

ANNUAL SALARY: $75,000, plus bonus

How did you get your job?

I got in the easy way. I did a summer internship and got an offer the following spring. I didn't have to go through the standard rigorous interview process. I had a phone interview for the internship, and then my boss recommended me for the full-time position.

Describe a typical day.

7:00 Participate in a conference call to Europe: four or six U.S. and European engineers plus an equipment supplier from Europe. Talk about what problems there are with the equipment and whether or not it's ready for testing.

9:00 Finish the call and bike in to work.

9:30 Attend an informal section meeting. Get together and eat muffins; listen to a marketer talk about a new marketing initiative, and have a discussion of how it will affect packaging.

11:00 Rush back to my desk and try to get through some of the thirty messages I've got to get through. Continue checking e-mail and voice mail whenever I have a free moment.

11:30 Lunch at the cafeteria.

12:30 Try to focus on some real work. There are design issues regarding safety in the machines we're working on right now. We're the ones responsible for making sure the equipment is safe. I need to explain a safety requirement regarding stopped machinery to a manufacturer. Check the safety manual before faxing him an explanation.

3:00 Take a break for juice.

3:30 Do some work on my safety certification. My company requires us to get lots of safety certificates.

4:30 Meet with another engineer to talk about a next-generation line of packaging.

5:30 Check for urgent e-mails, send a quick fax to the supplier about issues we talked about in the morning, and go home. Lots of times you get to end of the day and you feel like you haven't done much solid engineering work, just a lot of communication and facilitation. This is one of those days.

What are your career aspirations?

Find a more stable position with much less travel, doing something in pro-

---

sophisticated market, is the high-end professional and corporate market. Peripherals for these buyers include high-performance, networkable laser and color printers; backup and RAID storage; production-quality scanners; digital cameras; and other specialized audio and video accessories. Networks for the most part still focus on exacting IT and IS customers in the business markets. The big names here include Cisco, 3Com, and Lucent.

The differences in the markets have implications for job seekers. The consumer part of the business, like the computer hardware, is intensely competitive, with big players battling each other on price and service to sell commodity products. The sophisticated corporate market demands highly complex office systems designed to meet specific needs. This is not mass market, and you don't use the retail, mail-order, or Internet sales channels that most other hardware and software companies rely upon. CS/EE majors are the most obvious candidates for

duction or even better in R&D, where you have clear goals and time to achieve them. I'd like to do something sexier, like R&D. Manufacturing engineers don't have the rewards or respect that R&D engineers do.

What kinds of people do well in this business?

The people who do best are those who can work with the very abstract and who can bring people together to solve problems. Most problems involve our factories, product materials, product design, or suppliers, and they have no clear owners. The challenge is finding people who can keep their sanity and stay motivated in such an environment. Many people want a clear measure of success. Nowadays in our business there is a more nebulous measure of success. You also need to be able to work with people from very different cultures, since we have operations in so many different countries. You need to be a strong communicator and be able to go outside the bounds of your responsibility to solve problems. People who can do this are very hard to find.

What do you really like about your job?

I like having a very high level of responsibility at my age and experience level. From day one I have been responsible for millions of dollars worth of equipment. We had a lot of product introductions that depended on my team to stay on schedule. Also the personal relationships with the suppliers and company staff overseas; I feel at home when I go to the foreign locations.

What do you dislike?

The lack of clear measures for my success. I don't have any specific authority; I have to get people to buy into what needs to be done by persuading them that it's for the good of the company. Also, upper management doesn't understand the ill effects of outsourcing manufacturing on quality. They don't understand the problems we face in keeping projects on target.

What is the biggest misconception about your job?

People tend to think that travel is glamorous and fun. If you traveled once or twice a year and had a low-stress project then that might be true. But if you're traveling a lot, that means you're on an important, high-stress project. You often only know the road from the airport to the factory and that's about it. I feel like my life has been on hold recently because of all the travel.

Looking back on your career or job search, what do you wish you would have done differently?

The overwhelming thing is to have taken more advantage of professional development programs. There are lots of technical and management classes. There're probably a dozen courses that I wanted to take over the past six years, and I only took one.

How can someone get a job like yours?

The key part is the personal connection. So many résumés come in that it's hard to pick the good candidates. I've passed a lot of résumés of friends on to managers I know are hiring, and about 75 percent of them got hired. There are ways to submit résumés online, but honestly I doubt that managers look at them. They are so busy that they don't always take advantage of the flood of résumés. You need to follow through with a phone call or e-mail if you contact a person—an alum, say—in the company. If you don't follow up with people who are forwarding your résumé, then you won't seem like you really want in.

development and design jobs in both peripherals and networks; at the same time, there is also a growing demand for product marketers and sales teams, testers, senior managers, and systems consultants. Watch for an increasing number of success stories starring good listeners with an English degree, an analytical, problem-solving turn of mind, and an ability to fit people and networks together.

You also don't necessarily have to move to the San Francisco Bay Area to find the best jobs in this industry. Yes, many of the biggest firms—Hewlett-Packard, Cisco Systems, 3Com, Quantum—are headquartered in or near Silicon Valley, but IBM and Lucent are in New York and New Jersey, Novell is in Utah, and clusters of small companies are emerging in Denver, Austin, and North Carolina. Consultants who thoroughly research new products and know how to build and maintain customized networks for small and large companies can find work anywhere in the world—and if they're good, they can charge a lot of money for their services.

The 1996 Telecommunications Act opened the field to a host of new domestic competitors—publishers, TV networks, telecoms—and suddenly the convergence of all these media with computers is the industry's favorite new buzz. The next phase—where a lot of the money and jobs will be—is a much more public one, featuring the emergence of client/server computing, groupware applications, and the gradual blurring of the lines between networks and individual desktop PCs and accessories. "Think of it as a telephone," says one systems developer. "You can have pretty much any size or shape or color you want, and it can have lots of extra features or none. But the real point of the phone—or the next-generation computer—is the external connection, not its individual characteristics."

How It Breaks Down

This is a difficult industry to segment for several reasons. The first is that most companies sell across a wide spectrum of markets—consumers, graphic-arts professionals, huge corporations—with few overlaps in either their needs or problems. And products for networked environments confront very different, usually far more complex technical and marketing issues. Most of the larger manufacturers and developers also boast fairly broad product lines—everything from digital cameras to printers to networking solutions. The growing trend among many firms, big and small, is to partner with inexpensive, less-experienced manufacturing shops overseas. What used to be fairly important distinctions between competitors and their respective R&D and implementation efforts are now much less discernible, because they often share subcontractors.

Imaging Peripherals

These are the printers, scanners, digital cameras, and monitors which let people create, modify, and view text and graphic images. As networks grow in bandwidth and performance, imaging peripherals will become increasingly centralized and offer more shared services such as image posting, photofinishing, and high-quality printing. There are significant differences in pricing and markets, but the market leaders for these products, such as Epson, Kodak, Agfa, and Canon, will continue as strong employers for the foreseeable future. "Hewlett-Packard is going to be making printers in 2010," one industry analyst maintains. "Maybe the printer will be in the box, maybe it'll be in some remote location, maybe it'll be both: Almost certainly the technology will change. But they'll still be making printers."

Storage Peripherals

This is also a need that isn't going away; in fact, it's growing, as users increasingly create and share documents that contain graphics, video, and sound components requiring large amounts of disk space. Today, companies generally produce and share a far greater volume of documents than they used to, and they need even more powerful backup drives for protection and storage. Iomega's 100-meg Zip drive, which a few years ago seemed immense, is now common for many home users. CD-ROMs are also increasingly used for archival purposes. Again, where you look for work in this area depends on whether you opt for the consumer or the high-end and corporate market. SyQuest, Quantum, and Seagate are all useful starting points if this sector interests you.

Internal Peripherals

These are the options you can't see under the hood: hard drives, sound cards, LAN cards, video and graphic cards, among others. Previously seen and marketed as add-ons for the hobbyist, these are now increasingly bundled to accompany new PCs sold by companies such as Gateway and Dell. The market for internal peripherals is very good for producers who have strategic relationships with PC sellers; the predominant trend for most consumers now is to buy a new computer rather than two new peripherals.

Input and Other Peripherals

Everything else not covered above belongs here—from mice and graphics pens to digital cameras, speakers, microphones, and other tools and toys. Except for the most basic input devices, most customers tend to see these peripherals as extras. For some, they're worthwhile investments and necessary job tools; for others, they're bells and whistles. Logitech, Kensington, and Connectix all produce devices for this segment.

Networks

Networking and connectivity hardware are among the most dynamic areas for job seekers right now, certainly more so than most peripherals. And the ultimate integration of print, broadcast, and other media into these data streams makes the converging networks that much more important. Amazingly, only a few years ago AT&T and IBM were the undisputed kingpins here; no one could imagine a Lucent, 3Com, or Cisco controlling even a portion of the Network. Whatever happens next, experienced network engineers, testers, marketers, and managers have a promising future to look forward to.

What's Great

Systems Routers

Despite accolades in the press for Yahoo, Amazon.com, and a handful of other brand-name Internet content and commerce players, the real success stories in this space come from the players who've been providing the tools for the mammoth increase in traffic: that's right, the networking people. What Cisco did for routers, NetObjects is doing for Web authoring tools and RealNetworks for live audio and video on the Net. Lotus, Netscape, and Novell have also helped create the backbone for this industry, but the next big name could be the start-up staffing up right now. There is no shortage of either success stories or opportunities for job seekers in this industry.

A Better Mouse

You can earn good money helping develop a smaller, better, cheaper fill-in-the-blank peripheral that everyone will still want to buy next year. Although a number of giants populate this industry, there is still room for specialists with leading technologies to play the game. The endgame for these players may involve selling their products as an OEM (original equipment manufacturer) under the brand of one of the big players or getting acquired by a bigger player.

Your Big Ideas

If you enjoy collaborative decision making and have always wished you worked with people willing to listen to your ideas—even your zany ones—the smaller, more innovative companies in this industry want to hire you. "One of the better aspects of this business is that new ideas get heard," says one industry observer. "You're expected to get very involved, and relatively new people can be making significant decisions early on." As often as not, your great ideas get changed and changed again, and they may or may not be realized, but this industry is a meritocracy with a fairly flat reporting structure. If it's a really good idea, anything's possible.

What's to Hate

Road Kill on the Infobahn

People who've gone several rounds in this industry will tell you that the sky isn't always blue. "It's actually quite weird," says one veteran of several failed cable-delivery systems. "Very George Orwell, you know? All that money, all that work . . . didn't . . . ever . . . happen. But here's what's even worse," he adds. "No one ever seems to learn that this isn't possible." Would he sign up for another round? "Oh, sure, probably. If the money were good."

What's So Casual About These Guys?

Don't be fooled by the jeans and sweats. Almost none of the main players ever has been, or ever will be, a hotbed of enlightened creativity. IBM, Hewlett-Packard, Lucent, and virtually every other industry leader are out in front because they're highly disciplined, controlled, and controlling. "I always felt like that song, 'You're in the Army Now,'" says one former IBM employee. One good reason for this, of course, is that patent, copyright, and other trade-secret legal protections are at best inadequate in this business, and seldom enforceable. Loose lips lose market-share wars.

"Can You Explain That Again, Honey?"

Even though this industry offers some outstanding opportunities, you may have to get accustomed to the fact that your mom and dad may never understand exactly what you do. Oh sure, they may get as far as laser-jet printer, but just try explaining to them the function of a router or a packet-switching device. Even if you're at a very successful company that does, say, five times as much revenue as Amazon.com, you'll be known only in very select technical and investment circles. Then again, a couple of years back, nobody had ever heard of Intel.

KEY JOBS

The job outlook in peripherals and networking—as for the high-tech industry in general—is excellent. It's particularly strong for people with technical skills and degrees in computer science or electrical engineering. The opportunities vary quite a bit from company to company, but here are some typical jobs you might consider:

Product Marketing Associate

Marketing associates gather market and competitive data for the product marketing manager's overall marketing strategy. In this capacity, you're not as involved with product development (though you have to keep close tabs on what's going on) as you are with how your company positions the product for consumers or businesses. There's a lot of assisting others in this job, but it's a great way to learn a lot about the competitive landscape of the industry. Estimated salary range: $25,000 to $45,000.

Technical Support or Customer Service

Technical support staff are those patient souls who take questions from businesses or consumers who recently purchased your company's product. You know, the one that got shipped in a frenzied hurry with all the glitches that didn't get fixed. Intense competition in this industry means two things: Everything goes out the door too soon, and companies strive to have top-flight customer service to make up for it and set themselves apart from the pack. These positions are becoming increasingly important, and though a technical background isn't mandatory, it certainly helps make a tough job a little easier. Why does anyone want this job to begin with? Because it leads to some great slots in marketing. No one will know the customers as well as you after six months of this type of work. Salary range: $25,000 to $50,000.

Junior Engineer

In this entry-level position, you're the foot soldier in the long march to the pot of gold, the end of the rainbow: the perfect router or sound card. You're not so much coming up with ideas as implementing solutions developed by your superiors. Which will be changed and changed again. Still, this is an important foot in the door to more specialized, higher-paying engineering positions. This job category can also include software engineering—or programming—which involves writing the code built into the various systems and chips. Salary range: $40,000 to $60,000.

Systems Tester

If you have an electronic engineering (EE) degree and eventually want to design hardware, or if you have strong analytical skills in general, these jobs are always available. Testers ensure that the driver/modem/LAN/voice recognition/video display does what it's meant to. You work endless repetitions, looking for the one inconsistency, the one tiny flaw. There's lots of pressure coupled with a need for absolute accuracy—it's not an easy job. Plus, the amount of work in most test labs has more than doubled in the past five years, and staffing and time allocations have, of course, remained flat, according to one testing director. Why bother? Because most companies agree there is no better training. "Everyone knows it's hard and most people respect you for it," says one former tester, now a network consultant. Salary range: $30,000 to $35,000.

Product Manager

As a product manager, you're a key player in coming up with product ideas and working with engineers to make them a reality. This position requires some grasp

REAL PEOPLE PROFILE

WIN JACKSON

OCCUPATION:
Senior advisory programmer

YEARS IN BUSINESS: 20

AGE: 48

EDUCATION: BS in electrical engineering and computer science; MS in computer science, Syracuse University

HOURS PER WEEK:
50 to 75, 7:00 A.M. to
6:00 P.M.; 1 hour for lunch

SIZE OF COMPANY: 8,000

CERTIFICATION: None

ANNUAL SALARY:
$90,000, including bonus

How did you get your job?

When I got my EE degree, Bell Labs hired me. I started off designing power supplies for computers. I gradually became involved in networks and began moving around as a programmer in a variety of jobs all around the country. Now I design the architecture for communications subsystems. But I also design and write and test the actual code. This is unusual—most people at my level don't like to get their hands dirty—but in this company, you have a choice: You can be architectural and direct people, or you can have a much more hands-on systems role and not be penalized. I settled where I am now because I needed to be in one place and start putting some serious money away. But if you're good at writing software, you can actually live pretty much anywhere.

Describe a typical day.

7:00   Arrive at work and plunge into completing the design specs for a project we have under development. The group manager needs to see these at 10 A.M., and though I don't have to be the one to do the final review, I always like to anyway.

8:00   Answer e-mail and voice mail. Set up several teleconferences for next week with one of our facilities on the East Coast. If we already have a good working relationship with the implementers involved, we check in via a conference call, but this is a new team and "face to face" works better.

10:00   Meet with group manager and another architect. Talk about what stuff isn't working, how we're going to solve it, and what the priorities are. The biggest part of my work always comes down to solving problems. Interacting with other groups is a big part of this. We're a large organization. Nothing is simple, and if you don't force certain things through and yield on others, realistically you can't accomplish much.

11:30   Today's most immediate problem to solve is insufficient disk space. Sounds silly, doesn't it? Typically problems range from software bugs to architecture issues—how the design was supposed to work but isn't working. Ultimately everything has to function properly, and ultimately very few people are willing to take responsibility for making sure that happens.

12:00   Go to a gym and work out. We don't have one in our building, but even if we did, I think I'd prefer to be off-site for a while each day. This keeps me from going crazy and allows me to get a fresh perspective on things.

of technical matters, the ability to build consensus and teamwork (translation: if you're not good at office politics, don't raise your hand for this one), and a knack for spotting and anticipating market trends. Salary range: $45,000 to $75,000.

Financial Analyst

Financial analysis in computer hardware companies can take many forms: numerical analysis for production planning, industrial operations management, and general finance and accounting. In some cases, analysts evaluate other companies as

2:30	Work with several programmers on code for the operating system. This is different from the applications work most people do. Not many people get to go "inside."
4:00	Review completed design specs and begin planning the actual writing of the software so that we can begin to realize this project. More problems. More interruptions. More delays.
5:30	Tonight I can go home at a reasonable hour. Later in the development cycle I'll be here a lot later.

What are your career aspirations?

I want to be painting on the Mediterranean in Italy. My plan is to first study with master artists in Florence and then migrate to the coast over time. If this doesn't work out—and it may take a while longer than five years—I'd like to be doing what I'm doing now in a different location. It would be great to be near a much larger metropolitan area with many more things to do. I also think I'd like a wider spectrum of work.

What kinds of people do well in this business?

To do this for the long term and to be successful, you need a lot of drive, and that drive has to be closely in line with the company's values and goals.

You really have to be willing to do whatever is necessary to get the work done. Your goals have to coincide with the company's because if they don't, it's just too much—you won't be able to do it for more than a few years without it overwhelming you. You also have to be ruthless, I'm afraid. If you're not able to push people—and push them hard—to get the job done, it won't get done.

What do you really like about your job?

The money. It's actually no longer the security or being able to work on systems or having a lot of smart people around. A nice salary supports my "real" life.

What do you dislike?

Politics. The childish politics of trying to get the job done. There are a lot of very smart people with very big egos in this business. And when big elephants sit down in the road, it's very hard to get them to move.

What is the biggest misconception about this job?

It's actually not as cutting-edge or as tech oriented as you would think. There's lots of legacy in most computer systems. This means a lot of boring work, but it has to get done, and it's part of the job. You're not always dealing with new, innovative stuff, you know.

How can someone get a job like yours?

Assuming you can handle the corporate politics, you need to go to a reputable engineering school and get at least a master's in computer science. I'm also a big advocate of an electrical engineering degree. It involves a lot of nonsense, but in these jobs, you have to be able to solve problems. If you only know how to program, it's not the same. Write your résumé to highlight the problem solving. If you come in at the entry level, you'll generally be writing code someone else has designed, and you'll be fixing other people's problems. These are maintenance jobs. Don't complain. Just do it. Do it well. Do different jobs eagerly for scope. Keep plugging away. Unless you're a genius, the more experience you've got, the better off you are. Ultimately the key to success in these places is whether people come to you or you have to go to people. Your knowledge base is what matters. You also can't get personally and emotionally invested. You have to be a grown-up to do these jobs well. Finally, pay attention to what's happening in the outside world. What the competition is doing really matters. If you're not completely on top of the changes in technology, you'll lose your job.

potential merger or acquisition targets. These are expanding divisions in most of the larger companies right now and a good way to learn about the industry overall before you settle on a particular focus. Salary range: $50,000 to $70,000.

Sales Associate

The demands of this job vary widely depending on whether you're selling LANs, printers, or enhanced modems. Whatever it is, you need to know it cold. This job requires you to get up a steep learning curve about your product's technical specifications, but training is often provided. Salary range: $30,000 to $40,000 base; up to $45,000 to $60,000 with commission.

Systems Engineer (SE)

Engineers who combine technical expertise, strong people skills, and years of internal and external development experience do well in this job. SEs must know the technology inside out to be able to assist the sales staff in managing the relationship with the potential buyer. Sometimes an SE is paired with an individual salesperson, sometimes with a team of salespeople. Estimated salary range: $60,000 to $120,000.

Engineer

The middle ground between junior engineers and system architects, this position encompasses about 95 percent of the engineering workforce. These are the journeymen jobs—if you've done this before and you have a specific expertise already, you can get a job tomorrow morning and often name your price at close to six figures. In uncertain times, this is as close as it gets to guaranteed employment. Salary range: $55,000 to $100,000.

System Architect

This high-level engineering position—which usually reports to senior management or the chief technology officer—conceives new products and outlines their development plans. System architects possess extensive engineering experience and, in most cases, an advanced degree. As often as not, this is also a job which requires managerial and sales talent. You're always managing upward to sell your idea and your plan at the highest levels of the company. Salary range: $90,000 to $130,000.

Network or Technical Consultant

There are lots of desperate and confused folks out there in need of a network fix. This is where senior testers, engineers, and other burnouts go when they've had enough of corporate constraints and want more control over their lives and the work they produce. You'll need substantive experience, industry contacts, and a lot of patience to do this job well, but there's no shortage of small and large businesses right now who need a new LAN, an intranet, a start-from-scratch overhaul of their office systems. Salary range: $70,000 to $90,000 or more.

GETTING HIRED

- There's no such thing as being too analytical in this line of work. "You have to be smart and methodical in your thinking," says one insider. "You also have to be dedicated to solving problems, rather than just playing with toys." Show your interviewers that you know how to analyze. People skills matter, but careful attention to detail matters even more.

- A head for business is also increasingly seen as a desirable asset in this sector. In the past, engineers have often found it difficult to work with MBAs, particularly those in marketing. But this is changing as the industry leaders come to understand that a good product alone guarantees very little, and success over the long term requires significant support for strategic planning and implementation.

- You must play nicely with others. In general, this industry's companies possess a corporate culture in which "you can only say once or twice, 'I respect your opinion, but . . .,'" according to one engineer. "Dissenters—unless they're very, very careful—end up with a reputation." This is different from the world of software development and undoubtedly somewhat different from company to company. But just a word to the wise: Think collegial thoughts and test the collective opinion before you express your own views too emphatically.

- Be aware of the overall market trends, not just the precise technical specifications and the blue-sky power projections for various pieces of hardware. What are customers buying these days? How has this changed in the past two years? What systems will work best for them, their coworkers, and their families, not the early adapters and hobbyists? This is important for any job you're applying for, but a critical vantage point to remember if the position you want involves sales or working closely with clients.

Nonprofit and Government

Not in it for the money? Mad as hell and don't want to take it anymore? A nonprofit or government job might be just the place for you. And it's anything but impossible to find one; combined, the nonprofit and government sectors account for 20 percent of all economic activity in the United States.

Government jobs exist on the federal, state, and local levels; most opportunities are civil service positions at the many government agencies. This sector has shrunk in recent years, thanks to tighter federal budgets. But there are still plenty of government and other political positions available to job seekers, with a wide variety of job descriptions. For example, the various agencies and departments of the federal, state, and local governments handle issues as diverse as highway construction, the protection of wilderness areas, and public health programs—and hire people of diverse backgrounds as a result. And congressional and other elected officials hire staff to do everything from drafting legislation to studying policy to managing office operations.

In all, twenty million people have government jobs. Of those, people with federal jobs are often located in Washington, D.C., while those in state and local government jobs generally work in their state capital, county, city, or town.

REAL PEOPLE PROFILE

DENISE MORTON

OCCUPATION: Program director for a criminal justice nonprofit

YEARS IN BUSINESS: 8

AGE: 30

EDUCATION: BA in social sciences, MA in communications, San Francisco State University

HOURS PER WEEK: 45, 8:45 A.M. to 6:00 P.M.; working lunch

SIZE OF COMPANY: 24

CERTIFICATION: None

ANNUAL SALARY: 55,000

How did you get your job?

I'm the director of an alternative sentencing program in the criminal-justice system. I knew somebody who worked here through my old job. I had been looking for full-time work in either media policy or education, but wasn't having much luck. My friend told me about this nonprofit, which diverts people from trials and sentencing by placing them in various rehabilitation and community-service programs, and I thought it sounded interesting. Eight years later and I'm still here.

Describe a typical day.

8:45   Get to work, check e-mail.

9:00   Go to court and meet with judges. All of my clients have criminal court cases. Explain how clients are doing if they are in the system and why my organization is either rejecting or accepting candidates into the program.

11:30   Managers' meeting: personnel and staffing issues. Decide if someone should get transferred or get some special training.

Also, take a look at special violent cases. Assess them for public safety risks. We make recommendations to the court.

12:00   Do an interview to assess client for mental health, reason for the criminal incident, background, drug abuse, and potential for violence. We have doctors, teachers, lawyers, students—lots of students—and homeless. All kinds, really.

12:45   Eat a brown bag lunch at my desk.

1:00   Go to a local church that has a program for community service in its kitchen. Also talk to the manager of the anger-management classes it holds. I'm trying to see if we can include these programs in our service or not.

2:00   Go back to the office and review court reports to make sure clients are eligible. I'm responsible for final sign-off. Also spend a lot of time reviewing staff cases because the number one person isn't around much. Plan meetings.

Even though most of those in this sector enjoy excellent benefits, there can be downsides to working in government. For one thing, the pay is often lower in government positions than in their private-sector equivalents—especially if you're a staff member of an elected official or a higher-level civil servant. And in some positions, the priorities of your job can change as the election cycle progresses; in other words, the program you're working on or the representative you work for may not even be around next year—or next week.

Nonprofits are organizations that have been granted 501(c)3, or tax-exempt, status by the government. These organizations focus on a wide variety of causes, and include everything from the Africa Fund, which promotes human rights, education, and people-to-people exchanges with African countries, to the National Breast Cancer Foundation. Many nonprofit interest groups, such as the Clean Water Fund and the Center on Budget and Policy Priorities, are located in Washington, D.C., where they lobby government on behalf of their cause; others have offices near state legislatures, where, again, they lobby for the passage of legislation favorable to their cause. Operating revenues for nonprofits come

3:30 See clients and return phone calls. More planning of meetings. Do paperwork. Get ready for a panel on prostitution within the domestic violence community that I have tomorrow. Also do some reading to get ready for a meeting on jail overcrowding.

5:30 Make sure that the computer backups are set up. This is a technical thing that everyone in the office is afraid of, and it's not actually in my job description, but I like doing it. I'm not afraid to do what needs to be done in this job.

What are your career aspirations?

I'd like to go more into public administration or politics, perhaps the mayor's office of criminal justice. When I'm much older, I'd like to go into direct services. I run a support group for women in jail, so counseling is definitely something that's a big part of my life.

What kinds of people do well in this business?

Problem solvers, those with good follow-through. People who are compassionate and patient and who feel the obligation to help others. You have to be functional yourself—though many former drug abusers make great counselors, you absolutely have to be clean to do this job. To get to my level you really have to be motivated, even when you don't see a lot of support, even when you don't see a lot of forward motion. You have to be accountable for your actions. In general, either direct or indirect experience with the criminal justice system can also prepare you for the work.

What do you really like about your job?

Working with judges to solve problem cases. Working with clients to make a small difference in their lives. Working with staff to support their ideas. I like the responsibility. I feel that the work we do is important and that we have an impact in the criminal justice system.

What do you dislike?

Dealing with staff and personnel. Telling resistant personnel what to do. I'm younger than most of the people on staff, so that's hard.

What is the biggest misconception about your job?

You're not just helping people. You're also dealing with institutions and a lot of bureaucracy. There's also a lot of institutionalized suspicion and fear in our clients. It can be hard to overcome that so you can help them.

How can someone get a job like yours?

Start with volunteering at a drug treatment program or other organization that works in the criminal justice system. Being bilingual really helps. You don't need a degree in criminal justice, but a social work degree could help. Be enthusiastic about the organization you want to work for. If you don't really believe in the mission, it can be hard to stick with it.

from foundations, the government, membership dues, and fees they charge for services they provide. Nonprofits typically attract people passionate about solving social problems; the big upside of working in this sector is that you can make a positive impact on behalf of your organization's cause. The downside is that most jobs in the nonprofit sector, like many in the government sector, don't pay very well.

One of the reasons nonprofits don't pay so well is that funding sources are increasingly scarce. It's a catch-22 situation: As government cuts budgets, there's a greater need for the services provided by nonprofits—but at the same time, there's less government funding available for them. As a result, many nonprofits have sought new ways to get cash. In particular, they've begun looking at the private sector to learn how to operate more efficiently; some have even spun off businesses to help raise money and create jobs. For instance, Pioneer Human Services in Seattle, which provides a variety of services to the socially disadvantaged, has developed a number of business enterprises, including a real estate division and a metal factory.

How It Breaks Down

This is a vast industry, and there are many ways to break it down. Job seekers will be motivated by their interests. The breakdown that follows attempts to establish a framework of the different outlets for those interests.

Nonprofits

There are a number of ways to break down the nonprofit sector. For instance, nonprofits can be divided into those that focus on lobbying government on behalf of a cause (interest groups, such as the National Rifle Association) and those that focus on providing services to society (such as museums or homes for pregnant teens). But the best way to break down this sector is probably by cause. To get a sense of the variety of nonprofits, here's a short list of causes and the organizations that serve them: arts and education (Friends of the Library, the Washington Ballet, the New York Philharmonic, the Boy Scouts, the Girl Scouts, 4H, the National Center on Family Literacy), civil and human rights (Amnesty International, the American Civil Liberties Union, the National Immigration Forum, the NAACP, Planned Parenthood), the environment (the Environmental Defense Fund, the National Wildlife Federation, the Nature Conservacy, the Sierra Club), and economic and social justice (the American Association of Retired Persons, the Center for the Child Care Workforce, the National Low Income Housing Coalition, the Salvation Army, the United Way). Alongside the large national and international nonprofits are a myriad of locally based, smaller nonprofits; like their bigger cousins, these break down by mission and include everything from community theater troupes to women's shelters to convalescent homes.

Capitol Hill and Federal Government

Most federal government jobs are in one of the executive branch agencies, which include everything from the Social Security Administration, the Environmental Protection Agency, and the FBI to the National Endowment for the Humanities, the Bureau of Indian Affairs, and the Bureau of Engraving and Printing. (There are also jobs available in agencies under the aegis of the judicial and legislative branches, such as in the Library of Congress or the Congressional Budget Office.) There are two basic types of positions in the various government agencies: civil service positions, which require applicants to fill out a form called the SF-171 to get a job, and political appointments, also called Schedule C appointments.

Though many government agency jobs are located in Washington, many are not. (Just think of all those postal employees out on the streets of America, braving rain, sleet, and snow. Or the diplomat at the U.S. embassy in France. Or the park ranger in Yellowstone National Park.) Congressional jobs, however, are located almost exclusively on Capitol Hill. Congress is divided into the House, which consists of 435 members (and several nonvoting delegates), and the Senate, which is made up of 100 senators. Members of Congress each have an office and are assigned to one or more congressional committees, which are organized around issue areas; these include, for instance, the Committee on Appropriations, the Committee on Labor and Human Resources, and the Committee on Small Business. Each member of Congress hires staff to assist with his or her job; this is where many opportunities for young people exist in Washington.

State and Local Government

Like the federal government, the state governments consist of various executive-branch or state agencies along with a legislative body, all of which offer opportunities to job seekers. Similarly, local governments, including those of townships, counties, and cities, offer a range of political and agency job opportunities.

Nongovernment Political Jobs

In addition to the job opportunities that exist within government, there are plenty of political opportunities that are not technically within government. For example, many people work at lobbying firms (which lobby government on behalf of clients and include Patton, Boggs & Blow; Akin, Gump, Strauss, Hauer & Feld; and Verner, Liipfert, Bernhard, McPherson & Hand), nonprofit interest groups (such as the American Medical Association or the Teamsters Union), and think tanks (such as the Brookings Institute, the Heritage Foundation, and the Cato Institute) in Washington, D.C. and, to a lesser degree, in the various state capitals. And both the Democratic and the Republican parties have national committees and state and local offices where job seekers interested in working for a political party may find opportunities.

What's Great

Like-Minded People

In both the nonprofit and the government sectors, you'll have a chance to work with people who, like yourself, want to make a difference in government policy or in society. Says one nonprofit insider, "There is a spirit and camaraderie among the people who work here that I never had in my private-sector job." And in Washington, people at the beginning of their careers will find plenty of other recent college grads to play softball or go bar-hopping with.

Change the World

Jobs in government and at nonprofits give you a role in changing public policy and helping people. You might help craft legislation that affects millions of Americans; you might help feed hundreds who otherwise would have gone hungry. And at the end of the day, you can go home and say you've done something for people. Says an insider, "People who choose to work here are driven by the work, not by the money. They're willing to go that extra mile."

Continuing Education

Whether you work as a legislative staffer or in a nonprofit, you'll learn about key issues and develop expertise about them that few others have. And at some nonprofits, the loose structure can give those eager for experience a chance to take on responsibilities they wouldn't have been given the chance to take on elsewhere. That experience can look great on a résumé and serve you well as you move on in your career.

The Big Show

Politics is probably the closest thing to Hollywood around. The major players are written and talked about daily and are followed around the world by the media; it can be exciting to play a part in the show. One former Hill staffer says, "I never got over that butterflies-in-your-stomach feeling when a senator stepped onto the elevator." And working in politics, whether for the government or at a nonprofit political interest group (everything from the American Association of Retired Persons and the AFL-CIO to the NRA or the Tobacco Institute), is probably the best way around to feel like you're a part of history in the making.

What's to Hate

Man Cannot Live on Peanuts Alone

In much of the nonprofit and government sector, the pay is typically far lower than pay for comparable jobs in the private sector. Don't apply for jobs on the Hill or with a nonprofit if you're looking to get rich. Note that at federal and state agencies, the pay is generally better than elsewhere in this sector—and the benefits are typically excellent.

Organizationally Challenged

Nonprofits often suffer from a lack of structure and breakdowns in the lines of accountability. As a result, the work environment can be difficult. "This place is about chaos management," says an insider. "We're reactive instead of proactive, and I think that's typical."

The Wheel of Fortune

Legislative and government agency jobs are subject to the vicissitudes of the political cycle. In other words, a change in the political climate can put you out of work. And no matter what the political climate is like, if the legislator who's your boss isn't doing a good job, look for voters to boot him or her out of office . . . and you out of a job.

B Is for Bureaucracy

Perhaps the biggest frustration of working in the government and nonprofit sector is the bureaucracy. In legislative jobs, this will come in the form of bureaucrats unwilling to implement the legislation you worked so hard on. In government-agency jobs, you'll be a bureaucrat yourself—and job security and the low standards of those around you may tempt you to work at something less than your peak efficiency. (Just think back to your last visit to your Department of Motor Vehicles for an example.) And at nonprofits, the focus on the cause can cause employees to lose their sense of accountability and start acting like bureaucrats themselves. "People seem a bit sluggish," says one nonprofit insider.

KEY JOBS

Intern

Nonprofits, government agencies, and legislators all typically hire interns. The pay is low and the responsibilities are generally pretty administrative (Do you know your alphabet? Good, because you will be doing filing), but an internship can give you experience, as well as access to bigwigs, that can help with your future. Salary range: nonpaying to $2,000 per month.

Program Assistant

Program assistants assist program directors and work on analyzing issues and implementing programs for nonprofit organizations. These jobs include a lot of routine office work, but can also include substantive tasks, and they are a great way to learn about issues and get to know decision makers. Salary range: $22,000 to $50,000.

Program Analyst

People in these positions work at government agencies, where they analyze proposed or existing programs for presentation to the legislature. The job requires a knowledge of budgetary process as well as a financial background. Salary range: $48,000 to $75,000.

Program Director

Nonprofits hire program directors to oversee and manage specific programs. The job can include personnel management, public relations, fundraising, and other administrative and managerial duties. Generally, people in this position have an MBA or significant experience. Salary range: $50,000 to $75,000.

Project Manager

Government project managers work in regulatory agencies, where they manage the process of regulatory review through all its stages. (Think of IRS agents auditing a business or SEC officials investigating charges against a brokerage house.) The job typically requires experience in the regulated industry, an MBA, or equivalent skills. Salary range: $48,000 to $75,000.

Grant Writer

Nonprofits hire grant writers to write proposals to prospective funders, which can include the government or private foundations. The job requires the ability to synthesize information and write persuasively and well; don't look for work here if you've got problems with grammar. Salary range: $25,000 to $60,000.

REAL PEOPLE PROFILE

CARLA SUDBETTER

OCCUPATION:
Program analyst for a federal regulation agency

YEARS IN BUSINESS: 6

AGE: 28

EDUCATION: BA in financial management, University of Texas

HOURS PER WEEK:
40, 9:30 A.M. to 6:30 P.M.;
1 hour for lunch

SIZE OF COMPANY: 1,600

CERTIFICATION: None

ANNUAL SALARY: $65,000

How did you get your job?

I'd worked on the Hill for six years, and there was a law allowing people who had worked in Congress for five or more years and who had been laid off to compete on a level playing field with federal employees for agency jobs. A friend at the agency I was interested in heard about a job, and I applied for it. It wasn't a job I wanted, but it was a foot in the door, and I just kept my eyes open for opportunities to do what I really wanted to do (that is, strategic planning). Then I just started doing it and eventually got transferred to a different group that was doing strategic planning.

Describe a typical day.

9:30 Arrive, turn on my computer, check my e-mail. I read all the announcements sent by e-mail to FDA staff and to HHS (Health and Human Services) staff. I read any GAO (General Accounting Office) reports that have come in regarding the FDA, and any National Performance Review (the President's initiative to improve government) information. I've got to stay up-to-the-minute so I know what the center has to perform and on what budget.

10:30 Staff meeting with our associate director and four program analysts. This is just a routine weekly check-in.

11:30 Today, I'm unusually hungry, so I step out to get some fast food and run an errand.

12:30 Back in my office, I check my e-mail.

1:00 Work on proposal for a strategic management process for the center director.

2:00 Get in my car and drive to the other side of Rockville for a meeting.

Public Relations Manager or Press Secretary

Both nonprofits and legislative offices hire public relations managers (also called press secretaries) to work with the media to try to shape public perception of an elected representative or nonprofit group. The position requires excellent communications skills and knowledge of how the media works. Salary range: $35,000 to $120,000.

Family Advocate

These are social-work positions. Family advocates work directly with "clients" to deliver a nonprofit's service to them. If you have a strong desire to do good and can handle a low salary and the frequent frustrations associated with dealing with troubled clients in dysfunctional situations, this might be the job for you. Salary range: $25,000 to $32,000.

Legislative Correspondent

Legislative correspondents (LCs) work in congressional offices, where their responsibilities consist almost solely of answering the many pieces of correspon-

2:30 Go to an information meeting that describes the product quality assurance process of the FDA. I've got to understand this stuff so I can incorporate it into our planning and our budget needs.

4:00 Drive back to work.

4:30 Continue work on the strategic management proposal. The center director interrupts me by asking for help answering questions for someone at the agency who'll be testifying on the Hill in the morning. I run around looking for answers till quitting time.

6:30 Go home.

What are your career aspirations?

I'd like to stay where I'm at, as long as we continue to make progress toward implementing a strategic planning cycle.

What kinds of people do well in this business?

Energetic people can do well here if they are satisfied with incremental progress. There are still a lot of dinosaurs who need to die out, so resistance to change should be expected as a normal part of the process.

What do you really like about your job?

I like how my broad experience lets me see the big picture and understand the political realities. I also like that my boss lets me stay focused on the big picture, which is a luxury.

What do you dislike?

A lot of the things we must respond to squander our energy. Many planning exercises are disconnected and redundant. I've been vocal in meetings about this and the process has improved somewhat.

What is the biggest misconception about your job?

The scientists and doctors around here think planning is a waste of time. But the reality is our planning satisfies the outside constituencies that fund the work of these guys. Also, our planning is helping create a more dynamic place to work.

How can someone get a job like yours?

I had to take a job I didn't like to get my foot in the door. Another way is to try to get consulting work here and then see what's going on and what jobs are opening.

dence elected representatives receive each day. This entry-level position is a good place to start on Capitol Hill. Salary range: $20,000 to $25,000.

Legislative Assistant

One step above the LC is the LA, or legislative assistant. The LA deals with constituents, lobbyists, and other Members' staffs and can advise the Member on certain issues. Generally, prior experience working on Capitol Hill is required to become an LA, but sometimes strong issue expertise—or plain old right-place, right-time luck—can land you this job. Salary range: $25,000 to $40,000.

Scheduler

Schedulers are the personal assistants of elected representatives. People in these positions wield real power. After all, they're the gatekeepers to elected representatives; if somebody wants to meet with a given rep, that person needs to go through his or her scheduler first. Salary: $20,000 to $100,000.

GETTING HIRED

For most civil service jobs in federal and state government agencies, it's all about the paperwork: the first step to landing an agency job is saying the right things on the proper application form. At the federal level, this is the OF-612. On it, you'll be required to list your KSAs—knowledge, skills, and abilities; as agencies are looking for carefully defined skill sets in their employees, it's a good idea to check out the many books or computer software packages designed to help with this application process.

For staff jobs at nonprofits and in legislative bodies, there's no standard application procedure. (Currently, though, there is a move in many nonprofits toward formalizing the human resources function.) As in most industries, the best thing you can do to find a job is network. Find a person in an organization where you'd like to work, and try to get that person to help you get an informational interview with a program director or legislative staff member. Neither legislators nor nonprofits typically have a staff devoted to hiring, so initiative is key.

As you conduct your job search, you'll want to keep in mind the following:

- It's important to share the hiring organization or legislator's values. Nonprofits are typically cause-oriented organizations; legislators typically make their decisions based on where they stand on the political spectrum. You'll want to show that you know the organization or legislator's mission, that you care deeply about the work you'll be doing. Because nonprofits and legislative-staff positions generally don't pay as well as private-sector jobs, it's critical that you care about what you're getting into.

- Know what's going on. If you're applying for a job in government, know the key issues and current events that are shaping policy debates; if you're applying to a nonprofit, know what it does and study up on its latest work.

- If you're applying for a job on Capitol Hill, be patient and persistent and involve everyone you know in your job search. In D.C., the more people you know, the more power you'll have—and the more quickly you'll learn about opportunities.

- If you're applying for a job at a government agency, make sure your KSAs match the job description. It might just be worth it to take that night class in accounting, if that's what's required for that agency job you have your eye on. If you have considerable work experience, demonstrate hard-to-find knowledge or job skills. People who bring solid skills in finance or information technology to the table—or have particular industry or issue expertise—can be very attractive candidates, as most people with these skills and knowledge gravitate toward higher-paying private-sector jobs.

Personnel

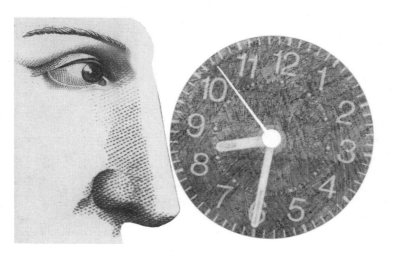

Whether you're an analytical whiz, a natural seller of ideas and concepts, or a good listener and shrewd judge of people, you may have a future in human resources (more commonly known as HR or, occasionally, personnel, although this name is not particularly popular). Having two of these traits would serve you better, and if you possess all three, you could make it to the top. For you to enjoy the field requires, ultimately, that you find it more satisfying to work with people than with products. However, as long as you're excited about the people aspect, the industry offers a vast array of opportunity. A few of the directions you might choose: recruitment (and its broader counterpart, staffing), employee relations, compensation and benefits, training, outplacement, and HR information systems.

Traditionally, companies handle their personnel needs with in-house staff. More recently, a whole industry has grown up to provide these services on a contract basis. These service providers cover a wide range of activities: Manpower and Adecco provide temporary staffing, Korn-Ferry International and Heidrick & Struggles offer executive recruitment, ADP provides payroll processing, Right Associates offer outplacement consulting, and numerous others, both large and small, provide a wide range of other services. This field has been marked by

BERNIE HULL

OCCUPATION:
Outplacement officer

YEARS IN BUSINESS: 10

AGE: 35

EDUCATION: BA in
psychology, State University
of New York

HOURS PER WEEK: 40,
8:00 A.M. to 5:00 P.M.;
1 hour for lunch

SIZE OF COMPANY: 5

CERTIFICATION: None

ANNUAL SALARY: $100,000

How did you get your job?

Networking! I went from running an ad agency to running a résumé service. I was tired of the résumé service and wanted to get more involved in the personnel search field. A friend of mine was planning to start an outplacement firm, so I hounded him until he eventually took me in.

Describe a typical day.

8:00 Arrive at work and check phone messages. Several referrals that need immediate attention. (We're lucky here—I don't have to spend any time marketing the business. It usually seems to come to us.) Difficult termination scheduled for this afternoon with one of our best clients. Call to check whether I should be there. Apparently I should be.

9:00 Interview with a new referral. She's going to need counseling as well as contacts. She also has to rethink her résumé. If my former job taught me nothing else, it trained me to spot a bad résumé almost before it comes out of an envelope.

10:30 More phone calls, this time to recruiters. I'm currently working with one candidate who is particularly strong. Hopefully we'll be able to place him quickly. Patience is an important part of this process, though. Too often people panic and grab at the first offer. This just ends them right back in this office or some other office in less than a year. We try very hard to help people find the right fit.

11:00 Time to finally focus on research and writing. I seem to spend more and more of my day sitting in front of my computer doing this. I like this part of my job, but I think ultimately I prefer talking and working with people.

1:15 Food! Sometimes if I'm really involved in researching a company, I forget to eat.

2:00 Another interview and some reference checking.

3:30 Ready to leave for client site. Quick call to a mediator we use for a few tips on how to deal with questions and issues which may arise in the termination interview. Jot down a few notes and make sure she's going to be available this afternoon if we need to clarify these points.

5:30 These things never go "well," but this is a good HR department and we've worked with

rapid growth. In 1997, temporary staffing organizations alone grew at a 15 percent clip, reaching $50 billion in revenues, and the number of headhunters has doubled in five years. At the same time, corporations have added to their ranks of in-house personnel specialists.

Underlying this growth is the remarkable change that has taken place in corporate America over the last two decades. People change jobs more frequently than they used to and companies have developed more-sophisticated employment practices and benefit programs. Also, legislation pertaining to a wide range of issues—age, race, and disability discrimination; health and safety requirements; employment security; confidentiality; and sexual harassment, to

them a lot in the past. He's also a strong candidate, receptive to suggestions, and he won't be difficult to place. We spend some time after his final interview making up a preliminary list of the work we need to do together.

What are your career aspirations?

I like what I'm doing and feel sustained by the variety of people I work with. I still find this job endlessly fascinating. I'm not sure I need to change anything.

What kinds of people do well in this business?

If you don't care about what happens to these people, you shouldn't do this job. In fact, you would be unable to do this job for more than a few months. Counseling is a very intuitive skill. If you don't have it, you will struggle and ultimately be ineffective. It is also vital that you have the sort of mind that can learn about people's jobs quickly. Rather than become intimately familiar with what someone does for a living, you must grasp the key concepts behind someone's work, assess a job, summarize someone's skills. Assertive people do better than shy types, particularly when it comes to finding a job for yourself! If you

find yourself working for a company that has to drum up new business all the time, you must be able to market your own skills and the value of your firm to potential clients.

What do you really like about your job?

I love the wide array of personalities and job candidates I help. My ten o'clock appointment could be an outplaced machine operator and my eleven o'clock appointment could be a former CEO. I enjoy tailoring my counseling to all walks of life; it's very challenging. There is a beginning, middle, and an end to every person's story in this business. It's a process, and I like watching it and being part of it. I find it enormously gratifying to see people leave here happier than when they came in. I guess I also enjoy knowing so much about all kinds of different careers and jobs, and having access to the top levels but being able to maintain a comfortable distance.

What do you dislike?

Trying to keep people motivated sometimes wears me down a bit. It's difficult, too, to watch them slide into depression or simply feel down about themselves. Once in a while, I encounter people who have been so brutalized by their job separation

that they never fully recover, which is very sad.

What is the biggest misconception about your job?

That it's fun and that you don't have to get involved in the lives of the people you're supposed to be helping. Make no mistake: it's hard work to keep people feeling positive! Outplacement is also not as hot a field as it used to be in the late 1980s and early 1990s. The focus now is on recruitment and retention.

How can someone get a job like yours?

Networking is a powerful tool. Work your way through professional organizations and talk to a lot of people. Let everyone you know and meet know that you're interested in doing this kind of work. In some cases, you may have to volunteer to get some good experience to build your résumé. These days, having the right educational background is important, too. Most people in this field have degrees in business or psychology, and backgrounds in corporate human resources or counseling.

name a few—has raised awareness of personnel issues across the country. More recently, the growth of the Internet has had a profound influence on the entire staffing world. These factors have brought personnel people increasingly to the front lines. Today, the top HR officer in a corporation is usually a key member of the executive team, sitting right alongside his or her counterparts in research, finance, operations, and sales and marketing. This change has also affected the rank and file. Personnel has become a nine-to-five job on Fridays only; you can expect to work from 8:00 to 6:30 most days—and on weekends several times a year.

For the purposes of this overview, we divide the opportunities in HR very broadly into in-house staff and service organizations. Within each of these broad segments, you'll want to think about the functional areas you'll pursue.

In-House HR Staff

The largest number of human resources positions, approximately one per hundred employees or 1.5 million for the economy as a whole, are on staff with the thousands of companies and other employers across the land. HR employees deal with all the following areas: staffing (everything from sourcing to orientation to retention), employee relations, compensation and benefits, training, and information systems. In larger organizations, each of these functions may have several or more employees (depending in part upon how much use the organization makes of outside service agencies). They may also include specialty areas—for example, the comps and benefits area may include everybody from people who handle the payroll to specialists in insurance and 401(k) plans. In smaller organizations, the HR person may wear many hats—but almost every company in the country has somebody on board to handle HR issues. As a job seeker, one thing you'll want to evaluate is the relative importance of the HR department to the specific company you're considering. If the HR office is still down in the basement, right next to the furnace, you may want to keep looking.

Staffing Firms

These include companies such as Manpower, Kelly, Interim, and other smaller organizations that focus on temporary positions, adding on a fee to the hourly rates of the candidates they place. It also includes the executive-recruitment firms (Heidrick & Struggles, Spencer Stuart, and others) that place higher-level candidates into full-time positions and charge clients a hefty percentage of the candidate's first-year salary. Jobs in these organizations usually require you to be a sharp judge of people and a good salesperson and negotiator. You also need the ability to think beyond the client's immediate needs.

Compensation and Benefits Consultants

The specific work here entails everything from policy development to the selection of providers to communication about programs to the rank and file. Players in this field include HR consulting firms like Hewitt, Hay, and Towers Perrin and specialists in managing other benefit programs, such as Ceridian, and even some of the investment houses and insurance companies. Required are an interest in research (what are other companies doing?), analytical ability, good communication and negotiating skills, and patience.

HR Information Systems (HRIS)

Players here include service bureaus, like ADP and Paychex for payroll, and IT firms that offer software and systems for operating the company's payroll, employee information, human resources management, and recruitment systems, along with related reports such as PeopleSoft and Resumix. HRIS has much in common with IT jobs elsewhere in the company—requiring the ability to work with users in defining needs and with vendors in understanding the capabilities and weaknesses of their wares, the ability to plan and implement appropriate training, and some technical knowledge about systems and software.

What's Great

People, Not Product

Like to help people? Not quite ready to be a Peace Corps volunteer in East Africa? Be an HR consultant or recruiter instead. The job is a rewarding one for those who enjoy working with people and solving people problems. Personnel jobs put you in a place where you can have a clear impact on the lives and happiness of others. Moreover, this industry attracts a friendly band of professionals who tend to behave in a considerate manner. They're typically happy to help with assistance, referrals, or ideas—or to just listen when that's what's needed.

Variety

You won't be bored, especially if you're inside an HR department. On a typical day you might schedule interviews, counsel a problem employee, help a new hire get a loan, plan a departmental function, create a memo for the general manager about employee punctuality, and so on. Besides, if you don't like your current role, it will likely change as a result of management changes, a reorganization, new management priorities, planned or unplanned job rotation.

You Can Take It with You!

HR is here to stay—in fact, its importance is growing. Companies will always need people to hire and train staff, deal with compensation and benefits, and assist with employee management. And unlike specific product knowledge, the skills you sharpen in an HR job can go with you anywhere and help you find your next job!

Expect the Unexpected

This is a field where new legislation, new management panaceas, complex relationships, and impossible timetables present constant intellectual demands. You and your colleagues are at your wit's end until you figure out how to deal with the issue of the moment and manage to sell your approach to top management. Even where the latter is impossible, the "what might have been" discussions are intellectually stimulating.

What's to Hate

Never the Last Word

Your role is that of adviser, not decider. Even when you make a decision, you're vulnerable to second-guessing by the rest of the executive team or the line managers. Guess what—that training schedule you carefully planned? Postponed. Quality-of-life recommendations based on your employee survey? Never implemented. The candidate you vetoed? Working in the finance department.

REAL PEOPLE PROFILE

GEOFF ANDERSON

OCCUPATION: VP at a temporary-personnel agency

AGE: 38

YEARS IN BUSINESS: 8

EDUCATION: BA in advertising and marketing, San Diego State University

HOURS PER WEEK: 40 to 45, 9:00 A.M. to 5:30 P.M.; 1 hour for lunch

SIZE OF COMPANY: 55

CERTIFICATION: None

ANNUAL SALARY: $75,000

How did you get your job?

I heard about the company from the temporary professionals who were being placed at the advertising agency where I worked. I was getting pretty burned out in advertising, but I liked the industry, I knew people, and I thought it might be fun to use those connections to find jobs for creative people. I contacted the agency my old firm was using, got an interview, and they gave me a job as a client-services manager.

Describe a typical day.

8:45 Arrive at work and open up. This is a new office and we still haven't established real routines yet. Most of the client service managers arrive around 9 A.M., Though I'm thinking maybe we should begin the day earlier to make sure someone is on hand to answer phone calls personally.

9:00 First interview with a potential associate. Articulate, with a nice portfolio. Computer graphics skills need to be stronger, however. Because our office is so new out here, I pitch in a lot and perform tasks that are typically client-service manager jobs in addition to my regular VP duties. (Usually CSMs do the interviews to determine if candidates have got the necessary experience for us to send them on to clients.)

10:00 More interviews. Complete duds. The New York ad agencies I used to work for were very competitive and I have fairly high standards. Clients need to know this if they're going to trust us. We're currently spending most of our time on these interviews in order to build up a strong database of names.

11:00 Summarize interviews for the associates' files. Pass these on to a CSM so he can get a better sense of what we're looking for. I'm also thinking of getting all our CSMs certified in Adobe graphics systems so that they really understand what we need when we test applicants and review their work.

12:00 Lots of phone time with prospective clients. We already have a base and have placed several associates, but a lot more work needs to be done in this domain. Follow up, follow up, follow up.

1:00 Quick lunch. Most days I try to get out for a while to clear my head. This job involves a lot of talking and listening. I need a break and some quiet time.

2:00 More interviews. Sometimes this gets discouraging. I look forward to having a group of associates whose work I like and whom I can count on. More summaries. No real gems today.

The Ladder Doesn't Reach the Top

An HR background qualifies you only for more-senior HR positions. CEOs and general managers tend to come from sales, finance, or engineering. And seldom will you get to switch to line management, unless you make the move early in your career. Early transfer options, if you should find you don't like HR, might be into sales, customer service, marketing, or operations. People with employment-agency or consulting-firm backgrounds do have growth possibilities in managing such operations, but seldom to move into a different line entirely.

4:15 Off to meet with a client to find out what worked and what didn't in a recent placement. "Oh, everything went fine" is seldom the whole story. For long-term assignments, we monitor our associates' performance while on the job. There's a fine line, though. We don't want to be too involved, but we do want to try and build trust and a reputation for reliability.

5:00 Useful conversation with the client. He has lots of other needs we can address as well.

6:30 Off to my evening class in marketing. In another two semesters, I hope to have an MBA.

What are your career aspirations?

I've been promoted quickly, and I've set my sights on becoming president—I would like to run this company someday! It's nice to know that, because the company is not a huge conglomerate, my goal is not unattainable. We're big, but not so big that I can't play a major role.

What kinds of people do well in this business?

People with relevant experience, such as advertising or graphic design. Basically whatever industry you're seeking to serve, you need to know a lot about it. We think it's vital to have professional credentials yourself before you start making placement decisions for others. Also, anybody who can be excited about their work and get others excited about it will be happy and will move up quickly. They need to be smart, interested, and interesting. If you don't like people, don't even think about this profession! It also helps if you don't take things too seriously or personally.

What do you really like about your job?

The firm is structured such that every employee owns a piece of the company, which makes us all work a little harder and take pride in what we do. This job also allows for more personal time and the energy to enjoy it than other jobs I know. There is some stress, but not nearly as much as in many jobs out there. The field of temporary personnel is still new enough to pose unique challenges, which I really enjoy. Also, I truly enjoy interviewing people!

What do you dislike?

Because we are so different from other personnel agencies, educating people about how we work can be trying. Otherwise, though, there really isn't much I don't like about my job.

What is the biggest misconception about this job?

People think we're headhunters. We don't pluck people from anywhere! There are legitimate agencies that work that way; it's a reality of the personnel business. Our firm doesn't work that way. We advertise that we place creative professionals in temporary positions, and we evaluate the applications. If someone has enough experience, we enter him or her into our database, and when we get a call from a client for a particular creative project, we check the database to see who might be best suited for the position. Our associates are freelance people who really can't be "stolen" from anywhere.

How can someone get a job like yours?

Having some HR experience would certainly be helpful. Having a background in the industry niches and specialties that you hope to serve is even more important. I worked my way up into this position, and I think that's usually more common than stepping into it from the outside. To get a job as a client-services manager (the person who interviews associates), you have to have a minimum of three years experience in some creative field like advertising, marketing, writing, or graphic design. Otherwise, you aren't credible to either your candidates or clients.

FICA Is All Your Fault

Guess who gets to explain social security taxes, insurance benefits (or lack thereof), and all the corporate policies? That's right—you! Don't be surprised if you suffer from guilt by association. HR workers snag a lot of grief and outrage for application-processing delays, unreimbursed medical claims, and the company's pregnancy-leave policy. They are also the line of first and last defense against problem employees and situations. If you need a lot of on-the-job positive feedback, this is not going to be a happy fit.

Dealing with Downsizing

Every company has its ups and downs—and you get to deal with the downsizing. A lot of work and considerable pain. During rapid growth you are frantic in your recruiting efforts, but at least it's a time when there's money, parties, and happy productivity. Downsizing is a downer, although a good outplacement program can make it easier.

KEY JOBS

Human Resources Manager

Many people in companies enter as human resources generalists. Specific responsibilities might include planning an off-site departmental meeting, leading a facilities planning team, or working with the department head to solve problems such as high turnover, accidents, or low morale. In a smaller organization, you will likely play the role of some or all of the specialized functions listed below. This position usually requires a college degree, not necessarily in a specific discipline. Salary range: $25,000 to $40,000 to start; managers earn $50,000 to $70,000; department heads in large companies can earn $100,000 or more.

Recruiter or Staffing Specialist

These jobs exist both within company HR departments and in staffing agencies, although the specific titles may vary. Within companies, recruiters may focus on a specific area such as campus recruiting. Key responsibilities include working with hiring managers to define their needs, sourcing candidates (via ads, the Internet, job fairs, or any way you can), managing résumés, flow, and interviewing. Skills required include an ability to judge people's abilities, sales capabilities (to deal with hiring managers and candidates), and the energy to deal with lots of people. Salary range: starts at $25,000 to $35,000 at temp agencies and companies and $30,000 to $45,000 at search firms. Because many search firms operate on a commission structure, senior partners can make several hundred thousand dollars per year.

HR Consultant

HR consulting firms hire people to provide clients advice about compensation, benefits administration, employee relations, training, HR information systems. Professional entry-level positions, usually involving analysis or report generation, exist in all of these categories except perhaps employee relations but are quite competitive. Salary range: entry-level positions start at $35,000 to $45,000, and senior consultants can earn $150,000 to $250,000 per year.

Benefits Manager

Benefits managers administer the compensation, insurance, pension, 401(k), and other programs. This job can involve reviewing competing plans and figuring out ways to save money for the corporation, as well as explaining programs to employees and helping them with enrollment. No advanced degree is required, but keeping abreast of employment trends, your direct competitors' packages, changes in social policy, and salaries at all levels in your industry is a vital part of this job. Salary range: $25,000 to $55,000.

Training Manager

Many larger organizations hire people to supervise and direct their employee-training programs, from new-employee orientation to skills training and professional-development classes. Skills required here are often the same as those required to be a good teacher, plus a talent for administration. Salary range: $30,000 to $60,000.

Outplacement Specialist

Outplacement firms provide company-sponsored assistance in identifying career directions, résumé preparation, and marketing assistance to employees whose employment is terminated by the sponsoring company. Job opportunities exist for those who can represent a firm (that is, sell and manage projects) to client companies and for those who prefer the role of counselor. Salary range: mid-career professionals earn $60,000 to $90,000.

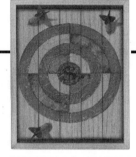

GETTING HIRED

- If you want to be in HR or join an agency or recruiting firm, sending in a résumé is one of the least effective ways to do it. Ultimately, you will need a résumé when you meet someone in the organization where you wish to work, but getting that opportunity is a matter of networking. HR people are a clubby bunch; a recommendation from someone known to the person you wish to meet is almost essential.

- If you're not yet a college senior, try networking to get hired into a summer job in the industry. The experience will make you a stronger candidate. It will also strengthen your interviewing skills and help you choose the right entry-level position.

- In your networking efforts, try to set up informational interviews. That way you can learn about various roles, get valuable advice and referrals, and simultaneously be looked over as a potential hire. Remember—good employees are hard to find!

Pharmaceuticals and Biotechnology

Drugs are good and getting better. The FDA's approval process takes almost half the time it used to. The number of new drugs given the green light last year has almost doubled from the early '90s. And as the over sixty-five age group grows—by almost 20 percent in the next decade—the $95 billion spent on pharmaceuticals in the United States in 1997 ($265 billion worldwide) is only going to increase. The biggest drug companies, known in the industry as Big Pharma, include Merck & Co., Glaxo Wellcome, Novartis, Bristol-Myers Squibb, Eli Lilly, Pfizer, and SmithKline Beecham. These multinational firms traditionally clear a whopping 30 percent in operating margins—that's twice what most S&P 500 companies can boast.

If some of the names above, such as Wellcome and Squibb, look more familiar to you as stand-alones, they were until recently—as were Sandoz and Ciba-Geigy. The past several years have been rife with mergers in this sector (twenty-seven in all, valued at close to $12 billion worldwide). Suddenly, this is no longer an industry of midsize firms, but an arena of giants—the top ten posted $127 billion in sales for '97. It's also an industry that is vertically integrated and becoming more so from initial drug development to marketing to health care to final distribution. (It's perhaps too integrated; the Justice Department is closely examining recent mergers between drug companies and distributors.) Add to this very successful

REAL PEOPLE PROFILE

REN GORDON

OCCUPATION:
Marketing manager for a
pharmaceuticals company

YEARS IN BUSINESS: 6

AGE: 35

EDUCATION: BA in philosophy, Stanford; MBA, Wharton

HOURS PER WEEK: 55,
9:00 A.M. to 7:30 P.M.;
30 minutes for lunch

SIZE OF COMPANY: 35,000

CERTIFICATION: None

ANNUAL SALARY: $75,000,
plus $10,000 bonus and stock
options

How did you get your job?

Shortly before the end of my first year
of business school, my company's CFO
gave a lecture on campus. I didn't
have a summer job lined up, so I went
up to her after her talk and asked if I
could work for her. She hooked me
up with a summer job, and at the end
of the summer I interviewed with the
marketing department, which offered
me a job to start when I finished B-
school. I'm currently in my third position with the company; all have been
in marketing.

Describe a typical day.

9:00 Come in, check e-mail and
      voice mail. Respond to twelve
      e-mails and four voice mails.

9:45 Senior management says I need
      to make cuts in this year's bud-
      get. I've been gathering infor-
      mation for a few weeks now,
      talking to team members about
      places to make cuts. Synthesize
      this data; begin working on
      report for management.

11:00 Meet with a vendor who
      published and distributed to
      pharmacists a write-up of a
      third-party study of our drug.
      Review the efficacy of the
      distribution and discuss possi-
      ble ways to work together in
      the future.

12:30 Grab lunch in the cafeteria.

1:00 Meet with an in-house fore-
      casting expert to discuss next
      year's sales projections and
      budget.

2:00 Catch up on voice mails and
      e-mails.

2:30 Meet with marketing intern
      to discuss direct consumer
      marketing.

3:00 Teleconference with a vendor
      to discuss a sales aid she's
      developing for us. Seems to be
      coming along well.

3:45 Meet with my boss to make
      sure my plans for the budget
      cut are in line with his
      thinking.

4:30 Settle in to finish the revised
      budget report.

7:00 Clean up last few voice mails
      and e-mails.

7:30 Go home.

What are your career aspirations?

I'm really not sure. I know I'd like to
stay in phamaceuticals, but I'd like to
relocate, which will probably mean I
won't be able to stay with my company. That makes me something of an

exception; the company treats its
employees well, and people tend to
stick around.

What kinds of people do well in this business?

People who work well in an orderly,
hierarchical, sometimes slow-moving
organization. That is, people who tend
to err on the side of perfection rather
than those who tend to err on the
side of getting things done quickly but
imperfectly.

What do you really like about your job?

My opinions and actions really matter
to the success of this product. And I'm
part of a company that makes things
that really, really improve the quality
of peoples' lives.

What do you dislike?

Around product launch time my hours
get pretty crazy. And I'm not making
as much money as my peers in other
industries.

What is the biggest misconception about your job?

That drug companies are full of
money-grubbing gougers who are
only out to get rich. Anyone who
spent a day here would know that
that's not true.

How can someone get a job like yours?

A lot of people come into the company through sales. A science background is helpful, but by no means
mandatory. Really the key prerequisite is a genuine belief in what the
company does, and a strong sense
of ethics.

mix the innovations of biotechnology—everything from new drugs like Viagra and Rogaine to criminal forensics—and you obviously have some very interesting job prospects. People with all sorts of backgrounds will find careers here—not only the scientists you'd expect, but also engineers to create and maintain all the machines used to research drugs; businesspeople to market and sell the ever-expanding array of products and coordinate with other companies' research efforts; computer programmers, who build the huge databases needed to track clinical trials, develop computer models, and maintain companies' systems; and health care professionals, who run clinical trials and work closely with hospitals, government agencies, and regulatory groups. There is also a growing need in specialized projects for nutritionists, environmentalists, and law-enforcement specialists, among others.

This is an industry poised for strong growth into the next millennium. The burn rate—the steep cost of research for the many products that don't make it to market—always affects who gets hired and when; it's important to review this aspect of your potential employers' financials as thoroughly as possible. And while most of the action in the industry is controlled by Big Pharma, you can opt to work in some of the more specialized areas of biotechnology, where companies range in size from a handful of employees to several thousand. Geographical constraints may be a factor here: biotech's home is in California (particularly the Bay Area), while Big Pharma is on the other side of the Mississippi.

How It Breaks Down

Big Pharma

These companies are the big daddies: huge multinationals that employ tens of thousands of people. Many pursue multiple business lines, selling medical devices and, ironically enough, pesticides. And though the trend in recent years has been for these firms to shed their peripheral businesses and concentrate on drugs, this focus includes pairing up with smaller biotech companies for research. For example, Glaxo Wellcome bought Spectra Biomedical. Another trend in this sector, mentioned in the overview, is consolidation. In recent years, large mergers have included Hoechst and Marion Roussel, Pharmacia and Upjohn, Glaxo and Wellcome, and Ciba-Geigy and Sandoz (together renamed Novartis). Despite these mergers, this remains a highly fragmented industry, with no single company garnering more than 7 percent of global revenues. On the employment front, these are good places to work if you like stability ("I don't think my company's ever had a round of layoffs," says one Big Pharma insider). Many people will spend whole careers at a single company and enjoy the traditional accoutrements of corporate life, including generous annual stock option grants for managers.

Biotech

Biotech is Big Pharma's adolescent sibling. Founded about twenty years ago to develop commercial uses for recombinant DNA (in other words, genetic engineering) technology, the sector includes about one thousand companies that range in size from fewer than ten to several hundred employees (some might say several thousand, but we've placed those into the middle tier). These companies typically have a heavy emphasis on research—in fact, many of the smaller companies operate solely as R&D shops, working on nothing but research. This means that most of the jobs in this sector go to scientists, though there are some positions for engineers and businesspeople.

Unlike the Big Pharma, most biotech companies are not profitable. Like high-tech start-ups, small biotech companies are funded by investors who hope that the company will make a great discovery that will bring in lots of money. A common source of funding is Big Pharma itself. (Centocor and Millenium Pharmaceuticals, for example, rely on American Home Products, Eli Lilly, and Bristol-Myers Squibb for cash in return for future royalties and profits.) Biotechnology covers a lot of ground: prescription and over-the-counter drugs, food products, hair restorers, environmental cleanup, and forensics. Basically any product that uses living organisms or cells to improve human health, modify the environment, or solve a problem is biotechnology.

If working for a major pharmaceutical company is like driving a Cadillac—smooth, comfortable, predictable—then working for a biotech company is like driving an Alfa Romeo—fast, wild, unreliable. You'll probably work on a wider variety of projects and have more responsibility early on at a biotech company, and on the slim chance that your company takes off, your stock options (which are often even more generous than Big Pharma management's) will be worth a lot of money. However, you may find yourself worried about where your next paycheck will come from.

The Middle Tier

Over the course of the last decade, a few biotech shops have managed to grow into small pharmaceutical companies. These companies—Amgen, Chiron, and Genentech—employ between five thousand and ten thousand people each and often turn a profit. R&D costs pose the biggest threat to earnings and long-term job security at these places. (Funds needed for research have been known to grow by close to 100 percent each year.) A large percentage of Chiron is owned by Novartis, a large pharmaceutical company; close to two-thirds of Genentech is owned by Roche. These alliances allow the smaller companies to distribute their products via the larger companies' global channels.

These companies are more stable then biotech start-ups, but still less predictable than the Big Pharma old guard. They hire plenty of businesspeople and engineers, though the focus is solidly on research. Additionally, unlike West Coast–averse Big Pharma, most of the major players in this tier call the Golden State their home.

What's Great

Get Paid to Help Others

People in this industry create products that ease suffering, save lives, make many foods cheaper and more accessible, and in certain instances improve the environment. If you have conflicting needs regarding altruism, results, and earning real money, biotechnology is one of the more viable compromises. Big Pharma also have plenty of worthy research efforts. None will ever be as worthy as those of socially enlightened nonprofits, but here you can pay your bills, maybe even buy a new car, and still feel reasonably good about what you're doing for a living.

Deep Thought

This is a brainy industry. It uses state-of-the-art manufacturing techniques to create sophisticated products. And an intensely complex and often lengthy research process precedes even the early prototypes. Very smart people still have to think very hard to do these jobs well. Many cite the intellectual nature of their work—and of the industry's atmosphere as a whole—as one of their favorite things about their job.

Magic Potions

Sick people will spend whatever money they have to numb the pain or make themselves healthy. Doctors and others in the health care industry will usually spend whatever their budgets will allow to have the best new technology. Drug and biotech stocks are notoriously volatile because of the high R&D costs and infrequent breakthroughs. But this doesn't mean that working in these areas isn't stable. Big Pharma are tough to beat in terms of job security, and even the mid-size biotech companies offer relative prosperity and safety. This is also an industry which, though constantly changing, doesn't seem to lay people off or need much technological reengineering.

What's to Hate

Produce or Perish

Though companies brag about their huge R&D budgets and work to cultivate a thriving intellectual environment, they must ultimately keep their eyes on the real prize: the new, revenue-generating drug; the bigger, better no-taste tomato; the carpet-fiber analysis to beat all existing fiber analyses. For some scientists, this means that profitability interferes regularly with truth, theory, and even ethics. Caveat emptor: This isn't an ivory tower. If you're most interested in the "why," not the new, improved "what," think hard before you proceed.

Shorter Doesn't Mean Short

The Food and Drug Administration may have streamlined its review process for new drugs from just over three years to a mere nineteen months. But that's still a mighty long while to wait for approval, especially if the clinical trials for your new drug took several years. If you're impatient and need to be in a fast-paced, results-oriented environment, you'll find most jobs in this industry to be variations of "Hurry up and wait."

Rules, Rules, Rules

This is one of the most highly regulated industries around. This applies not only to the science side of things, but to sales and marketing as well. One marketing insider at a pharmaceutical giant remarks, "Every piece of promotional material that goes out has to conform to an incredibly strict set of guidelines." No room for creative embellishment here. Innovation is a risky business, particularly where human health is concerned. Don't be fooled by the R&D budgets at Big Pharma or the glamour and energy of biotech. No one wants the Big Mistake emerging from their labs. So they take great pains that it won't.

KEY JOBS

A note about salaries: At large pharmaceutical companies, people in management positions earn significant bonuses in cash and stock options. At many biotech companies, all employees receive stock options, which, if the company does well, can be lucrative. These bonuses are not reflected in the salary ranges below.

Lab Tech

Lab techs perform the routine maintenance tasks—cleaning and maintaining glassware, working with animal colonies, and operating lab equipment, among other things—needed to keep labs functioning. A high school diploma is required, and many people with college degrees start here as well. Salary range: $25,000 to $35,000.

Research Associate

This is the entry-level science position; a BS in some form of chemistry or biology is typically required. Associates work at the bench, conducting experiments under the guidance of PhD scientists. These jobs typically don't require previous work experience, though experience in certain scientific specialties is often required or preferred. Salary range: $35,000 to $45,000.

Research Scientist

After receiving a PhD and completing a post-doc, a scientist can get a real job as a research scientist, designing and conducting experiments in a given field and, when appropriate, writing up results for publication. Salary range: $65,000 to $85,000, often in the low six figures at large companies.

Sales Rep

Sales reps work with physicians, hospitals, HMOs, and other medical institutions to keep health-care professionals abreast of and interested in a given company's line of drugs. Some of these jobs require extensive travel; others don't. Drug reps typically have bachelor's degrees, usually in the sciences. Big Pharma companies have huge staffs of reps, making this position a good entrée into the industry. Salary range: $35,000 to $80,000.

Marketing Analyst

Job seekers without backgrounds in science can find work in Big Pharma or smaller biotech companies on the marketing side. A marketing analyst might perform market research, analyze product performance, and design and help the marketing team implement campaigns for specific drugs or specific audiences. Many MBAs come into the industry this way. Salary range: $50,000 to $75,000.

Marketing Managers

These are the brand managers for the products. In this job, you'll not only manage your promotional team and the analysts, but also will help determine price, distribution, brand image, forecasting, and overall strategy for several, or in some cases, a large family of products. Salary range: $60,000 to $100,000.

Systems Analyst

This is something of a catch-all title that refers to a wide variety of jobs, but put simply, systems analysts are computer folks. There's a lot of complex database work to be done in this industry, particularly in clinical trials. Computers are also increasingly used to model chemical and physiological processes, which puts job seekers who combine backgrounds in science with computer know-how in particularly high demand. And of course everybody needs IT people to keep their systems up and running. Bachelor's degrees are usually, but not always, required here; familiarity with UNIX, NT, and SQL is very helpful. Salary range: $30,000 to $90,000.

Regulatory Affairs Associate

Regulatory affairs offers a career path for job seekers with backgrounds in science who don't want to do lab work. Regulatory affairs associates ensure that their company's development and manufacturing processes are in accordance with the detailed and complex regulations imposed by the FDA on pharmaceutical and other related companies. A BS in science is typically required for this position. Those with law degrees come in at a higher level with more responsibility but fundamentally the same job description. Salary range: $35,000 to $50,000. JDs can expect double this range.

Clinical Research Physician (CRP)

Clinical research physicians are MDs who develop and implement plans for bringing drugs through clinical trials. They work on cross-functional teams in order to understand the pharmacological, regulatory, and clinical dimensions of the drug being studied. Salary range: $90,000 to $200,000.

GETTING HIRED

- Know whom you're talking to. A tiny biotech company will want you to be willing to roll up your sleeves and turn on a dime. A huge pharmaceutical company will want you to be comfortable with hierarchy and process. Even within a given sector, each company will have its own specific traits: research-driven, egalitarian, highly structured. By familiarizing yourself with these before the interview you will be able to present yourself in the best possible light—and figure out if you really want to work there.

- Be flexible. There is plenty of horizontal movement in this industry, particularly in more-junior positions. If you can't find a job doing exactly what you want, consider taking a job doing something else with the intention of working your way into your ideal job over the course of a year or two.

REAL PEOPLE PROFILE

BONNIE WASSERSTEIN

OCCUPATION:
Research associate in biotech

YEARS IN BUSINESS: 3

AGE: 25

EDUCATION: BS in chemistry, MIT

HOURS PER WEEK:
40, 9:00 A.M. to 5:30 P.M.;
30 minutes for lunch

SIZE OF COMPANY: 30,000

CERTIFICATION: None

ANNUAL SALARY:
$45,000, plus bonus

How did you get your job?

My senior year of college, I didn't have a job lined up, so I went to see the counselor in the chemistry department. The next day, as I was walking by her office, she said "Hey, Bonnie, I think I've got a job for you." Turns out the guy who is now my boss had called her, just after I left her office, looking to hire someone coming out with a BS in chemistry. I interviewed with him and persuaded him that I was bright and ready to learn. He offered me the job if I'd give him a two-year commitment, which I did. That was three years ago.

Describe a typical day.

9:00   Come in, collect the appropriate glassware from down the hall to set up a continuous extraction (a process of transferring a compound dissolved in water into an organic solvent by continuously boiling, condensing, and dripping the organic solvent through the water, and recollecting the solvent to boil once more).

9:45   Check e-mail. Seven new messages: one from my dad, six from my lab.

9:50   Call Dad. Chat about a book he recommended.

10:00   Concentrate and attempt to recrystallize a solution I've been working with for several days. This entails playing around with different solvent mixtures in order to find the one that the compound will crystallize from. Lots of trial and error. Dissolving and removing solvent.

10:30   Set up a new reaction; set it to stir under an atmosphere of nitrogen at 100 degrees Celsius.

11:00   Prepare a flash chromatography column to purify a reaction that I completed yesterday. What I do here is pack a glass column with silica gel, load the compound onto the column, and start the automatic fraction collector, a machine that will collect the solvent into small test tubes.

12:00   Grab a newspaper, head to the cafeteria.

12:30   Back to the lab. I need to determine the appropriate reagent to use in the next reaction I am going to set up. Go to my boss for help.

1:15   After discussing the possibilities, my boss recommends that I search the literature for previous examples. Do a search of the literature on my computer; find a relevant article. Head to the company library, photocopy the article, bring it back to the lab, and read it.

2:15   Fortunately, we have the correct reagent in stock, so I get it from a lab down the hall. Add it; set the mixture stirring at room temperature under nitrogen. I'll find out tomorrow if it works.

- Scientists: PhDs should have publications under their belts, preferably as first author. Also, a PhD from a North American university is more valuable than one from anywhere else in the world. BS and MS job seekers should have some experience doing research in a lab. And the more relevant your experience is to the lab to which you're applying, the better.

2:45 Take another reaction that's been stirring since yesterday. Work it up: extract it, remove all residual water, and remove the organic solvent to give me my crude (unpurified) product.

3:15 Check each test tube from the column chromatography I did before lunch to determine which tubes contain my purified product. Collect contents of the appropriate tubes into one large flask, remove the solvent, find the mass, and calculate the yield of the reaction. Take an NMR (nuclear magnetic resonance, a test that allows me to determine a compound's structure) of the compound to confirm that it's what I think it is.

4:00 Take the compound I worked up at 2:45 and combine it with a compound my boss made. This part's a little nerve-wracking: These two compounds represent several days of work each, so if I mess it up . . . Anyway, I set the mixture of the compounds to stir until tomorrow and hope that the reaction runs smoothly.

4:30 There's this compound that I've been trying to recrystallize for days: dissolving it, drying it, scratching it, filtering it. It just doesn't want to be a solid. Work on it for a while, trying every trick I can think of.

5:15 No luck today with that recrystallization. Maybe tomorrow. Check on the several reactions I have stirring to make sure they are at the right temperature and all set to continue running overnight.

5:30 Wash my hands, close the hood sash, turn off the rotovap, shut down my computer, hit the lights, and go home.

What are your career aspirations?

I really don't know yet; sometimes I feel like there are too many options. Probably something different than what I'm doing, though; maybe go back and get my PhD, maybe get a master's and teach at a small college. I really like teaching.

What kinds of people do well in this business?

At my level, persistence is important. Things don't work a lot of the time, or bog down at the end, and you've got to keep pushing to make the compound you're trying to make. So a high tolerance for frustration is key. Creativity is important too—particularly for higher-level scientists. There are a limited number of basic structures to start with, and a lot of them have already been tested, so it takes a creative intelligence to keep coming up with ideas for new possibilities. Generally speaking, creative, intelligent people who work hard do well.

What do you really like about your job?

It's always interesting. Every compound I make is new, every reaction I run is unique, and unexpected things happen. So I get to improvise a lot, which is fun. Another cool thing is that my work is physical: I boil things, smash things, grind things—sometimes I feel like a kid playing in a backyard sandbox. And there's a beauty, an elegance to what I do; the compounds I create are like microscopic sculptures. I also like the atmosphere. There's no one looking over my shoulder; it's okay for me to pay my bills at work or to take off in the middle of the day and go for a jog.

What do you dislike?

There is some pressure to put in more than forty hours a week. Also, I handle carcinogens every day, which is scary. And, even though I don't do it directly, the animal testing that my company does disturbs me.

What is the biggest misconception about this job?

That it's boring or repetitive and that I merely operate machinery all day. My work is always different and almost always interesting.

How can someone get a job like yours?

A BS in chemistry is a minimum; an MS is better. Get experience in an organic chemistry lab. Demonstrate a genuine intellectual interest and a solid work ethic. That's pretty much it.

Real Estate

Real estate, the source of almost half the privately owned wealth in the United States, is an industry famous for making people filthy rich. It is also responsible for over five million jobs in the United States, in the sales, management, and analysis of land and property. The industry is a cyclical one, with booms and busts tied closely to the economy's overall performance. In the late 1980s and early 1990s, the real estate industry struggled through a devastating recession; but the industry, like the economy, has recovered. Spurred on by high-tech companies in the northwest and Silicon Valley and strong financial and business-services performance in New York, L.A., Miami, and Dallas, demand for office space is once again strong. In many major U.S. cities investors are even looking to long-forgotten downtown areas for space. And with a generation of aging baby boomers set to enter their high-earning years, the residential real estate market should remain steady as well. Still, real estate veterans remain cautious, wary of the type of oversupply that crippled the industry in the late '80s.

Although it's experiencing one of its strongest growth periods ever, real estate has been undergoing a major restructuring. Aggressive consolidation and a wave of strategic alliances have resulted in two tiers of players in the industry. At the

REAL PEOPLE PROFILE

ARNOLD GRIEG

OCCUPATION: Project manager at a commercial real estate development company

YEARS IN BUSINESS: 8

AGE: 30

EDUCATION: BA in finance, Stanford University

HOURS PER WEEK: 65, 8:00 A.M. to 7:00 P.M. with some weekends; 1 hour for lunch

SIZE OF COMPANY: 25

CERTIFICATION: None

ANNUAL SALARY: $80,000, including bonus

How did you get your job?

I interned in college with the firm I'm at now. After college I started out as an assistant project manager, which I was for three years. Then I moved on to become a project manager. My firm is a very small company, so I was fortunate to get an opportunity early on to show what I could do.

Describe a typical day.

8:00 Arrive at work after having avoided the usual monster line at the coffee shop. Immediately begin looking into a piece of property that I currently have in escrow, pouring over various reports which affect the way we can use the property. These reports include soils, environmental, title, and survey reports, as well as taking a look at the zoning history of the property. All this information is geared toward figuring out how we can best use this property.

10:30 Meet with our land-use attorney to devise a strategy for our rezoning case to make use of property the way we want to. Afterwards, head over to a neighborhood zoning meeting which could directly affect the property. After the meeting, meet up with city council staff to go over site plans.

12:30 Grab a quick bite to eat at a local sandwich place while on my way to meet with the architects and engineers regarding the design of another project which is farther along. After okaying the final design, I head back to the office for a meeting with a broker about negotiating the sale of a pad to a fast-food user.

2:00 After my meeting with the broker, I again go over covenants, conditions, and restrictions relating to the property from this morning. Turns out the condition of title is more restrictive than initially thought and we may have to alter our initial design plans.

4:00 Head out to a fourth piece of property that is in the construction phase for a meeting with the contractor. I check on construction progress and compare it with the agreed-upon project-completion schedule.

6:00 Back at the office I take a call from a lender about negotiating the loan documents on another property.

7:00 Take a minute to catch my breath and then head home, hoping to get in a quick run before dinner.

---

top are large multiservice firms, such as Trammell Crow and Lasalle Partners, with enough capital and resources to withstand economic downturns. The bottom tier includes smaller developers and agencies that are more flexible and better able to service local markets. Meanwhile, midlevel operators are getting pushed out. For job seekers, this means you can expect to work for either a regional or a more national firm.

Real estate investment trusts (REITs) have been another big industry development. They provide investors the opportunity to pool their money to invest in an array of properties; their access to massive amounts of capital allows them to buy and develop large amounts of property. Two of the largest owners of office and residential property in the United States, Equity Office Properties Trust and Equity Residential Properties Trust, are REITs.

What are your career aspirations?

My present position as project manager is ideal for me as far as what my job entails. I am involved in every conceivable aspect of the development process and no two days are alike. Eventually I hope to get a piece of the action—that is, have ownership of the projects that I am working on and get a cut of the money made. If you're senior enough that's what you get. Most companies are very small at the top, with one or two people putting in a whole lot of time and putting up a large amount of capital. They are typically reluctant to give up ownership. They would prefer to hire quality people and pay them a salary and bonus.

What kinds of people do well in this business?

People who do well are very detail oriented. They must be able to see the big picture while also being able to see the details. I like to compare it to the aperture of a camera. You need to open up the lens wide enough to capture everything, but you also must be able to tighten it up to catch all the details. You also have to be able to work long hours and not be afraid to take on risk. A person who doesn't need a lot of structure will do well. There are not very many training programs in this business. You also have to be very intelligent.

What do you really like about your job?

I like everything, but most of all I like the fact that I get to see the product of my labor. I can drive around town and almost everywhere I go I can look at projects that my company has developed. I can think back to the couple of years that it took to complete it. Those buildings are now providing employment, and they look great. It's different from almost any other job. I am involved in a product that I can see and touch. It's very entrepreneurial. There are a lot of opportunities, I can see them and then go after them. There's more variety than you can shake a stick at. I might have six or eight projects going at once, all at different stages of development. It is a content-rich experience. I am a high-energy person, and I get my appetite satisfied.

What do you dislike?

There are honestly very few things that I dislike about my job. The stress and the long hours can get to me sometimes. There can't be many things that you dislike about this job or you won't be successful. There are too many other people who want to do this. If you don't love it, they will run circles around you.

What is the biggest misconception about this job?

That it's easy. This is really hard work. Most people think developers are all like Donald Trump, making lots of money without taking on much risk. Lots of people see a building in progress and don't have a clue about all that's involved in getting it built. The construction is the easy part. The risks are large, there are a whole lot of things that can happen and go wrong before the building ever gets put up. Is it possible to make a million dollars on a piece of property? Sure. Not always, but it can happen. But you could also lose $5 million. Most people assume that all developers are rich people. Certainly some are, but there are more people who aren't.

How can someone get a job like yours?

Real estate development is an extremely tough industry to break into. The companies like to be lean and mean and keep overhead down for when the market turns down. Most people start out going to work for one of the large commercial brokerage firms as brokers. From there, they hope to make contacts, preferably developer clients, who will then offer them a job.

Even though there is a lot of money to be made in this industry—after all, a third of the world's wealth is tied up in real estate—one should not enter it expecting to become the next Donald Trump, at least not right away. On average, real estate salaries are low. Most positions require several years to build up experience, contacts, and responsibility. To be successful you'll need to be self-motivated, focused, and able to take the good times with the bad. Job opportunities exist mainly in sales and property acquisition and analysis.

If you want to enter on the sales side, you'll need to get a license and then go to work for a commercial or residential broker, both of which act as intermediaries between buyers and sellers. To work in property acquisition and analysis, you'll probably need a college or advanced degree; only then will you be able to find a job at a property management company or an REIT. A recent trend of note:

One effect of the industry's growing complexity, and the resulting dependence on financial analysis, is an increase in job opportunities for people from non–real estate backgrounds.

How It Breaks Down

The real estate industry is awash in mergers, acquisitions, and strategic alliances. But even with widespread consolidation, job opportunities in the industry remain divided into four distinct fields: sales, management, development, and acquisition and analysis. Although crossover between these sectors is possible, most people start out specializing in a specific area.

Sales and Leasing

A number of factors have combined to place enormous upward pressure on property sales in recent years: REITs and their elephantine appetite for property, rising revenues among U.S. corporations, and strong demand for residential real estate. This segment, which has benefited enormously from rising real estate prices, includes everything from residential real estate brokers such as Century 21 and Coldwell Banker to larger corporations that broker bigger commercial properties such as office towers. Grubb and Ellis Company has one of the largest global brokerage divisions, offering sales and leasing services in sixty-nine U.S. markets and in Europe. Cushman and Wakefield is another giant, with forty-five offices nationwide. Its clients are primarily corporations and other institutions, for which it negotiates sales and leases.

Management

Property managers are those responsible for maintaining property values. This involves dealing with tenants, managing finances, and physically tending to the property. The management sector has been hit hardest by the wave of mergers and acquisitions sweeping the industry. In 1996, two dozen firms were absorbed by others. Some industry insiders are predicting that 75 percent of the property management firms in operation in 1990 will be out of business by the year 2007. Much of this can be attributed to clients' using fewer management firms and the increased costs caused by technology. For job seekers, this means fewer jobs as companies look to become more efficient and cut redundant staff. One of the largest acquisitions in recent years was the 1997 merger of CB Commercials and Koll, then the fifth-largest property management company in the United States. Today CB Richard Ellis Commercial/Koll Management Services is the second-largest property manager, behind Insignia Financial Group, Inc. One of the largest residential property managers is Lefrak Organization, which manages more than sixty thousand apartments in New York City.

Development

Developers are responsible for taking a property idea and making it a reality. This is a complex process involving architects, engineers, zoning officials, builders, lenders, and prospective tenants. Development is not always the gravy train some make it out to be. In the early 1990s, when real estate prices crashed, construction dried up and a lot of commercial office space was left vacant. This oversupply had developers scrambling for survival. Many endured the down time by venturing into other areas of real estate. Today, many of the largest real estate developers are also property owners and managers. Hines Interest LP, the largest office developer in the United States, also manages over seventy-five million square feet of real estate. Other major players in this segment include the Lincoln Property Company, which offers development and investment services in both residential and commercial real estate, and Del Webb, the largest U.S. developer.

Acquisition and Analysis

As the 1990s draw to a close, the market for REITs—which are in essence securitized real estate investment opportunities—is booming. By the end of 1997, REITs had accumulated $50 billion in real estate; that same year, REITs accounted for more than a quarter of the $18 billion in total real estate transactions. The opportunities here are for finance types, often MBAs, who are charged with evaluating and arranging for the purchase of properties for REITs and other investment purposes.

What's Great

Matinees and Day Games

Positions in real estate, particularly those in sales, are not your typical nine-to-five jobs. "If it's a nice day and I want to leave early to go surfing or hit the gym, I can," says one broker. Because you make your money off commissions on sales, rather than on the number of hours per week you sit at a desk, you can decide just when you will and won't work.

Moving Made Easy

The career options in real estate are numerous; you can work in everything from development to sales to management. "I started in sales and leasing, but have moved into property management over time. It lets me stay involved in projects longer," says one insider.

Schmoozapalooza

Much of real estate involves dealing with clients or potential clients. "This industry is completely relationship driven. I love getting out and meeting people and hearing their stories," explains one insider. If you like being social and are good at it, real estate may be the place for you.

What's to Hate

The Dark Side of Sales

For those in sales positions that operate on commission, the lack of a steady paycheck can be stressful—as those of you who've seen the film *Glengarry Glen Ross* know. "Its disheartening to know you put in a sixty- to seventy-hour workweek and have absolutely nothing to show for it," says one young sales agent.

REAL PEOPLE PROFILE

JAMES GLADSTONE

OCCUPATION:
Commercial sales associate

YEARS IN BUSINESS: 2

EDUCATION: BA in history and economics

HOURS PER WEEK:
65, 7:30 A.M. to 6:30 P.M., some weekends; 30 minutes for lunch

SIZE OF COMPANY: 450 brokers in 28 offices

CERTIFICATION: Sales license

ANNUAL SALARY:
Commissions only

How did you get your job?

I got in the door through an ex-girlfriend whose brother had been an intern at my company and whose father was a close friend of one of the owners of the company. After spending a year as an assistant, I became an agent.

Describe a typical day.

6:30   Wake up, shower, and eat breakfast.

7:30   Arrive at work and begin making calls on available properties listed in the *Wall Street Journal*, the *San Francisco Chronicle*, and other papers. I specialize in small retail properties, so I'm on the lookout for listings that match that description in my geographic area. That might be a Burger King, a Walgreen's, a Safeway, or a Blockbuster Video. I only call owners whose properties I have seen first-hand, so I make plans to visit those properties I don't already know.

8:00   Call title companies to get ownership information on a couple of properties that I've learned about in the papers.

8:30   Research my database to find more phone numbers of own-ers of properties I have already scouted in person. My database is my lifeline; it includes all the contacts I have made.

9:15   Search the tax rolls on the computer looking for any own-ers that pay taxes and own retail properties valued at over $500,000.

10:00 Cold-call property owners with the hope of eventually repre-senting them in the sales of their property. Also known as canvassing or farming, this is basically sending out phone feelers hoping for a bite.

12:00 Get a super burrito from the place around the corner, bring it back to the office, and eat at my desk. While eating, read the paper or surf the Internet for any new developments or leads on properties. Loopnet is one of the more popular real estate sites on the Web.

1:00   Back to the phones. You guessed it—more cold-calling of owners.

3:30   Write correspondence. These are mostly follow-up letters to owners I have already spoken or met with. Often they include responses to requests for information about the mar-

Good Times, Bad Times

Real estate is cyclical. Although times are good now, they will inevitably slump. "You may be very good at your job, but there is little you can do about a down market other than wait for it to recover," says an insider.

Paying Your Dues

Much of real estate is about building contacts and forging relationships. That takes time. People just starting out or relocating to a new area may have a tough time breaking into the local scene. As an industry insider puts it, "Starting out in

ket, including recent sales, rents in the area, and other properties available for sale.

5:00 Prepare marketing packages on available property listings for distribution to potential buyers.

6:00 More research and working on proposals and property analysis—all geared toward building up my database.

7:30 Head out to meet a friend for drinks.

What are your career aspirations?

I'd like to learn as much about the business as I can and make enough money as a broker to live comfortably. Down the line, I hope to use my commissions to become an investor in real estate myself. Ultimately, my goal is to become a successful real estate developer, focusing on the redevelopment and renovation of existing property.

What kinds of people do really well at this business?

You have to be very driven and self-motivated to survive in this business. If you need supervision, you're in the wrong place. You can't rely on anyone else, so you have to be focused, very efficient with your time, and willing to crank out the work no matter how frustrating and long-term it may be.

What do you really like about your job?

I don't have to rely on anyone for anything. My success or failure is not restricted by a set career path like it is in a lot of professions. I also like the flexibility. This is not a typical nine-to-five job. If I need to leave work early or take a vacation, I can. And my job requires me to get in front of and meet all different types of people; it's great to hear their stories.

What do you dislike?

No salary; it's completely commission-based compensation. Commissions are typically 6 percent, split between the buying and selling agent. In the past ten months I haven't made anything, but I've had several near misses. The smallest property I deal with is $500,000, so on one sale I can make $50,000 or more. There's a lot of pressure and stress that comes with no steady paycheck. It can be disheartening to work a seventy-hour week, sleeping and eating very little, and to make absolutely no money.

What is the biggest misconception about the job?

How easy it is to make a lot of money. This is a very difficult industry to break into, especially for someone right out of college. It's tough to establish credibility. There's also this stereotype that real estate salespeople are dishonest, slippery creatures. Sure, I'm trying to make money, but there's a professional way to go about it. The industry has become a lot more professional in recent years.

How can someone get a job like yours?

Call all the big brokerage firms and ask to speak to the manager. Be extremely enthusiastic and interested in the profession and see where it leads. You should also ask about any mentor programs or internships where you can work under a broker. I definitely recommend being an assistant before becoming an agent.

real estate is a lot like starting a new business. It takes about three years to get up and running."

KEY JOBS

The great thing about real estate is it's not going away. It's the level of demand and how many jobs the market can support that will fluctuate. A strong economy creates lots of opportunities. But for salespeople, it also means plenty of competition. On the management side, the popularity of rental housing and the rising number of elderly should create job opportunities in apartment and assisted-living management. Those who want security can find work as appraisers, as these jobs are less affected by the industry cycle. There is currently an oversupply of residential appraisers; their number is expected to be cut in half by 2000.

Residential or Commercial Agent or Broker

These are individual sales professionals who provide their services to brokers for a commission, usually 6 percent. To be an agent you must be eighteen years old and have graduated from high school and passed a written test on property laws and real estate transactions. Some states require additional classroom training. To become a broker you need a broker's license, which allows you to open your own agency. Commercial sales professionals typically specialize in a specific property type: apartments, retail, office, and so on. Salaries vary according to location, level of effort, and luck. Salary range: $50,000 to $100,000 or more.

Appraiser

Appraisers provide estimates of a property's value and quality, and typically specialize in residential or commercial real estate. Most appraisers work for banks or appraisal firms. The majority of appraisals are done for mortgage-lending purposes and involve finding comparable sales. All states require appraisers to be licensed. Salary range: up to $75,000.

Property Manager

Although some property owners manage their own investments, the majority hire professional management companies to do it. Property managers are in charge of maintaining a property's value. This is done through finding tenants, satisfying tenants, negotiating leases, making sure rents are in line with the market, and maintaining the physical property. Most people enter as assistant managers and work their way up. Salary range: $20,000 to $80,000.

Consultant or Adviser

With the increase in institutional investing, real estate advisers are becoming more and more in demand. Prior experience in investing or management is necessary. Real estate advisers are generally good with statistics and excel at dealing with clients. Salary range: $50,000 and up.

Developer

Developers are the ones who make property plans come to life. To become a developer you'll need excellent communication skills and a strong understanding of all aspects of the real estate industry. Most developers start out in entry-level positions with a developer or contractor and then work their way up. Salary range: $50,000 to $100,000 or more.

Entrepreneur

Real estate entrepreneurs buy property for the purpose of making money. Success as an entrepreneur takes an equal mix of industry smarts and good fortune.

Just remember: Although many people have made fortunes in real estate, an equal number haven't. Salary range: the sky's the limit, but the threat of bankruptcy is very real.

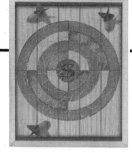

GETTING HIRED

In real estate you start at the bottom and work your way up. Whether it's as an assistant sales agent or in an entry-level position with a developer or property management company, that initial experience is generally a springboard to your first sale or promotion. Exhibiting strong motivation and communication skills will help speed up that process. Note that many people enter real estate after several years in another profession, and that making a few investments on your own is a good way to gain experience in the industry. If you're interested in getting into real estate, keep the following in mind:

- Check with brokerage, management, and development firms about internship programs. After you get one, be open, enthusiastic, and willing to learn. Much of the real estate industry revolves around relationships. If people like you and know you can do the job, they'll hire you.

- Try to get an entry-level paid position with a property management or development company. This will save you the stress and pressure of working on commission while you're just starting out.

- Find a mentor who can show you the ropes of the industry and help you make contacts. Working under someone is the ideal way to learn the industry and develop contacts. Be persistent, unassuming, and willing to take rejection. You can't assume anything about real estate without making an effort first.

Retail and Wholesale

D o you love clothes? Do linens, cookware, and beautiful furniture appeal to you just as much if not more? Are you ahead of the curve in music and books? Do you think that human behavior, particularly human buying behavior, is intriguing and ultimately what marketing is really all about? Is 40 percent off all merchandise a big enough incentive for you to work just about anywhere, for just about any pay?

If the answers are yes, a lot of job seekers would agree with you; retail executive-training programs are crammed with energetic twentysomethings, all hoping to be sales and merchandise managers, buyers, and marketers. But the retail and wholesale world is much larger than that. According to the U.S. Department of Labor, twenty-eight million people in the United States were employed in these two sectors in 1998 (that's approximately one in every four workers!). Most of these people are, of course, salespeople and clerks. However, the industry also has opportunities for people interested in determining what goods will be sold; in getting them to the right place at the right time; and in managing the operations, finances, and administration of retail companies. There are several significant trends that will affect the market for job seekers

LEE KASTEN

OCCUPATION: Senior buyer

YEARS IN BUSINESS: 9

AGE: 37

EDUCATION: BA in sociology, UCLA

CERTIFICATION: None

SIZE OF COMPANY: Privately held specialty store with 85 locations nationwide

HOURS PER WEEK: 50, 8:00 A.M. to 6:30 P.M.; 1 hour for lunch

ANNUAL SALARY: $75,000

How did you get your job?

I began as a department manager in a department store and then moved into buying. Today, there are a variety of ways to get into it. Knowing someone always helps, but starting in another operational area and transferring into buying is still an effective and common entry point. Some people can get into buying right out of college, but they generally have an education tailored to this kind of work, such as a business or even a retailing degree.

Describe a typical day.

Because I am a merchant rather than a buyer, my days may be less varied and hectic than those of a traditional buyer. The reason for that lies in the distinction between merchant and buyer. A buyer buys, whereas a merchant selects merchandise and participates in the design and development of the product. More and more stores are turning to private labeling, which means that skills beyond buying are necessary to create a product that will appeal to a specific store's customer. The term "buyer" is becoming obsolete, since it no longer fully describes what is required of you in this position at many stores. Here's what a typical day looks like:

9:00   I usually start by reviewing inventory levels. If they're higher or lower than expected, I need to find out why and talk to the people responsible.

10:00   Next I spend some time going over various sales-analysis reports and sales trends. Planners create specific reports at the merchant's request, and I spend the majority of my time with those reports to learn what's in the stores, what's on its way, what we need.

11:00   Realize from my reading that we're going to have to make a few important changes. Assuming that trends will not change much, especially within a season, is the biggest mistake a merchant can make. Constant, ongoing analysis is necessary to stay on top of what the customer wants and what the customer will buy.

12:00   Lots of phone calls in the afternoon. My position does not require me to deal with many vendors, because we develop in-house most of what we sell in-house. But I do work with merchants and buyers who still acquire most of their merchandise from the outside. This means they travel quite a bit and are on the phone for the better part of the day. I have to travel only about one

in this industry. Although the $727 billion retail industry has enjoyed robust growth, averaging 4 percent per year between 1992 and 1996, experts call for the growth to slow. In particular, many point to the fact that retail space has grown at four times the rate of sales as an indication that there will be a shakeout in the industry in the next several years.

Other significant trends include a change in the retail landscape as new store categories start to dominate the marketplace. Discounters (Wal-Mart, Kmart, and Target), mass retailers (Costco), "category killers" (Home Depot, Barnes & Noble, Staples), and specialty retailers (J. Crew, Coach) have all developed successful retail models. At the same time, smaller mom-and-pop stores and traditional department stores have found the competition intense. This has contributed to a third trend in the industry: consolidation among players. Finally, nontraditional retail concepts have had an increasingly large impact on the way people shop.

month out of the year, which isn't much compared to my counterparts. Most of them travel roughly three or four months out of every year.

6:00: Though often I go home much later than this, especially if there are meetings or I have more reading to do, I try to leave at a reasonable hour when I don't have a lot of pressing commitments.

What are your career aspirations?

I have endured the long hours, low pay, and grueling work, so I am finally at a point where I am paid well and have some semblance of a personal life. My aspirations now are to maintain what I have!

What kinds of people do well in this business?

You must love fashion. You have to enjoy studying all the fashion magazines, because depending on an editor's loyalty or affiliation, what one magazine presents may not be indicative of a trend. Nobody measures you by how well you dress or what good taste you have. The merchandise you buy has to sell and make profits for the company. You have to be bottom-line oriented. You must also accept the notion that this is a career rather than a job. Viewing it as a job will cause you to burn out quickly. Your passion has to drive you. You need to be competitive, thick-skinned, and confident. You have to tolerate humiliation, handle criticism delivered in the most degrading manner possible, and love it enough to persevere. If you don't make your sales plan one month, you should immediately strategize how you'll make it the next month. This business can be good to people who are ambitious and hungry. If you eat and sleep the business, you will move up quickly and make more money.

What do you really like about your job?

I love the challenge of living on the edge. I never really know if I will make my sales plan. I like the specific goal of trying to make money for the company and managing that process myself. The environment meshes well with my achievement work ethic. I also like the fact that this business financially rewards those who meet their goals.

What do you dislike?

Many managers display a tremendous lack of sensitivity for our personal lives; meetings are often called at five or six o'clock in the evening. You find that you live the same kind of life as the person you report to. If that person has no balance in his or her life, neither will you, unfortunately.

What is the biggest misconception about this job?

People think it's fun to have a job where you shop all day. That's not what this is all about. They also believe it's a glamorous job because they associate it with glossy fashion magazines. There is very little that is glamorous about this work.

How can someone get a job like yours?

This company, like many smaller retailers, would probably only hire merchants and buyers who had gained some experience with the bigger retailers. People right out of school have a better chance of getting hired with a large store which has the training resources. So, my advice would be to start with the big guys. They are also more likely to have internships and training programs.

Potentially the most significant of these is the advent of the Internet, which has quickly achieved widespread acceptance as a retail channel.

These trends suggest that there will be significant dislocations as the landscape changes and that layoffs will occur as a result of consolidation and automation of a number of functions. But this also means that there will be opportunities for businesspeople able to navigate through the troubled waters and for people who can get products to consumers in creative ways. Among other areas, the following should be in high demand: distribution specialists and merchandise planners; buyers with product development and private-label experience; anyone who understands data-interpretation technology and tracking systems such as Quick Response, Electronic Data Interchange, and POS terminals; and all you managers with either e-commerce or overseas marketing expertise.

Retailing and wholesaling cover a lot of consumer goods; we'll focus here on three areas: general merchandise, apparel, and furniture. These categories include computers, clothes, sports equipment, beauty products, jewelry, and home furnishings, but leave out food, autos, and building materials. Most online sales efforts thus far are simply electronic extensions of one of the categories listed below or mentioned in the overview. Here are the main types of employers you should be aware of:

Wholesalers

Wholesalers are often called middlemen because they bridge the gap between manufacturer and retailer. A wholesaler can be a manufacturer's representative or the liaison that works to match merchandise to retailers. Their ranks are dwindling in apparel and home furnishings as retail buyers increasingly use electronic purchasing and inventory-tracking systems, eliminating the need to order through wholesalers. The buyers are also less dependent on the wholesalers to scour the markets. But the major players in technology want to concentrate on manufacturing, not sales. Consequently, huge distributors of computer technology exist to take orders from retailers.

Department Stores

A few years ago, names like Sears, JC Penney, Macy's, and Montgomery Ward dominated malls and downtowns all over America. Over the last decade or so, however, the department stores have suffered. In part this is a result of increased competition and changing shopping patterns. It has also come from the financial burden of companies that acquired competitors and grew too soon. It's unlikely that these players will disappear from the market. However, expect more bumps as the strong get stronger and the weak get absorbed.

Discount Stores

These are giants such as Wal-Mart, the largest retailer in the world, and warehouses such as Costco. Originally set up to serve members only, the deep discounters now face competition from category killers, nonmembership warehouses, and mass merchandisers like Ross. Even more alarming is the growing realization among their harried shoppers that traipsing through endless aisles of merchandise just to buy a roll of tape and some underwear isn't worth the savings. Discount stores and warehouse jobs will teach you a lot about inventory, bulk-purchase sales, and customer behavior, but their future may be too uncertain to offer solid career prospects for many younger jobs seekers.

Category Killers

These are the giant retailers that dominate one area of merchandise (Office Depot, Tower Records, and The Sports Authority). They are able to buy bathroom tiles, file cabinets, electronic goods, or pet food in such huge volume that they can then sell them at prices even fairly large competitors can't match. The outlook for this category is better than for many of the more general discounters, but the same employment caveats apply. For most job seekers, these companies offer "earn and learn" experiences with vendors and distributors, before you move onward and upward.

Specialty Stores

These include Crate & Barrel, the Body Shop, and Victoria's Secret. These stores concentrate on one type of merchandise and offer it in some manner that makes it "special." Some are very high end (Louis Vuitton), others cater to the price-conscious masses (Old Navy). Many are so successful that department stores have started to emulate their buying, marketing, and merchandise-display strategies. Industry experts predict continued growth in this segment, particularly for home furnishings, and it seems to attract many of the best and brightest in retail. Promotion and responsibility come quickly to those willing to work hard, and in many of these stores, the heavy hand of bureaucracy weighs less heavily than in other types.

What's Great

First on the Block

In retailing and wholesaling, you get to see what's coming before the consumer does. There's something exciting about being the first to know what's new. For anyone interested in music or software, this is an even stronger draw than it is for the clothes mavens. Depending on where you work, this can also mean access to designer showrooms, fashion shows, and gala parties where designers are the guests of honor.

Such a Deal

Employee discounts with retailers range anywhere from 10 percent to a whopping 40 percent. This intoxicating fact of life is often the basis for employee loyalty, particularly in high-end apparel and home-furnishings. One insider who works in jewelry hastens to mention that she uses these discounts mostly for Christmas and birthdays, not for herself. "I actually don't wear much [jewelry] at all," she admits, "but I have friends who think this job is wonderful!"

Fly by Night

In the middle employment ranks of this industry, travel to the major markets is a given: New York, Los Angeles, Hong Kong, to name a few. Even if you're not in haute couture, many buyers also go to Paris and Milan at least once a year, if not more often, just to keep abreast of international trends in clothes and accessories. Where you go will depend on what you buy or sell, but rest assured you'll be traveling somewhere.

Up the Down Escalator

Something about this business attracts zany personalities: actors, writers, students, musicians, and other interesting types who need steady part-time work. If you like order, predictability, and decorum, you probably won't be happy in retailing. A rather twisted sense of humor thrives in this environment.

Oh, You Wanted Money Too?

In retail, especially apparel, expect to work ten- and twelve-hour days and expect inadequate compensation for it—as in $9 to $12 an hour. To add insult to injury, you'll most likely work weekends, and all the holidays everyone else in the world gets off. Wholesale jobs tend to pay a bit more at the entry level because of the commission structure. Decent salaries don't begin on the retail side until you become a buyer, and even then, they aren't great.

Quickly, Now! Quickly!

It just looks glamorous. If you're a retailer, you spend a good portion of your day haranguing vendors about missed shipping dates. Expect to do a lot of schlepping as well, through airports, through the stores, even through those so-called gala parties. Buyers and managers also have to be able to process information quickly and then act. If you can't handle a fair amount of pressure, if you don't like people screaming at you ("for no apparent reason, they just seem to scream a lot," says one insider), then this is not a career path to pursue.

Chapter 11: In Which You Lose Your Job

There's not much job security in this business right now. Due to over expansion in recent years in most segments of the industry and to mounting consumer debt, bankruptcies are on the rise. The famous ones include Woolworth and Montgomery Ward, but innumerable smaller stores have closed their doors in the past decade as well. Designers are also faring badly. Anne Klein, Adrienne Vittadini, Isaac Mizrahi, and Kenar are among the big names which are either for sale or out of business. This is risky business. High stakes, high reward, even higher rates of failure.

Inventory Shrinkage

This is the polite way to say shoplifting, vendor fraud, and employee theft. This is a $43.7 billion problem and guess who accounts for most of it. That's right, employees, not lawless shoppers. If inventory is missing, you are indeed the first and most logical suspect. Many of these places have less bureaucracy and fewer rules than corporate environments, but trust is earned and even then not automatic. Too often, one insider notes, "You're guilty till you're proven innocent, and usually it's impossible to prove you're innocent."

KEY JOBS

Many jobs in retail and wholesale don't require a college degree, particularly if you did well in one of the many high-school work-study programs available around the country. Those with college degrees are eligible for the executive-track management-training programs that most large chain and department stores offer. (Increasingly, the successful specialty stores do as well.) More people find entry-level jobs in retailing than any other industry, according to the U.S. Department of Labor.

Assistant Buyer

If buying is your goal, this is where you begin. Assistant buyers typically help in merchandise selection, deal with vendors, write orders, and learn how to operate within a budget. You'll need a good head for numbers and the ability to juggle too little time and too much information in stressful situations. Be advised that some retailers are even eliminating this position, relying instead on automated processes for some of the more mundane order-taking, delivery, and follow-up aspects of this job. Most assistant buyers have a college degree, and many major in retail management or business. Salary range: $18,000 to $25,000.

Buyer

This is the person who is involved with and responsible for planning sales, monitoring inventory, selecting the merchandise, and writing and pricing orders to vendors. Being a buyer is the ultimate exercise in living on a budget. You'll be told what you have to spend for a season, and your job will be to get the most and best for your buck. Buyers get their positions after spending two to five years as an assistant or by completing a management-training program sponsored by the store. A lot of people want this job, despite its increased emphasis on sales and inventory management and the relatively low pay. Be prepared for some fairly stiff competition. Salary range: $28,000 to $36,000.

Sales Associate

Retail sales can be lucrative with certain high-end retailers or with electronics because of the generous commissions, but to qualify, you'll need to be well versed in the products you're selling. This is less true for most noncommissioned sales positions. If you like pleasing people and don't mind standing most of the day, this job offers flexibility and an entrance into retailing. Students and others in need of part-time or seasonal work make up a full third of these sales teams. A college degree is rarely required for these positions, and those who work hard and do well can usually advance within a few years to sales or department manager or, in larger organizations, a management-training program. Salary range: $10,000 to $18,000, not including commission.

Retail Management Trainee

If you're accepted into a store's management training program, this is your title for the four to nine months you're learning merchandising, finance, marketing, operations, and personnel management. Typically, sales associates and others who excel in various departments get first crack at these programs, though company recruiters hire college grads and other outside experienced talent as well for the openings that remain. Salary range: $18,000 to $24,000.

Department or Sales Manager

For management training program graduates and for very successful sales associates, this is typically the first rung in the retail ladder. This is one of the lowest levels of management, but a useful one for those who want a long-term career in the industry. Department managers supervise the sales staff, control the sales floor inventory, and often work closely with buyers. A college degree is rarely required for this position; candidates need only to prove they can sell, work with people well, and keep careful track of inventory. As technology becomes increas-

REAL PEOPLE PROFILE

ROSEANNE ZABENOFF

OCCUPATION:
Sales representative

YEARS IN BUSINESS: 5

AGE: 33

EDUCATION: BS in sociology, New York University

HOURS PER WEEK:
40, 8:30 A.M. to 5:30 P.M.;
30 minutes for lunch

SIZE OF COMPANY: 9

CERTIFICATION: None

ANNUAL SALARY:
$50,000

How did you get your job?

Through another sales job actually. I was working in a furniture manufacturer's showroom. I'd been doing it for about two years and reached about as high a level as I was going to get. I was also a little bored and wanted a challenge. Working out of my own home really appealed to me.

Describe a typical day.

8:30   Get up, have breakfast, and then move over to my office area.

9:00   Make several phone calls. Sometimes I talk to established contacts; other times, to customer service. Between calls, I begin organizing samples I'll need to bring out on the road. Start writing up orders I know are probably solid.

10:00   Jot down some thoughts about developing strategies to meet my quota. My quota is my sales goal. It varies from month to month and is based on past history. Certain months are much busier in wholesale. By early November, I've already lived though Christmas. January-

February and August-September are busiest.

10:30   Take off to make some calls. I usually see two to three customers a day on the road and try to hit three different types of retailers. I always plan in advance what I'm going to show them. Some of relationships started at gift shows, but I also just pop in to introduce myself. Cold calling is about 15 percent of my work

12:00   Lunch is always at home or in my car. I almost never take a long, leisurely lunch. I do occasionally schmooze with clients, but people in retail are really busy. You're lucky if you can get an hour of their time. After an hour, most lose all ability to focus.

12:30   Back on the road. Stop by to see one particularly close contact, someone I met at a show years ago. I've actually been interacting with same people for five years now, so with many of them we have a real friendship.

2:00   Stop to make a call to one of my bosses about one of our

ingly a part of sales and customer analysis, a facility with data and systems is also a big plus. Salary range: $18,000 to $25,000.

Sales Representative or Vendor

These are the people who "move" merchandise from manufacturer to retailer. Sometimes they represent the manufacturer, sometimes they are the middlemen. The rise in private labels and computerized ordering systems has forced many middlemen into new careers. But electronics and computers are a notable exception, as they still rely heavily on middlemen to get their product to the retail market. A strong customer-service ethic is necessary to do this job well. The more you sell, the more likely you'll get promoted, which means hungry salespeople experience the fastest career movement. As you move up, your commission base improves as well. A college degree is rarely required for this position; an aggressive, energetic, not easily discouraged personality is a must. Salary range: $21,000 to $27,000.

manufacturers. Need to know if there's been a change in the line. I generally represent fifteen to twenty different manufacturers. I meet them at the various shows I go to and usually the manufacturers approach us. The company has two principals who set up all relationships, and I don't deal with them directly as a rule.

4:00   Read through a manufacturer's report and review where we are in terms of their sales numbers and goals.

5:30   Everyone goes home around now, so I usually quit, too. It seems like a short day, but selling is hard, and you can't do it if you're tired. I try to quit while I'm ahead.

What are your career aspirations?

Hopefully I won't be doing this at all in five years. I'm actually a musician and this job is a very good way to pay the bills. Not much stress and good experience. Someday I'd really like to administer a volunteer program and play my guitar. But no matter what you do, it's more effec-tive if you know how to sell. I'm hoping this will help me a lot in whatever I do next.

What kinds of people do well in this business?

People who are very numbers ori-ented. And a people person who likes dealing constantly with a lot of different types. You can't be driven by the money. I get excited by products I'm selling and the interactions I have with people. Outside interests are actually a big help. You can't get too caught up in this stuff or take it too much to heart when you're not sell-ing well.

What do you really like about your job?

I enjoy working with people. I really like the freedom and the great rela-tionships that I have built. I also like people I work with, though what I really love is being able to work at home and on the road.

What do you dislike?

I dislike feeling that you can never do enough. I could work twenty-four hours a day, and there would still be more to do. I also dislike the unpre-dictability. This is a strictly commission basis and sometimes I wish I just had a regular paycheck.

What is the biggest misconception about your job?

That sales reps are lazy. I've been doing this for a while, and I don't know any myself . . . well, maybe one who was a jerk, but he's long gone.

How can someone get a job like yours?

Obviously sales experience is very important. You also need to know what's out there in terms of products. Being familiar with the market is key. If you're a big shopper, you'll like this job.

Merchandise Manager

Often known as a divisional merchandise manager (DMM), this job oversees several merchandise departments and their respective buyers. Buyers typically move into this position after six to ten years. They help to ensure consistent quality, the proper amount of merchandise, and value and price points to customers. They also manage vendor relations, market visits, and the ongoing education and development of their buying teams. This is a senior slot, and if you do well, your next step is the upper ranks of executive retail management. Salary range: $46,000 to $55,000.

Market Analyst

Both retail and wholesale have a growing need for accurate and ongoing analysis of what customers are buying; when and how they're buying; and what all the data mean for buyers, advertisers, and strategic planning. Marketing majors who understand how to model demographic information and analyze the volumes of transactional data generated by customer purchases will find numerous opportunities in this field, both inside large companies and in a proliferating number of independent research groups. Salary range: $25,000 to $40,000.

Director of Marketing

Many retailers are now focusing on loyalty programs and efforts to more accurately predict their customers needs and behavior. Seen as distinctly separate from sales, marketing directors and their staff manage external research and coordinate all the internal sources of information to retain their best customers and attract new ones. This is an increasingly visible slot, and e-commerce is now an integral part of the job. Salary range: $55,000 and up.

Information Technology

Someone has to develop, maintain, and fine-tune all the electronic systems that track goods from warehouse to customer to returns desk. Even very small operations now rely heavily on Quick Response and EDI. For those of you interested in networks and systems, this is still a relatively open arena. As online opportunities emerge, those with both technical and e-commerce experience will be in ever greater demand. Salary range: $30,000 and up.

GETTING HIRED

Many retailers offer internships that often develop into buying positions or a place in their management-training programs. Your high school or college may also offer similar arrangements with selected retailers. Here's what most employers look for when they hire at all levels:

- People skills. With the ever-increasing focus on keeping customers happy, you need to enjoy serving people and be perpetually alert as to how to serve them better. There is also a lot of teamwork in these jobs, often under fairly stressful conditions.

- Flexibility. These marketplaces are constantly changing and so are the customers. The more attuned you are to the shifts, the more successful your retailing career will be. Resourcefulness under pressure counts as a key part of flexibility.

- Decisiveness. You need to be self-motivated and aggressive—whether you're making a sale or improving the new orders and transactions systems. And when you take on new responsibilities or make decisions under deadline pressure and they don't work out, you have to know how to handle the repercussions.

- Analytical skills. Perhaps even more sought after than the ability to sell just about anything to just about anyone are the problem-solving and data-analysis skills that marketing needs. You're also eminently hirable these days if you understand technology and enjoy the architecture of systems and networks.

- Loyalty and enthusiasm. Love the store, love the merchandise it sells, love the prestige and cachet of your particular niche in the industry. The pay is low, the hours are long, and advancement is never easy. Insiders are unanimous: If you'd buy what this company is selling, you're a much stronger potential hire.

Semiconductors

Gordon Moore, one of Intel's founders, said the power of semiconductors would double every eighteen months. Known throughout the industry as Moore's Law, this pronouncement has largely held true since he made it in 1965. By virtue of this doubling—and the applications which this increase in power has made possible—the semiconductor industry has thrived: $153 billion worldwide and about $50 billion in the United States in 1997. Semiconductors have accounted for roughly 8 percent of the total growth of the U.S. manufacturing sector since 1991, and experts predict a 17 percent jump in revenues by 2000.

The industry is hungry for trained workers. The majority of jobs go to chip designers with computer science or electrical engineering degrees, but there are other opportunities in machine design, factory design, finance, marketing, operations, purchasing, information technology, and strategic planning. Chemical engineers and technicians find work in manufacturing. Those with backgrounds in chemistry, physics, and other physical sciences can find jobs making semiconductor materials and packaging. On the marketing side, there are plenty of sales and marketing jobs—especially for individuals with technical backgrounds. Like other high-tech industries, this is a fast-paced, rapidly changing field, and you can

REAL PEOPLE PROFILE

JAMES SEARLE

OCCUPATION: VP of marketing for a semiconductor equipment manufacturer

YEARS IN BUSINESS: 11

AGE: 39

EDUCATION: BS in engineering, UC Berkeley; MBA, Andersen School of Business

HOURS PER WEEK: 60, 7:00 A.M. to 7:00 P.M.; 1 hour for lunch

SIZE OF COMPANY: 6,000

CERTIFICATION: None

ANNUAL SALARY: $160,000, with stock options and a $50,000–$100,000 year-end bonus

How did you get your job?

I started out as a process engineer for a chip maker. I did that for two years before going to business school. After business school, I was recruited by a person who I worked with at the company where I worked before business school. This is pretty typical. (As an equipment manufacturer, we're selling to semiconductor companies, and we often look to them for prospective employees; sometimes this gets us into trouble.) I started out as an applications engineer and moved up from there.

Describe a typical day.

7:00 Arrive at work and check e-mail and voice mail. E-mail people in the factory; talk to customers. Need to schedule meetings for a trip I'm taking at the beginning of next week. The technology in this industry changes quickly. We work with all types of manufacturers, and we're working with the most advanced technology, so it requires a dynamic and responsive organization. No day is like any other and the challenges are always changing.

9:00 Customer meeting. I do a lot of customer meetings, taking care of customers who are visiting our factories and checking out our equipment. I don't ever feel like I spend enough time with our customers. Generally, they take up 30 to 40 percent of my time. The sale cycle is pretty long. We sell capital equipment for more than a million dollars a shot. There are a number of technical decision makers and others in charge of the budget, and we talk to them all. When I go on the road, I spend time with our sales force. I'll also spend time with customers, educating them, dissuading them from buying competitors' products, persuading them to buy ours.

11:00 Meet with engineers. I spend a lot of time working with engineers to drive new product development, either talking over enhancements to new products or new product definition. There are different aspects of this depending on where the product is in its lifecycle. Marketing works closely with engineering to give a clear definition of what the product is going to look like. Marketing drives the product introduction, determines who we're going to work with, and involves managing that process as the product ships. We make sure the bugs are fixed during

expect to work hard; workweeks often exceed fifty hours. In return, you'll make a competitive salary and can expect stock options—and if you land at the next Intel, these could quickly make you rich.

Semiconductors power everything from PCs and cellular phones to aircraft navigational systems and elevators. Increasingly, they are showing up in every imaginable electronic consumer good, from toys to refrigerators. Due in part to the capital-intensive nature of semiconductor manufacturers, the industry regularly faces temporary slumps and shakeouts. The one which just occurred, compounded by the Asian financial crisis, hurt memory chip makers in particular. Though the Semiconductor Industry Association projects that in 1998 sales would decrease 1.8 percent from 1997, the industry should grow in 1999 and over the long term—as will the industry's thirst for engineers and other qualified

alpha and beta testing, do PR, get articles in tech journals. It's not too different from other marketing jobs in high tech.

3:00 Conference call with people in the factory. I spend some time every day communicating via e-mail and conference calls with people in the factory.

5:30 Plan for a trip later this month in Asia. About 40 percent of the market is in the U.S., and a lot of the rest is in Asia. To be competitive you need to be a player worldwide and bring in enough revenues to drive R&D for the next phase of products. It's very cyclical. In general, the worldwide demand for electronics is growing, but it grows in fits and starts. There's a big difference in chip manufacturing based on oversupply or undersupply. The oversupply of memory chips has hurt profitability of a lot of chip makers, which trickles down to hurt us at the tail of the cycle and is a unique part of our industry. Semiconductor manufacturing averages 20 percent growth, but it's uneven. It can be 50 percent one year, then it contracts the next. This leads to a lot of challenges for managing the business.

7:00 Go home.

What are your career aspirations?

I would like to be a general manager or run a business.

What kinds of people do well in this business?

Generally people that either have a technical or technology background or are interested in learning. It's hard to be successful unless you can be comfortable with the technology. That usually translates into having a computer science or electrical engineering degree as an undergrad.

What do you really like about your job?

The challenge of it, because it changes quickly and it is growing fast. That causes a lot of opportunities both professionally and personally. It means there's never a dull moment.

What do you dislike?

There's some politics and bureaucracy in any mid- to large-size company that makes decision making slower than it needs to be sometimes. Nor does it allow the autonomy some of us would like.

What is the biggest misconception about this job?

The critical thing is to understand what marketing means at a specific company. A lot of people go to business school and become interested in marketing. You need to look at who is running the company and see if they are technology driven or customer driven. Also, what role does the customer play in new product development? If you're not able to quickly innovate and develop new products, you're going to be out of a job. Understanding how a company does that is pretty important.

How can someone get a job like yours?

Marketing in this business is pretty industry specific. Generally we hire people either from other semiconductor equipment companies or from semiconductor makers, who are our customers. We hire both out of business school and undergrad to work in entry-level roles in engineering, manufacturing, and customer support. Experience managing people is important and knowledge of the semiconductor business is useful. Experience as a process engineer or in product marketing, or general high-tech marketing experience can lead to my job.

personnel. Overall, this is a robust segment creating products with an increasing number of applications.

The largest share of the market—about 74 percent—is in integrated circuits (IC). These devices combine millions of transistors, go by different names, and perform a wide range of functions; logic chips do mathematical calculations, memory chips remember information, microprocessors run computers and microcontrollers run electronic devices such as VCRs. Within the IC world, PC microprocessors account for the largest part of the market. Intel is the industry leader, holding 90 percent of the desktop market. Other key players include Advanced Micro Devices, Motorola, and Cyrix. A smaller but faster-growing segment is digital signal microprocessors, the stand-alone microprocessors used in cell phones and PC modems, which some estimate will be a $50 billion market in the next decade. Texas Instruments owns 40 percent of this market, with Lucent Technologies, Analog Devices, and Motorola chasing it. More and more intellectual property is going onto chips, increasing their functions and giving them even greater applications, especially in consumer electronics. This industry segment should grow huge as more digital products go to market.

How It Breaks Down

Testing and assembly operations—both labor-intensive activities—are generally located in Asian countries and other places where labor and materials are cheap. If you want to travel, get into assembly or packaging. Fabrication and R&D generally take place in the United States and other industrial countries, because both require a technically sophisticated workforce attuned to American market needs. Here's a more detailed breakdown of the industry:

Fabs

From the early days of the industry, talented engineers have had a passport to travel—ex–Fairchild Semiconductor execs (including Moore) left to form companies like Intel. Even today, top design engineers with great ideas can go into business for themselves, setting up a small design shop and selling their design—rather than manufacturing services. However, over the last several decades, the cost of going into—or staying in—the manufacturing end of the business has become huge. Today, a fab, or chip factory, costs more than $1 billion to build. As a result, this forms its own segment of the industry and is populated by a relatively small number of huge players, including the microprocessor and memory chip makers (Intel, Motorola, Zilog, Texas Instruments, Micron, and Asian makers) and ASIC (Application Specific IC) makers like LSI and VLSI.

Fabless

At the other end of the spectrum are the fabless shops, which tend to focus on design rather than manufacturing. These companies either outsource production of their chips to the companies with fabs or rely on sales of intellectual property (that is, chip design) to the growing number of companies seeking to license specific designs. The fabless segment includes makers of PLD (programmable logic devices—chips that can be programmed after being created), such as Altera, Xilinx, and Lattice, as well as the numerous small design shops that have been started by design engineers who have left the bigger players. Although these companies lack the stability of the bigger companies in the mature segments, there are more possibilities for growth here and a good likelihood that they might be acquired by one of the bigger companies.

The Semiconductor Manufacturing Equipment Industry

The semiconductor industry relies on the $28 billion semiconductor manufacturing equipment (SME) industry for the equipment used to manufacture and test semiconductors. This industry follows the rough four-year boom-and-bust cycle of the semiconductor market. Some of its leading players are Applied Materials, which makes wafer-fabrication equipment; Etec, which produces the equipment used for photolithography mask patterns; Cadence Design Systems and Mentor Graphics, which focus on Electronic Design Automation (a rapidly growing segment); and Photronics, which creates the quartz plates used as stencils to transfer circuit patterns onto wafers during production. A subset of the SME industry is testing equipment; KLA-Tencor and Teradyne are leaders in this area. Finally, an overview of the industry would be incomplete without mentioning the companies that manufacture packaging such as Integrated Packaging Assembly and distributors such as Arrow Electronics.

What's Great

The Challenge

On both the marketing and the engineering sides of the semiconductor industry, you'll be forced to adapt to new technologies and competitive topographies. "If you're someone who values a lot of change, classic technology trends and strategies, there's a whole lot of it here," says an insider. And the intellectual challenge of creating a new chip can be exhilarating. "[This business is all about] constantly evolving and adapting and introducing new technologies that can shape and change the world," says another insider.

Triple 7s

One thing driving the companies and players in this industry is the opportunity to hit the jackpot. Create a successful new chip and you'll turn your company into a major player. "It's a mobile workforce and everybody's chasing the magic buck," says an insider. This can cause trouble with your team, but it also can make you rich. If you're in the right place at the right time, you may be able to create a design for a next-generation chip and make your company, and yourself, rich in the process.

Continuing Ed

If you're interested in a particular area of study that dovetails with the semiconductor industry, those in development can find exceptional opportunities to learn. To begin, the equipment is top-of-the-line. "There are some things that I would have drooled to get my hands on when I was in graduate school," says one developmental engineer. And unlike many academic programs, the spirit of cooperation is high: "Everyone works toward a common goal." The downside? "We're very, very empirical at times because the time pressure is so strong."

What's to Hate

Keeping Up

If you can't adapt to new technologies quickly and aren't willing to throw away outdated designs, this may not be the industry for you. "It's rapidly changing," says an insider. "You have to be able to deal with it. The chip industry is definitely accelerating quite a bit as the tools get easier. Just keeping up with that change can be tough."

The Men's Club

An insider puts it bluntly: "There are no women in the profession." That may be an overstatement—there are women here, especially in marketing—but overall, the semiconductor industry is a male game. This can make work less interesting if you're a man and hugely frustrating if you're a woman who wants female role models.

Hours

The semiconductor industry, like most of the high-tech world, can be taxing and exhausting. You'll work long hours—insiders estimate ten or eleven a day. That can be a bummer, at least until your company's IPO is a huge success and you can turn in your silicon for gold. Says an insider, "The hours suck."

KEY JOBS

Jobs fall into two general areas: technical and nontechnical, or business. About 80 percent of the jobs in this industry are on the technical side. Salary levels listed below are base salaries only; compensation generally exceeds the base. And don't forget those options. "Compensation in this sector has a lot to do with stocks," says an insider. Performance bonuses are also common.

Design Engineer

Design engineers work on chip designs on the software or hardware side. The position includes computer-aided design (CAD), digital signal processor (DSP) design, application-specific integrated circuit (ASIC) design, logic design, and microprocessor design jobs, among others. Integrated circuit design pays better than other design jobs in the high-tech sector. This position generally requires a bachelor's or master's in electrical engineering or computer science. Salary range: $40,000 to $60,000 to start. Those with two or three years' experience, depending on their specialty, can earn up to $85,000. Really good PhDs can make more. "The sky's the limit," says an insider. Those with management responsibilities, and three to ten years under their belts, may well be paid in the six figures.

Process Engineer

Process engineers work on photolithography, diffusion, etching, implant, thin films, or other processes that go into developing semiconductor materials and manufacturing processes at equipment manufacturers or fabrication facilities. Backgrounds required for these positions include physical sciences, chemical engineering, and electrical engineering, with experience in some aspect of the semiconductor manufacturing process. Salary range: $65,000 to $85,000 to start.

Product Engineer or Test Engineer

Test engineers evaluate chip designs, creating programs to test designs. Product engineers make sure the product tests out and often work with others in design engineering and on the applications side to release a new product; they also seek out ways to make production processes more efficient. The job generally requires a background in computer science and electrical engineering and experience in design. Salary range: $50,000 and up.

Designer or Content Developer

This role has several titles and in the past was often shared by the project manager, senior programmers, and others on the development team. But now usually one person is in charge of the user experience and logic flow—how all the text, graphics, sound, and other information fit together. Like a magazine with a very good art director, well-designed content feels natural, inviting, and easily understandable. Software companies are increasingly willing to spend time and money finding just the right writer, artist, or interface expert with significant technical experience for this slot. Salary range: $55,000 to $80,000.

Product Development Engineer

Product development engineers develop; this can be test equipment, manufacturing equipment, and semiconductor products. The job generally requires a PhD and involves working with a lot of data, generally in a lab. Material-science backgrounds, particularly chemical engineering backgrounds, are required. Salary range: $60,000 to start; managers with three to ten years of experience may make $80,000 to $100,000 or more.

Field Service Engineer

Field service engineers install, repair, and maintain semiconductor equipment for equipment manufacturers and their customers. They also train customers in using the equipment. Experience in semiconductor equipment manufacturing and operation is required. Salary range: $60,000 and up.

Applications Engineer

This job is in the marketing department, although it requires technical know-how. Applications engineers work with customers, demonstrating equipment or fine-tuning it to customer specifications. Requires two to five years experience. Salary range: $50,000 to $75,000.

Project Manager or Product Manager

This position manages a cross-functional team, acting as a mini–general manager of a product while managing pricing, promotion, and definition; determining customers; and facing competition. The project manager enhances and manages the product over time. This job requires five years experience or an MBA and a technical background. Salary range: $60,000 to $90,000.

Account Manager

This is a sales job. Account managers manage existing accounts and seek out opportunities to develop relationships with new accounts for both equipment and chip makers. A technical background in the semiconductor industry or another sales position in the high-tech sector is necessary. Salary range: Those with two or three years' experience in industry start at $65,000 to $85,000, base plus commissions; sales managers, responsible for selling equipment or processes, start at $90,000, plus commissions.

REAL PEOPLE PROFILE

LARRY VOCINI

OCCUPATION:
Fabless chip designer

YEARS IN BUSINESS: 3½

AGE: 31

EDUCATION: BS in engineering, University of Pennsylvania; MA in electrical engineering, specializing in logic design, chip design, and computer architecture, Stanford University

HOURS PER WEEK:
50 to 70, 9:00 A.M. to 8:00 P.M.; 30 minutes for lunch

SIZE OF COMPANY: 200

CERTIFICATION: None

ANNUAL SALARY: $80,000

How did you get your job?

Through the university résumé bank. I submitted my name, résumé, and career objective to the electrical engineering career planning office. They publish this. Companies like the one I'm now at buy it. The companies browse the résumés and contact the people with résumés who match their needs.

Describe a typical day.

9:00   In general, the first thing I do is check e-mails and voice mails. I usually get about three or four e-mails when I come in and maybe five or six throughout the day.

9:30   Depending upon where we are in the product cycle, I'll be doing one of three things: designing new chips, debugging old chips, writing test software. I'm mostly doing design work. The only thing you need to do is interface with others who are creating designs. The process of designing chips is pretty straightforward. Once we have a description of the chip to design (usually after getting feedback from the project

manager, marketing, and software engineers), we design the overall chip architecture. Once every member of the design team agrees with the architecture, we implement the design. We use Verilog to describe the chip architecture and behaviors. Verilog is a hardware description language (HDL). Once we have a Verilog RTL model of the chip, we debug and test the model, verifying both its functionality and performance. (RTL is short for Register Transfer Level, which is a way of describing the architecture and behaviors of a design.) Normally we write a lot of C-codes to accomplish this. After we're sure that the chip functionality is correct, then we synthesize the Verilog RTL model into a gate-level model. Normally we use a synthesis tool such as Synopsys to do this. Once we have the gate-level model, we do static timing analysis on the model in order to confirm that the chip can perform at the targeted clock frequency. Finally, after all of the above is done, the chip gate level is ready to be

Management, Director-Level

This could involve managing product managers, planning future product launches, managing strategic-marketing initiatives, or directing field operations. Requires six to ten years experience. Salary range: $90,000 to $150,000.

Business Administration, Entry-Level

This could involve anything from working on financial models to administrative support for others. Requires a four-year degree. Salary range: $30,000 to $40,000.

laid out and mapped into silicon. We usually do one more static timing analysis on the laid-out netlist before the final chip netlist is taped out (that is, sent to fab for manufacture).

11:00 Doing this work, I'm mostly sitting in the office at my computer. Once in a while I'll talk to other members of the group.

12:00 Every two hours or so I like to sit up, walk to the other side of the building, and talk to people. I usually take a half hour for lunch at noon.

4:00 Exercise a half hour. This is one of the great things about design. You don't have to sit in the office waiting for a phone call all day.

4:30 I'll keep working on the chip design until I leave.

8:00 Head home.

What are your career aspirations?

Someday I'd like to be a project manager and hopefully start my own company. But that's years down the road.

What kinds of people do well in this business?

People who have a strong background in math and science.

People who have good quantitative skills. And people who can think independently, solve problems, and explore new things. When I was in school, my emphasis was on computer architecture. Now I'm doing data compression. It's kind of exciting to do new things.

What do you really like about your job?

The thing I like most about the job is I can learn new things. It's exciting to study and understand new stuff that's happening in electrical engineering in general. In design work, you can do your work any time you want. You can go home to work there and take time off if you finish early. I like that flexibility.

What do you dislike?

One thing: in general, I don't like doing repetitive things. After a chip comes back and you have to debug it and run the tests over and over, it's slightly boring. That's a minor dislike.

What is the biggest misconception about this job?

I live in Silicon Valley, so most people are somewhat technical and understand these things. Most of my friends are technical people, and they get what I do. I can't think of a big misconception.

How can someone get a job like yours?

My job requires a background in electrical engineering or computer science. The easiest path is to get a bachelor's or master's degree and take a lot of computer-architecture, logic-design, or circuit-design classes. Anything in addition to that you can learn by yourself by reading books. The most important thing is the electrical engineering or computer science degree. That will open the door for you.

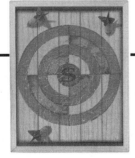

GETTING HIRED

If you want a job in the semiconductor industry, your best bet is to get a degree in computer science or electrical engineering. Electrical engineering degrees have long been the industry standard, but increasingly work is done with software. "If I had my choice between a guy with a pure electrical engineering background, I would rather have a computer scientist, someone who understands C++ and

Perl. You can teach them to use Verilog really easily." Those with a background in the physical sciences should consider working at a fab. To get hired, move up, and move around, here's what you should know:

- Companies want people who are excited to work in the high-tech sector. If you're looking for a job on the corporate or administrative side, you'll need this interest to thrive—and to get hired. Says an insider, "I look for people who basically are very excited about the industry. They really wanted to work in the high-tech sector and can explain why. They don't need to know all the technology."

- Semiconductor companies look for people who can deal with ambiguity. Things change quickly in this industry, and you need to be able to change and learn with it.

- Leadership qualities are at a premium. There are a lot of management positions, and those who can drive and lead teams will be valuable employees.

- More so than other industries, this one's a meritocracy. Once you're in, your degree won't matter; what matters is what you can contribute. There's no hard-and-fast timetable for advancement. If you show you can do the work, you can find an opportunity to do it.

Telecommunications

In 1877 Alexander Graham Bell founded AT&T. Today, the telecommunications industry generates more than $400 billion in revenues in the United States. In 1997 about $106 billion went to telecommunications equipment—voice mail–messaging systems, as well as the transmitters, switches, and routers that send your communications to the right place. A little more than $300 billion went to telecommunication services—the regional Bell operating companies (RBOCs, which include Baby Bells such as Bell Atlantic, BellSouth, and Ameritech); long-distance service providers such as AT&T, Sprint, and MCI Worldcom; and all variety of wireless and data services. Worldwide, telecommunications spending for both services and equipment hit about a trillion dollars in 1997.

All that money represents a lot of phone calls, e-mails, and faxes. It's also good news for job seekers: this industry is hot, and it's going to stay that way for some time to come. Two key factors are fueling the rapid growth and major change the industry is experiencing: regulation and technology. "In some respects, they influence each other," says one industry expert. "It's partly that regulation is changing, abetting technology; but it's also that people use the technology to circumvent the regulation." The Telecommunications Act of 1996

REAL
PEOPLE
PROFILE

YOLANDA VELASQUEZ

OCCUPATION:
Marketing manager for a
telecommunications company

YEARS IN BUSINESS: 6

AGE: 31

EDUCATION: BA in international affairs and Spanish literature, MA in Spanish literature and linguistics, Cal Berkeley; MBA, Monterey Institute

HOURS PER WEEK: 80
(including travel time),
7:30 A.M. to 2:00 P.M.;
30 minutes for lunch

SIZE OF COMPANY:
141,600

CERTIFICATION: None

ANNUAL SALARY: $95,000,
plus $28,000 in bonuses

How did you get your job?

I don't know. I came to a career day here. I was working for a competitor at the time; this company happened to be looking for somebody with my experience.

Describe a typical day.

7:30   Trying to catch up with voice mail and prioritizing on the way to work. Once I arrive, I answer my e-mails.

8:00   The day is very different if I'm traveling or if I'm in the office. If I'm in the office, I go to various meetings. These can be with the sales team, marketing, or marketing communications. If it's a sales meeting, we'll discuss revenue targets, customer deals, requirements from customers, positioning our products, working with financing packages, and how to help service providers drive revenue with our products. We'll also discuss problems and resolutions for what's happened at the customer site. If it's a marketing meeting, then we'll talk about the product requirements that weren't met, implementations that need to happen if we're going to sell a product, and related issues. In a marketing communications

meeting, we'd discuss speaking opportunities (I give presentations and sit on panels at trade shows), marketing collateral, and new products with segmented needs.

10:00   I spend about two weeks out of every month on the road. If I'm traveling, my day would have started at 6:30 or so, and I'd probably have had a breakfast meeting. Then I would have returned to the customer and work with its marketing and technical team, figuring out how to help them use our equipment, making sure it has the right connectivity, and turning the product into something that's going to sell in the marketplace.

12:00   Lunch. My job is to consult with our customers and help them use our products to help themselves. When I'm traveling, I'm usually training a salesperson, who I'll manage. They'll watch me present to customers several times, and then I'll generally watch them work. Eventually I hope to spend more time in the corporate office.

1:00   Generally, I'll spend the afternoon on the same issues I worked on in the morning. On the road, I'll go back to the

deregulated local phone markets with the intent to make telecommunications services—an industry known for its bureaucracy—competitive. So far, the Bells have resisted, trying to prevent outsiders from stealing their captive audience away. Nevertheless, a variety of smaller players—for example, wireless companies using a wireless-local-loop, which circumvents the local phone network—have offered a foreshadowing of the competition to come.

Other technologies, in particular the Internet, are fundamentally transforming this industry. Industry analysts predict that by 2001, 90 percent of traffic over networks will be data—despite the fact that voice traffic is growing at between 8 and 15 percent a year. Over the past few years, this industry has experienced mergers, acquisitions, alliances, and restructurings, and it's not through yet. Global markets are moving toward free-market telecommunications, and

hotel and try to catch up on communications. I need to make sure everything's going smoothly with the team. Usually we'll spend two or three days at the customer site and then go to another customer nearby. At some point in the afternoon, I make it to the hotel gym for a workout.

2:00 If I'm in the office, I'll give feedback to various products and work on others, such as find data on the regional segmented view of the market, identifying our segmented customer targets, and get feedback from different groups of customers. Do some shopping on the way home.

What are your career aspirations?

At some point, I'd like to have more of an international accountability for programs happening across the world and not just one region. After that, I'd like to have my own consulting firm, and do marketing consulting in the telecommunications industry. It's a big opportunity.

What kinds of people do well in this business?

People who are strong willed, entrepreneurial in spirit, who don't wait around for people to tell them what to do, and who can find creative ways around the status quo. People who aren't afraid of hard work and who have a vision of where they see things going and can drive toward that.

What do you really like about your job?

I like that it's challenging. There's new things happening every day. I like finding new ways to do things. I like the area we're in with wireless technology. New applications are being rolled out every quarter; it's exciting to bring these technologies to countries that have not yet had communications.

What do you dislike?

Long hours; I think the strain these have on me in my personal life by not giving me a chance to work toward my personal goals, that's what I don't like most. And the internal politics. There are so many decisions to be made and so many people who have ideas on how things should be done, it's a challenge to deal with the political machinations.

What is the biggest misconception about your job?

That we can solve the problems for everyone and that we're a catch-all for anything termed marketing. We're the voice of the customer, in my position. We work with them and consult with them, but we don't control the product. Marketing is a lot of different things; it's not only the product but concepts and business strategy.

How can someone get a job like yours?

If I look at the people I'm looking to hire, you've got to have five years industry background, working with implementing technology in the marketplace. It can by any kind of technology. If you're a product manager for a service provider, or if you know the marketplace after, say, having worked as an analyst for a research company, that's good background. We're looking for people who know the market well. A person with an international focus, who understands the dynamics of culture on technology, that's an important quality too.

throughout the world major players are jockeying for position as they endeavor to offer one-stop services for all your telecommunication needs. Upstart players have thrown their hats in the ring, hoping to use the latest technology to catapult themselves into industry leadership as new digital systems replace the hardwired, mechanical switching systems that have been the industry norm. The imminent rise in high-speed data services, voice communications over the Internet, and data networks will all mean more R&D and competition and, as leaders emerge, consolidation. Finally, look for foreign companies to compete in an increasing array of markets as formerly state-owned telecom companies like Deutsche Telekom look abroad for new business. If you want an industry that's going to require you to learn fast and adapt quickly, this is it.

A prediction: In ten years, you won't recognize this industry. Think back ten years to see what we mean. Who used a pager, mobile phone, or the Internet in 1989? These devices mark just the beginning of a convergence of technologies that will create a worldwide network in which video, data, and voice communications are omnipresent and information instantly accessible—don't be surprised that for instant newspaper delivery, you'll merely need to press a button on a wireless, paper-thick screen that you can carry about your house. In fact, the converging technologies, including semiconductors, speech recognition, fiber-optic networks, and satellite relays, will eventually make your telephone touch pad irrelevant. To call Grandma Emmie, all you'll have to do is speak into your telephone the words "Call Grandma."

How It Breaks Down

Prior to the Telecommunications Act of 1996, a variety of regulations divided telecommunications artificially—cable companies were prohibited from offering local telephone service, video programming was banned, and local service companies and long-distance service providers were forbidden from competing in each other's markets. The Telecommunications Act lifted these competitive restrictions. One regulatory barrier that remains prohibits service providers from manufacturing telecommunications equipment. The cleanest way to break this industry down, then, is between those who make the software and hardware and those who provide various services—purchasing the equipment from the manufacturers to do so.

Service Providers

These provide local and long-distance wireline telephone service. Industry insiders call this POTS for plain old telephone service. Wireline providers include the large long-distance service providers—AT&T, which has 55 percent of this market in the United States, followed by MCI Worldcom and Sprint—and the RBOCs—SBC Communications and Ameritech (which are merging), Bell Atlantic (which is merging with GTE, a non-RBOC local service provider), Bell-South, and U.S. West. These firms rely on their extensive copper wire networks that connect your local calls as well as the transnational and transoceanic wire networks. A new generation of companies is laying fiber-optic wire networks to handle the rapidly increasing data traffic, including Qwest, Level 3, and the Williams Companies.

Wireless Service Providers

Marked by carrier consolidation and partnering to augment geographic reach and gain economies of scale, wireless communication services have shaken up the telecom service industry. They have also brought telecommunications to the far corners of the earth, including parts of Africa and South America where there's no existing wireline infrastructure, and have made local markets far more competitive in the United States. Among the fastest-growing segments of telecommunications, wireless service comes in analog or digital form. Most people in the United States are familiar with cellular services that are analog; however, PCS, or digital wireless, offers the potential of all-in-one consumer information appliances capable of transmitting e-mail and voice messages. The largest players in wireless communication are, not surprisingly, wireless divisions of the largest players in wireline: AT&T Wireless, Sprint PCS, Bell Atlantic Nynex Mobile, and

GTE Wireless, as well as a number of newer players, including AirTouch Communications and regional service companies like Western Wireless, Nextel, and United States Cellular. As one of the first telecommunications sectors to be opened to competition, wireless communication services have spurred change and provided a variety of new bundled services to their markets such as advanced messaging, data transmission, and location services.

Satellite Telecommunication Services

Satellite telecom services breaks down into fixed satellite services such as INTELSAT; mobile satellite services such as Comstat; low earth orbit companies (LEOs), which include Iridium and mega-LEO Teledesic; direct broadcast satellite companies such as DirecTV and Primestar; and the global positioning system (GPS). Satellite services include everything from navigation systems (which you can expect to find in the dash of your automobile sometime in the near future) to video broadcast and data transmission.

Internet Service Providers (ISPs)

These consist of those companies that make it possible for you to go online—Microsoft, AOL, Earthlink, MindSpring, and the RBOCs. The Internet, which has run headlong into telecommunications backfield as if it were a blitzing linebacker, is also responsible for adding a huge dose of talent and energy to telecom as voice and data networks converge.

Customer Premise Equipment (CPE) Manufacturers

Telecommunication service providers are the biggest customers of telecommunications equipment makers. When they sell a service to a company, for instance, they purchase the switch, which can serve anywhere from 15 to 100,000 people, as well as other customer premise equipment (CPE)—everything from telephones, voice processing, video communication, private branch exchanges (PBXs), and telephones. Local area networks (LAN) require their own routers, switches, and hubs. The big players here include Lucent Technologies, Nortel, Fujitsu, Siemens, and Alcatel.

Networking Equipment and Fiber Optics Manufacturers

Networking equipment includes the stuff that makes the local area network operative, including routers, hubs, switches, and servers. Fiber optics consists of the optical fiber and fiber optic cable, transmitters, receivers, and connectors that carry data and voice messages. The biggest switch makers are Nortel and Lucent. Cisco, Bay Networks, and 3Com are the biggest makers of networking equipment.

Wireless and Satellite Communication Equipment Manufacturers

These are different categories that we've grouped together. The radio-based communications systems, the switches, transmission, and subscriber equipment for this sector differ from what the wireline service providers use. Large players in wireless equipment include Motorola, Qualcom, Hughes Electronics, Sony, and NEC. Satellite communication equipment makers include Comcast and Loral Space, as well as a number of cable companies, such as Cox Communications, DirecTV, Primestar, and the TCI Network.

What's Great

Reach Out and Touch Someone

In telecommunications, you're working with products that people know and use. Everybody knows what voice mail, caller ID, and portable phones are. One insider says, "It's stuff I identify with and my friends identify with." As a consequence, your work more than reaches out and touches someone—it touches a lot of people.

So Many Ways to Call

"The products are varied," says an insider. "It's changing incredibly fast. That's not unique to telecom, but it's certainly true of telecom." Wireless, speech recognition, Internet calls, computer telephony—the list of new products driving change in this industry is long and the impact on our lives will be huge. If you can deal with the ambiguity that comes with change and get a charge from the excitement that goes along with all the new opportunities, then this is a great industry in which to work.

New Directions

"Where does telecommunications end and the Internet start?" asks an industry insider. Because the Internet has drawn a lot of talented, innovative employees and workers, it has injected new life and energy into telecommunications as well. This makes both new products and the work environment particularly exciting, while bringing a variety of industries together.

What's to Hate

Old Bells

The monopolies that the Bells held for so long didn't exactly make telecom a stimulating industry. New technology and deregulation have changed this, but there's still a lot of holdover. "Telecom was so regulated for so long, you didn't have to be good to go far," says an insider. "It was such an inbred industry." Join a newer company if you want to be sure to avoid this aspect of the industry.

Red Tape

Historically, telecommunications has been one of the most regulated industries. "One thing that's kind of a love-hate thing is the regulatory environment," says an insider. "It impacts just about every company in the industry. Some days I think it's an added challenge to deal with the industry and also with this complexity. Some days I wish it weren't there."

The Hugeness

The biggest players in telecom are huge. "That's not for everybody," says an insider. In particular, the Bells and major long-distance service providers are large, often bureaucratic organizations where you'll need lots of people to sign off before you can get a project approved. In contrast, there's a huge number of smaller companies, many of which have found niches or picked off market share exactly because of their mobility.

KEY JOBS

Engineer

Engineers of various types are in great demand in this industry. Although the specifics of different assignments will vary (for example, field engineers will install equipment at a customer site, and network engineers will plan out network needs), most positions will require a degree in computer science, electrical engineering, or system engineering, as well as knowledge of Windows NT, C++, Unix, and other programming languages. Salary range: $40,000 to $100,000.

Test Engineer

The test engineer makes sure the product works, especially the switches, which are critical. If e-mail or voice mail doesn't work, it is, after all, considered mission critical. The test cycle is often as long as the development cycle. Salary range: $50,000 to $80,000.

Software or Applications Engineer

These engineers concentrate on writing code. Most companies require code to be written on Unix-based machines, although Microsoft has been pushing hard to get telecom companies to use an NT platform, and many newer companies have changed. Salary range: $50,000 to $80,000.

Product Manager

Essentially, product managers make the product happen. Product managers determine what service or product they'll sell to the end user, then help develop it, be it wireless service, DSL, caller ID, or voice mail. On the manufacturing side, they need to know the technology or show some knowledge about it. This position generally requires an MBA or similar experience with another company, preferably in networking or data communications. Salary range: $70,000 to $90,000.

Sales

Salespeople sell the product to the customer. They usually have a smaller base salary and larger commission than their counterpart, the technical sales rep or sales engineer, who often accompanies the sales rep in order to answer the customer's technical questions. Salary range: $40,000 to $80,000, plus commissions.

Customer Support Staff

Customer support answers customer phone calls or e-mails, helping to solve problems. This includes everything from identifying problems to fixing bugs. This is often a good place to start a career in telecom, particularly if you lack an engineering background. Customer service managers make at the high end of the scale. Salary range: $25,000 to $50,000.

REAL PEOPLE PROFILE

JACK FARMER

OCCUPATION:
District sales manager for a multimedia communications company

YEARS IN BUSINESS: 2

AGE: 40

EDUCATION: BA in marketing, University of Florida; technical courses in telecommunications

HOURS PER WEEK:
40, 8:15 A.M. to 5:00 P.M.; 1 hour for lunch

SIZE OF COMPANY: 100

CERTIFICATION: None

ANNUAL SALARY: $70,000

How did you get your job?

I've been in sales and marketing for fifteen years. I was with a Fortune 500 company and it was stable. But realistically, you get bored with it. That's where I took a career change. The computer was becoming big. We've come a long way in ten years. I took some technical courses and found a job in computer hardware sales. The area I'm in now looked really exciting.

Describe a typical day.

8:15   I'm usually in the office by now. The product I'm selling integrates your telephone with your PC, so that you can use one system to do two things you'd formerly used two systems to do. If somebody calls, for instance, your computer will ID that person and bring up the history on your screen. You can decide to take the call, let the call go to voice mail, whatever. It's supposed to make life more productive. There's going to be a huge number of products that work with the telephone coming out in the next year. The product I'm selling hasn't been released yet. What I do largely depends on where we're at in the cycle.

8:30   Usually I'll contact the sales manager. Right now we're working on the marketing side, so we've got to put together a dealer handbook, training materials, that sort of thing. That way when the product hits the market, we can teach people how to use it. We'll also be developing a sales model, trying to figure out what the end-user will need for training, trying to make it as simple as possible, creating a CD-ROM to help.

10:00   This week I'm reporting on what types of things a seller needs. I'm putting together a wish list of things we'd like for showing the system to potential buyers: phones connected to an NT server, laptops to show it working. If I can show everything I want, it will be a pretty impressive demo.

Public Relations and Government Relations

The role the government has played in regulating telecommunications has resulted in a number of jobs within the major companies to work with the government and press to enhance relations. These include lobbying government officials, helping draft legislation, and working with the press to garner favorable coverage for regulations your company supports. Salary range: $50,000 to $150,000.

GETTING HIRED

Here are a few things to think about before you start looking for a job in telecommunications:

- If you want a job in telecom, your best bet is to study up on the industry. There's a host of industry trade magazines covering a variety of areas, and these will provide you with a sense for the peculiar argot of the industry.

11:00 We've spent the last two months figuring out what's the ideal distributor. Increasingly, we're getting into sales issues. What do we need to make the product successful?

1:30 As we move toward the commercial release, I spend more time on the phone, talking to people in the industry. Who are the end-users? Who are the commercial-users? Who are the best dealers to supply the end-users? Who are the best distributors to supply the dealers? So usually I'm on the phone, marketing the product. I'm also trying to get the beta sites going and testing the product, so that people can see what it does and how it works.

5:00 Go home.

What are your career aspirations?

My career goal is to stay in this industry and land with a company that is successful and hopefully rise with that company.

What kinds of people do well in this business?

You definitely have to be a go-getter. The more you can find out about the industry and where it's going, the more you know, the better off you're going to be. It helps if you can learn quickly.

What do you really like about your job?

Every day is challenging and different. The industry is changing all the time. I can't wait to get the trade industry magazines. Can you imagine looking at your screen and seeing your voice mails and e-mails on your screen? Here's this industry, the PC is on one side, the telephone on the other. When you put those two together, this is a new industry. I like that.

What do you dislike?

If you don't have a product that works, that can be difficult.

What is the biggest misconception about your job?

They think that everything has to do with the phone company. That's not really what I'm into at all. What I do is make your telephone speak to your computer.

How can someone get a job like yours?

The best source of information that I can think of is go to these trade shows that the industry magazines, *CTI* and *Computer Telephony*, list. Bring your résumé. The career fairs are great places, great sources of information. The industry is so new that nobody's really been in it for longer than twenty years.

- The bigger companies, such as AT&T and the RBOCs, recruit on college campuses. A good place to make contacts is through career fairs at your school.

- Smaller companies typically look for people with experience in some aspect of the industry. If you do have experience in the industry, including such areas as networks or computer telephony, this will give you a leg up in finding work.

- Insiders in the industry say that your best route to finding a job is networking. Although this is true in most industries, it's particularly true for telecommunications. Companies talk to each other a lot. If you know a few people in the industry, you can pretty easily get additional contacts.

- Be careful about going to work for a company that's a potential takeover target. If there are lots of articles speculating that a company is a buyout candidate, it's probably going to get bought out within two years. If you work in corporate sales or another area where there will be serious duplication—line installers shouldn't worry—you may want to think twice about accepting an offer.

Transportation

Transportation may at first seem like a rather pedestrian industry. Its purpose, after all, is merely *transportation*: moving people and goods, by land, sea, or air, from one point to another. But consider: In addition to the package deliverer, truck driver, and airline attendant—the ambassadors of the industry—there is a beehive of behind-the-scenes workers bustling to load containers, fuel airplanes, coordinate the logistics of thousands of airplanes, and chart the best routes for truck drivers to take across the United States.

The transportation industry has come a long way from the days of the spice trade. Virtually everything that surrounds us—including our clothes—comes from somewhere else. Your computer's components, manufactured in multiple countries, all had to be transported to the computer manufacturer, assembled, and then transported to a store or perhaps your front door. The newspaper you read this morning could not have been produced (think of the trucks delivering logs to the paper mill; think of the paper and ink being delivered to the printing press) or delivered without the transportation industry. And then there's passenger travel—the airlines, trains, boats, and buses that people use every day to get from place to place. Transportation may not at first appear sexy, but it pervades nearly every

REAL
PEOPLE
PROFILE

JANE SHADDUCK

OCCUPATION:
Vessel planner

YEARS IN BUSINESS: 6

AGE: 29

EDUCATION: BA, Merchant
Marine Academy

HOURS PER WEEK: 40,
6:00 P.M. to 4:00 A.M.,
Monday through Thursday

SIZE OF COMPANY: 1,400

CERTIFICATION: None

ANNUAL SALARY: $45,000

How did you get your job?

I went to two shipping companies and initiated half-time internships so that I spent half the week at one company and half at the other. Because of my experience at the Merchant Marine Academy, I knew what I was looking for; I picked the company whose operations I preferred, and they hired me after a few months. Then they prepared me for work with a six-month training program.

Describe a typical night.

6:00 Arrive in my office after taking a shuttle from the parking lot; we can't park near the shipping yard because it's too busy with cranes and trucks loading and unloading the boats. The day planner briefs me on how the day shift went.

6:30 While studying a computer profile of the ship that's loading tonight, I call the captain; we discuss the ship's capacity. I also arrange a time later on tonight to come onboard and supervise loading activities.

7:00 I call the logistics department. I'm actually working in logistics, myself, although my department is called Ship Loading and Unloading. The logistics department coordinates between different shipping companies that have shipping agreements. My company has traded space on one of our ships bound for Marseilles for space on another company's liner bound for Lisbon; I'm calling to find out how much we'll be shipping for that other company and to let them know how much they need to ship for us.

8:00 Talk to the captain again, confirming that the heavy containers are being stacked on the bottom. We both have computer profiles of the ship, showing how much volume it can hold and weight it can carry, which are the most important factors to keep in mind when loading a ship.

8:30 Talk to the ship supervisor on the phone to ensure that the refrigerated containers, or "reefers," are stored adequately. There are a limited number of outlets, so it is vital to manage space efficiently.

9:00 Meet with union clerks in the yard. I explain to them what operations I am planning, and how much labor will be needed, and coordinate my plans with available labor

area of our lives. Indeed, in 1996, $847 billion was spent on transportation in the United States—more than 11 percent of the U.S. gross domestic product (GDP). Without the transportation industry, the global economy would disintegrate, taking many domestic ones with it.

No doubt about it: There are job opportunities aplenty in transportation. This is an industry that employs some ten million people in the United States. If you want to hop aboard, however, you'll want to keep some things in mind. Those interested in having direct contact with cargo and vehicles should think about jobs in operations, which are often set outdoors and can involve loud noise and physically strenuous work—for example, loading or unloading a boat or train. Logistics, which involves planning and managing efficient transportation for everything from individual shipments (such as a book from your favorite e-com-resources. Although I try to work according to a time table, it's usually impossible since each shipment is different and the numbers of people available to load and unload them fluctuate as well.

1:00 I call the container yard department, which stacks containers on piles or on wheels; they can then be outgated to the trains. (Trucks move the freight between the trains and our ships.) Then I call the maintenance department to ensure that trucks will be ready to unload the train at 3 A.M.

2:00 Board the ship to supervise the remaining activities for my shift. Approximately a third of my time is spent supervising the crew and speaking to union clerks.

3:00 Find the supervisor of truck loading and talk to him about making a smooth handoff to the next shift. Discuss the night's operations with a ship planner; confirm that we've covered everything that we needed to cover for this operation.

4:00 Head home.

What are your career aspirations?

Eventually, after getting an MBA—which my company is paying for—I want to work in a foreign ship terminal. In school, I am learning how foreign markets affect trade, and I hope to use this knowledge abroad as a ship planner.

What kinds of people do well in this business?

People who like having lots of responsibility, who are good at multitasking, and who can deal well with different kinds of people. People who can handle a steep learning curve and don't mind the long and late hours.

What do you really like about your job?

I like that I can move around a lot instead of sitting in an office. Being on a ship is also exciting because there is so much activity. I can see the results of my efforts to organize a loading or unloading operation, and that's satisfying.

What do you dislike?

I don't like the hours, but soon I'll be switched to the day shift.

What is the biggest misconception about this job?

That it's hard working with longshoreman. Many people think they're difficult and even dangerous. But I've found them to be friendly and to have loads of experience to share. However, it's important to cultivate a working relationship with them by understanding their part of the loading operations. They won't take to bossy novices.

How can someone get a job like yours?

If you love ships and enjoy the challenge of thinking on your feet, then you'll make a good impression when you apply for a job like this. A BA in international trade relations will help, but the best qualification is a degree from the Merchant Marine Academy. Another way into this industry is an unpaid internship, which will teach you what the business is and make you contacts within a company that could lead to a job.

merce site) to entire fleets of trucks, has been booming as information technology advances have swept the industry; today, it's possible to track shipments by satellite and thus improve the efficiency of the transportation and shipment process. Be aware that for many positions, you'll need to join a union—and in recent years, strikes have been a part of life in the industry (just ask Northwest and American Airlines).

The opportunities in the industry can be classified geographically—as being local (local jobs are referred to as being "in the field" by insiders), regional, or national. Often, you'll need to pay your dues in the field before moving up to a regional transportation outfit, and work at a regional one before moving to a national one. Finally, if you go into freight transportation, be aware that this sector, like other industries where companies are seeking to become global players, has been consolidating, with companies merging to become giant, full-service transportation integrators, combining ships, trains, boats, and rail. This hasn't really lessened the number of jobs available except in the rail sector, where a spate of mergers in 1996 hit hard and led to layoffs of a quarter of all employees.

How It Breaks Down

There are two sides of the transportation industry: companies that move goods (freight and shipping companies) and companies that move people (passenger transportation companies). The biggest of the shipping companies are the ones that integrate several types of transportation services to offer clients efficient door-to-door service. Meanwhile, on the passenger side of the transportation industry, there is no such thing as an integrated system. Here is how the two sides of the transportation industry look when broken down by the type of vehicle used:

Plane

The biggest shipping players in this segment—FDX Corporation (FedEx), Airborne Freight Corporation, DHL, and Worldwide Express—integrate air transportation with other types of transportation. This segment of the market has been doing very well lately, with companies registering strong double-digit growth in revenues and staff.

On the passenger side, the airline industry has consolidated in the years since it was deregulated in 1978. Currently, American Airlines, Continental Airlines, Delta Airlines, Northwest Airlines, and United Airlines earn over half of U.S. airline revenues. Of these, United is the leader of the pack, with 1998 revenues of $17.6 billion. The remainder of this sector comprises regional carriers, which fly people between rural areas and bigger airports. Biggest among regional carriers: Southwest Airlines, which had revenues of $4.2 billion in 1998.

Ship

Freight shipping by deep-sea liners, nonliners, and tankers accounts for three quarters of the water transportation industry. The biggest shipping companies are based outside the United States: Taiwan's Evergreen Marine, Japan's Nippon Yusen Kabushiki Kaisha, and Denmark's AP Moller move more containers than anyone else. Although the federal government is revitalizing U.S. performance in this segment through the use of advanced technology, opportunities at the foreign companies, where annual employment growth rates are in general much higher, are still a better bet for job seekers.

Passenger transportation, which accounts for less than 5 percent of total water transportation revenues, includes modes of transportation such as ferries and cruise liners. Carnival Cruise Lines is easily the biggest cruise company in the world. The ferry business is not as consolidated as the cruise business, with most companies owned regionally. Both businesses are predicted to grow slowly in coming years.

Truck and Bus

The $360 billion trucking industry carried 80 percent of all consumer goods. The biggest players in this segment are integrated-transportation parcel-delivery companies such as United Parcel Services (UPS), FDX Corporation, DHL, and Worldwide Express; trucking companies like Schneider Nation, Consolidated Freightways, J. Hunt, and Yellow Freight; and truck rental companies such as Amerco (best known for its U-Haul trucks) and Ryder.

On the passenger side, the biggest bus company in the United States is Greyhound. Greyhound, which also offers express package delivery, employs about twelve thousand people.

Rail

Freight trains mainly carry coal, grain, and lumber. After a period of intense consolidation in this segment, the four leading companies are Burlington Northern Santa Fe, CSX, Norfolk Southern, and Union Pacific.

Passenger rail transportation in the United States is dominated by the federally funded Amtrak, which makes stops in 45 states. In an attempt to be more self-sufficient, Amtrak is trying to rely less on Congress and more on profits to fund operations.

What's Great

Smells Like Team Spirit

As in many other industries, in transportation, the network of coworkers you develop will not only be important for your success, it'll be what makes the work fun. But transportation differs from some other industries in that there's very little snobbishness among the people in it. An insider explains, "We help each other, wherever we are. This makes work easier and more enjoyable."

The Power of Technology

Technology has changed the face of the transportation industry. If you're in logistics, for instance, you can expect to work using 3–D graphics or special software to help you arrange the placement of billions of tons of freight onboard a ship, or plan global shipping routes, or monitor shipments by satellite. An insider describes the innovative technology as "awesome," adding, "There are so many cutting-edge tools being developed every day to enhance tracking performance that it's a great challenge to be working with them."

Join the Industry, See the World

As you might expect, opportunities to see the world abound in this industry. If you steer the plane, train, or ship, or if you assist on board, you'll definitely get to see new places. As an added bonus, family members can come with you or do their own traveling—often for free.

What's to Hate

The Hours

This is a twenty-four-hour industry; as a result, the work can be unusually strenuous. People at the corporate level complain of twelve-hour days that keep them in the office until late at night, while people in operations complain about the stress of working night shifts. "I hate the hours," says one insider who otherwise likes his

REAL PEOPLE PROFILE

SALLY MARSHALL

OCCUPATION:
Outside sales manager

YEARS IN BUSINESS: 5

AGE: 29

EDUCATION: BA in economics and history, University of Michigan

HOURS PER WEEK:
50, 8:30 A.M. to 6:30 P.M.;
1 hour for lunch

SIZE OF COMPANY: 5,000

CERTIFICATION: None

ANNUAL SALARY:
$70,000

How did you get your job?

I started working as an account developer and gained enough experience to become an inside sales representative. To advance you have to be well-rounded in the business, so afterwards I worked in the pricing department, which works out the rates for shipments. Then I got my current job.

Describe a typical day.

8:30   Come in and e-mail clients. To be in sales you have to contact your clients all the time, letting them know how well your company's service is coming along. Unlike customer service, which is reactive and fields general questions, to succeed in sales you need to be proactive. This means I have to call our client, not the other way around, and make sure that a client's specific needs are being met.

10:00   Read some trade magazines and the *Journal* over coffee.

11:00   Have a sales meeting with other salespeople. Basically check up on how everyone's doing and plan for some sales classes for the junior salespeople to take.

12:30   Go out to lunch with another salesperson. Actually, we're treating a client who gave us a little business two months ago. We'd like to be their regular provider, so we stop by their office—this is the third time so far—and try to find out what they're not getting already in terms of service so that we can try to offer that to them. After chatting up the clients in their office, we all go to a Chinese restaurant. At this point we don't talk business; we're trying to develop a relationship.

2:30   Back to the office. An older, very important client calls up upset. A clerk at our company has made a lot of mistakes on a recent shipment and has been very uncooperative in resolving the situation. I know the person in question, and let's just say he's not one of our better or more-pleasant employees. Although it's not my fault, I have to smooth things over.

job. If you like to keep vampire's hours, this industry might be the perfect place for you; if you find yourself nodding off at ten every night, most likely it isn't.

Tons of Pressure

Managing huge operations, solving problems on short notice, multitasking—the typical transportation industry job description may appeal to some, but to others it's a nightmare. Deadlines in transportation come fast and are inflexible, and the pressure to meet them can seem huge—whether you're dealing with millions of dollars in cargo or cranky passengers that need to be in Des Moines three hours ago. "There are so many things to do, sometimes, that I am on the verge of losing my cool," says an insider.

Join the Industry, See a Blur

Although insiders in this industry usually think the travel's great, there are times when they're more likely to hate it. Often, people in the transportation industry are moving around too much and too fast to really see any of the new places

3:15 Talk to the general manager of my office to get his advice on the problem. He'll talk to the employee, and he suggests that I give the client a really good price on their next shipment. Also, he's going to call up the main contact at the client and invite him to play golf.

4:00 Talk to the pricing department to find out how low a rate I can give the client. They'll get back to me.

4:30 Go back to my desk to look at faxes that have come in. (We don't have e-mail yet.) Nothing much important, so I plan out my day tomorrow. Two sales calls in the morning, so I do a little research on the clients to jog my memory of times they've used us in the past.

5:00 Duck out of the office a little early.

What are your career aspirations?

I'm not sure. The great thing about my job is that it could lead to different fields. I could work in consulting or work as a salesperson in a different field. Once you're in sales you can transfer to the sales department of a totally different company fairly easily.

What kinds of people do well in this business?

Sales is sales, so basic things like charisma, perseverance, and customer focus are important. Beyond that, the thing to know about sales in my industry is that it's very, very competitive. It's very hard to make your company's services stand out as being different from those of others. Basically, most transportation companies are pretty similar. That means that your sales skills, customer focus, and ability to build relationships are all you have to go on.

What do you really like about your job?

I enjoy the interactive part of this job. In the day-to-day I get to talk to lots of different people, both those in my company and those who are part of our client's team. I also like the fact that there is never a dull moment. I'm always busy and challenged.

What do you dislike?

The fact that there is never a dull moment works both ways. Sometimes I wish things would quiet down a little. Politics, the weather, and economics, which are factors we need to account for anytime we're making a shipment, are constantly changing, and we need to take them into account when we price things and ship things for clients. It can be tough to stay on top of the ball.

What is the biggest misconception about your job?

That all salespeople do is wine and dine customers.

How can someone get a job like yours?

An internship is a good place to start; that's a way to get experience. A college degree won't land you a job immediately. It's important to know exactly what you are selling. Investigate a company before you interview with it.

they visit. Some find too much travel positively depressing. "I wouldn't want to be on the road all the time anymore," says one insider. "You're away from your family and friends too much of the time."

KEY JOBS

Opportunities in transportation fall generally into five categories: sales, marketing, documentation, information technology, logistics, and driving and piloting.

Sales

Sales representatives work closely with their clients—companies with something to transport. They spend a lot of time visiting clients, developing relationships, quoting prices, and working with their company's pricing department to determine prices for deliveries based on weight, volume, and delivery time. Charisma and confidence are more important in sales positions than a college degree. Salary range: $25,000 or more, plus commission.

Documentation

People in these positions work on pricing and rating. Pricing personnel determine the rates clients will pay, which vary based on the weight and volume of freight, transit time, and other factors. The rating department steps in once goods reach their destination; rating department personnel deal with bills of lading—the final computation of the price charged of clients. Documentation personnel working with international accounts also deal with customs-related issues. Entry-level documentation positions require a college degree. Salary range: $20,000 to $40,000.

Information Technology

Jobs in IT involve database management, the development and maintenance of warehouse systems, and supply chain management. Many companies outsource the management of their IT systems, so these jobs aren't always technically within the transportation industry. IT work requires a strong background in programming; a degree in computer science is often a requirement. Salary range: $40,000 and up.

Logistics

Logistics personnel manage the movement of people and goods—that is, logistics makes sure the plains and trains arrive and leave on time. At the field level, dispatchers schedule pickups and deliveries. In more strategy-intensive positions, logistics people use computer systems to track shipments around the globe or to limit the amount of time products stay in warehouses or distribution centers. Jobs in logistics generally require a college degree or military experience; some positions require an MBA. Salary range: $25,000 and up.

Marketing

People in marketing promote their company to current and potential clients and investors. Most often, marketers cite either the efficiencies—or the lower prices—their company can bring to shipping processes. An insider stresses the importance of imagination, strategic thinking, and keen perception for people in these jobs. A college degree is required, as is a marketing portfolio. Salary range: $30,000 and up.

Driving and Piloting

People in these positions do everything from driving a UPS truck or an 18-wheeler to piloting a boat or an airplane. Truck drivers and bus drivers need a commercial driving license (CDL), which can take a few weeks to obtain, while pilots require a commercial pilot license (CPL), which can take up to three years to get. Train engineers usually start as yard crew, then work for at least ten years before driving a train. Although truck and bus drivers usually work alone, ship captains and plane pilots generally require assistance from at least one other person. Salary range: $20,000 to $80,000.

GETTING HIRED

There are a lot of different people doing a lot of different jobs in transportation, so qualifications for entry-level positions vary—but in general, even though training programs exist at all levels, the more-advanced positions nearly always require an MBA or prior experience in the field. Many insiders claim that sales is the quickest way into transportation—but once you are in the industry, it's possible to jump from one career track to another. Whatever job you're looking for, expect to start in the field—at the local level—and keep the following in mind:

- Research the company you're applying to and its competitors. It will impress an interviewer if you show a knowledge about the company and how it's different from others.

- If you want a job in marketing, learn how the company presents itself to its clients and what strengths it emphasizes by studying its marketing collateral, then prepare a portfolio that shows how you would sell the company's strengths to potential clients and investors.

- Understand the basic measurements used in logistics, and have a good grasp of geography.

- Timeliness is something people in the industry strive for, so be punctual for your interview.

Venture Capital

Meet the new Masters of the Universe. What Tom Wolfe's suspenders-clad bond traders were to the 1980s, venture capitalists are to the 1990s: a well-educated group of relatively young hotshots making an astronomical amount of money. VCs, who invest in start-up companies in return for a piece of the profits, have been behind some of corporate America's greatest success stories—Compaq Computer, FedEx, Intel Corporation, Sun Microsystems, and Apple, to name a few. The risks are enormous, but for legions of brilliant young people with MBAs—yes, you'll probably need one, and from a top school—the potential rewards are even bigger.

Essentially, venture capitalists raise money from other investors such as corporations, financial institutions, private foundations, university endowments, and wealthy individuals and families and then sort through stacks of business plans before deciding which lucky companies to invest in. After investing in a company, venture capitalists are usually involved in important business decisions and often take a seat on the company's board of directors. The goal of venture capital is simple: to make money for the fund by investing in promising companies early. VCs make their money by helping the company grow and then selling it

REAL PEOPLE PROFILE

VIKRAM AGRAWAL

OCCUPATION: Associate at a venture firm

YEARS IN BUSINESS: 6 months

AGE: 26

EDUCATION: BS in business administration, Georgetown University

HOURS PER WEEK: 55, 8:30 A.M. to 7:00 P.M.; working lunch

SIZE OF COMPANY: 18 professionals

CERTIFICATION: None

ANNUAL SALARY: $70,000, plus deal bonuses

How did you get your job?

While I was in I-banking, I told a friend at another private-equity firm that I wanted a job in VC. He told me about an opening at this firm, and I sent in my résumé.

Describe a typical day.

8:30 Arrive at the office, then check e-mail and voice mail and surf the Web for business headlines relevant to my research.

10:00 Call companies I've heard about or that have been referred to us. Explicitly, I'm trying to find out from CEOs about what their product is, who's on their team, what the market opportunity is, and how much they're trying to raise and the terms of the deal. Implicitly, I'm trying to learn about the market they're in so I'll be more intelligent for the next call I make.

12:00 Lunch meeting with a couple of members of a company that I'm interested in. I try to see if there's as much of a fit between my firm and their company as I initially thought.

2:00 Do some due diligence on a company we're already talking with. This mainly consists of calling customers and industry analysts.

4:00 Spend some time going over other deals with other associates or partners. We talk about what stage the projects are in and what needs to be done.

6:00 Try to catch up on voice mail and e-mail messages, and plan my day for tomorrow.

7:30 Head home.

What are your career aspirations?

Either to become a partner in a venture firm or to take the knowledge that I've learned through my involvement at a VC firm to get involved with an early-stage company.

to a larger company or taking the company public in an initial public stock offering (IPO).

As the 1990s draw to a close, the venture capital industry is exploding. According to PricewaterhouseCoopers, in 1998, 2,856 companies received venture-backed investments. These investments were up 24 percent from 1997 and 78 percent from 1996, for a total of $14.3 billion. Blame technology: To meet their lofty return on capital goals (many venture firms aim for ten-to-one returns on investments and 20 to 30 percent average annual rates of return), venture capitalists have focused increasingly on high-tech companies, which in 1998 accounted for 76 percent of total VC investments. Not surprisingly, many of the top funds (including Institutional Venture Partners, the Mayfield Fund, and Sequoia Capital) have headquarters in Silicon Valley.

Does the enormous growth in the venture capital industry mean that the industry is hungry for fresh hires? Unfortunately, no. In general, venture capital funds are extremely flat organizations, often consisting solely of partners and low-level support staff (secretaries, office managers, and receptionists). Even the largest funds have only a handful of professional positions. Kleiner Perkins Cau-

What kinds of people do well in this business?

You have to marry three abilities: You have to know the tech and business side to evaluate new technologies; you have to have a basic understanding of how financing and growing a company works; and most importantly, you have to be very good at talking and listening to people to draw out their knowledge to increase your own. You can't hope to learn everything by reading things off the Web or in magazines.

What do you really like about your job?

The very high level of independence. I am really responsible for a lot of what happens to get deals in front of the partners. The only thing I'm judged on is whether I'm bringing quality deals to the partnership. How I do that and how I spend my time day to day is completely up to me. I also like the number of incredibly intelligent and motivated VCs and entrepreneurs I get to talk to at every turn.

What do you dislike?

There are not enough hours in the day. It can be very hectic, especially when there's travel. Honestly, there can often be many more things to do than you have time for. You often have to pass up opportunities that you don't have the time to devote enough attention to.

What is the biggest misconception about your job?

That every deal you do is a winner and that it's easy to get good deals. There's a lot of hard work and dumb luck that goes into making an Amazon or an eBay. It's not easy to take an unpolished start-up and have it turn into a big name. You can't just throw money at a start-up and expect it to succeed.

How can someone get a job like yours?

There are two tracks. First, the analytical side: Get experience at an I-bank, a top-tier consulting firm, or a research firm like Gartner or Yankee.

Then there's the industry side, especially technology. A lot of VCs have experience in industry, either at a start-up or a big player. Most hiring is done by personal introduction and on a case-by-case basis. VC openings are few and far between, sometimes. Find opportunities to meet VCs either through personal introductions or at VC events. VCs often talk about possible hires to other VCs, so the important thing is to meet some and network from there.

field & Byers, which has raised more than $1.2 billion and been involved in over a hundred IPOs, has only seventeen partners.

Established funds generally hire people with proven entrepreneurial backgrounds, high net worth (William Randolph Hearst III is a partner at Kleiner Perkins), or MBA degrees from either Harvard or Stanford, both of which offer specialized venture capital tracks. Even then, the competition is intense. Draper Fisher Jurvetson, a venture capital firm based in Redwood City, California, interviewed more than 250 prospects before hiring a new partner candidate. Not surprisingly, the successful hire had an MBA from Stanford.

But don't despair if your last name isn't Hearst or if you don't have an MBA from Harvard or Stanford. As the industry matures, opportunities for graduates from other business schools and even for undergraduates will increase. TA Associates, a Boston-based fund that also has offices in Menlo Park, California, hires undergraduates with some business experience as associates and fresh B-school grads as vice presidents. Additionally, some high-tech companies, notably Cisco, Microsoft, and Intel, have started their own internal venture capital operations, as have many financial-services firms.

There are many kinds of players in the VC world, from traditional VC firms to funds operated by publicly owned corporations. Some are tightly focused—by stage of investment, region, or type of industry—but most have a much broader focus. Here's a rough breakdown of the industry:

Private VC Firms (Early- to Mid-Stage)

Firms in this segment follow the classic VC model: Find an entrepreneur with a great idea and business plan, sprinkle with cash, bake for several years, and sell to someone else for a hefty chunk of change. Early-stage (or seed) investments are the riskiest, as many start-ups tank. Still, they often provide the highest returns because investors coming in early can demand a lower price for equity. As many traditional VC firms raise larger funds and start to focus on middle- and late-stage investments, seed financing has increasingly become the province of newer firms and angel investors—entrepreneurs who've made it big and have money to spend. Some firms known for seed and early investing are Altos Ventures, Onset Ventures, and Hummer Winblad Venture Partners.

Private VC Firms (Mid- to Late-Stage)

These firms, many of which also operate at the seed level, provide funds to companies that are already established—those that have a product, sufficient employees, and perhaps even revenues. At these stages, firms inject more capital into the company to help it become profitable so that it will attract enough interest to either be acquired by a larger company or go public. The trend is for VC firms to make larger investments in more-stable firms, reducing risk and shortening payoff time.

Growth Buyout Funds

Some VCs have moved into growth buyouts of larger private companies or divisions of public companies. These funds invest larger amounts of capital—up to $100 million—in exchange for a significant minority or majority position in the company. By focusing on stable, growing (and often profitable) companies, buyout funds don't have to wait long before they can cash in on the company's IPO or sale. There's less risk—unless market factors cause the delay of an IPO, for example. The funded company and its earlier investors benefit from having a prestigious late-stage investor add credibility on Wall Street come IPO time. Some firms that specialize in growth buyouts are Summit Partners, J.H. Whitney, Housatonic Partners, and Chase Capital Partners.

Financial-Services Firms

Where there's money, of course you'll find I-bankers. Banks such as Morgan Stanley Dean Witter, and Citicorp will invest in the later stages. Their aim is pretty much the same as those of the VCs: to make a killing through either an IPO or an acquisition.

Corporate Funds

As opposed to private funds, whose primary goal is monetary gain, corporate funds have the added goal of strategically investing in companies whose technology relates in some way to the corporation's business. For example, Microsoft invested in Qwest Communications, a telecom company that is building a fiber-optic network, to help it deliver NT-based software. Other companies with similar strategic investment funds include Intel and Hewlett-Packard.

Venture Capital–Related Companies

The tremendous growth in VC has resulted in a number of companies that serve to support, facilitate, and otherwise make a buck out of VCs and entrepreneurs making a buck out of each other. Myriad consultants help entrepreneurs develop eye-catching business plans and flashy presentations; one, Garage.com, goes one step further by matching entrepreneurs with investors at the seed level. There are also numerous research companies that help investors learn about hot industries and promising young companies. PricewaterhouseCoopers does a quarterly survey of the industry, as does Venture One.

What's Great

The Green Stuff

Put quite plainly, venture capitalists make more money than just about anyone else excepting, perhaps, entrepreneurs. Even better, unlike entrepreneurs, venture capitalists don't run the risk of personal bankruptcy if a company fails.

Cherry-Picking

What could be better than getting a sneak peek at the business plans of the brightest and most motivated businesspeople and investing in only the best? Many corporate venture funds, such as those run by Microsoft and Adobe Systems, exist primarily to give them first dibs on the next hot technology.

On a Mission

Maybe it's just guilt over those seven-figure paychecks, but venture capitalists will often tell you that they have a mission. For some it is to build a better, electronic world—Microsoft cofounder Paul Allen, who invests in start-up companies through his Vulcan fund, sees himself helping create a "wired world." Others want to bring breakthroughs in medicine to market. Still others claim that venture capital is the lubricant powering our entire economy.

What's to Hate

Workin' Nine to Nine

Being a venture capitalist is by no means a nine-to-five job. Depending on the fund and the deals that are currently active, you can expect to put in your fair

REAL PEOPLE PROFILE

RICK BREMMER

OCCUPATION:
Managing partner of a
venture capital company

YEARS IN BUSINESS: 7

AGE: 36

EDUCATION: BS in electrical
engineering, UC Berkeley;
MS in electrical engineering
and MBA, Stanford University

HOURS PER WEEK:
75, 7:00 A.M. to 8:00 P.M. at
office and 9:30 P.M. to 11:30
P.M. at home; working lunch

SIZE OF COMPANY: 7

CERTIFICATION: None

ANNUAL SALARY:
Total compensation of
$185,000

How did you get your job?

I worked at a consulting firm that catered to private-equity firms. I developed a lot of relationships there and eventually went to work with one of my clients. From there I transferred to a VC firm as a principal. Finally, a B-school classmate of my current partnership called me to join him and his partners in raising a new fund. He and I have known each other for several years and had worked together on a couple of transactions while I was at my first private-equity firm.

Describe a typical day.

6:30 On the way to work I check voice mail and call the Boston office if there's any urgent business. Get to work about seven, check e-mail, check my calendar for the day and respond to e-mail, and read the *Journal* and other papers.

8:00 Phone starts ringing. Have a conference call discussing the budget for the next twelve months with a portfolio company.

8:45 Send some more e-mail: to portfolio company CEOs, entrepreneurs looking for capital, and investors.

9:00 First appointment. An entrepreneur comes in to tell me his story. I've reviewed his business plan and have invited him in. One of my partners in the San Francisco office joins me for the meeting.

11:00 On the phone working down my list of calls—the oldest calls are backlogged three or four days. Urgent matters include a portfolio company CEO who wants advice on finding a new VP of sales. Another CEO wants to discuss an acquisition that the company is working on. Call one of my Boston-based partners to catch up with him.

11:45 Head for a restaurant three blocks away to meet with an I-banker who wants to learn about my firm to figure out how we can do some business together.

1:15 Back to the office. Check voice mails that I know I have since my pager's been vibrating me all through lunch.

1:30 Interview a CFO candidate for a portfolio company.

2:15 Go to a portfolio company board meeting.

6:00 Meet with the same company's CEO one-on-one to see how he's doing.

6:15 Back to the office. Process e-mails and respond to voice mails. Add the ones that aren't urgent to my to-call list to be followed up on in the next few days.

7:00 Head to the East Bay and home.

7:30 Dinner and family time.

share of eighty-hour weeks. That said, the hours aren't as consistently brutal as those in other elite industries such as law, management consulting, or software programming.

Risky Business

One of the reasons venture capital investing is growing at an exponential pace is the sky-high valuation the current bull market is putting on technology compa-

9:30 Put the kids to bed and then go to my home office. Prepare term sheets for two opportunities which look promising. Send and respond to e-mails and faxes and leave voice mails for people who need info. I do talk to people in person when possible to maintain relationships, but leaving voice mails is more time efficient.

11:30 Lights out.

What are your career aspirations?

To be a great investor. If I had as much money in the bank today as I could ever spend in my life, I would still do what I'm doing today. I might be getting more sleep, but I'd be doing exactly the same thing. Now I just focus on building great companies. Most of this is finding great entrepreneurs who need and want my help and with whom I would enjoy working.

What kinds of people do well in this business?

You've got to be a team participant. If you're going to help companies through your advice, you've got to be good at delivering that advice in such a way that they'll listen. You can't be driven to have your name plastered all over the *Wall Street Journal*. Ninety-nine percent of the people in this business you've never heard of. Your job is to help make CEOs become heroes. You're not the hero. You've also got to be inspired by the whole notion of capitalism, because what we're doing is at the very root of what makes this whole system work: the American dream. If you're not excited by that merging of great people, great ideas, and growth capital, then it'll never get your juices flowing.

What do you really like about your job?

The best part about it is the people you get to work with—from CEOs and management teams to other investors to very bright and creative lawyers and other service providers.

What do you dislike?

The travel can sometimes be difficult. So is removing somebody who has put their heart into a business but who isn't suited to lead it. That's the worst. Even when everyone agrees that it's the right thing to do, it's not easy.

What is the biggest misconception about your job?

People outside of the money world sometimes use the phrase "vulture capitalist" to describe us. This implies that we're stealing businesses away from entrepreneurs. Nobody is ever going to agree to sell a company or a portion of one unless they want to. Our firm doesn't do turnarounds or bankruptcies or other distressed investment situations. In 95 percent or more of the investments by private-equity firms, both sides are dealing from a position of some strength to reach a reasonable deal. Portrayals like *Barbarians at the Gate* just make us all look like idiots in private equity, like it's all about ego and doing the biggest, highest-visibility deal, treating people like they don't mean anything. If we find people like that, we don't ever do business with them. For bankers, the common misconception is that the principal people like me don't work a lot of hours. Sure, I don't have the stresses of a client hanging over me, but I don't get any extra sleep.

How can someone get a job like yours?

I think there are two common routes. One is a consulting or operating background. Figure out how businesses work, how to improve them and how to recruit and motivate management teams. The other side is the financial side. Spend a couple years as an analyst at an investment bank. In either avenue, try to begin developing your relationships with people in the private-equity world. Get to know other entrepreneurs' investors. If you're in I-banking, get to know the private-equity firms that your bank does business with. Plan on getting an MBA if you don't already have one. Consider it a long-term job search process. It's probably going to take you years before your contacts and an appropriate opening come together.

nies. This won't last forever—and a venture capitalist's compensation is directly tied to the performance of the fund, and indirectly to the market as a whole.

Always the Bridesmaid . . .

Venture capitalists are always one step removed from being the CEO of a successful public company. In terms of excitement and prestige, would you rather be the guys who founded Yahoo (Jerry Yang and David Filo) or the guy who invested in it (Michael Moritz at Sequoia Capital)?

KEY JOBS

Staffing needs and titles vary greatly from one venture capital firm to the next. Many funds consist solely of partners and support staff. Others hire a limited number of undergraduates and MBAs as analysts and associates, with the expectation that most will return to get their business degrees or join start-ups within a few years. (Keep in mind that while the terms "analyst" and "associate" usually refer to undergrads and MBAs or experienced hires, respectively, at some firms the titles are reversed.) Even at the lowest professional levels, compensation is tied to the performance of the fund. If the fund is performing poorly, the partners suffer along with it. But because of built-in fund-management fees, no one ever starves at a venture capital firm—and as a rule, venture capitalists do very, very well for themselves. Top-tier partners at major funds are worth many millions of dollars. Lower-level professional staff and junior partners can expect total compensation exceeding (often vastly exceeding) $250,000 per year. Compensation at corporate venture funds is lower.

General Partner

These are the guys with their names on the door. General partners raise the money for the fund and make the final decisions on which companies to invest in. General partners are expected to provide a wealth of business advice and industry contacts to the entrepreneurs they back. They often sit on the boards of many companies and are deeply involved in decisions about "exit strategies"—that is, when to cash out by taking the company public or selling it. Salary range: $150,000 to $200,000 and up, plus the potential of millions in profits.

Limited (or Junior) Partner

Junior partners are just that: junior versions of the general partners. Usually, junior partnerships are viewed as training for general partnerships and junior partners perform similar duties albeit on a reduced scale. Also reduced is their personal stake in the fund itself. Salary range: $100,000 to $130,000, plus a limited amount of carry, or percentage of profits.

VP or Associate

Some firms hire MBAs or people with business experience (usually in leveraged buyouts or investment banking) as vice presidents or associates. Associates screen business plans, make cold calls on prospective investments, and on occasion make on-site visits to portfolio companies. At this level, compensation, while still tied to the overall performance of the fund, can take the form of a flat bonus rather than a percentage of the fund. Salary range: $50,000 to $100,000, including bonus; VPs earn at the higher end.

Analyst

A very few venture capital funds—generally those that are more established or are later-stage investors—hire undergraduates as analysts. Analysts screen business plans before passing them on to senior staff and do due diligence, or research, on promising industries and entrepreneurs. A background in finance and some outstanding college internship or business experience are musts, but venture capitalists also stress the interpersonal and networking skills that are essential to anyone working in VC. The typical stay for an analyst at a VC firm is three years, after which most get an MBA, work for a portfolio company, or move over to another VC firm. Salary range: $30,000 to $70,000, plus bonus.

GETTING HIRED

As mentioned earlier, this is not the easiest industry to get into. VCs don't recruit on campus, and they don't put out ads in the newspaper or online. As a rule, you have to have a top school and relevant industry experience on your résumé to get a shot at a coveted spot at a VC firm. Even then, you'll have a lot of competition. Here are a few things you can do to improve your chances:

- Work at a start-up. After college, while your friends are trekking in Nepal on $20 a day or sucking it up on Wall Street for $100,000 a year, you could be working for a sexy cutting-edge company for not much money but a lot of responsibility. Oh, and did we mention exposure to the company's investors? Maximize that—and the experience you've gained—and you could actually become a blip on a VC's radar screen. One insider says that his experience interning at a failed start-up helped him get a job at a VC firm. Operating experience and a sense of reality are prerequisites to a VC career.

- Become an expert. If you're already working in an industry VC likes, you may be able to turn your experience into a VC job. Physicians can evaluate health care and biotech start-ups, and software engineers can evaluate high-tech start-ups, for example.

- Start networking. That's really what this business is all about, anyway. Classmates, friends, acquaintances—ask whoever you know who might know someone in VC. There are also a number of formal and informal professional organizations. And don't forget your company's investors; they may have contacts in the VC community or may be VCs themselves.

- Aim small. If you don't mind working for a smaller regional firm—say, in Texas or Illinois—you might be able to shift over to a bigger firm after a few years and a good track record. One thing to remember: Industry knowledge is very important to most VC firms. If you know all about cutting-edge oil-extraction technologies from your stay in a Dallas VC firm, don't expect to get hired by a Silicon Valley firm that focuses on the Internet or health care.

RESOURCES

Know What You Want

The WetFeet.com Job-Finding Self-Assessment

The WetFeet.com Self-Assessment has been designed to help you narrow your search and personalize the information in this book to your specific situation. Most people develop an interest pattern early on in their lives that suggests the types of skills they have and enjoy using; if you can figure out what your pattern is, you'll find it much easier to find the job you want—not to mention convince your interviewers to hire you. By reflecting on the various industries and Real People Profiles in this book, you'll be able to make some decisions about where in the working world you might best fit. The three-step process we take you through requires you to think hard about yourself, your experiences, and your interests. The more energy you spend identifying what you're looking for, the better able you'll be to talk about your skills with hiring managers and the more knowledge you'll have about what you're able to do.

Step One

The first step in finding the job you want is taking an inventory of your interests, experiences, and skills. The more you know about what you like to do and the conditions in which you like to do it, the better equipped you'll be to find the best industry for you.

Interests

- What five activities do you most enjoy? (For example, do you like to write? read? do crossword puzzles? cook? paint? learn about new cultures?)

  1. _____

  2. _____

  3. _____

  4. _____

  5. _____

- What do you like most about these activities? (Try to think hard about how the activities you like engage you. Do they require problem-solving skills? Do they require creative-thinking skills? Do they require you to use your hands?)

  _____

  _____

  _____

  _____

  _____

  _____

  _____

- What five activities do you least enjoy?

  1. _____

  2. _____

  3. _____

  4. _____

  5. _____

- What do you dislike about these activities? (Try to be specific about what you dislike and why.)

  _____

  _____

  _____

- Under what conditions do you work best? Do you work best when there's pressure or no pressure? Do you prefer a fast-paced work environment? Do you like to work alone or with others?

_____

_____

_____

_____

_____

- What types of people do you work best with? Do you enjoy more-creative people or more-analytical people? Do you want to work in an environment that has mostly young people or would you prefer a mix of different ages?

_____

_____

_____

_____

_____

- What types of work do you admire? When you hear different people talking about their jobs, what jobs are the ones that fascinate you?

_____

_____

_____

_____

_____

- When you think about the lifestyle you want to lead, what is it? Do you want to make a lot of money? Would you rather make money than have free time to pursue your hobbies and other interests?

_____

_____

_____

_____

_____

_____

Experiences and Skills

- List classes you took in school, extracurricular activities, and any organizations, professional or personal, of which you're a member.

_____

_____

_____

_____

_____

- What classes or extracurricular activities were your favorite in school?

_____

_____

_____

_____

_____

- List all of your previous work experience.

_____

_____

_____

_____

_____

- What parts of your previous jobs have you been best at? What skills did you use in those jobs? (This might include organizing, communicating, initiating changes, or managing a project.)

_____

_____

_____

_____

_____

■ List any accomplishments or leadership experience. This should include leadership that is both formal, such as being class president, and informal, such as organizing your friends to go bowling.

_____

_____

_____

_____

_____

■ What are your strengths in the different leadership situations you've been in?

_____

_____

_____

_____

_____

■ In what circumstances do you lead best? Try to identify the reasons you're able to lead.

_____

_____

_____

_____

_____

Now that you've given some thought to what you like doing, think more about the jobs you've had and skills you've developed. The following list of job attributes delineate the issues you'll face in most work situations. Answer the questions that follow them to get an idea of what situation you'd most like to be in.

1. **Security versus risk.** Do you want the security of knowing your job will be there for you tomorrow no matter what? Or are you willing to work in a more volatile industry where you may lose your job, but where the payoff may be much higher in terms of personal challenge and economic reward? Under what circumstance would you be willing to put up with more risk and less job security? Under what circumstance would you want job security and feel uncomfortable

with risk? (How you answer these questions will tell you a couple of things. The first is whether or not you'd prefer a relatively stable industry, such as aerospace, or a more rapidly evolving industry, such as telecommunications. The second is the type of company you'd work best at: a larger company with a defined career path or a smaller company where the changes of success—and the ability to weather a downturn—are more questionable.)

2. **Technology jobs versus nontechnology jobs.** Do you love to play with the latest technology? Do you like to take apart and put together electronic gadgets or do you avoid computers and anything that blinks? (If you're not technologically savvy, that doesn't necessarily preclude a career in the high-tech industry. However, how you answer these questions will tell you if you have a propensity and desire for talking about, learning about, or playing with technology or if you'd rather avoid this industry.)

3. **Hours and lifestyle.** What hours do you most like to work? Do you prefer to set your own hours? Do you prefer to work forty hours a week or are you willing to put in more time to get ahead? Do you prefer to dress casually or formally? What sort of lifestyle do you want to lead? (Many of the industries in the high-tech sector, including computer hardware and software and Internet and new media, require long hours. In other industries such as heavy manufacturing and pharmaceuticals, people typically work a forty-hour week. Think about what you'd like your time commitment at work to be. Also, think about your work environment. While there's a trend toward more-casual attire at work, some industries, such as law, consulting, and investment banking, still require people to dress formally. Finally, keep in mind that in some industries, you'll have much less free time while in others, you'll have more. At different points in your life, too, you may require different work environments. How you think through these issues will be crucial in identifying the industry and job that's best for you.)

4. **Compensation.** How important is making a lot of money to you? Can you do something you love for limited compensation, or do you need to get paid a lot no matter what you do? How much will your level of compensation affect your happiness? Would you work for less money in exchange for stock options and the chance to strike gold if your company has an IPO? (When thinking about compensation, keep in mind that it is not exclusively money. How much—if at all—a company will match your earnings in a 401(k) plan and how much time you get off are both part of your compensation package. As with hours, how much you need to make will in part depend upon where you are in your life.)

5. **Workplace diversity.** What type of working environment do you see yourself in? Is it a laid-back atmosphere filled with people from diverse backgrounds, or is it a highly formal and professional environment, filled with people just like you? For women, will you be comfortable working in a male-dominated industry? Minorities face similar questions. In industries such as management consulting and investment banking, few minorities are in positions of power; in the pharmaceutical industry there's comparably a better representation of minorities in upper management (although minorities are still underrepresented in these positions when compared to the general populace). Do you feel that you need role models of the same ethnicity to succeed or would you like to be a pathfinder in an industry that historically hasn't been as open to minorities? (In diverse work environments, there's far more room to learn and grow from the people who surround you. Much of corporate America remains very white and very male. If you're a woman or a minority in the venture capital industry, for instance, you'll very likely feel outside of the old boys network. That shouldn't discourage any-

body from entering this or any other industry. But keep in mind that the less diverse the industry, the less you'll have to learn from others and the more restricted your worldview will be.)

6. **Hierarchical versus nonhierarchical.** Do you hate red tape? Does it drive you crazy when you have to go through five different people to get something approved? Do you prefer structure or do you work better in fluid environments? What do you think about hierarchy? (Many fast-growing industries are less hierarchical; many older industries have rigid hierarchies and well-defined career paths. Hierarchical industries and companies tend to be far more bureaucratic than nonhierarchical ones.)

7. **Creative opportunities.** How creative are you? Do you need outlets for your creativity in your daily working life? Do you enjoy being around creative people? (Some industries and some jobs require more creativity; in others, there's much less opportunity to be creative. Think about what kind of balance would be right for you.)

8. **Educational opportunities.** What importance do you place on taking classes and developing new skills in a job? (Many industries require you to constantly be learning new things. Some industries, such as publishing, provide constant learning opportunities; others, such as computer software, require you to be fluent in the latest programming languages. In almost any industry, you'll need to keep learning to keep pace in your career, but the type of learning, and how much you do, can vary enormously. You'll fit best and last longest in an industry where you enjoy the learning you'll do.)

9. **Mobility and flexibility.** Do you like the idea of being able to change jobs or companies frequently? Do you want to work in an industry where you can move up quickly? Are you willing to pay your dues for a few years in order to reach your career goal? (If you want a stable job, you might go into pharmaceuticals, but if you'd like to change jobs often, try a high-tech or related industry.)

10. **Job variety.** Would you like to build up a skill base that can transfer easily into different fields and positions? Are you worried about being pigeonholed into a specific department or job type? (Some jobs are repetitive; others require a lot of multitasking. Knowing which you'd prefer will help you figure out where you will best fit into an industry.)

11. **Travel.** Do you want a job that allows you to travel and see the world? Do you enjoy spending extended periods of time in strange cities and countries? Or do you prefer to save traveling for vacations, and stay close to home the rest of the time? (Some jobs require a lot of travel; in others you won't travel at all. Think about how important traveling—or not traveling—is going to be for you.)

12. **Pace of business.** Do you work best in a chaotic environment? Do you want to work in an industry that is always changing, forcing you to constantly adapt to a changing work environment? Do you prefer the comfort of a slower-paced industry? (Many high-tech industries require constant learning and adjusting. More-mature industries, like consumer products and real estate, change more slowly.)

13. **The human factor.** Do you want a career that makes a difference in society? Is your happiness directly related to your ability to help other individuals? Will your conscious be troubled by the ruthless aspects of an industry? (If you want to change the world, it's unlikely you'll find a job designing T-shirts as satisfying as one in health care. Think about what you want to contribute to society and where your skills will best fit in.)

- Pick the three attributes from the previous list that are most important to you. What are the specific characteristics you desire in your job? Make a list.

    1. _____

    2. _____

    3. _____

- Pick the three attributes from the list that are least important to you. What are the specific things you don't want to do? Make a list.

    1. _____

    2. _____

    3. _____

Step Two

Now that you've explored your skills, interests, and work preferences, you'll need to match them with the industries in this book. After reading this book, you've probably developed some ideas about where you would best fit in. Return to the Industry Insiders and Real People Profiles. Which ones match up with your profile? Keep in mind that an exact match is unlikely. You have already prioritized what you think is most important in a career, so look for those key characteristics. If you are drawn to a particular Real People Profile, ask yourself if the What's Great for that industry agree with your interests and lifestyle desires. How do these compare to the What's to Hate for that industry? Below, write out the pluses and minuses of the top three industries that interest you.

INDUSTRY NUMBER ONE

Major pluses: _____

_____

Drawbacks: _____

_____

Relevant skills: _____

_____

Related past experiences: _____

_____

Industry number two: _____

_____

Major pluses: _____

_____

Drawbacks: _____

_____

Relevant skills: _____

_____

Related past experiences: _____

_____

Industry number three: _____

_____

Major pluses: _____

_____

Drawbacks: _____

_____

Relevant skills: _____

_____

Related past experiences: _____

_____

Step Three

Now that you've narrowed the list of industries, it's time to go out and learn more. Look over the Getting Hired and Real People Profiles in the industries you've selected to get a sense of what you'll need to do to land a job. In all industries, your best way in the door is by networking and informational interviewing (the resources in the next section provide more detail on networking and informational interviewing). However, to prepare for that process, and to better think through what you need before embarking on a new career—or a career in a new industry—you should answer the following questions:

■ What additional schooling or training might you need to get into the industries you've selected?

_____

_____

_____

_____

_____

■ What areas of the industry are good entry points?

_____

_____

_____

_____

_____

■ What is the current industry outlook? How fast is it growing?

_____

_____

_____

_____

_____

■ What is the job that you think you're best suited for?

_____

_____

_____

_____

_____

■ What questions do you have about that job?

_____

_____

_____

_____

_____

■ What questions do you have about the industry?

_____

_____

_____

_____

_____

- Who do you know who works in this industry who could answer your questions?

- Who do you know who knows somebody who works in this industry who might be able to answer your questions?

- Who do you know who is likely to know somebody in this industry who might be able to answer your questions?

Get on the Fast Track

Networking and Informational Interviewing

You've read through this book and identified some industries and jobs you're interested in. Your next step is to find the best job at the best place for you. How do you go about it? What's the most sure-fire way to find the job you want—and then get hired to do it?

First, you should understand how companies work. The typical company recognizes that it needs to hire a person long before it draws up the job specifications or resorts to classified ads or a recruiter. Often, the hiring manager will do an informal search to see if anybody within the company knows of a talented person who might fill the spot. He or she will consult advisers, vendors, customers, even friends. And candidates who present themselves on their own will likely find a receptive audience. If the candidate comes with an introduction from somebody the hiring manager knows or respects, so much the better. In other words, the hiring manager will network to find a candidate.

Your aim as a job seeker should be to create a network that intersects the network of those doing the hiring. The jobs you'll find through the standard employment resources—classified ads, Internet listings, and recruiters—may have been difficult for the organization to fill through networking because they are undesirable in some way. They'll also put you in competition with many other candidates—often a hundred or more. And by the time you become aware of the opening, it might be close to being filled. But through networking you'll have an earlier look at an opportunity at a time when you can still shape the job description and influence the level and pay range of the position. You'll have less competition because usually only a handful of others will have been brought in through the organizations' networking activities. Because most of those other candidates will already be employed elsewhere, they won't have the time to prepare for the interview as thoroughly as you will—provided you make the time. Networking also gives you access to people who might not be responsive to a more direct approach by providing you with the advantage of a recommendation from someone they know. If somebody they respect referred you, they'll be more likely to view you more favorably.

How to Network

Start networking with people you know. Don't expect them to point you to specific jobs, but realize that your friends and relatives are excellent resources for helping you improve how you present yourself, and your résumé, or for identifying your skills. Those in your immediate network include friends, relatives, friends and relatives' friends and relatives, alumni of your college, professors, professionals you know, neighbors, former coworkers, and anyone who you think might be interested in something you've done, such as volunteer work or research. Call these people and ask them for referrals to people they know in the industries you've targeted, or people who might work with people in the industries you've targeted.

The people your immediate network refers you to may or may not know of specific jobs, but they can provide useful information about where the jobs are, what skills are in demand, what to emphasize in interviews, what you need to learn, and other resources (including other people in the industry) you might access. Try to make a good impression on these contacts; they can refer you to those who can hire you, provided there's an opening and you're qualified. Keep in mind that there may not be an immediate need for your skills, but that a well-conducted information interview with a hiring manager might lead to an interview a month or two later, as well as introductions to others with whom you can further extend your network.

The Informational Interview

Often the best way to contact the people you've been referred to is to send them a letter or e-mail requesting an informational interview and saying that you'll follow up with a telephone call. The letter gives them some warning and the call commits them to setting up a time for the interview. You'll be surprised at how willing many people will be to share their experiences and knowledge with you. Make sure to mention who referred you; busy people will be more willing to carve out time for someone who graduated from the same college or who knows one of their friends than for a complete stranger. If they don't have time or are unwilling to see you, however, then you should be sure to ask them if they know anybody else with whom you could discuss the company or industry. That way your effort isn't wasted. Most people will be happy to refer you to others who can answer your questions.

Keep in mind that in scheduling informational interviews that the person you'll be talking to has as much to gain from the meeting as you do. Specifically, that person may be looking for talented employees but hasn't had time to shape a specific job description; enjoys sharing information with people; is impressed that you've researched their industry and wants to help you along (because, who knows, you may one day be in a position to help them along); and respects the person who referred you to them.

Of course, you have a number of things to gain from the interview as well. The fact that it's an informational and not a job interview takes off some of the pressure you might otherwise feel, but gives you a chance to hone your interviewing skills and learn more about an industry in a relaxed environment. You'll define the agenda, so you'll get a chance to have specific questions relating to your skills and interests answered. While you won't be explicitly asking about job opportunities at the company, in the course of the conversation you might learn about something interesting—or get referred to another person in the company who might be in a position to hire you. By creating a favorable impression, you might generate interest in yourself as a candidate—or you might find the person you speak to refers you to somebody else in another organization who can hire you.

The Interview

Informational interviews can last anywhere from fifteen minutes to an hour or more. To be safe, plan on a shorter meeting. With family, friends, and others you know well, you will generally have more time to discuss your career interests and plans. But with people you don't know as well, you should be especially sensitive to the fact that they are busy and may not have too much time to share with you. Try to keep those meetings to a short fifteen minutes unless the person explicitly invites you to stay and talk longer.

Before you go into an informational interview, you should draw up a list of questions you'd like to have answered in the time you've allotted yourself. Your goal should be clearly defined at the outset, such as finding out information about how the company operates, what the major companies in the industry are and how they differ, and what the best place for somebody with your skills and experience would be to start out. You'll also want to have done some research on the person with whom you'll be talking and the industry about which you'll be asking questions. Having read this book will help: you'll have a base of information to show that you're generally informed, and this will allow you to ask specific and informed questions. Also, pay attention to how you dress. You want to make a good impression, and the best way to do this is to look good. Looking good, of course, means different things for different industries; in banking, it means a nice wool suit and a tie. In publishing, it means a tie and shined shoes. Ask around to find out what's considered standard in the industry you're interested in.

At the information interview, don't bring up the issue of jobs. If the person does mention jobs, it's up to you whether or not you want to follow along. You will seem more purposeful—and attractive—if you remind your contact that you're simply gathering information at this point. You might suggest setting up a separate meeting to discuss employment opportunities. (Don't forget to bring several résumés, though; your contact may want to send them around to others in the company.) For this meeting, you want to explain who you are and what you're looking for in a short, two-minute presentation, and then get answers to specific questions. This should also be an excellent way to find out how the person you're talking with got his or her job. The questions in the Real People Profiles are a good starting point. But come up with your own questions, too.

At the end of the interview, be sure to ask for names of others with whom you might talk to get more information. This is very important; people at companies and in industries you're interested in know a lot of people who might be able to help you—and the more people you talk to, the more information you'll have about what recruiters look for and what you need to do to land a job. And, of course, the more people who know you're looking for a job, the better your chance of finding out about a job in the future.

Following Up

After the interview, follow up with a personal thank-you card. You can type this or handwrite it; if you're applying in a high-tech industry, you should e-mail it. Be careful to proofread the thank-you note carefully, however you send it. Promptly call the contacts' whose names you were given and set up interviews with them—it shows your respect for the contact's time and recommends you as somebody who is serious about your job search. Plus, searching for a full-time job is itself a full-time job and the more people you involve in helping you, the better your chance of finding the job you want.

The World Is Your Oyster

More Research Opportunities

Contacts

Of course, we've already discussed these. At first, don't consider them potential employers. Think of them as valuable sources of information, and you'll be using them the right way.

Company Websites

Though usually aimed at investors and customers, company websites are an essential resource for job seekers as well. Depending on how elaborate a site is, you can download an annual report, check out product and business lines, or look at archived press releases. Many companies have employment information available online: recruiting schedules, a heavy-handed "work for us" pitch, and even interviewing tips. And many now list jobs online and accept electronic résumés. And don't forget to check out the sites of competitors—that's an extra step many of your own competitors won't think to take.

Career Fairs

If you're a college student, you'll have ready access to career fairs, to which companies send representatives—often alumni—to talk about internships and full-time opportunities, hand out knickknacks with the company logo on them, and collect résumés. If you're not a college student, you may still be able to attend career fairs at local universities. There are also career fairs held at hotels and convention centers in most cities; anyone can attend. Check your local paper for announcements. No matter where the career fair is held, it will probably be your initial contact with a company. Don't treat the recruiter as a drop-off for you résumé. Ask a couple of questions—nothing fancy—and ask for a business card. Getting one is tacit permission to follow up with a phone call or an e-mail.

Download *Selling Your Stuff: The WetFeet Mini-Insider Guide to Career Fairs* for free at www.wetfeet.com.

On-Campus Info Sessions

Unlike career fairs, info sessions are sponsored by an individual company and attendance is usually limited to graduating seniors or some other such group. Here is your chance to not only learn a lot about a company you're interested in but also to stand out in the recruiter's mind with your thoughtful questions and good manners. It's an open secret that for some companies, attending the info sessions is mandatory; recruiters often look at info-session attendance sheets when evaluating candidates after the first-round interview. If your name's not on the list, recruiters might decide you're not serious enough about working for their company.

Trade and Business Magazines

Go to the library or do a search on the Internet to find relevant publications for the industry you're interested in. You'll learn about its players, trends, and culture, which will give you the background information you need to ask smart questions and impress your interviewers.

Professional Organizations

Professional organizations often offer networking, mentoring, and industry information. The Internet and your college's career center are the best places to find out about them.

Minority Organizations

If you belong to a minority group, you have a great resource at your fingertips. Minority organizations such as Inroads offer seminars, internships, and networking opportunities. Many minority organizations are industry based, and many have a presence on college campuses.

Schmoozing

You schmooze when you network and make contacts, so why the separate category? Just to drive home how important it is that you work overtime during your full-time job of job hunting. Anytime you meet someone—at a party, at a bar, at the gym—strike up a conversation. Without being pushy, find out what the person does, or at the very least, mention that you're looking for work in such-and-such industry. You never know when you'll hear, "Oh, really? My husband is a defense attorney. I know all about the Public Defender's office." Or "My brother's girlfriend is a regional sales manager for that company. Let me give you her e-mail address." It happens every day.

In this book you've seen the industry-focused research we've assembled to help you decide on a career. Visit our website to find out more about companies in the industries you're interested in. Our CompanyQuicks give you an at-a-glance overview of employment opportunities you'll find at specific companies. Our NewsCenter will keep you up-to-date on recent news and the effect it has on job seekers. Finally, our Insider Guide series—our flagship product—provides in-depth insider's perspectives on hot industries and companies to help you ace your interviews.